The Shakespeare Almanac

The Shakespeare Almanac

Gregory Doran

To Mary

Greg Doran

Hutchinson
London

Published by Hutchinson 2009

2 4 6 8 10 9 7 5 3 1

Grateful acknowledgement is made for permission to reproduce lines from the following:

Extract from *Thomas Tusser*, edited and with an introduction by Dorothy Hartley © 1931 by Dorothy Hartley, is reproduced by permission of Sheil Land Associates Ltd.

Caroline F.E. Spurgeon, *Shakespeare's Imagery and What It Tells Us* © Cambridge University Press 1935, reproduced with permission.

J C Trewin, *Portrait of the Shakespeare Country* © The Estate of J C Trewin. Reprinted by permission of The Estate Of J C Trewin.

From *The Diary of Virginia Woolf*, published by The Hogarth Press. Reprinted by permission of the Random House Group Ltd.

Extract from *Reach For Tomorrow* by Arthur C Clarke © 1956, published by Gollancz, reproduced with permission.

The quotations from the autobiography of Dame Laura Knight – *The Magic of a Line* are Copyright © 2009 Dame Laura Knight and are produced with permission of The Trustees of The Estate Dame Laura Knight DBE RA RWS.

Extracts from the Blue Guide New York, 4th edition. Reproduced with permission.

Excerpt by J B Priestley from *Apes and Angels* (© J B Priestley, 1928) is reproduced by permission of PFD (www.pfd.co.uk) on behalf of The Estate of J B Priestley.

The extract from Kenneth Tynan's review of *Titus Andronicus* reproduced by kind permission of the Estate of Kenneth Tynan

First published in Great Britain in 2009 by Hutchinson
Random House, 20 Vauxhall Bridge Road, London SW1V 2SA

www.rbooks.co.uk

Addresses for companies within The Random House Group Limited can be found at:
www.randomhouse.co.uk/offices.htm

The Random House Group Limited Reg. No. 954009

A CIP catalogue record for this book
is available from the British Library

ISBN 9780091926199

The Random House Group Limited supports The Forest Stewardship
Council (FSC), the leading international forest certification organisation. All our
titles that are printed on Greenpeace approved FSC certified paper carry the FSC logo. Our paper procurement
policy can be found at www.rbooks.co.uk/environment

Book design by Anthony Cohen

Printed and bound in Great Britain by
Butler Tanner and Dennis Ltd, Frome, Somerset

For Tony
with whom I spend the ever-running year

Acknowledgements

Jane Tassell, my personal assistant at Stratford, for organising my time,
and chasing every loose end.

Sylvia Morris (Head of Shakespeare Collections) with Helen Hargest and Jo Wilding
at the Shakespeare Centre Library and Archive, and David Howells, Curator of the
RSC Theatre Collection, for their help, above and beyond the call of duty.

Mic Cheetham, my literary agent, for encouraging me to write this book, Paul Sidey,
at Hutchinson, for his enthusiasm and for editing it, Tess Callaway for checking it so
thoroughly, and Anthony Cohen for designing it so beautifully.

Alec Cobbe, for permission to use the new Shakespeare portrait on the cover,
which belongs to his family.

And the RSC for a lifetime of inspiration.

WHEN I FIRST JOINED THE ROYAL SHAKESPEARE COMPANY, as an actor, we began rehearsing for the season in February in London, and moved up to Stratford-upon-Avon in April. Dashing backwards and forwards on the tube to Waterloo, where we then rehearsed, I paid very little heed to the growing year, noticing only the soggy weather and narrow patches of sky. But in Stratford suddenly spring had arrived and the horse chestnut trees in Chestnut Walk were in full and splendid bloom. A line from the play we were about to open caught my own sense of excitement at the prospect of a summer stretching ahead in the Warwickshire countryside:

A day in April never came so sweet
To show how costly summer was at hand.

This is one of the loveliest lines in *The Merchant of Venice*, and Shakespeare has given it to one of the lowliest of servants.

As spring turned to summer, that year, and summer to childing autumn, and angry winter, I watched the seasons change through Shakespeare's eyes. In his own home town, I sought out the violets dim, and the daffodils that come before the swallow dare, the azur'd

harebells and the darling buds of May. We heard the cuckoo herald midsummer in midmost England. Then 'summer's green all girded up in sheaves', yielded to the approach of autumn:

When yellow leaves or none, or few do hang
Upon those boughs which shake against the cold.

Finally, with 'old December's bareness everywhere', the season came to an end.

Since then I have directed a whole seasonal gamut of plays by Shakespeare in Stratford from *A Midsummer Night's Dream* to *The Winter's Tale*. Every play seems to have its own elemental characteristics, whether it be the sunny playful May-lit *Love's Labour's Lost* or the light-thickening darkness of *Macbeth*, and with each play a sense of Shakespeare's profound relationship with his surroundings has been further impressed upon me. And that became the starting point for this book.

I wanted to chart the year through Shakespeare's words. I wanted to understand the way Elizabethans understood the cycle of the zodiac, and marked the changing seasons with high days and holy days; festivals, ceremonies and superstitions, many of which are unknown to us now, and which were archaic even then. We may still celebrate Christmas, we may observe Easter, but few now may know the significance of Candlemas or Lammastide, of Hocktide or Hallowmas. I started to put together a calendar of Shakespeare's year, and to fill in the important dates in his life, the birth of his children, the deaths of his parents. And then to expand out from the festivities associated with the farming or ecclesiastical year, to the major civic events of his city career: the Lord Mayor's procession; the Accession Day tilts celebrated in Elizabeth's reign; and the Coronation of King James. Then followed some of the important historical events which occurred in his lifetime: the Spanish Armada, the Essex Rebellion, and the Gunpowder Plot. I tried to piece together a mental landscape of Shakespeare's world, from diaries, letters, pamphlets, and broadsides. Somehow, reading first-hand eye-witness accounts makes the events and the beliefs of the period so much more immediate. I included a series of insights into the world elsewhere, from merchants, mercenaries, and missionaries encountering life in the Virginia Colonies, Moghul India, the Shah's Persia, the Ottoman Empire, and Shogunate Japan. And alongside stories of the plague, of torture, and execution, I tried to include the very ordinary: a letter from an actor on tour, a tourist having to tip the attendants at the Tower of London, an accident at the bear pit.

I have been alerted to some of these extracts by actors, designers and other directors I have worked with. Many have been given to me because they in some way illuminate both how close we are to Shakespeare's world, and how far away from it. I've always been a bit of a magpie, 'a snapper up of unconsider'd trifles', a squitterbook (the Elizabethan word for a bookworm), and I've plundered the work of Thomas Nashe, Robert Greene and Thomas Dekker, and the writers we tend only to read about in footnotes – Robert Burton, Gervase Markham, and John Aubrey – to share what I have found either useful or fascinating.

Almanacs in Elizabethan and Jacobean London were hugely popular, readily available, and filled with all sorts of information. They could be bought in sheet form to pin up on the wall like a calendar, or as a pamphlet, for a penny. They were part horoscope, part Filofax. Almanacs provided data on when to plant seeds, or shear sheep, and left space for you to make notes of debts or payments due the next quarter day. They might furnish you with a table containing the legal terms, or the dates of the next fair, or the distance from one town to another. They were full of sententious morality, scurrilous gossip, and as the period went on, political propaganda.

They could inform you of the changes of the Moon (as in *A Midsummer Night's Dream*), of planetary motions and conjunctions, or warn you, if you were planning to marry, of which unlucky days to avoid. In Middleton's play *No Wit, No Help Like a Woman's*, there is a character called Weatherwise, who leads his entire life by the Almanac, including his love life.

In an age when astrology was part of the dominant pattern of beliefs, almanacs made much of their often dodgy prognostication. Thomas Overbury's *Character of an Almanac-maker* satirizes such a man as 'the key to unlock terms and law days, a dumb Mercury to point out highways, and a bailiff of all the marts and fairs in England. But for judging all the uncertainty of the weather, any old shepherd shall make a dunce of him', and Overbury concludes, 'the rest of him you shall know next year, for what he will be then, he himself knows not'. However, Rev. John Ward,

who was the Vicar of Holy Trinity after the Restoration, writing in 1667, warns the sceptical not to underestimate almanac-makers: 'Sir Edward Walker confessed that most of them did foretell the fire of London last year, but he caused it to be put out.'

I now spend much of the year living in Stratford, next to the weir on the River Avon at Lucy's Mill. Part of this almanac then is a diary of my own observations of the changing year as I walk in and out to work, past Holy Trinity Church where Shakespeare was baptized and is buried.

Reading Elizabethan almanacs gives me an insight into the world of the ordinary folk of Shakespeare's time. I hope my almanac, in some small way, does this too. It is not an academic exercise; it is far too irresponsible for that. It is rather an anthology of some of the things which intrigue and delight me about the world, and the fluctuating cycles of the year in Shakespeare's day.

Gregory Doran
Candlemas 2009

Towards a Bibliography

I<small>N RESEARCHING THIS BOOK</small>, I have been led back to a whole library of writers I had neglected; and became familiar with books I generally only refer to in footnotes. Some I would probably never even have bothered to pick up again. Some I can now not put down. The authors that have become precious to me, whom I feel I know a little, like the pragmatic but canny theatre entrepreneur Philip Henslowe, the hands-on herbalist John Gerard, and the obsessively thorough historian John Stow, have earned a special place on my bookshelves, as has the anarchic firecracker wit and master of extravagant opinionated tumbling prose, Thomas Nashe. I was about to describe him as irrepressible, but that would not be true, as he was thoroughly and fatally repressed by the church authorities in 1599.

I even enjoyed the rantings of the splenetic Puritan Phillip Stubbes, and the doggerel translations of the rabidly anti-Catholic Barnabe Googe. Robert Burton's *Anatomy of Melancholy* surprised me by making me laugh out loud, and the sometimes fanciful Edward Topsell, Perpetual Curate of St Botolph's, Aldersgate, who compiled his huge volumes on the history of the four-footed beasts, frequently made me chortle.

Thomas Dekker's *The Wonderful Year*, and his *Gull's Hornbook*, proved really engaging, as did Robert Greene's *The Art of Coney-Catching*, although for a real insight into some of the low life of the period, the sober Thomas Harman's *Caveat for Common Cursitors* was chock full of incredible characters. Thomas Deloney's short novel *Thomas of Reading* had much to recommend it too.

I re-read the superbly crafted sermons of Lancelot Andrewes and John Donne, and the elegant essays of Bacon and Montaigne; the startling case books and diaries of the occultists Dr John Dee and Simon Forman, and the charming emblematica of Henry Peacham. The letters of the self-confessed gossip and Paul's Walker, John Chamberlain, were endlessly intriguing as were the *Brief Lives* and *Miscellanies* of the frankly unreliable, but irresistible, John Aubrey.

The receipt books of Elinor Fettiplace and Sir Kenelm Digby made mouth-watering reading, while the household and farmyard tips of Gervase Markham had a great domestic appeal. Intrepid travellers' tales were supplied by the pioneering propagandist Richard Hakluyt, and I gleaned fascinating insights into Elizabethan London from foreign visitors such as the German Paul Hentzer, and the Swiss Thomas Platter, as well as thoroughly enjoying the self-promoting travels of Thomas Coryate, and the hilarious homely exploits of John Taylor the (frankly atrocious) Water Poet. I became addicted to the *Nine Days' Wonder* of Will Kemp, and had to be weaned off him, and I even embarked upon poor Michael Drayton's neglected topographical epic *Poly-Olbion*.

I may never otherwise have bothered to read the fabulous *Golden Legend of Saints* nor Foxe's sensationalist *Book of Martyrs*. For a book which examines the cycle of the year, Robert Herrick provided ample material, Nicholas Breton's bouncy *Fantasticks* was a surprising delight, and I found that rough, tough Thomas Tusser had an enduring earthy appeal, beautifully described by Dorothy Hartley in 1932.

I have rendered the Elizabethan prose mainly in modern English spelling, retaining capitals sometimes, punctuating for ease of reading and cutting where I saw fit, without necessarily bothering to alert the reader to any excisions.

G D

You'd be so lean, that blasts of January
Would blow you through and through.
The Winter's Tale (Act 4 Scene 3)

'It is now January, and Time begins to turn the wheel of his Revolution, the woods begin to lose the beauty of their spreading boughs, and the proud oak must stoop to the axe: the squirrel now surveyeth the nut and the maple, and the hedgehog rolls himself up like a football: an apple and a nutmeg make a gossips cup: and the ale and the faggot are the victuallers merchandise: The Northern black dust is the during fuel, and the fruit of the grape heats the stomach of the aged: Down beds and quilted caps are now in the pride of their service, and the cook and the pantler are men of no mean office: The ox and the fat weather now furnish the market, and the coney is so ferreted that she cannot keep in her burrow: the curier and the lime rod are the death of the fowl and the falcon bells ring the death of the mallard: the trotting gelding makes a way through the moor, and the hare and the hound put the huntsman to his horn: the barren doe subscribes to the dish and the smallest seed makes sauce to the greatest flesh: the dried grass is the horses ordinary, and the meal of beans makes him go through with his travel: Fishermen now have a cold trade, and travellers a foul journey: the Cook room now is not the worst place in the ship, and the shepherd hath a bleak seat on the mountain: the blackbird leaveth not a berry on the thorn, and the garden earth is turned up for her roots: the water floods run over the proud banks, and the gaping oyster leaves his shell in the streets, while the proud peacock leaps into the pie: Muscovia commodities are now much in request, and the water spaniel is a necessary servant: the load horse to the mill has his full back burden: and the thresher in the barn tries the strength of his flail: the woodcock and the pheasant pay their lives for their feed, and the hare after a course makes his hearse in a pie: the shoulder of the hog is a shoeing horn to a good drink, and a cold alms makes a beggar shrug. To conclude, I hold it time of little comfort, the rich man's charge, and the poor man's misery. Farewell.'
From Fantasticks: Serving for a Perpetual Prognostication,
Nicholas Breton (1554 - 1626)

'January should be clad all in white like the colour of the earth at this season, blowing his nails, in his left arm a billet, the sign of Aquarius standing by his side.'
Emblems, Henry Peacham

New Year's Gifts

I'll have my brains ta'en out and buttered
and give them to a dog for a New Year's gift.
The Merry Wives of Windsor (Act 3 Scene 5)

Enter New-Year's Gift in a blue coat, (serving-man like), with an orange, and a sprig of rosemary on his head, his hat full of brooches, with a collar of gingerbread, his torch-bearer carrying a marchpane, with a bottle of wine on either arm.
The Masque of Christmas, Ben Jonson

Gifts were traditionally given on New Year's Day, rather than at Christmas, in Shakespeare's day. An orange stuck with cloves was a common New Year's present. It was thought that hanging an orange or lemon stuck full of cloves into a jug of wine (but not actually touching the liquor) would preserve it from mouldiness, and improve the flavour. A gilt nutmeg (a nutmeg glazed with the white of an egg) was also a common present for lovers and used for spicing drinks.

Gloves were a popular New Year's gift or a sum of money (often called glove money), as were metal pins, which were first introduced at the beginning of the sixteenth century. In *The Two Noble Kinsmen*, one of the countrymen is so displeased with his sweetheart that he promises the next pair of gloves he gives her will be of dogskin. Shakespeare's father, a glover by trade, must have been particularly busy around New Year, making gloves for New Year's gifts.

Portrait of Johanna Le Maire by Nicolaes Eliasz Pickenoy

Whilst some in golden letters write their love,
Some speak affection by a ring or glove,
Or pins and points (for every peasant may,
After his ruder fashion be as gay
As the brisk courtly sir), and thinks that he
Cannot without gross absurdity
Be this day frugal, and not spare his friend
Some gift to show his love finds not an end
With the deceased year.
Poole's English Parnassus

Let others look for pearl and gold,
Tissues, or tabbies manifold :
One only lock of that sweet hay
Whereon the blessed baby lay,
Or one poor swaddling-clout, shall be
The richest New-Year's gift to me.
The New Year's Gift, Robert Herrick

Gardens for All Months of the Year

Gardener's servant:
Why should we in the compass of a pale
Keep law and form and due proportion,
Showing, as in a model, our firm estate,
When our sea-walled garden, the whole land,
Is full of weeds, her fairest flowers chok'd up,
Her fruit trees all unprun'd, her hedges ruin'd,
Her knots disorder'd, and her wholesome herbs
Swarming with caterpillars?
Richard II (Act 3 Scene 4)

The great philosopher, scholar, statesman and natural scientist, Francis Bacon, writes about gardening throughout the year, in his famous book of *Essays*:
'God Almighty first planted a garden. And indeed it is the purest of human pleasures. It is the greatest refreshment to the spirits of man, without which buildings and palaces are but gross handy-works, and a man shall ever see that when ages grow to civility and elegancy, men come to build stately sooner than to garden finely, as if gardening were the greater perfection. I do hold it, in the royal ordering of gardens, there ought to be gardens for all the months in the year, in which severally things of beauty may be then in season.

'For December and January, you must take such things as are green all winter: holly, ivy, bays, juniper, cypress trees, yew, pineapple trees; fir-trees; rosemary, lavender; periwinkle, (the white, the purple, and the blue); germander, flags; orange trees, lemon trees; and myrtles, if they be stoved; and sweet marjoram, warm set.'

John Aubrey, in his *Brief Lives*, tells us that Bacon was fond of marking the changing season even at his table:
'At every meal, according to the season of the year, he had his table strewed with sweet herbs and flowers, which he said did refresh his spirits and memory.'

We might be surprised by the look of an Elizabethan garden. At Hampton Court, for example, Thomas Platter visiting in 1599 describes what he saw:
'By the entrance I noticed numerous patches where square cavities had been scooped, as for paving stones; some of these were filled with red brick-dust, some with white sand, and some with green lawn, very much resembling a chess board. The hedges and surrounds were of hawthorn, bush firs, ivy, roses, juniper, holly, English or common elm, box, and other shrubs, very gay and attractive.

'There were all manner of shapes, men and women, half men and half horse, sirens, serving-maids with baskets, French lilies and delicate crenellations all round, made from the dry twigs bound together and the afore-said evergreen quick-set shrubs, or entirely of rosemary, all true to the life, mingled and grown together, trimmed and arranged picture-wise that their equal would be difficult to find.'

Actresses

'Early in the morning to the Exchequer, where I told over what money I have of my Lord's and my own there... thence to Will's, where Spicer and I ate our dinner of a roasted leg of pork which Will did give us. And after that, I to the Theatre where was acted *Beggars Bush* - it being very well done; and here the first time that ever I saw women come upon the stage.'
Samuel Pepys, January 3rd, 1661

Pepys saw actresses for the first time at the Tennis Court Theatre in Vere Street just after the Restoration, in a play by John Fletcher. In fact, the previous month, Margaret Hughes had the honour of making the first professional appearance by a woman on that very same stage, on Saturday December 8th, 1660. The actor and dramatist, Colley Cibber, tells us that it took a while for the actresses to fulfil all

the roles previously played by boys, and that young men still played many of the parts for some time.
'Though women were not admitted to the stage till the return of King Charles, yet it could not be so suddenly supplied with them, but that there was still a necessity, for some time, to put the handsomest young men into petticoats which Kynaston was said to have then worn with success; particularly in the part of Evadne in *The Maid's Tragedy*.
'The king, coming before his usual time to a tragedy, found the actors not ready to begin; when his

Frontispiece from *The Maid's Tragedy* by Beaumont and Fletcher, in which Kynaston played Evadne

Majesty, not choosing to have as much patience as his good subjects, sent to them to know the meaning of it; upon which the master of the company came to the box, and rightly judging that the best excuse for their default would be the true one, fairly told his Majesty that the queen was not shaved yet.
'The king, whose good humour loved to laugh at a jest as well as make one, accepted the excuse, which served to divert him till the male queen could be effeminated. Kynaston was at that time so beautiful a youth, that the ladies of quality prided themselves in taking him with them in their coaches to Hyde Park in his theatrical habit, after the play, which in those days they might have sufficient time to do, because plays then were used to begin at four o'clock.'

In the 1590s, Thomas Nashe had decried the use of women on the stage, on the continent:
'Our players are not as the players beyond the sea, a sort of squirting, bawdy comedians, that have whores and common courtesans to play women's parts, and forebear no immodest speech or unchaste action that may procure laughter.'

Prognostication

This is the excellent foppery of the world, that when we are sick in fortune, – often the surfeits of our own behaviour, – we make guilty of our disasters the sun, the moon and the stars; as if we were villains on necessity, fools by heavenly compulsion, knaves, thieves and treachers by spherical predominance, drunkards, liars, and adulterers by an enforced obedience of planetary influence...

King Lear (Act 1 Scene 2)

One of the most popular features of almanacs in Shakespeare's day were astrological prognostications for the year ahead. Here, Thomas Nashe savagely attacks the author of a book of such prophecies, the scholar Richard Harvey. In the *Astrological Discourse*, Harvey warned of the potential effects of a rare conjunction of Saturn and Jupiter, due on April 28th of that year. His doom-laden forecasts caused near-panic, but when the conjunction passed off quietly Harvey became a laughing-stock.

'Gentlemen, I am sure you have heard of a ridiculous ass that many years since wrote an absurd Astrological Discourse of the terrible conjunction of Saturn and Jupiter; wherein, (as if he had lately cast the heaven's water or been at the anatomizing of the sky's entrails in Surgeons' Hall), he prophesieth of such strange wonders to ensue from stars' distemperature and the unusual adultery of planets, as none but he that is a bawd to those celestial bodies could ever descry. What expectation there was of it in both town and country, the amazement of those times may testify; and the rather because he pawned his credit upon it, in these express terms: "If these things fall not out in every point as I have wrote, let me for ever hereafter lose the credit of my astronomy."

'The whole university hissed at him, Tarleton at the theatre made jests at him, and Elderton consumed his ale-crammed nose to nothing in bearbaiting him with whole bundle of ballads. Would you, in likely reason, guess it were possible for any shame-swollen toad to have the spit-proof face to live out this disgrace? ... and which is more, he is a vicar.'

Pierce Penniless

Later Nashe addresses Harvey directly:
'I have read over thy sheepish discourse and could not refrain but bequeath it to the privy, leaf by leaf as I read it, it was so ugly, dorbellical, and lumpish.'

Nashe, under the assumed name of Adam Fouleweather, is also the probable author of a pamphlet called *A Wonderful Astrological Prognostication*, which ridiculed almanac-makers.

Twelfth-day Eve

Hang there like fruit my soul,
Till the tree die!
Cymbeline (Act 5 Scene 5)

Blessing the Apple Trees
An old country custom on Twelfth-day Eve was to bless the apple trees, as recorded here:
'On the eve of the Epiphany, the farmer, attended by his workmen, with a large pitcher of cider, goes to the orchard, and there encircling one of the best bearing trees, they drink the following toast three several times:
Here's to thee, old apple-tree,
Whence thou mayst bud,
And whence thou mayst blow!
And whence thou mayst bear apples enow!
Hat-fulls! Cap-fulls!
Peck-fulls, bushels, bag-fulls,
And my pockets full too! Huzza!

'This done, they return to the house, the doors of which they are sure to find bolted by the females, who, be the weather what it may, are inexorable to all entreaties to open them till some one has guessed at what is on the spit, which is generally some nice little thing, difficult to be hit on, and is the reward of him who first names it. The doors are then thrown open, and the lucky clod-pole receives the tit-bit as his

recompense. Some are so superstitious as to believe, that if they neglect this custom, the trees will bear no apples that year.'
The Gentleman's Magazine

The Wassail Cup or Bowl was an indispensable part of Twelfth-day Eve. It was a large punch bowl containing ale in which roasted crab apples fizzed

about. Shakespeare makes mention of it in Love's Labour's Lost ('When roasted crabs hiss in the bowl'), and Puck in A Midsummer Night's Dream disguises himself thus to frighten the villagers:
Sometimes lurk I in a gossip's bowl
In very likeness of a roasted crab,
And when she drinks against her lips I bob
And on her wither'd dewlap pour the ale.
A Midsummer Night's Dream (Act 2 Scene 1)

Herrick in his poem Twelfth Night, or King and Queen, also mentions the wassail bowl, full of 'lamb's wool' (a drink spiced with sugar, nutmeg and ginger), as well as another custom. A plum cake was baked containing a bean and a pea. Whoever found the bean would be king, whoever the pea would be the queen for the night, and they would run the feast:
Now, now the mirth comes
With the cake full of plums,
Where bean's the king of the sport here;
Beside we must know
The pea also
Must revel as queen of the court here.

Epiphany: Twelfth Night

Epiphany celebrates the day the Christ child was made manifest to the Magi. It is also the twelfth day after Christmas, when the last of the revels takes place.

The Queen Blacks Up

In the Jacobean period, masques were frequently performed on Twelfth Night, at Whitehall for the Court. They were lavish affairs. One of the first of these entertainments was also one of the most extraordinary.

Inigo Jones' design for a daughter of Niger from *The Masque of Blackness*

Queen Anne, James I's tall, blonde, Danish wife, brought together two of the most distinguished artistic talents of the age, Ben Jonson and Inigo Jones, and asked them to work together to create a court masque for Twelfth Night 1605 in which she and her ladies might appear. But the most curious element of her brief to them was that she and her ladies wanted to 'black up'.

Jonson and Jones therefore, in their first collaboration together, created *The Masque of Blackness*. Jonson managed to fulfil the Queen's express wish to appear in black-face with great ingenuity. She and her ladies were to present the daughters of the River Niger, who have been blackened by the sun. But now dissatisfied with being black, they have been advised to seek out a place lit with a greater light than the sun. The Moon points out that this blessed plot is Britannia. Thus they appear at the court of King James, to express their fervent desire to be turned white by the power of the king.

The Masque cost up to £3,000 for just one performance, which was as much as the cost of the Earl of Leicester's state funeral.

Sir Dudley Carleton described the evening to a friend:
'Their black faces and hands which were painted and bare up to the elbows, were a very loathsome sight and I am sorry that strangers [he means foreign ambassadors] **should see our court so strangely disguised.'**

And later, the evening ends on a rather raucous note:
'In the coming out, a banquet which was prepared for the king was overturned, table and all, before it was scarce touched. It were infinite to tell you what losses there were of chains, jewels, purses and such loose ware, and one woman amongst the rest lost her honesty for which she was carried to the porter's lodge being surprised at her business.'

The Masque of Blackness

This is a most majestic vision, and
Harmonious charmingly.
The Tempest (Act 4 Scene 1)

Here, Ben Jonson himself describes the previous night's exquisite masque:

'First, for the scene, was drawn a Landscape consisting of small woods; which falling, an artificial sea was seen to shoot forth, as if it flowed to the land, raised with waves which seemed to move, and in some places the billow to break, as imitating that orderly disorder, which is common in nature. In front of this sea were placed six tritons, in moving and sprightly actions; their upper bodies human, their desinent parts fish. From their backs were borne out certain light pieces of taffeta, as if carried by the wind, and their music made out of wreathed shells. Behind these, a pair of sea maids, for song, were as conspicuously seated; between which two great sea horses, as big as the life, put forth themselves; the one mounting aloft, and writhing his head from the other, which seemed to sink forwards. Upon their backs Oceanus and Niger were advanced.

'Oceanus, the colour of his flesh blue, and shadowed with a robe of sea green, his head grey and horned, as he is described by the ancients. He was garlanded with algae or sea grass, and in his hand a trident. Niger, in form and colour of an Ethiop, his hair and rare beard curled, shadowed with a blue and

An Oceania as a light-bearer by Inigo Jones

bright mantle; his front, neck and wrists adorned with pearl; and crowned with an artificial wreath of cane and paper-rush. These induced the masquers which were twelve nymphs, negroes and daughters of Niger, attended by so many of the Oceaniae, which were their light-bearers.

'The masquers were placed in a great concave shell, like mother of pearl, curiously made to move on those waters, and rise with the billow: the top thereof was stuck with a chevron of lights, which struck a glorious beam upon them, as they were seated one above another, so that they were all seen but in an extravagant order. On sides of the shell did swim six huge sea monsters, bearing on their backs the twelve torch bearers, all having their lights burning out of whelks or murex shells.

'The attire of the masquers was alike in all without difference; the colours azure and silver, their hair thick and curled upright in tresses, like pyramids, but returned at the top with a scroll and antique dressing of feathers, and jewels interlaced with ropes of pearl. And for the front, ear, neck and wrists, the ornament was of the most choice and orient pearl, best setting off from the black.

'The Queen, playing the nymph Euphoris, descended and danced on the shore with her eleven ladies. Then a song composed by Alfonso Ferrabosco, and sung by a tenor voice (representing the sea), summoned them back to their shell on the billows which then "went out".'

John Chamberlain and the Frozen Thames

Not till a hot January.
Much Ado About Nothing (Act 1 Scene 1)

On this day in 1608, John Chamberlain wrote to his younger friend, Dudley Carleton, about the frozen River Thames.
'**Above Westminster the Thames is quite frozen over and the Archbishop came from Lambeth on Twelfthday over the ice to the Court. Many fantastical experiments are daily put in practice, as certain youths burnt a gallon of wine upon the ice and made all the passengers partakers. But the best is of an honest woman (they say) that had a great longing to have her husband get her with child upon the Thames.'**

The Chronicler, Raphael Holinshed, describes how the Thames had frozen the winter William Shakespeare was born:
'**On New Year's even people went over and along the**

Thames on the ice from London Bridge to Westminster. Some played at the foot-ball as boldly there as if it had been on dry land. Divers of the court, being daily at Westminster, shot daily at pricks set upon the Thames; and the people, both men and women, went daily on the Thames in greater number than in any street of the city of London. On the 3rd day of January it began to thaw, and on the 5th day was no ice to be seen between London Bridge and Lambeth; which sudden thaw caused great floods and high waters, that bare down bridges and houses, and drowned many people, especially in Yorkshire.'

John Chamberlain was a bachelor, a gossip, a newsgatherer and a brilliant letter writer. He called himself a 'Paul's Walker', who for thirty years had picked up all the tittle-tattle in the aisles of St Paul's Cathedral.

Thomas Dekker, in his satirical manual *The Gull's Hornbook*, gives advice about how a young fop should display himself in St Paul's, walking up and down the aisles, in his finest attire, and strutting into the choir to tip the choristers. 'Be sure your silver spurs dog your heels, and then the boys will swarm about you like so many white butterflies.' He also suggests paying a penny for a trip up the steeple (which the Cathedral then had) to add to the graffiti:
'**And when you have mounted there take heed how you look down into the yard, for the rails are rotten as your great-grandfather. Before you come down again, I would desire you to draw your knife, and grave your name, or, for want of a name the mark which you clap upon your sheep, in great characters upon the leads. Indeed the top of Paul's contains more names than Stow's Chronicles.'**

Another Frozen River, in Russia

Anthony Jenkinson describes witnessing Tsar Ivan the Terrible attending a ceremony on the frozen river in Moscow in 1557:

'Every year upon the twelfth day they use to bless or sanctify the river Moscua, which runneth through the city of Mosco, after this manner.

'First they make a square hole in the ice about 3 fathoms large every way, which is trimmed about the sides and edges with white boards. Then about 9 of the clock they come out of the church with procession towards the river in this wise.

'First and foremost there go certain young men with wax tapers burning, and one carrying a great lantern; then followed certain banners, then the cross, then the images of our Lady, of St Nicholas, and of other saints, which images men carried upon their shoulders: after the images followed certain priests of the number of 100 or more; after them the Metropolitan who is led between two priests; and after the Metropolitan came the Emperor with his crown upon his head, and after his majesty all his noblemen orderly. Thus they followed the procession unto the water, and when they came unto the hole that was made, the priests set themselves in order round

Ivan IV Vasiliech, 'Ivan the Terrible', unknown artist

about it. And at one side of the same pool there was a scaffold of boards made, upon which stood a fair chair in which the Metropolitan was set, but the Emperor's majesty stood upon the ice.

'After this the priest began to sing, to bless and to cense, and did their service, and so by that time that they had done, the water was holy, which being sanctified, the Metropolitan took a little thereof in his hands, and cast it on the Emperor, likewise upon certain dukes, and then returned again to the church with the priests that sat about the water: but that press that there was about the water when the Emperor was gone, was wonderful to behold, for there came above 5000 pots to be filled of that water: for that Moscovite which hath no part of that water, thinks himself unhappy.

'And very many went naked into the water, both men and women and children: after the press was a little gone, the Emperor's jennets and horses were brought to drink of the same water, and by that means they make their way, they make their horses as holy as themselves.'

Hakluyt's Voyages, Anthony Jenkinson

Plough Monday

To business that we love we rise betime
And go to't with delight.
Antony and Cleopatra (Act 4 Scene 4)

If all the year were playing holidays,
To sport would be as tedious as to work;
But when they seldom come, they wish'd for come,
And nothing pleaseth but rare accidents.
Henry IV Part One (Act 1 Scene 2)

It was also known as St Distaff's Day:
Partly work and partly play
You must on St Distaff's Day:
From the plough soon free your team;
Then cane home and fother them:
If the maids a-spinning go,
Burn the flax and fire the tow.
Bring in pails of water then,
Let the maids bewash the men.
Give St Distaff's all the right:
Then bid Christmas sport good night,
And next morrow every one
To his own vocation.
Robert Herrick

Plough Monday, the next after Twelftide be past,
Biddeth out with the plough, the worst husband is last.
If ploughman get hatchet or whip to the screen
Maids loseth their Cock if no water be seen.
The Farmer's Feast Days, Thomas Tusser, 1571

Plough Monday, the next Monday after Twelfth Night, marked the end of the Christmas festivities, and was traditionally the day everyone went back to work.

A distaff is a tool used in spinning. It holds the unspun fibres of flax or wool, keeping them untangled, and easing the spinning process. It thus became a symbol of the housewife.
Goneril, in *King Lear*, scoffs at her mild husband's 'cowish terror' in the face of the invading army of Cordelia and the King of France. She tells Edmund:
I must change arms at home, and give the distaff
Into my husband's hands.
King Lear (Act 4 Scene 2)

We still use the term the 'distaff side' referring to the female side of the family.

Giants

●●●●●●●

... it is excellent
To have a giant's strength; but it is tyrannous
To use it like a giant.
Measure for Measure (Act 2 Scene 2)

On this day in 1613, in the French province of Dauphiné, some workmen digging in a field in the grounds of an old castle discovered the bones of a giant. The field had been known since ancient times as *Le Terroir du Géant* or *The Giant's Field*. They came across a tomb, built of brick, thirty feet long and twelve feet wide. When they opened the tomb, they found a complete human skelton, more than twenty-five feet long and ten feet wide across the shouders. The giant's teeth were the size of an ox's hoof. Several ornaments and urns were also found, as well as a grey stone block with the inscription 'Teutobochus Rex'.

The local surgeon and the village clerk went to examine the remains. The erudite surgeon realized that the remains must be those of King Teutobochus of Cimbria, a legendary giant, who was defeated by a Roman army under Marius and taken to Rome as a prisoner of war. In the triumphal procession, the giant's head had towered over the trophies carried atop the long spears of the legionnaires. Apparently Teutobochus could vault over four or even six horses at a time.

In Shakespeare's day, London was very familiar with giants. When Philip and Mary made their public entry into London in 1554, two giant statues named Corineus and Gogmagog stood upon London Bridge; and when Elizabeth passed through the city the day before her coronation the two giant statues were placed at Temple Bar. They made regular appearances in midsummer pageants, as Puttenham describes, in 1589 'where to make people wonder are set forth great ugly giants, marching as if they are alive'. They ended up in the Guildhall.

John Stow describes a real giant in London in 1581: **'This year were to be seen in London two Dutchmen of strange statures, the one in height seven foot and seven inches, in breadth betwixt the shoulders three quarters of a yard and two inches, the compass of his breast one yard half and two inches, and about the waist one yard, quarter and one inch, the length of his arm to the hands a full yard, a comely man of person, but lame of his legs, for he had broken them lifting a barrel of beer. The other was in height but three foot had never a good foot nor any knee at all, and yet could dance a galliard, he had no arm, but a stump to the elbow or little more on the right side, on which singing he would dance a cup, and after toss it about three or four times, and every time receive the same on the said stump, he would shoot an arrow near the mark, flourish with a rapier, throw a bowl, beat with a hammer, hew with an axe, sound with a trumpet, and drink every day ten quarts of the best beer, if he could get it.'**
Chronicles, John Stow

Pretty Boys

I'll have no worse a name than Jove's own page
And therefore look you call me Ganymede.
As You Like It (Act 1 Scene 3)

As the Sun has by now entered Aquarius (in Shakespeare's day at any rate; nowadays it is ten days later), here is the myth of Ganymede: Jupiter disguised as an eagle is said to have carried the beautiful youth to Olympus, to be his cup-bearer. Ganymede was set among the heavens as the constellation Aquarius, to prevent Jupiter's wife, Juno, from hurting him. Ganymede is the name Rosalind chooses to call herself in As You Like It, when she is dressed as a boy.

Here is the story as it is told by Ovid in The Metamorphoses translated by Arthur Golding:
But now I need a milder style to tell of pretty boys
That were the darlings of the Gods, and of unlawful joys
That burned in the breasts of Girls, who for their wicked lust
According as they did deserve, received penance just.

The King of Gods did burn erewhile in love of Ganymede
The Phrygian, and the thing was found which Jupiter that stead
Had rather be than that he was. Yet could he not beteem
The shape of any bird than eagle for to seem
And so he soaring in the air with borrowed wings, trussed up
The Trojan boy who still in heaven even yet doth bear his cup,
And brings him Nectar though against Dame Juno's will it be.

Ovid goes on to tell the story of Apollo and his beloved boy, Hyacinth (see March 18th).

NON EST MORTALE QUOD OPTO.

ΓΑΝΥΜΗΔΗΣ.

'This Woeful Spectacle'

They have tied me to a stake; I cannot fly,
But bear-like I must fight the course.
Macbeth (Act 5 Scene 7)

On this day in 1583, disaster occurred at a bear baiting in Paris Garden as the stage collapsed. Here is the puritan Phillip Stubbes' gruesome account:

'Upon the 13th day of January last, being the sabbath day, Anno 1583, the people, men, women and children, both young and old, an infinite number flocking to those infamous places, where these wicked exercises are usually practised, when they were all come together and mounted aloft upon their scaffolds and galleries, and in the midst of all their

jollity and pastime, all the whole building (not one stick standing) fell down with a most wonderful and fearsome confusion; so that either two or three hundred men, women, and children (by estimation) whereof seven were killed dead, some were wounded, some lamed, and other some bruised and crushed almost to death. Some had their brains dashed out, some their heads all to-squashed, some their legs broken, some their arms, some their backs, some their shoulders, some one hurt, some another. So that you should have heard a woeful cry, even piercing the skies. This woeful spectacle and heavy judgement, (pitiful to hear of, but most rueful to behold), did the Lord send down from Heaven to show unto the whole world how grievously he is offended with those that spend the sabbath in such wicked exercises; in the meantime leaving his temple desolate and empty. God grant all men may take warning hereby, to shun the same for fear of like or worser Judgement to come!'

There also exists an account of this same accident in the writings of William Clowes, a surgeon at St Bartholomew's Hospital:

'The cure of a man, which received a notable wound in his head with great fracture of the skull; by a fall out of a gallery at the Bear Garden, at that time when all the gallery there did fall down and killed and hurt many.

'At the beginning of this cure, I did cut and shave away the hair round about the wound. Then with my fingers I made further probation into the wound, and there I did manifestly feel a notable fracture or breach in the skull on the left side of his head, upon the bone called *os petrosum*, which was depressed upon the *pannicle dura mater*. I filled the wound with pledgets and runlets made of lint and very fine tow, wet with whites of eggs mixed with Galen his powder then with good bolstering and rolling he thus remained until the next day.'

Hilary
• • • • • • •

Day Two of Dr Clowes' Treatment of his Patient

Asked by the man's master what danger he was in, Clowes replied:

'I told them he was not without great danger, partly by reason the brain was sore shaken with the fall, and partly for that the bone was broken and depressed upon the *dura mater*, which were the causes that did hinder his speeches. Howbeit, I did hope of some amendment after I had pierced the skull with the trepan. I caused them to hang all his chamber with carpets and coverlets, and made it very dark, without light or air but only by a candle because in this case the air was very hurtful.

'I caused a strong man steadfastly to hold and stay his head with his hands, and having stopped his ears with wool, I then did set on the trepan, and so orderly pierced the skull through in two places. Then with an instrument called a levator, I raised up the depressed bone, which being done, immediately his speech amended.'

Clowes went on to clean the wound with 'fomentations of wine' and placed 'a piece of fine lawn dipped in *mel rosarum* between the *dura mater* and the skull'. He filled the wound with wet lint, then applied a plaster of Betony and finishes off the dressing by annointing the head with *oleo rosarum*. **'And thus I continued with this dressing until all the blackness was taken away from the *dura mater* by the foresaid honey or roses.**

'This wounded man was in the more danger, for that he received his hurt very near unto the full moon, whereby this evil followed, that *dura mater* did rise and thrust itself out of those places of the skull that I did perforate or pierce with the trepan.'

Addressing the fracture of the man's thigh bone, Clowes managed to place splints on the leg: **'of light willow well wrapped about and also bolstered with tow, gently bound with good strong tape, which being done I laid or placed the member as seemly and decently as possibly might be, in a double linen towel rolled up at both ends, with a good quantity of good long rushes, such as chandlers use to put into their watching candles.**

'To conclude, after I had fully ended the cure of my patient, then both he and his friends seemed to be discontented with me for that the fractured member was somewhat shorter than his other leg. So they departed from me, being not well pleased with the shortness of his leg, and I much more discontented for their base minded payment for healing of so great and dangerous a cure.'

Today is the Feast Day of St Hilary (the fourth-century Bishop of Poitiers), an eminent doctor of the church, who gave his name to this term in the High Court of Justice and in the universities. The Hilary term is one Sunday to nine Sundays after this feast day. Traditionally, it's the coldest day of the year.

A Turkish Massacre

·······················

This new and gorgeous garment, majesty,
Sits not as easy on me as you think.
Brothers, you mix your sadness with some fear:
This is the English, not the Turkish Court;
Not Amurath an Amurath succeeds,
But Harry, Harry.

Henry IV Part Two (Act 5 Scene 2)

On this day in 1595 the Ottoman Sultan Murad III died. He was the grandson of Suleyman the Magnificent, but had little in common with his illustrious forebear. He was controlled by the Queen Mother, the redoubtable Nur Banu, and his favourite wife, the Venetian-born Sultana Baffo. The power of these women, and the in-fighting between them in the harem, would lead to the Kadinlar Sultanati, or the Sultanate of Women.

Murad had been addicted to sex. His mother supplied him with a new slave girl every Friday. Some say there were up to 1200 women in his harem, and

that he fathered up to 103 children. Certainly at his death twenty of his sons and twenty-seven of his daughters survived him. But Sultana Baffo had the interests of her own son, Mahomet, most at heart.

On hearing of his father's death, Mahomet returned to Istanbul. He landed at the Grand Seraglio, and immediately ordered the spot to be planted with half a million hyacinth bulbs from Aleppo. After his father's funeral in Haghia Sophia, Mahomet went to see his mother. She had not seen him for twelve years because he had been banished by his father for his ungovernable temper. He was twenty-nine. At that private meeting it would seem his mother told him to summon his other nineteen brothers to 'kiss his hand'.

The boys arrived, the youngest of whom was only eleven. Mahomet assured them they had nothing to fear. The next morning however nineteen corpses littered the palace. They had all been strangled with silken bowstrings by the deaf mutes, who were the Sultan's bodyguard.

Mahomet (or Amurath, as he was referred to, like his father) had acted within the law. One of his ancestors had instituted the *Zanan-nameh*, to avoid the dangers of a disputed succession.

Writing just a couple of years after this terrible event, it is no surprise that Shakespeare should imagine that the brothers of the newly crowned Henry V might be nervous.

Poets' Corner

Thou art a monument without a tomb.
To the memory of my beloved, the author Mr William
Shakespeare: and what he has left us.
Ben Jonson

The poet Edmund Spenser was buried on this day in 1599, in the South Transept of Westminster Abbey. He was 46.

The nearby tomb of Geoffrey Chaucer had been erected nearly half a century before, during the reign of Queen Mary, although in fact 'the Father of English Literature' died in 1400. Chaucer had originally been laid to rest in Westminster Abbey because he was Clerk of Works to the Palace of Westminster, not because he had written *The Canterbury Tales*. However, with Spenser and Chaucer now in eternal proximity, a tradition began which was to develop during the succeeding centuries, and this area of the Abbey became known as Poets' Corner. Spenser's coffin was carried by other poets, who strew his grave with pens and pieces of poetry.

Burial or commemoration in the Abbey did not always occur at or soon after the time of death. Shakespeare had to wait until the mid-eighteenth century before his monument appeared. He was even preceded by the playwright Francis Beaumont, John Fletcher's collaborator, who was shipped straight into the Abbey on his early death, just a month before Shakespeare in 1616. Ben Jonson, with a note of indignation, writes:
My Shakespeare, rise, I will not lodge thee by
Chaucer or Spenser, or bid Beaumont lie
A little further to make thee a room
Thou art a monument without a tomb.

Shakespeare, however, had to wait in line. Even his first editor and biographer Nicholas Rowe got there before him, in 1718. But eventually a fan base called the Shakespeare Ladies' Club secured a public subscription and the Swan of Avon was duly commemorated in Poets' Corner in 1740 with a monument designed by William Kent, and sculpted by Peter Scheemakers. Poor old Christopher Marlowe only received recognition in a window unveiled in 2002, beneath one dedicated to Oscar Wilde.

Edmund Spenser was author of *The Faerie Queen* and also *The Shepherd's Calendar*, 'containing twelve eclogues proportionable to the twelve months'.

Edmund Spenser: Artist unknown

In the final cantos of *The Faerie Queen*, Spenser strikes an unsettling note of chaotic change, introducing the titaness, Mutabilitie, who claims sovereignty over the world. Before her are paraded the four seasons: lusty spring, jolly summer, autumn in yellow clad, and winter clothed in frieze, and 'chattering his teeth for cold'. This procession is followed by all the months of the year, riding on their respective signs of the zodiac. Here is January, ready to cut back and prune with his hatchet, and standing on the stone water jar of Aquarius:
Then came old January, wrapped well
In many weeds to keep the cold away;
Yet did he quake and quiver like to quell,
And blow his nails to warm them if he may:
For, they were numbed with holding all the day
An hatchet keen, with which he felled wood,
And from the trees did lop the needless spray:
Upon an huge great Earth-pot steane he stood;
From whose wide mouth, there flowed forth the Roman flood.
Mutabilitie Cantos, VII: XLII

St Antony

The Feast of St Antony, the patron saint of pigs and swineherds.

I' faith, and thou follow'dst him like a church. Thou whoreson little tidy Batholomew boarpig, when wilt thou leave fighting a days and foining a nights, and begin to patch up thine old body for heaven?
Henry IV Part Two (Act 2 Scene 4)

John Stow, in his *Survey of London*, makes reference to a custom in the London markets:
'The officers in this city, did divers times take from the market people, pigs starved or otherwise unwholesome for man's sustenance; these they did slit in the ear. One of the proctors of St Anthony's Hospital tied a bell about the neck, and let it feed upon the dunghills; no one would hurt or take it up; but if any one gave it bread or other feeding, such it would know, watch for, and daily follow, whining till it had somewhat given it; whereupon was raised a proverb, such a one will follow such a one, and whine as if it were an Anthony pig.'

A Tantony pig was generally the smallest pig in the litter, which according to the proverb will follow you wherever you go.

Launcelot Gobbo complains about the adverse effects of converting the Jews to Christianity in *The Merchant of Venice*:
This making of Christians will raise the price of hogs: if we grow all to be pork-eaters, we shall not shortly have a rasher on the coals for money.
The Merchant of Venice (Act 3 Scene 5)

Gobbos were hunchbacks in Renaissance Venice. *Il Gobbo di Rialto* or the *Hunchback of the Rialto* is a granite statue of a hunchback found opposite the Church of San Giacomo. A punishment for minor offences was to be stripped naked and made to run, from Piazza San Marco to the Rialto, through a gauntlet of jeering citizens ending at the statue, which you then would have to kiss to save yourself from further humiliation. *Il Gobbo* is still a lucky charm in Italy today.

The hunchbacked Richard III is insulted by Queen Margaret:
Thou elvish-mark'd, abortive, rooting hog!
Richard III (Act 1 Scene 3)

Shakespeare in the Bible

In this week in 1604, King James convened a conference at Hampton Court, at which a new translation of the Bible was proposed. An authorized and correct version of the Bible was greatly needed. There were at least four different English translations, not one of which had any absolute authority over any other. The proposal originated with the Puritans. James embraced the project eagerly, and with his own pen drew up the rules for translating. He appointed a commission of learned men selected from the two universities and from Westminster. Each was given a portion of the Scriptures to translate. They began their labours in the spring of 1607; and then a select committee was appointed, who met at Stationers' Hall in London, to correct the work of the rest. The new King James Bible appeared in 1611, perhaps the most influential book, next to *Shakespeare's Plays*, in the English language.

In 1610, the year before the Bible was published, Shakespeare was 46 years old.

If you count 46 words in from the beginning of Psalm 46 and count 46 words back from the end, you get the words *shake*, and *spear*.

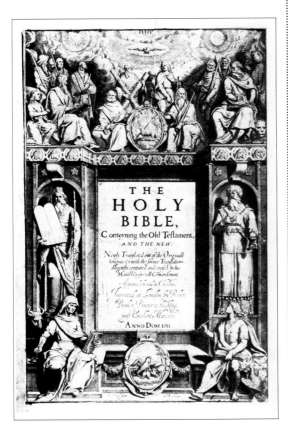

God is our refuge and strength,
a very present help in trouble.
Therefore will not we fear,
though the earth be removed,
and though the mountains be carried into the midst of
    the sea;
though the waters thereof roar and be troubled
though the mountains SHAKE with the swelling thereof.
There is a river, the streams whereof shall make glad the city
    of God,
the holy place of the tabernacles of the Most High.
God is in the midst of her;
she shall not be moved:
God shall help her, and that right early.
The heathen raged, the kingdoms were moved:
he uttered his voice, the earth melted.
The Lord of hosts is with us
the God of Jacob is our refuge.
Come, behold the works of the Lord,
what desolations he hath made in the earth.
He maketh wars to cease unto the end of the earth;
he breaketh the bow, and cutteth the SPEAR in sunder;
he burneth the chariot in the fire.
Be still, and know that I am God:
I will be exalted among the heathen,
I will be exalted in the earth.
The Lord of hosts is with us;
the God of Jacob is our refuge.

Whales
•••••••••

What tempest, I trow, threw this whale, with so many tons of oil in his belly, ashore at Windsor?

The Merry Wives of Windsor (Act 2 Scene 1)

On Thursday January 19th, 2006 staff at the Thames Barrier reported that a whale had come through the gates. It turned out to be a bottlenose whale, which swam up the Thames as far as Battersea, and into the imagination of the entire British public. Unfortunately attempts to rescue the confused mammal failed and it died two days later.

Whales have swum up the Thames to London many times over the centuries – but never before perhaps with such sympathetic support. In fact when a 'beast of prodigious size' swam under London Bridge in 1240, Londoners chased it upstream and harpooned it. Indeed in Shakespeare's lifetime England launched its first whaling fleet. In 1611, Jonas Poole captained the *Elizabeth* and the *Mary Margaret*, to Spitsbergen to fish the whale stocks there. They caught the first whale on June 12th, and captured thirteen in all, though the voyage itself was a complete disaster. Both ships were lost, one capsized and the other was driven ashore by ice.

Nevertheless, London was soon home to a flourishing whaling industry that killed tens of thousands of these leviathans a year simply to extract their oil for lighting. Barrels of whale oil were placed around the streets and lit each night, winning the city a reputation as one of the best lit in Europe.

Here is an early account of a whaling trip:

'I might here recreate your wearied eyes with a hunting spectacle of the greatest chase which Nature yieldeth, I mean, the killing of the whale. When they espy him on the top of the water (which he is forced to, for to take breath) they row towards him in a shallop, in which the harpooner stands ready, with both his hands to dart his harping iron, to which is fastened a line of such length that the whale, (which suddenly feeling himself hurt, sinketh to the bottom), may carry it down with him, being before fitted, that the shallop therewith be not therewith endangered; coming up again, they again strike him with lances made for that purpose about twelve foot long, the iron eight thereof, and the blade eighteen inches; the

harping iron principally serving to fasten him to the shallop: and thus they hold him in such pursuit, till after streams of water, and next that of blood, cast up into the air and water (as angry with both elements, which have brought hither such weak hands to his destruction) he at last yieldeth his slain carcass as meed to the conquerors. They tow him to the ship with two or three shallops made fast to one another: and then floating at the stern of the ship, they cut the blubber or fat from the flesh, in pieces three or four foot long, which after at shore are cut smaller, and boiled in coppers, which done they take them out and put them in wicker baskets, which are set in shallops half full of water, into which the oil runneth, and is thence put into buts. This whale fishing is yearly now used by our men in Greenland, with great profit. The ordinary length of a whale is sixty foot.'

Purchas His Pilgrimes, Samuel Puchas

St Agnes' Eve

And on sweet St Agnes' night
Please you with the promis'd sight
Some of husband, some of lovers
Which an empty dream discovers.

The Satyr, Ben Jonson

Upon St Agnes' Night you take a row of pins, and pull out every one, one after another, saying a Pater Noster, sticking a pin in your sleeve, and you will dream of him or her you shall marry.

Miscellanies, John Aubrey

The feast of St Agnes was a special holiday for women. St Agnes was a Roman virgin and martyr, condemned to be debauched in the public stews before her execution. Her virginity was miraculously preserved, however, by lightning and thunder from heaven.

John Keats based his poem, *The Eve of St Agnes*, on this superstition.

They told her how, upon St Agnes's Eve,
Young virgins might have visions of delight,
And soft adorings from their loves receive
Upon the honey'd middle of the night,
If ceremonies due they did aright;
As, supperless to bed they must retire,
And couch supine their beauties, lily white;
Nor look behind, nor sideways, but require
Of Heaven with upward eyes for all that they desire.

Out went the taper as she hurried in;
Its little smoke, in pallid moonshine, died:
She closed the door, she panted, all akin
To spirits of the air, and visions wide.
No utter'd syllable, or, woe betide!
But to her heart, her heart was voluble,
Paining with eloquence her balmy side;
As though a tongueless nightingale should swell
Her throat in vain, and die, heart-stifled, in her dell.

Sewing patterns from Trevelyon's Miscellany

St Agnes' Day

The Hunters in the Snow by Pieter Brueghel the Elder, 1565

Snow

Shakespeare makes many references to the snow and the cold at this time of year:

O, that I were a mockery king of snow,
Standing before the sun of Bolingbroke,
To melt myself away in waterdrops!

Richard II (Act 4 Scene 1)

When icicles hang by the wall,
And Dick the shepherd blows his nail
And Tom bears logs into the hall
And milk comes frozen home in pail,
When blood is nipped and ways be foul,
Then nightly sings the staring owl:
'Tu-whit, tu-whoo'
A merry note,
While greasy Joan doth keel the pot.
When all aloud the wind doth blow

And coughing drowns the parson's saw
And birds sit brooding in the snow
And Marian's nose looks red and raw,
When roasted crabs hiss in the bowl,
Then nightly sings the staring owl:
'Tu-whit, tu-whoo'
A merry note,
While greasy Joan doth keel the pot.

Love's Labour's Lost (Act 5 Scene 2)

Yea, like the stag when snow the pasture sheets
The barks of trees thou browsed'st.

Antony and Cleopatra (Act 1 Scene 4)

As chaste as the icicle
That's curdied by the frost from purest snow
And hangs upon Dian's temple.

Coriolanus (Act 5 Scene 3)

St Vincent's Day

Remember on St Vincent's Day
If that the Sun his beams display
For tis a token bright and clear
Of prosperous weather all the year
Traditional Verse

St Vincent was a Spanish martyr who died by fire in 304 AD.

On St Vincent's Day in 1607 (according to to the Stationers' Register), the rights to publish *Love's Labour's Lost* (originally printed in 1598) were transferred from the bookseller Cuthbert Burby to one Nicholas Long. He also handed over *Romeo and Juliet.*

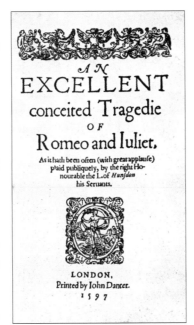

AN
EXCELLENT
conceited Tragedie
OF
Romeo and Iuliet.

As it hath been often (with great applause)
plaid publiquely, by the right Honourable the L. of *Hunsdon*
his Seruants.

LONDON,
Printed by Iohn Dancer.
1597

There is an anecdote about a performance of *Romeo and Juliet* after the Restoration, in John Downes' *Roscius Anglicanus*:

Note: There being a fight and scuffle in this play, between the House of Capulet, and the House of Paris; Mrs Holden acting his wife, enter'd in a hurry, crying 'O, my dear Count!' She inadvertently left out 'O' in the pronunciation of the word Count, giving it a vehement accent, put the house into such laughter, that London Bridge at low tide was silence to it.

The following letter, sent to Robert Cecil, from Sir Walter Cope, gives a little insight into the everyday workings of Shakespeare's company. Cope had been scuttling around London, trying to rustle up some new entertainment for King James' wife, Queen Anne of Denmark. Richard Burbage, head of the newly titled King's Men, it seems was the messenger.

To the Right Honourable the Lord Viscount Cranborne at the court.★
Sir Walter Cope to my Lord.
Sir,
I have sent and been all this morning hunting for players, jugglers, and such kind of creatures, but find them hard to find, wherefore (leaving notes for them to seek me), Burbage is come and says there is no new play that the queen has not seen, but they have revived an old one, called *Love's Labour's Lost* which for wit and mirth he says will please her exceedingly. And this is appointed to be played tomorrow night at my Lord of Southampton's unless you send a writ to remove the Corpus Cum Causa to your house in Strand. Burbage is my messenger ready attending your pleasure.
Yours most humbly,
Walter Cope

Cope was a gentleman, adventurer, and member of the Society of Antiquaries. He also had a Cabinet of Curiosities, like the Tradescants in Lambeth (see February 18th), which included 'a round horn which had grown on an English woman's forehead, and a flying rhinoceros'.

★King James had made Robert Cecil Viscount Cranborne in 1604.

The Gloomiest Day of the Year

As today is often described as the gloomiest day of the year, here to cheer everyone up is an extract from Robert Burton's *Anatomy of Melancholy*. Burton describes the condition of Love Melancholy, which distorts one's perceptions. As he says, 'Jupiter himself cannot love and be wise together.' Burton then writes a sentence of such vivacious and misogynistic vitriol it deserves noting:

'Every lover admires his mistress, though she be very deformed of herself, ill-favoured, wrinkled, pimpled, pale, red, yellow, tanned, tallow-faced, have a swollen juggler's platter face, or a thin, lean, chitty face, have clouds in her face, be crooked, dry, bald, goggle-eyed, blear-eyed, or with staring eyes, she looks like a squis'd

cat, hold her head still awry, heavy, dull, hollow-eyed, black or yellow about the eyes, or squint eyes, sparrow mouthed, Persian hook-nosed, have a sharp fox nose, a red nose, China flat, great nose, a nose like a promontory, gubber-tushed, rotten teeth, black, uneven, brown teeth, beetle browed, a witch's beard, her breath stink all over the room, her nose drop in winter and summer, with a Bavarian poke under her chin, a sharp chin, lave-eared, with a long crane's neck, which stands awry too, her dugs like two double jugs, or else no dugs, in that other extreme, bloody fallen fingers, she have filthy, long unpared nails, scabbed hands or wrists, a tanned skin, a rotten carcass, crooked back, she stoops, is lame, splay-footed, as slender in the middle as a cow in the waist, gouty legs, her ankles hang over her shoes, her feet stink, she breed lice, a mere changeling, a very monster, an oaf imperfect, her whole complexion savours, a harsh voice, incondite gestures, vile gait, a vast virago, or an ugly tit, a slug, a fat fustylugs, a truss, a long lean rawbone, a skeleton, a sneaker, and to thy judgement looks like a mard in a lantern, whom thou couldst not fancy for a world, but hatest, loathest, and wouldst have spit in her face, or blow thy nose in her bosom, remedium amoris to another man, a dowdy, a slut, a scold, a nasty rank, rammy, filthy, beastly quean, dishonest, peradventure, obscene, base, beggarly, rude, foolish, untaught, peevish, Irus' daughter, Thersites' sister, Grobian's scholar, if he loves her once, he admires her for all this, he takes no notice of any such errors, or imperfections of body and mind. He had rather have her than any woman in the world.'

The *Anatomy of Melancholy* was the only work which Burton produced. Dr Johnson said it was the one book that ever took him out of bed two hours sooner than he wished to rise.

This melancholy finds rather gentler expression by Jacques in *As You Like It*:
I have neither the scholar's melancholy which is emulation; nor the musician's which is fantastical; nor the courtier's which is proud; nor the soldier's which is ambitious; nor the lawyer's which is politic; nor the lady's which is nice; nor the lover's which is all these; but it is a melancholy of mine own, compounded of many simples, extracted from many objects; and indeed the sundry contemplation of my travels, which, by often rumination, wraps me in a most humorous sadness.
As You Like It (Act 4 Scene 1)

Henslowe and Titus Andronicus

On this day in 1594, Philip Henslowe, the great entrepreneur who ran the Rose Theatre on Bankside in Shakespeare's day, recorded the following in his diary: 'Ne – Rd at titus & ondronicus the 2[4] of jeneway iij viijs'

'Ne' indicates a 'new' play. 'Rd' ('received') at 'Titus Andronicus', on 'the' (Thursday) 24th of January, iijli viijs (three pounds and eight shillings).

Even though Henslowe wasn't too sure about the title, he knew that it was good 'get penny' box office. Indeed, when they repeated it at the Rose the following Tuesday, January 29th, and the Wednesday of the following week, February 6th, the receipts yielded forty shillings (two pounds) per performance. Unfortunately the next day, Thursday February 7th, the Rose was closed, because of plague. The company sold the play to a printer, who rushed it out, and copies were soon to be had at the Sign of the Gun, a bookstall (or station) outside the little north door of St Paul's. Though Henslowe never mentioned his name in the diaries, the play was by Shakespeare, and this was the first time one of his plays had been published. As he was not famous yet, his name did not actually appear on the cover.

Henry Peacham's drawing of *Titus Andronicus*, the earliest known illustration of a Shakespeare play.

Philip Henslowe's diaries give a fascinating insight into the world of the theatre in Shakespeare's day. They are written on the blank pages of an old account book, which Henslowe's brother had kept for his brother-in-law's ironworks. As a careful businessman, Henslowe made use of the spare paper. The pages record not only the receipts of the 1592 season at the Rose, but also his notes, jotted down sporadically over the next seventeen years until 1609. They show the dealings Henslowe had with some twenty-seven playwrights, payments for their work, and commissions for sequels, as well as private loans. Henslowe scribbled a telling note which revealed something of his attitude to his stable of writers: 'Should these fellows come out of my debt, I should have no rule over them.'

Henslowe had bought a property called the Little Rose in 1584. It was probably a brothel, with a rose garden attached, near the home he shared with his wife Agnes, opposite the Clink in Southwark. Three years later in 1587, he opened the Rose Theatre, and by 1591 he had partnered with the Admiral's Men. Their lead actor, Edward Alleyn, had married his step-daughter Joan. When Burbage built the Globe Theatre, rather too close by, in 1598, Henslowe moved his company to the Fortune Theatre, north of the city, on the other of the river.

Henslowe was an entrepreneur with his fingers in many pies. He and Alleyn purchased the office of Keeper of the Royal Game, when King James came to the throne, and ran the bull and bear baiting operation at Paris Garden. In 1614 they built the Hope Theatre as a dual purpose theatre cum bear pit. Ben Jonson complained (in his introduction to *Bartholomew Fair* which played at the Hope), that the place was 'as dirty as Smithfield and as stinking every wit'. In the same introduction he also referred to *Andronicus*, which was still holding the stage twenty years later.

St Paul's Day
••••••••••••••

If St Paul's Day be fair and clear,
It does betide a happy year;
But if it chance to snow or rain,
Then will be dear all kind of grain;
Antiquities of the Common People, Henry Bourne

Ben Jonson

Thomas Dekker gave a vivid description of his rival playwright as having a face like a bruised, rotten russet apple, or a badly pock-marked warming pan.

Ben Jonson, after Abraham van Blyenberch, 1618

In 1619, Ben Jonson walked from London to Scotland to stay with his friend William Drummond of Hawthornden. On this day he set off home again. Much of Drummond's observations are in note form. Here is his description of Jonson, happily sozzled one night, imagining all sorts of wonders:

⚙ He hath consumed a whole night in lying looking to his great toe, about which he hath seen Tartars & Turks, Romans and Cathaginians fight in his imagination.

⚙ Of all his plays he never gained 2 hundred pounds.

⚙ He esteemeth John Donne the first poet in the world in some things, his verses *The Lost Chain*, he hath by heart & the passage of the calm, that dust and feathers do not stir, all was so quiet. Affirmeth Donne to have written all his best pieces ere he was 25 years old.

⚙ He is a great lover and praiser of himself, a contemner and scorner of others, given rather to lose a friend than a jest, jealous of every word and action of those about him (especially after drink) which is one of those elements in which he liveth, a dissembler of ill parts which reign in him, a bragger of some good that he wanteth, thinketh nothing well but what either he himself, or some of his friends and countrymen hath said or done. He is passionately kind and angry, careless either to gain or keep, vindictive, but if he be well answered, at himself.

⚙ He went from Leith homeward the 25 of January 1619 in a pair of shoes, which he told lasted him since he came from Darnton (Darlington), which he minded to take back that far again.

Duels

· · · · · ·

God bless me from a challenge.
Much Ado About Nothing (Act 5 Scene 1)

On this day in 1614, King James banned duelling.
The previous September, Edward Sackville, the Earl
of Dorset, and the Scottish Lord Bruce had fought a
duel over the beautiful Venetia Stanley. In order to
avoid King James' displeasure they travelled to
Bergen-op-zoom, a village outside Antwerp, to fight.
Here is Sackville's own account:

'I bade him alight, and then, in a meadow, ankle deep
in water at the least, bidding farewell to our doublets,
in our shirts began to charge each other; having afore
commanded our surgeons to withdraw themselves a
pretty distance from us: conjuring them, besides, (as
they respected our favours or their own safeties) not
to stir, but to suffer us to execute our pleasures, we
being fully resolved, God forgive us, to dispatch each
other by what means we could.

'I made a thrust at my enemy, but was short, and in
drawing back my arm, I received a great wound
thereon, which I interpreted as a reward for my short
shooting, but in revenge I pressed in to him, though
then missed him also, and then receiving a wound in
my right pap, which passed level through my body
and almost to my back. And there we wrestled for the
two greatest and dearest prizes we could ever expect
trial for: Honour and Life. In which struggling, my
hand having but an ordinary glove on it, lost one of
her servants, though the meanest, which hung by a
skin, and to sight yet remaineth as before, and I am
put in hope, one day to recover the use of it again.

'But at last, breathless, yet keeping our holds, there
past on both sides propositions of quitting each
other's sword. But when amity was dead, confidence
could not live; and who should quit first was the
question: which on neither part, either would
perform, and re-striving again afresh, with a kick and
a wrinch together, I freed my long captivated weapon.

Which incontinently levying at his throat, being
master still of his, I demanded if he would ask his life,
or yield his sword; both which, though in imminent
danger, he bravely denied so to do. Myself being
wounded, and feeling loss of blood, having three
conduits running on me, began to make me faint: and
he courageously persisting not to accord to either of
my propositions, I struck at his heart; but with his
avoiding missed my aim, yet passed through his body,
and drawing through my sword, repast it through
again, through another place, when he cried, "O, I am
slain."

'This thus ended; I retired to my surgeon, in whose
arms after I had remained a while for want of blood, I
lost my sight, and withal, as I then thought, my life
also. But strong water and his diligence, quickly
revived me, when I escaped a great danger.'

Lord Bruce's heart was interred in a heart-shaped
leaden box. Sackville returned to England, but
Venetia Stanley had married someone else in his
absence.

The First Westerner in the Forbidden City
••

I will fetch you a toothpicker from the farthest inch of Asia, bring you the length of Prester John's foot, fetch you a hair from the great Cham's beard, do you any embassage to the pigmies...

Much Ado About Nothing (Act 2 Scene 1)

On this day in 1601, the Jesuit priest, Matteo Ricci, presented a letter to accompany a series of gifts to the Ming Emperor of China, Wan Li.

These presents included a painting of Christ, one of the Madonna and child, a cross inlaid with precious stones also containing relics of the saints, an Atlas (the *Theatrum Orbis Terrarum of Ortelius*), eight mirrors, a rhinoceros tusk, and two clocks: a large one, worked by weights, and a small striking one worked by springs and made of gilded metal.

He ended the memorial signing off: **'Your majesty's grateful servant awaits orders: he has written this letter in all humility: dated the twenty-fourth day of the twelfth moon of the twenty-eighth year of the Kingdom of Wan Li.'**

The letter, carefully wrapped between two yellow tablets and covered with a piece of yellow silk, was handed in at the principal gate of the palace in Peking.

Initially, Fr Ricci was not granted an audience with the Emperor. But the chiming clock impressed, and Ricci was finally allowed to present

himself at the Imperial court. Thus he became the first Westerner to be invited into the Forbidden City. Vincent Cronin continues the story:

'Since he refused to see the foreigners, the Emperor gave orders that their portraits should be painted. From the college of mathematicians they were escorted to the imperial studios, still inside the palace. Here Ricci and Pantoja stayed several days, while they were both painted full length on rolls of silk. At the end of the sitting they inspected the finished portraits, then looked at each other in silent astonishment. It was impossible to tell which was which: they were unrecognisable, without the smallest likeness; just as Chinese annalists made unprecedented events conform to past tradition, the account of any one year reading like those of the past two millennia, so the painters, working in a period of artistic decline and slavish imitation of the past calligraphic masters, had portrayed two Chinese graduates, distinctive only by their having slightly larger eyes and thicker beards. They had drawn barbarians within the orbit of the Flowery kingdom.

'Proudly the painters carried their work to the Emperor, and reported his approval: When His majesty saw the pictures, he said, "They are Hoeihoei": that is saracens of Persia, who trade with the Middle Kingdom. But a secretary replied, "Surely not, Your majesty, for these foreigners eat pork."'

The Wise Man from the West,
Vincent Cronin

Covered Jar with Carp Design, 1522-66, Ming Dynasty

The War of the Theatres

Words, words, words.

Hamlet (Act 2 Scene 2)

The so-called *War of the Theatres* involved a dispute between Ben Jonson and his fellow writers John Marston and Thomas Dekker. They caricatured each other in a number of plays written between 1599 and 1602. Here is my favourite skirmish which comes from Jonson's *The Poetaster*. Horace (Jonson) has brought two false poets, Crispinius (Marston: 'full of lewd solecisms and worded trash') and Demetrius (Dekker) to trial for calumny. Horace gives the poets a purgative drug, which makes them vomit up all their made-up words.

Tibullus: How now Crispinius?

Crispinius: O, I am sick!

Horace: A basin, a basin, quickly, our physic works. Faint not man.

Crispinius: O – retrograde – reciprocal - incubus.

Caesar: What's that, Horace?

Horace: Retrograde, reciprocal and incubus are come up.

Gallus: Thanks be to Jupiter.

Crispinius: O – glibbery – lubrical – defunct – O!

Horace: Well said. Here's some store.

Virgil: What are they?

Horace: Glibbery, lubrical and defunct.

Gallus: O, they came up easy.

Crispinius: O, O...!

Tibullus: What's that?

Horace: Nothing yet.

Crispinius: Magnificate –

Horace: What cheer, Crispinius?

Crispinius: O! I shall cast up my – spurious – snotteries.

Horace: Good, again?

Crispinius: Chillblained –O –O – Clumsie –

Horace: That clumsie stuck horribly.

Gallus: Who would have thought there should have been such a deal of filth in a poet?

Crispinius: O – balmy froth.

Caesar: What's that?

Crispinius: Puffle – inflate – turgidous – ventosity.

Tibullus: O terrible windy words!

The Poetaster (Act 5)

Scholars used to suggest that Shakespeare was satirizing Jonson as Ajax in *Troilus and Cressida* and Marston as Thersites. Be that as it may, on this day in 1609, *Troilus and Cressida* was re-entered for publication in the Stationers' Register.

Hilliard Blues
·················

Painting is welcome.
Timon of Athens (Act 1 Scene 1)

The great miniaturist painter, Nicholas Hilliard, died aged 73 in January 1618 and was buried in St Martin's in the Fields. For thirty-five years, he had lived and worked in a house called The Maidenhead in Gutter Lane in the parish of Ludgate.

In his *Treatise On the Art of Limning*, Hilliard describes how to make the blues for which he is famous. Ultramarine was made of lapis lazuli, and was very costly:

'For limning, the darkest and highest blue is ultramarine of Venice. Of the best I have paid three shillings and eightpence a carat, which is but four grains – eleven pounds and ten shillings the ounce; and the worst is but bad, will cost two shillings and sixpence the carat – seven pounds ten shillings the ounce. Instead whereof we use smalt, of the best; blue bices of divers sorts, some paler than others, some seven or six degrees one above the other. These may be grinded, but better broken like enamel in a stone mortar of flint excellent smooth, with a pestle of flint or agate, well stirred till it be fine, with gum water only, and washed; so have you many sorts and all good. Shadowing blues are litmus and indigo, and florey; these need no washing, nor litmus any grinding, but steeped in lye of soap-ashes; use gum at discretion as aforesaid.'

Here Hilliard also suplies some trade secrets about how to grind colours:

'India lake to be ground with gum water and spread thin about the shell; umber and some other colours are much subject to crackle and fall from the shell in pieces. When you find it so, take a little white sugar candy reduced to white powder, and with a few drops of fair water you must temper the colour again as it is in the shell, till both the colour and the sugar candy be

Sir Walter Raleigh by Nicholas Hilliard

both thoroughly dissolved; which being once dry will lie fast in the shell. English Ochre will lie fast in the shell and works well if well ground.

'Pink is also a very good colour, and works sharp and neat, and must be ground as the rest. Umber, being a foul and greasy colour, if when you have bought it you burn it in a crucible or goldsmith's pot, it is cleansed, and being ground as the rest works well. Terra de Collana is easy to work when it is new ground, and is very good to close up the last and deepest touches in the shadowed places of pictures by the life. Cherry stone and ivory are both to be burned and so ground; the first is a very good black, especially for draperies and black apparel, but if you make satin it must be tempered with a little India lake or indigo, but only to make it appear with a more beautiful gloss, which heightened with a lighter mixture of more whiteish in stronger touches and hard reflections, and deepened with ivory, will show marvellous well. Ivory black must be well tempered with sugar candy to prevent cracking.'

Tsunami in Bristol Channel, 1607

Though you untie the winds and let them fight
Against the churches; though the yesty waves
Confound and swallow navigation up;
Though bladed corn be lodged and trees blown down;
Though castles topple on their warders' heads;
Though palaces and pyramids do slope
Their heads to their foundations, though the treasure
Of Nature's germens tumble altogether
Even till destruction sicken, answer me
To what I ask you.
Macbeth (Act 4 Scene 1)

An astonishing recent discovery reveals that the West Country experienced a tsunami in Shakespeare's lifetime, with terrible loss of life and livelihood.

On this day in 1607 the Bristol Channel floods resulted in the drowning of an estimated 2,000 or more people, with houses and whole villages swept away, farmland inundated and livestock destroyed, wrecking the local economy along the coast.

There remain plaques up to 8 feet above sea level to show how high the waters rose on the sides of the surviving churches. The disaster was commemorated in a contemporary pamphlet: 'God's warning to the people of England by the great overflowing of the waters or floods'.

'In January last (towards the end of the month) the sea at a flowing water meeting with Land-floods, strove so violently together, that bearing down all things that were built to withstand and hinder the force of them, the banks were eaten through and a rupture made into Somerset-shire. No sooner was this furious invader entered, but he got up high into the Land, and encountering with the River Severn, they both boiled in such pride that many miles, (to the quantity of 10 in length, and 4 or 5 at least in breadth) were in a short time swallowed up in this torrent. This Inundation began in the morning, & within few hours after, covered the face of the earth thereabouts to the depths of 11 or 12 foot in some places, in others more.'

Written evidence from the time describes events that were uncannily similar to the tragedy that unfolded in South-east Asia in 2005. The sea receded, then a wave of water rushed in faster than people could run.

And here's another example of disastrous tides from 1613:

'On All Hallows Day, at night a vehement northwest wind that had lasted two or three days, meeting with the spring tides, brought in the greatest tide that hath been seen here by Kent, Essex, Norfolk, and other places, as well by overflowing their marshes, bearing down their walls, and making breaches, as by carrying away stacks of hay, many houses, and drowning great numbers of sheep and other cattle, insomuch as one man hath lost above 1500 sheep, besides other losses. And they make account that Kent alone is damnified to the value of £200,000; for not only along the Thames side, but about Sandwich and that way there is great harm done, and six houses were carried away at Margate.'
Letter from John Chamberlain to Dudley Carleton

Heads on London Bridge

Behold, where stands the usurper's cursed head.
Macbeth (Act 5 Scene 7)

Detail from Visscher's Panoramic View of London (1616)

After they were hanged on January 31st 1606, Guy Fawkes and the other gunpowder conspirators had their heads chopped off and mounted on pikes on London Bridge.

'Over the river at London, there is a beautiful long bridge, with quite splendid, handsome, and well-built houses, which are occupied by merchants of consequence. Upon one of the towers, nearly in the middle of the bridge, are stuck up about thirty-four heads of persons of distinction, who had in former times been condemned and beheaded for creating riots and from other causes.'
Frederick, Duke of Württemberg, 1592

Back in the reign of Henry VIII, John Fisher, who had supported Katherine of Aragon, was executed for high treason. His body was buried, but his head was put on show.
'The head being somewhat parboiled in hot water, was pricked upon a pole and set on high upon London Bridge. The miraculous sight of this head, which after

it had stand up the space of 14 days upon the bridge, could not be perceived to waste nor consume, neither for the weather, which was then very hot, neither for the parboiling in hot water, but grew daily fresher and fresher, so that in his lifetime he never looked so well, whereby was notified to the whole world the innocency and holiness of this blessed father.'
Life of Fisher, Richard Hall

In his *Brief Lives*, Aubrey mentions the story of Thomas More's head:
'After he was beheaded his trunk was interred in Chelsea church, near the middle of the south wall, where was some slight Monument erected. His head was upon London Bridge. There goes this story in the family viz. that one day as one of his daughters was passing under the Bridge, looking on her father's head, said she, "That head has lain many a time in my lap, would to God it would fall into my lap, as I pass under." She had her wish, and it did fall into her lap, and is now preserved in the vault in the cathedral at Canterbury.'

Thomas Platter is bemused by the custom of pointing out relatives:
'And their descendants are accustomed to boast of this, themselves even pointing out to one their ancestors' heads on this same bridge, believing that they will be esteemed the more because their antecedents were of such high descent that they could even covet the crown, but being too weak to attain it were executed for rebels; thus they make an honour for themselves of what was set up to be a disgrace and an example.'

The head of one of Shakespeare's own ancestors had been placed on London Bridge: Edward Arden, High Sheriff of Warwickshire, was executed in 1583, just four years before Will arrived in London.

You have such a February face
So full of frost, storm.
Much Ado About Nothing (Act 5 Scene 4)

'It is now February, and the Sun is gotten up a cock-
stride of his climbing, the valleys now are painted
white, and the brooks are full of water: the frog goes
to seek out the paddock, and the crow and the rook
begin to mislike their old makes: forward conies
begin now to kindle, and the fat grounds are not
without lambs: the gardener falls to sorting of his
seeds, and the husbandsman falls afresh to scouring
of his plough share: the term travellers make the
shoemaker's harvest, and the chaundler's cheese
makes the chalk walk apace: the fishmonger sorts his
wares against lent: and a lambskin is good for a lame
arm; the waters now alter the nature of their
softness, and the soft earth is made stony hard: The
air is sharp and piercing, and the winds blow cold:
The taverns and the inns seldom lack guests, and the
ostler knows how to gain by his hay: the hunting
horse is at the heels of the hound, while the ambling
nag carries the physician with his foot cloth: the
youth of blood begins to spring, and the honour of
art is gotten by experience: the trees a little begin to
bud, and the sap begins to rise up out of the root:
Physic now hath work among weak bodies, and the
apothecary's drugs are very gainful: there is hope of a
better time not far off, for this in itself is little
comfortable: and for the small pleasure that I find in
it, I will thus briefly conclude of it: It is the poor
man's pick-purse, and the miser's cut-throat, the
enemy to pleasure, and the time of patience.
Farewell.'
Fantasticks, Nicholas Breton

'There followeth for the latter part of January and
February, the mezereon-tree, which then blossoms,
crocus vernus, both the yellow and grey; primroses,
anemones, the early tulippa, hyacinthus orientalis,
chamairis, fritillaria.'
Of Gardens, Francis Bacon

'February shall be clothed in a dark sky colour
carrying in his right hand with a fair grace the sign of
Pisces.'
Emblems, Henry Peacham

The Life of an Actor/Musician

'Mr Phillips, this is your call'

There is a plat which still exists for an Elizabethan play called *Sardanapalus*. A plat is a backstage reminder of what scene went next in the running order, and it reads like a contemporary call sheet. I can imagine one of our stage managers reading the latter part out, and hearing it backstage at Stratford: **'Enter Sardanapalus, Abractus, Nicanor and Captains, marching: Mr Phillips, Mr Pope, Robert Pallant, John Holland.'**

Though Phillips played the splendid Assyrian King himself (presumably the lead), he generally played more supporting roles. We know nothing else about *Sardanapalus*, but we do know a little bit about Phillips himself. For example, we know he wrote a little jig called *The Jig of the Slippers*, though we don't know what it sounded like.

Augustine Phillips was one of the original sharers in the Globe, and he lived nearby in Southwark: in Horseshoe Court near Bullhead Alley in the Liberty of the Clink to be exact. He and his wife Anne and their two girls (Rebecca and Magdalen) moved briefly over the river to the parish of St Botolph without Aldgate, near Houndsditch (where they buried a stillborn child, another daughter). Eventually, after having another girl, they moved back across the river and baptised a son whom they called Austin like his dad. Tragically little Austin died before his third birthday. After his death, Phillips moved his wife and the girls out of town. He bought a house way upstream at Mortlake.

Austin Phillips made his will in May 1605, '*being at this present sick and weak of body*'. Generously, he left £5 to the hired men in the *King's Men* to be distributed among them. The hired men were the extras, basically, who played all the crowd parts, and the soldiers – the spear carriers if you like. He left both Will Shakespeare and Harry Condell thirty shillings in gold and the same amount to his servant Chris

Beeston (see November 4th, he's the 'I've-slept-with-over-a-hundred-women' bloke). And a pound each to six of his other mates in the company, including Robert Armin.

To Sam Gilburne, his apprentice, he left two pounds and some clothes (which might be costumes): 'my mouse-coloured

The Flute Player by Hendrick Terbrugghen, 1621

velvet hose, and a white taffeta doublet, a black taffeta suit, my purple cloak, sword and dagger', and then as a bit of an afterthought 'and my bass viol'. To his second apprentice, Jim Sands, as well as another two pounds, he left the rest of his musical instruments: 'a cittern, a bandore, and a lute'. Sadly there was a squabble over the will.

Last in Spenser's parade of the months comes cold February drawn by the fish of Pisces:

And lastly, came cold February, sitting
In an old wagon, for he could not ride;
Drawn of two fishes for the season fitting,
Which through the flood before did softly slide
And swim away: yet had he by his side
His plough and harness fit to till the ground,
And tools to prune the trees, before the pride
Of hasting Prime did make them burgeon round:
So past the twelve Months forth, & their dew places found.
Mutabilitie Cantos, VII: XLIII

Candlemas

If Candlemas be fair and bright
Come winter have another flight
If Candlemas brings cloud and rain
Go, winter and come not again.
Traditional Verse

Candlemas was the festival of the purification of the Virgin Mary, when candles were blessed. You might have thought that candles would have been considered part of the panoply of Catholic superstition, and that at the Reformation, the ceremonials of Candlemas would have been banned. However, in 1539 Henry VIII proclaimed:
'On Candlemas Day it shall be declared that the bearing of candles is done in memory of Christ, the spiritual light, whom Simeon did prophesy, as it is read in the church that day.'

On this day in 1585, Shakespeare's wife, Anne, gave birth to twins: Hamnet and Judith.
And exactly fifteen years later, to the very day, on Candlemas in 1600, *Twelfth Night* was performed at Middle Temple. Shakespeare had written a play about another set of twins, Viola and Sebastian, who are separated in a shipwreck. The Middle Temple performance should have taken place on the fifteenth birthday of his own twins. But by then Judith and Hamnet had been separated for ever. Hamnet died when he was only eleven.

One eye-witness to that performance was John Manningham, who was a member of the Temple. He thought it worth recording in his diary. He wrote:
'Feb 2 at our feast (Candlemas) we had a play called Twelfth Night or What You Will, much like the Comedy of
Errors or Menaechmi in Plautus... A good practise is it to make the steward believe his Lady widow was in Love with him by counterfeiting a letter, as from his Lady, in general terms, telling him what she liked best in him and prescribing his gesture in smiling his apparel etc. And then when he came to practise, making him believe they took him to be mad.'

Robert Herrick alludes to the customs of Candlemas Eve. All the green Christmas decorations had to be taken down on this evening.
Down with the rosemary and bays,
Down with the mistletoe;
Instead of holly now upraise
The greener box for show.

The holly hitherto did sway,
Let box now domineer,
Until the dancing Easter day
Or Easter's eve appear.

The snowdrop was called the *Purification Flower* (also the *Fair Maid of February*), from its blossoming about Candlemas.

St Blaise's Day

St Blaise his day, about Candelmas, when country women go about to make good cheer; and if they find any of their neighbour women a spinning that day, they burn and make a blaze of fire of the distaff, and thereof called St Blaise his day.

Minshew's Dictionary

Blaise was an Armenian bishop persecuted under Diocletian, by being tormented with iron combs. He was a healer of men and beasts. He is patron saint of sore throats. A Blessing of the Throats ceremony is still held on this day in his honour, at St Etheldreda's Church in London.

Brothers and Sisters

I am all the daughters of my father's house and all the brothers too.

Twelfth Night (Act 2 Scene 4)

On this day in 1612 Shakespeare's brother Gilbert was buried. He was just over two years younger than William. He had become a seller of men's clothing; hats, shirts, gloves and such, and died (aged 45) a bachelor. We know little more about him.

Exactly a year and a day later, on February 4th 1613, his remaining brother Richard was buried too. Richard was ten years his junior, and had not yet reached his fortieth birthday. William was the first of John and Mary's children to survive infancy. Two daughters, Joan, their first-born child, and Margaret, had died before he was born, and another sister, Anne, had died aged seven when William was fourteen. Now he was left alone with only his sister, another Joan, remaining. Joan was the longest-living of all the siblings and was still alive in 1646 aged 77. (For the fate of his youngest brother Edmund see December 31st).

⧗

Dead Man Walking

Towards the end of February 1586, John Stow records:

'A man hanged for felony, at St Thomas Waterings, being begged by the surgeons of London, to have made of him an anatomy, after he was dead to all men's thinking, cut down, stripped, laid naked in a chest, thrown in a car, and so brought from the place of execution through the borough of Southwark, and the city of London, to the Surgeons' Hall near unto Aldersgate, the chest being there opened and the weather extreme cold he was found to be alive, and lived till Thursday next following, and then died.'

Malt
......

When brewers mar their malt with water.

King Lear (Act 3 Scene 2)

On this day in 1598, Shakespeare is named among a list of hoarders, as having illegally held 10 quarters (80 bushels) of malt or corn during a shortage. Between 1594 and 1597 there were three catastrophic harvest failures in a row in England. A national prohibition on malt-making was imposed, to ensure that grain reached the markets. But Stratford was 'one of the chiefest towns in England for malt-making'. So the town appealed against the ban. The Corporation petition pleaded that *for time beyond man's memory* Stratford had *no other special trade.*

Here William Harrison (in 1577) describes the process of malt-making: the roasting and grinding of grain, usually barley, for use in brewing:

'Our drink is made of barley, water, and hops, sodden and mingled together, by the industry of our brewers. But, before our barley do come into their hands, it is converted into malt, the making whereof I will here set down in such order as my skill therein may extend unto (for I am scarce a good maltster).

'Our malt is made all the year long in some great towns; but in gentlemen's and yeomen's houses, who commonly make sufficient for their own expenses only, the winter half is thought most meet for that commodity: howbeit the malt that is made when the willow doth bud is commonly worst of all.

'Nevertheless each one endeavoureth to make it of the best barley, which is steeped in a cistern, in greater or less quantity, by the space of three days and three nights, until it be thoroughly soaked. This being done, the water is drained from it by little and little, till it be quite gone. Afterward they take it out, and, laying it upon the clean floor on a round heap, it resteth so until it be ready to shoot at the root end, which maltsters call combing. When it beginneth

therefore to shoot in this manner, they say it is come, and then forthwith they spread it abroad, first thick, and afterwards thinner and thinner upon the said floor, and there it lieth (with turning every day four or five times) by the space of one and twenty days at the least, the workmen not suffering it in any wise to take any heat, whereby the bud end should spire, that bringeth forth the blade, and by which hurt of the malt would be spoiled and turn small commodity to the brewer.

'When it hath been turned, so long upon the floor, they carry it to a kiln covered with hair cloth, where they give it gentle heats till it be dry. For the more it be dried (yet must it be done with soft fire) the sweeter and better the malt is, and the longer it will continue, whereas, if it be not dried down, but slackly handled, it will breed a kind of worm called a weevil, which groweth in the flour of the corn, and in process of time will so eat out itself that nothing shall remain of the grain but even the very rind or husk. The best malt is tried by the hardness and colour; for, if it look fresh with a yellow hue, and thereto will write like a piece of chalk, after you have bitten a kernel in sunder in the midst, then you may assure yourself that it is dried down. The wood-dried malt when it is brewed, beside that the drink is higher of colour, it doth annoy the head of him that is not used thereto, because of the smoke.'

Banks' Wonderful Performing Horse

The dancing horse will tell you.
Love's Labour's Lost (Act 1 Scene 2)

In 1595, a young bay, or chestnut-coloured nag called Morocco performed tricks in the yard of the Bell Savage Inn in Fleet Street. It could stand on its hind legs and 'dance the Canaries'.

'A glove being thrown down, its master would command it to take it to some particular person: to the lady in the green mantle or the gentleman in the large ruff, and this order it would correctly execute. Some coins being put in the glove, it would tell how many they were by raps of its foot. It could in like manner tell the numbers on the upper face of a dice. As an example of comic performance, it would be desired to single out the gentleman who was the greatest slave to the fair sex; and this it was sure to do satisfactorily enough.'

From a brochure published under the name of Maroccus Exstaticus: or Banks Bay horse in a traunce; a Discourse set down in a merry dialogue between Banks and his Beast... intituled to Mine Host of the Belsauage and all his honest guests.

Morocco was taken by John Banks to be exhibited in Scotland in 1596, and there it was thought to be animated by a spirit. On this day in 1600, a man called John Banks rode his horse to the top of St Paul's Cathedral.

While this capering performance was going on before an enormous crowd, a serving man came to his master walking about in the middle aisle, and entreated him to come out and see the spectacle. 'Away, you fool!' answered the gentleman. 'What need I go so far to see a horse on the top when I can see so many asses on the bottom?'

Banks also exhibited his horse in France, and there, by way of stimulating popular curiosity, professed to believe that the animal really was a spirit in equine form. This, however, 'very nearly led to unpleasant consequences, in raising an alarm that there was something diabolic in the case'. Banks very dexterously saved himself for this once by causing the horse to select a man from the crowd with a cross on his hat, and pay homage to the sacred emblem.

Owing perhaps to this incident, a rumour afterwards prevailed that Banks and his curtal nag had been burned as subjects of the Black Power of the World, at Rome, by order of the Pope. Other stories say that Banks ended his days as a vintner in Cheapside in the reign of King Charles I.

According to John Stow's *Chronicles*, a man called Antony Finch walked 35 miles from Lewes in Sussex, 'followed by a covey of partridges, over London Bridge, through new Fish Street, Crooked Lane, Candlewick Street and into My Lord's house by Downegate, where he delivered them 8 in number'.

A fortnight later the partridges 'followed him up to the top of Paul's steeple, and then he gave them to the Bishop of London.'

The Essex Rebellion

Here is the actor, Augustine Phillips' account of the part played by the Lord Chamberlain's Men in the Essex Rebellion of 1601. Examined by Lord Chief Justice Popham:

'He sayeth that on Friday last, or Thursday, Sir Charles Percy, Sir Jocelyn Percy, and the Lord Mounteagle, with some three more, spake to some of the players in the presence of this examinant to have the play of the deposing and killing of King Richard the Second to be played the Saturday next, promising to give them forty shillings more than their ordinary to play it. Where this examinant and his friends were determined to have played some other play holding that play of King Richard to be so old and so long out of use as that they should have small or no company at it. But at their request this examinant and his friends were content to play it the Saturday and had their 40 shillings more than the ordinary for it and so played it accordingly.'

I have a vivid impression of the Lord Chamberlain's Men spending this Friday in 1601 trying to mug up *Richard II* for the specially commissioned performance the following day. Some of the company were doubtless grumpy at the decision to take the commission, which entailed so much re-learning of lines, and re-rehearsal. They would already be preparing the season's new work, and may have had over 30 plays in their playing repertoire. For example, the Admiral's Men in 1594-5 performed 38 plays, 21 of which were new that season.

Here, cousin, seize the crown.

Richard II (Act 4 Scene 1)

The performance of *Richard II* went ahead that Saturday afternoon, attended by some of the Essex conspirators. Presumably they believed the scene depicting the deposition of King Richard would inspire their followers to overthrow Queen Elizabeth.

The Earl of Essex, after Marcus Gheeraerts the Younger, circa 1596

The next morning, Sunday, February 8th, the Essex Rebellion shook London. The Lord Chief Justice Sir John Popham and three other officials were taken hostage at Essex House. Essex and his followers marched on the City but (despite the performance of *Richard II*) failed to gather enough popular support for an uprising. By evening the revolt had ended in utter failure. The Earls of Essex and Southampton retreated to Essex House, where they finally surrendered to the authorities.

Later in a conversation recorded by the antiquarian Lambarde, Elizabeth referred to the play:

'Her majesty fell upon the reign of Richard II. Saying, "I am Richard II. Know ye not that?"'

The Trial of Essex and Southampton

The courtier's, soldier's, scholar's, eye, tongue, sword,
The expectancy and rose of the fair state,
The glass of fashion and the mould of form,
Th'observed of all observers, quite quite down.

Hamlet (Act 3 Scene 1)

'The 19 hereof the Earls of Essex and Southampton were arraigned at Westminster, before the Lord Treasurer – Lord High Steward of England for that day, and 25 of their peers, whereof were 9 earls and 16 barons. The only matters objected

The Earl of Southampton in the Tower of London, by John de Critz, 1603

were his [Essex's] practice to surprise the Court, his coming in arms to London to raise rebellion, and the defending his house against the Queen's forces. To the two latter he answered that he was driven for safety of his life, to the former that it was a matter only in consultation and not resolved upon, and if it had taken effect it was only to prostrate himself at her majesty's feet, and there manifest such matters against his enemies as should make them odious and remove them from about her person, and recall him to her favour.

'This was the sum of his answer, but delivered with such bravery and so many words, that a man might easily perceive that, as he had ever lived popularly, so his chief care was to leave a good opinion in the people's minds now at parting.

'The Earl of Southampton spake very well (but methought somewhat too much as well as the other),

and as a man that would fain live, pleaded hard to acquit himself, but all in vain for it would not be; whereupon he descended to entreaty, and moved great commiseration, and though he were generally well liked, yet methought he was somewhat too low and submiss, and seemed too loath to die before a proud enemy…

'Yet the general opinion is there will be no great executions, for the Queen is very gracious and inclines much to mercy.'

Letter, John Chamberlain, February 24th, 1601

Essex was condemned to death. Shakespeare's patron, Southampton, was imprisoned in the Tower.

Dudley Carleton replied to Chamberlain from Holland, telling him of the Dutch reaction to Essex's execution:

'The earl's fall is generally bewailed, but his fault so ill understood by the people, that no reason can beat it into their maudlin drunken heads, but that he lost his head wrongfully.'

The Execution of The Earl of Essex

Mary Queen of Scots Beheaded

On this day in 1587, Mary Queen of Scots was executed.

'The gown in which the Queen was attired was of exquisite black velvet, which she had likewise worn when she appeared before the gentlemen. In her hand she held a small cross of wood or of ivory with the picture of Christ thereon and a book. On her neck hung a golden crucifix, and from her girdle a rosary.

'Thereupon she stood up and prepared herself for death. She doffed her jewels and her gown, with the help of two women. When the executioner wished to assist her, she said to him that it was not her wont to be disrobed in the presence of such a crowd, nor with the help of such hand-maidens. She herself took off her robe and pushed it down as far as the waist. The bodice of the underskirt was cut low and tied together at the back. She hastened to undo this.

'Thereafter she kissed her ladies, commended them to God, and because one of them was weeping too loudly, she said to her: "Have I not told you that you should not weep ? Be comforted." To her she gave her hand and bade her leave the dais. When she was thus prepared, she turned to her servitors, who were

kneeling not far off, blessed them and made them all witnesses that she died a Catholic and begged them to pray for her. After, she fell on her knees with great courage, did not change colour and likewise gave no sign of fear. One of her tirewomen bound a kerchief before her eyes. As she knelt down she repeated the 70th psalm: *In te Domine, speravi...* When she had said this to the end, she, full of courage, bent down with her body and laid her head on the block, exclaiming in *manuas tuas, Domine, commendo spiritum meum.* Then one of the executioners held down her hands and the other cut off her head with two strokes of the chopper. Thus ended her life.

'The executioner took the head and showed it to the people who cried: "God spare our Queen of England!"

'When the executioner held up the head, it fell in disarray so that it could be seen that her hair was quite grey and had been closely cropped.

'Everything that had been sprinkled with her blood, also the garments of the executioner and other objects, were promptly taken away and washed. The planks of the dais, the black cloth and all else were thrown into the fire, at once, so that no superstitious practices could be carried on therewith.'

Described by Emanuel Tomascon, who was present at the happenings.

The Phoenix and Other Wonderful Birds

... in Arabia
There is one tree, the phoenix throne, one phoenix
At this hour reigning there...
The Tempest (Act 3 Scene 3)

On this day in 1544, William Turner dedicated his *History of Birds* to Edward, son and heir to Henry VIII. In this rare treatise, between descriptions of the Partridge and the Pica (the Magpie), Turner describes the Phoenix:

'The Ethiopians and Indians tell of birds of very varied colouring and indescribable, and of the phoenix of Arabia, most noteworthy of all: I know not whether falsely, that there is but one in the

whole world, and this not often seen. It is declared to be of the size of the eagle, with golden sheen around the neck, but purple otherwise, varied with roseate feathers on a tail of blue; tufts beautifying the face, a feathery crown the head. First of our citizens and with great care, Manilius wrote of it, that noted senator, of such high birth; of his own knowledge he asserts that nobody exists who ever saw it eat. He says that in Arabia it is considered sacred to the sun, and lives for six hundred and sixty years. When it grows old it makes itself a nest of cassia and twigs of frankincense, this nest it stores with scents and on the top it dies. Then from its bones and marrow is produced what seems a little worm that afterwards becomes a chick.'

Turner is translating from Pliny, and makes no other personal comment.

But the Phoenix is not the only strange bird that Turner describes. Here for instance is the Caprimulgus, once described by Aristotle and Pliny: 'When I was in Switzerland I saw an aged man, who fed his goats upon the Mountains, which I had gone up intent on search of plants: I asked him whether he knew of a bird of the size of a blackbird, blind in the day time, keen of sight at night, which in the dark is wont to suck goats' udders so that afterwards the animals go blind. Now he replied that he himself had seen many in the Swiss Mountains fourteen years before, that he had suffered many losses from those very birds; so that he had once had six she-goats blinded by Caprimulgi, but that one and all they now had flown away from Switzerland to Lower Germany, where nowadays they did not only steal the milk of she-goats, making them go blind, but killed the sheep besides. And, on my asking the bird's name, he said it was called the Paphus, otherwise the Priest. But possibly that aged man was jesting with me. Yet whether he was jesting or spoke gravely, still I have no other German name than what he gave to me for Caprimalgus. If there be any then who have in readiness a better or a fitter name, let them produce it.'

In Francis Willughby's *Ornithology* of 1676, the Caprimulgus is referred to as the Goat-sucker

Shakespeare's Daughter Marries a Rogue

Prospero: *Take my daughter, but*
If thou dost break her virgin knot before
All sanctimonious ceremonies may
With full and holy rite be minister'd,
No sweet aspersion shall the heavens let fall
To make this contract grow; but barren hate
Sour-eye'd disdain and discord shall bestrew
The union of thy bed with weeds so loathly
That you shall hate it both.
The Tempest (Act 4 Scene 1)

On this day in 1616, Shakespeare's daughter Judith married Thomas Quinney, a local vintner – in Lent. You had to have a special licence to marry in Lent and the couple had failed to obtain it. They were duly summoned to appear before the ecclesiastical court in Worcester. Quinney didn't appear and was excommunicated.

This verse helped minister and congregation remember when marriages could happen:
Advent marriages doth deny
But Hilary gives thee liberty.
Septuagesima says thee nay,
Eight days from Easter says you may.
Rogation bids thee to contain
But Trinity sets you free again.

Unbeknownst to Judith, Quinney had a mistress, Margaret Wheeler, whom he had made pregnant. Margaret gave birth to the baby, but mother and child both died. When the story came out, Judith's husband was prosecuted for incontinence, and sentenced by the vicar to stand in front of the whole congregation at Holy Trinity in a gown of humility, a white sheet. He was told do so for the next three Sundays. Within two months, Shakespeare was dead.

In November, Judith's first child was baptised in Holy Trinity Church. It was a son, and they christened him 'Shakespeare', after his grandfather who had passed away just seven months before. Unfortunately, the infant died the following May. William's own sisters, Joan, Margaret and Anne, had also died in infancy. The Quinneys were unlucky. They went on to have two boys, Richard and Thomas, who both grew into early manhood, but then died within a month of each other (aged 21 and 19 respectively) in 1639, probably of the plague. So none of Judith's family survived her to continue the Shakespeare line.

The Quinneys lived in a house on the corner of Bridge Street and High Street. It was bought and renovated by W.H.Smith and Sons in 1923. It is currently owned by Crabtree and Evelyn.

The Headmaster of Morris Dancers: Kemp's Nine Days' Wonder

On this day in 1600, the actor and clown Will Kemp set out for his jig to Norwich:

'The first Monday in Lent, the close morning promising a clear day, attended on by Thomas Slye (my Taborer), William Bee (my servant), and George Sprat, appointed for my overseer, that I should take no other ease but my prescribed order, myself, that's I, (otherwise called Cavaliero Kemp, head-Master of Morris-dancers, high Head-borough of heighs, and only tricker of your Trill-lilles, and best bell-shangles between Sion and Mount Surrey), began frolickly to foot it, from the right Honorable the Lord Mayor's of London, towards the right worshipful (and truly bountiful) Master Mayor's of Norwich.

'Somewhat before seven in the morning, my Taborer struck up merrily, and through London I leapt. By the way many good old people, and divers others of younger years, gave me bowed sixpences and groats, blessing me with their hearty prayers and God-speeds.

'Being past Whitechapel, and having left fair London, multitudes of Londoners left not me: or else for love they bear toward me, or perhaps to make themselves merry, if I should chance (as many thought) to give over my Morris within a mile of Mile-

end. However, many a thousand brought me to Bow, where I rested a while from dancing.

'The Taborer strikes alarum. Tickle it, good Tom, I'll follow thee. Farewell Bowe, have over the Bridge, let's now along to Stratford Langton. Many good fellows being there met, had prepared a Bear-baiting: but so unreasonable were the multitudes of people, that I could only hear the Bear roar, and the dogs howl: therefore forward I went with my hay-de-gays to Ilford , where I again rested, and was by the people of the town and country thereabout, very very well welcomed. I soberly gave my boon companions the slip.

'From Ilford by Moon-shine, I set forward, dancing within a quarter of a mile of Romford: where in the high way, two strong jades were beating & biting either of other. And such was my good hap, that I escaped their hooves both being raised with their fore-feet over my head, like two Smiths over an Anvil.

'There being the end of my first day's Morris, a kind Gentleman of London alighting from his horse, would have no nay but I should leap into his saddle. To be plain with ye, I was not proud, but kindly took his kindlier offer, chiefly thereto urged by my weariness: so I rid to my Inn at Romford. In that town, to give rest to my well laboured limbs, I continued two days, being much beholding to the towns-men for their love, but more to the Londoners, that came hourly thither in great numbers to visit me: offering much more kindness than I was willing to accept.'

It seems that Kemp had left the Lord Chamberlain's Men, after some sort of dispute. His 'Nine Days' Wonder' (which actually took from February 11th to March 8th) was both an exercise in self-promotion and a sponsored fundraiser for himself.

The Tyger Sets Sail

Her husband's to Aleppo gone, master o' th' Tyger:
But in a sieve I'll thither sail,
And like a rat without a tail,
I'll do, I'll do, and I'll do!

Macbeth (Act 1 Scene 3)

On this day in 1583, a merchant ship called the *Tyger* set sail from the Pool of London. On board the *Tyger* was Ralph Fitch. He was to be one of the first Englishmen to visit India, and he left his account of his travels.

'In the year of Our Lord 1583, I Ralph Fitch of London merchant being desirous to see the countries of the East India, did ship myself in a ship of London called the *Tyger*, wherein we went for Tripolis in Syria: and from thence we took the way for Aleppo, and finding good company we went from thence to Birra, which is two days and a half travel with camels.'

Fitch travelled on via Fellujah, Babylon (where he visited the ruins of the Tower of Babel), Basra and Ormuz, arriving at Goa within the year, where he was imprisoned for a time.

In *Macbeth*, one of the weird sisters curses a ship called the *Tyger*. The following account comes from a description of the World Trade Center's twin towers: **'During excavations in this vicinity in 1916, construction workers came across some of the charred timbers of the *Tyger*, the trading ship captained by Adriaen Block that burned in the harbour in 1613. Block and his followers spent the winter in New Amsterdam and built themselves another vessel, the *Onrust* (usually translated as Restless), which carried them back to Holland. A half century later, in 1967, during excavations for the World Trade Center, workmen unloaded a bronze breech-loading swivel-necked gun, bearing the mark of the Dutch East India Company, also probably from the *Tyger*, for the loss of whose cannon Adriaen Block was sued by the Dutch admiralty. The exhumed relics are now on view at the Museum of the City of New York, while the rest of the *Tyger* still lies buried some 20 ft below the World Trade Center.'**

From The Blue Guide to New York, second edition, 1991

Ralph Fitch's the *Tyger* belonged to the Levant Company. The *Tyger* that was abandoned in New Amsterdam belonged to the Dutch East India Company. So it cannot have been the same ship the witches cursed… nevertheless!

Kissing Comfits

Ophelia's Lament

To-morrow is Saint Valentine's day,
All in the morning betime,
And I a maid at your window,
To be your Valentine.
Then up he rose, and donn'd his clothes,
And dupp'd the chamber-door;
Let in the maid, that out a maid
Never departed more.

By Gis and by Saint Charity,
Alack, and fie for shame!
Young men will do't, if they come to't;
By cock, they are to blame.
Quoth she, before you tumbled me,
You promised me to wed.
So would I ha' done, by yonder sun,
An thou hadst not come to my bed.

Hamlet, (Act 4, Scene 5)

Sweetmeats and Aphrodisiacs

Shakespeare mentions a number of sweetmeats and confectioneries. Some of these might be made in preparation for St Valentine's Day. Falstaff greeting Mrs Ford at Herne's Oak in Windsor Forest cries:
'*Let the sky rain potatoes; let it thunder to the tune of Greensleeves; hail kissing comfits and snow eringoes. Let there come a tempest of provocation, I will shelter me here.*'
The Merry Wives of Windsor (Act 5 Scene 5)

Kissing comfits were perfumed sugar plums used as breath sweeteners. Eringoes were made from the candied roots of sea holly, which had aphrodisiac properties, as, apparently, had sweet potatoes. Although John Gerard in his *Herbal* warns that eringoes make goats stand still.

Adspicis exiguæ illustres in imagine vultus,
Magna Palatini scilicet ora ducis:
Qui superat magnis teneros virtutibus annos,
Et quoque magnanimos nil nisi spirat avos.
Crisp. Pass. fig. sculp. et excudit.

Federick V, Elector Palantine, married James's daughter Elizabeth in 1613 and was elected King of Bohemia in 1618

Valentine Gifts

And if you were thinking of buying some flowers for your sweetheart, the crocus was the flower dedicated to St Valentine. A more traditional Valentine's gift was a pair of gloves. Venison was also regarded as an appropriate Valentine's Day gift. Valentine's Day was also a popular day for weddings, as long as it did not fall in Lent (see February 10th), and was the day chosen for the wedding of Frederick Elector Palatine and Princess Elizabeth in 1610.

Valentine's Day

The Special Marks of Love

Valentine: *Why, how know you that I am in love?*
Speed: *Marry, by these special marks: first, you have learned, like Sir Proteus, to wreathe your arms, like a malcontent; to relish a love-song, like a robin-redbreast; to walk alone, like one that had the pestilence; to sigh, like a school-boy that had lost his A B C; to weep, like a young wench that had buried her grandam; to fast, like one that takes diet; to watch, like one that fears robbing; to speak puling, like a beggar at Hallowmas. You were wont, when you laughed, to crow like a cock; when you walked, to walk like one of the lions; when you fasted, it was presently after dinner; when you looked sadly, it was for want of money: and now you are metamorphosed with a mistress, that, when I look on you, I can hardly think you my master.*

The Two Gentlemen of Verona (Act 2 Scene 1)

In *As You Like It*, Rosalind, dressed as the boy Ganymede, teases the 'love-shaked' Orlando:
Rosalind: *There is none of my uncle's marks upon you: he taught me how to know a man in love; in which cage of rushes I am sure you are not prisoner.*
Orlando: *What were his marks?*
Rosalind: *A lean cheek, which you have not, a blue eye and sunken, which you have not, an unquestionable spirit, which you have not, a beard neglected, which you have not; but I pardon you for that, for simply your having in beard is a younger brother's revenue: then your hose should be ungartered, your bonnet unbanded, your sleeve unbuttoned, your shoe untied and every thing about you demonstrating a careless desolation; but you are no such man; you are rather point-device in your accoutrements as loving yourself than seeming the lover of any other.*

As You Like it (Act 3 Scene 2)

Now on my faith, old Bishop Valentine,
You have brought us nipping weather. 'February
Doth cut and shear' - your day and diocese
Are very cold. All your parishioners
Had need to keep their feather beds,
If they be sped to loves: this is no season
To seek new mates in.
Ben Jonson's *Tale of a Tub* begins thus, on a cold St Valentine's morning. The speech refers to the tradition of seeking new mates on Valentine's Day.

Good morrow, friends! St Valentine is past
Begin these woodbirds but to couple now ?
A Midsummer Night's Dream (Act 4 Scene 1)

Stratford-upon-Avon is loud with birdsong now. Traditionally, St Valentine's Day heralded the start of the mating season among birds.

Our English Housewife: She Must Know All Herbs

O mickle is the powerful grace that lies
In herbs.
Romeo and Juliet (Act 2 Scene 3)

I knew a wench married in an afternoon as she went to the
garden for parsley to stuff a rabbit.
The Taming of the Shrew (Act 4 Scene 4)

'She shall know the time of year, month and moon in which all herbs are to be sown; and when they are in their best flourishing, that, gathering all herbs in their height of goodness, she may have the prime use of the same. And because I will enable and not burden her memory, I will here give her a short epitome of all that knowledge.

'First then, let our English housewife know that she may at all times of the month and moon, generally sow asparagus, coleworts, spinach, lettuce, parsnips, radish and chives.

'In February, in the new of the moon, she may sow spike, garlic, borage, bugloss, chervil, coriander, gourds, cresses, marjoram, palma Christi, flower-gentle, white poppy, purslane, radish, rocket, rosemary, sorrel, double marigolds, and thyme. The moon full, she may sow aniseeds, musked violets, bleets, skirrets, white succory, fennel and parsley. The moon old, sew holy thistle, cole cabbage, white cole, green cole, cucumbers, harsthorn, dyer's grain, cabbage-lettuce, melons, onions, parsnips, lark-heel, burnet, and leeks.

'In March, the moon new, sow garlic, borage, bugloss, chervil, coriander, gourds, marjoram, white poppy, purslane, radish, sorrel, double marigolds, thyme, violets. At the full moon, aniseeds, bleets, skirrets, succory, fennel, apples of love, and marvellous apples. At the wane, artichokes, basil, blessed thistle, cole, cabbage, white cole, green cole, citrons, cucumbers, hartshorn, samphire, spinach, gillyflowers, hyssop, cabbage-lettuce, melons,

muggets, onions, flower-gentle, burnet, leeks and savory.

'In the month of April, the moon being new, sow marjoram, flower-gentle, thyme, violets; in the full of the moon, apples of love, and marvellous apples, and in the wane, artichokes, holy thistle, cabbage-cole, citrons, hartshorn, samphire, gillyflowers, muggets, and parsnips.

'In May, the moon old, sow blessed thistle. In June, the moon new, sow gourds and radishes. The moon old, sow cucumbers, melons, parsnips. In July, the moon at full, sow white succory, and the moon old, sow cabbage lettuce. Lastly in August, the moon at full, sow white succory.'
The English Housewife, Gervase Markham (1615)

Also on this day in 1564, Galileo, the great Italian scientist and mathematician, was born in Pisa, two months before William Shakespeare.

Funeral of a National Hero

There's a great spirit gone.

Antony and Cleopatra (Act 1 Scene 2)

Sir Philip Sidney, courtier, soldier, poet, and patron of the arts, by an unknown artist

On this day in 1587, the great soldier poet, Sir Philip Sidney, was buried in St Paul's in a ceremony of unprecedented splendour. He had been killed fighting at Zutphen in the Netherlands.

Many years later, John Aubrey recalled seeing a singular record of this great state funeral:

'When I was a boy of 9 years old, I was with my father and one Mr Singleton, an Alderman and Woolen-draper in Gloucester, who had in his parlour, over the chimney, the whole description of the funeral, engraved and printed on papers pasted together, which was, I believe the length of the room at least: but he had contrived it to be turned upon two pins, that running one of them made the figures march all in order. It did make such a strong impression on my tender fantasy that I remember it as if it were but yesterday. I could never see it elsewhere. The house is in Great Long Street, over against the high steeple, and 'tis likely it remains there still. 'Tis pity it is not redone.'

Here is an official account of the order of the funeral procession which gives some idea of the pomp and magnificence of the occasion, with the Heraldic officers, Portcullis, Bluemantle and Rouge Dragon all playing their part:

'His burial was ordered by Robert Cook, Clarencieux King of Arms; first proceeded 32 poor men in black gowns, according to his age; the Sergeants of the Band, fife and drum, ensigns trailed; Lieutenant of Foot, Corporals, trumpets, guidon (standard) trailed; Lieutenant of his Horse, conductors to his servants; the standard borne by the gentleman; his gentlemen, and yeoman servants, 60; physicians and surgeons, steward of his house, esquires, of his kindred and friends, 12; preacher and chaplains; the pennon of his arms borne, the horse of the field, led by a footman; a page riding with a broken lance; a barbed horse led by a footman; a page on horseback carrying a battle-axe, the head downward; yeomen-ushers to the Heralds; the great banner borne by a gentleman; Portcullis bearing the gilt spurs; Bluemantle the gauntlets, Rouge Dragon the helmet and crest; Richmond the shield of arms; Somerset the coat of arms... the corpse covered with a velvet pall, carried by 14 yeomen; 2 bannerols following; Sir Robert Sidney, chief mourner; mourner assistants; 4 knights; two gentlemen-ushers to the noblemen.

'So general was the lamentation for him, that for many months after it was accounted indecent for any gentleman of quality to appear at Court or City, in any light or gaudy attire.'

An anonymous letter dated February 16th, 1587

A Murderer Elected Tsar
....

So shall you hear of carnal, bloody, and unnatural acts.
Hamlet (Act 5 Scene 2)

On this day in 1598, in Moscow, Boris Godunov was elected Tsar.

A contemporary report (written in 1605, the year Boris died) compared the historic events surrounding his reign to the story of Hamlet still playing on the London stages.

'His father's (Boris Godunov) empire and government was but as the poetical fury in a stage action, complete yet with horrid and woeful tragedies: a first, but no second to any Hamlet; and that now Revenge, just Revenge was coming with his sword drawn against his royal mother, and dearest sister, to fill up those murdering scenes, the embryon whereof was long since modeled, yea digested, (but unlawfully and too, too vively) by his dead self murdering father: such and so many being their fears and demons.'

Ivan the Terrible and Boris Godunov by C.L. Doughty, 1913-85

Voyage and Entertainment in Russia 1605, Sir Thomas Smythe

Boris Godunov allegedly obtained the throne of Russia by poisoning the Tsarevich Dimitri, the rightful heir. In 1605 he died suddenly, and the empire passed to his son Theodor. However, a false Dimitri then appeared, a pretender to the crown, claiming to be the lost Tsarevich, and set on revenging himself on Boris' heirs. This led ultimately to the fall of the dynasty, and the rise of the Romanov family.

Alexander Pushkin, Russia's greatest poet, wrote a play called *Boris Godunov* based on the story, published in 1831, which Mussorgsky then turned into an opera.

Kemp's Jig: Day Four
'On Monday morning I had the heaviest way that ever mad Morris-dancer trod: yet
With hey and ho, through thick and thin,
the hobby horse quite forgotten,
I follow'd, as I did begin,
although the way were rotten.

'This foul way I could find no ease in, thick woods being on either side of the lane: the lane likewise being full of deep holes, sometimes I skipped up to the waist: but I had some mirth by an unlooked for accident.

'It was the custom of honest Country fellows my unknown friends, upon hearing of my Pipe (which might well be heard in a still morning or evening a mile) to get up and bear me company a little way. In this foul way two pretty plain youths watched me, and with their kindness somewhat hindered me. One, a fine light fellow would be still before me, the other ever at my heels. At length coming to a broad plash of water and mud, which could not be avoided, I fetched a rise, yet fell in over the ankles at the further end. My youth that follow'd me, took his jump, and stuck fast in the midst, crying out to his companion, "Come George, call ye this dancing, I'll go no further": for indeed he could go no further, till his fellow was fain to wade and help him out. I could not choose but laugh to see how like two frogs they laboured: a hearty farewell I gave them, and they faintly bade God speed me, saying if I danced that dirty way this seven years again, they would never dance after me. Well, with much ado I got unto Braintree.'

The Tradescants' Ark
....

... your gallery
Have we pass'd through, not without much content
In many singularities.
The Winter's Tale (Act 5 Scene 3)

The John Tradescants (father and son) were great gardeners, botanists, and collectors. From their house in Lambeth they collected rarities from all over the world. The Ark, as it was known, was the first museum open to the public in England.

From the introduction to *Tradescant's Catalogue*:
I was resolved to take a catalogue of those Rarities and Curiosities which my father had sedulously collected, and myself with continual diligence have augmented, and hitherto preserved together: The enumeration of these rarities (being more for variety than any one place known in Europe could afford) would be an honour to our Nation, and a benefit to such ingenious persons as would become further enquirers into the various modes of Nature's admirable works, and the curious imitators thereof. Your ready friend,
John Tradescant

Tradescant's Cabinet of Curiosities included:
❀ The claw of the bird Roc, who, as authors report, is able to truss an elephant.
❀ A Cherry stone, upon one side St George and his dragon, perfectly cut, and on the other side 88 emperors' faces.
❀ Hippopotamus.
❀ Divers sorts of ambers with flies, spiders etc.
❀ Turkish Al-Koran in a silver box.
❀ Half a hazelnut with 70 pieces of household stuff in it.
❀ Flea chains of silver and gold with 300 links, and yet but an inch long.

❀ A Book of Mr Tradescant's choicest plants and flowers, exquisitely limned on vellum.
❀ A bundle of Tobacco Amazonian.
❀ Birds' nests from China.
❀ Blood that rained in the Isle of Wight.
❀ Powhatan, King of Virginia's, habit, all embroidered with shells.
❀ Rich vest from the great Moghul.
❀ Edward the Confessor's knit-gloves.
❀ A bracelet made of the thighs of Indian flies.
❀ Knife wherewith Hudson was killed in the North West Passage.
❀ An Umbrella.

A twenty-four-year-old German student called Georg Christoph Stirn recorded this visit to the Ark in his diary in July 1638:
'In the art museum of Mr John Tradescant the following things: first in the courtyard lie two ribs of a whale, also a very ingenious little boat of bark. We saw a salamander, a chameleon, a pelican, a remora, a lanhado from Africa, a white partridge, a goose which has grown in Scotland on a tree, a flying squirrel... the hand of a mermaid, the hand of a mummy... a small piece of wood from the cross of Christ ...poisoned arrows such as are used by the executioners in the West Indies...an instrument used by the Jews in circumcision ...a scourge which Charles V is said to have scourged himself, a hat band of snake bones.'

Also on this day, in 1564, two months before Shakespeare was born, Michelangelo died.

Christenings
....

On this day in 1608, in all possibility, Shakespeare's grand-daughter, Elizabeth Hall, was born. A few years later, Shakespeare (and his collaborator Fletcher) would write a scene in which a baby called Elizabeth is christened Princess Elizabeth in *All is True* (or *Henry VIII*).

King Henry made Cranmer, Archbishop of Canterbury, a godparent to his new daughter. But when Cranmer protested his unworthiness for such an honour, Henry retorted:

Come, come, my lord, you'd spare your spoons.

All is True (Act 5 Scene 3)

Gossip spoons, or apostle spoons, were traditionally given by godparents to new-born babies. Apostle spoons were very popular thoughout the sixteenth century. They are spoons with an image of an apostle at the end of the handle, each bearing his distinctive emblem.

At the Princess's christening in *All is True*, the Porter and his man are having trouble holding back the excited crowds:

Porter: You'll leave your noise anon, ye rascals.
Do you take the Court for Paris Garden, ye rude slaves?
Leave your gaping... (to his man)
Fetch me a dozen crab-tree staves, and strong ones,
These are but switches to 'em. I'll scratch your heads,
You must be seeing Christenings? Do you look
For ale and cakes here, you rude rascals?
Man: Pray sir be patient. 'Tis as much impossible
Unless we sweep 'em from the door with cannons,
To scatter 'em, as 'tis to make 'em sleep
On May-day morning - which will never be
We may as well push against Paul's as stir 'em.
Porter: How got they in?...

Man: Alas, I know not. How gets the tide in?...
What would you have me do?
Porter: What should you do, but knock 'em down by the dozens? Is this Moorfields to muster in? Or have we some strange Indian with the great tool come to Court, the women so besiege us? Bless me, what a fry of fornication is at door! On my Christian conscience, this one christening will beget a thousand. Here will be father, godfather, and all together.

All is True (Act 5 Scene 3)

Nuntia Chriſticolis venturæ cladis, inermes
Æthere ab armatis nocte perire videt. ꞵ: 6.7

Shrovetide
· · · · · · · · · · · ·

The word Shrovetide comes from the old English word to *shrive* meaning to *hear confession*. And though the Catholic sacrament of Confession was abolished in Protestant England after the Reformation, the word was still used to describe the period before Lent. Shrovetide celebrations could last for four days leading up to Shrove Tuesday.

In 1570, Thomas Kirchmaier's *The Popish Kingdom* (written in Latin verse in 1553) was 'englyshed by Barnabe Googe'. It lists all the popular superstitions and customs related to the Saints' Days and Holy Days in 'Papist Lands'. Here is the account of carnival revels at Shrovetide. Note, among all the dressing up, the ceremony of carrying the turd at the end:

Now when at length the pleasant time of Shrovetide
    comes in place,
And cruel fasting days at hand approach with solemn grace:
Then young and old are both as mad as guests of
    Bacchus feast,
And four days long they tipple square, and feed and
    never rest
Down go the hogs in every place, and puddings everywhere
Do swarm: the dice are shaked and tossed, and cards
    apace they tear:
In every house are shouts and cries, and mirth
    and revel rout,
And dainty tables spread, and all be set with guests about.

But some again the dreadful shape of devils on them take,
And chase such as they meet, and make poor boys to fear
    and quake.
Some naked run about the streets, their faces hid alone,
With visors close, that so disguised, they might be
    known of none.
Both men and women change their weed, the men
    in maid's array,
And wanton wenches dressed like men, do travel
    by the way,

And to their neighbours houses go, or where it likes
    them best
Perhaps unto some ancient friend or old acquainted guest,
Unknown and speaking but few words, the meat
    devour they up,
That is before them set, and clean they swinge of every cup.

Some run about the streets attired like monks, and
    some like kings,
Accompanied with pomp and guard and other stately
    things,
Some like wild beasts do run abroad in skins that divers be
Arrayed and eke with loathsome shapes, that dreadful
    are to see:
They counterfeit both bears and wolves, and lions
    fierce to fight,
And raging bulls. Some play the cranes with wings and
    stilts upright.
Some like the filthy form of apes, and some like fools
    dressed,
Which best beseem these papists all, that thus keep
    Bacchus feast.
But others bear a turd, that on a cushion soft they lay,
And one there is that with a flap doth keep the flies away,
I would there might another be, an officer of those,
Whose room might serve to take away the scent from
    every nose.

Collop Monday: Jack-a-Lent and Roguery Night

I will not say you shall see a masque; but if you do, then it was not for nothing that my nose fell a bleeding on Black Monday last, at six o'clock i' the morning, falling out that year on Ash Wednesday was four year in the afternoon.
The Merchant of Venice (Act 2 Scene 5)

You little Jack-a-Lent, have you been true to us?
The Merry Wives of Windsor (Act 3 Scene 3)
The day before Shrove Tuesday was Collop Monday. In some places it is called Nickanan Night or Roguery night. The name Nickanan may come from the practice of knocking on doors and running away, known as *Nick Nack*. During Nickanan, a *Jack-a-Lent*, or figure made of straw, was paraded through the villages, pelted and then burned on a bonfire. Fire rituals such as those associated with the Jack-a-Lent may also indicate Celtic pagan origins and may be related to the Imbolc festival.

'On the day termed Hall Monday, which precedes Shrove Tuesday, about the dusk of the evening, it is the custom for boys, and, in some cases, for those who are above the age of boys, to prowl about the streets with short clubs, and to knock loudly at every door, running off to escape detection on the slightest sign of a motion within. If, however, no attention be excited, and especially if any article be discovered negligently exposed, or carelessly guarded, then the things are carried away; and on the following day are discovered displayed in some conspicuous place, to expose the disgraceful want of vigilance supposed to characterize the owner. The time when this is practised is called "Nickanan night" and the individuals concerned are supposed to represent some imps of darkness, that seize on and expose unguarded moments.'
Glossary of Words in Use in Cornwall, Margaret Ann Courtney, and Thomas Quiller Couch (1880)

This rhyme was used by children during Nickanan Night and the following day, Shrove Tuesday:
Nicka nicka nan
Give me some pancake, and then I'll be gone
But if you give me none
I'll throw a great stone
And down your door shall come.

Shrove Tuesday: Carnivals and Cock-throwing

Today was Shrove Tuesday in the year Shakespeare was born.

'By that time that the clock strikes eleven, then there is a bell rung, called the Pancake bell, the sound whereof makes thousands of people distracted, and forgetful of either manners or of humanity, then there is a thing called wheaten flour, which the sulphury necromantic cooks do mingle with water, eggs, spice, and other tragical, magical enchantments, and then they put it, by little and little, into a frying pan of boiling suet, where it makes a confused dismal hissing (like the Lemean snakes in the reeds of Acheron, Styx or Phlegethon), until at last, by the skill of the cooks, it is transformed into the form of a Flap-Jack, which in our translation is called a Pancake, which ominous incantation the ignorant people do devour very greedily.'

Letter from Edward Sherburne to John Chamberlain, 1617

Merrymakers at Shrovetide by Frans Hals, 1615

Shrovetide in England never quite matched up to the excesses of Carnival on the Continent, and Pancake Tuesday may seem a pale shadow of Mardi Gras. Mass football matches were often played, and still are in places like Workington in Cumbria.

Cock-throwing, or cock-shying, was widely practised in England until the late eighteenth century. A cockerel was tied to a post and people took turns throwing specially weighted sticks called coksteles at the poor bird until it died. Even Sir Thomas More referred to his skill as a boy in casting a cokstele. The cock was also sometimes placed inside an earthenware jar to prevent it moving. As the cock was the traditional symbol of the French, it may be an emblematic piece of xenophobia. But there were regional variations such as goose-quailing or cat- and dog-tossing.

Also on this day in 1617, a mob of apprentices broke into the new Phoenix Theatre:

'On Shrove Tuesday last, three or four thousand apprentices committed extreme insolencies. Part of this number, taking their course for Wapping did there pull down to the ground four houses; and a justice of the peace coming to appease them, while he was reading a proclamation, had his head broke with a brickbat. Th'other part, making for Drury Lane (where lately a new playhouse is erected), they beset the house round, broke in, wounded divers of the players, broke open their trunks, and what apparel, books or other things they found they burned and cut in pieces.'

Letter from Edward Sherburne to John Chamberlain, 1617

Ash Wednesday
·················

... what Lenten entertainment the players shall receive from you.
Hamlet (Act 2 Scene 2)

Today would have been Ash Wednesday, in 1564, the year Shakespeare was born, the start of Lent, a period of forty days of fasting and abstinence leading up to Easter. Meat was banned, and fish was much in demand.

The Wednesday next a solemn day, to Church they
*   early go,*
To sponge out all the foolish deeds by them committed so.
Some bear about a herring on a staff and loud do roar,
'Herrings, herrings, stinking herrings, puddings now
*   no more,'*
And hereto join they foolish plays, and doltish doggerel
*   rhymes*
And what beside they can invent, belonging to the times.
Then (O poor wretches) fastings long approaching
*   do appear:*
In forty days they neither milk, nor flesh, nor eggs do eat
And butter with their lips to touch, is thought a trespass
*   great.*
The Popish Kingdom, translated by Barnabe Googe

Kemp's Jig : Day Five & Six
'Wednesday of the second week: I tripped it to Sudbury. In this town, there came a lusty tall butcher, that would in a Morris keep me company to Bury: but ere we had measured half a mile he gave me over, protesting, that if he might get a 100 pound, he would not hold out with me; for indeed my pace in dancing is not ordinary. As we were parting, a lusty Country lass called him faint hearted lout: saying, "If I had begun to dance, I would have held out one mile though it had cost my life." At which words many laughed. "Nay," saith she, "if the Dancer will lend me a leash of his bells, I'll venture to tread one mile with

him my self." I looked upon her, saw mirth in her eyes, heard boldness in her words, and beheld her ready to tuck up her russet petticoat, I fitted her with bells: which she merrily taking, garnished her thick short legs, and with  a smooth brow bade the Taborer begin. The Drum struck, forward marched I with my merry Maid Marian: who shook her fat sides: and footed it merrily to Melford, being a long mile. There parting with her, I gave her an English crown to buy more drink, for good wench she was in a piteous heat: my kindness she requited with dropping some dozen of short curtsies, and bidding "God bless the Dancer," I bade her adieu: and to give her her due, she had a good ear, danced truly, and we parted friendly.

'Saturday of the second week. In the morning I took my leave, and was accompanied with many Gentlemen a mile of my way. Which mile Master Colts his fool would needs dance with me, and had his desire, where leaving me, two fools parted fair in a foul way. I danced to Bury. By reason of the great snow that then fell I stayed at Bury from Saturday in the second week of my setting forth, til Thursday night the week following.'

Jog on, jog on, the footpathway,
And merrily hent the stile-a
A merry heart goes all the day,
Your sad tires in a mile-a.
The Winter's Tale (Act 4 Scene 2)

Biblical Plague of Flies and Beetles on the Avon

At Tewkesbury, down river from Stratford-upon-Avon on this day in 1575, according to John Stow in his *Chronicles*, a strange thing happened:

'...After a flood which was not great, in the afternoon there came down the river of Avon great number of flies and beetles such as in summer evenings use to strike men in the face, in great heaps, a foot thick upon the water, so that to credible men's judgement, they were in a pair of butts' length of those flies above a hundred quarters. The mills there about were damned up with them for the space of four days after, and then were cleansed by digging them out with shovels, from whence they came, yet unknown, but the day was cold and a hard frost.'

Stow refers to other plagues that pestered England in his lifetime:

A Vexation of Mice

'1581: About Hallontide last past, in the marshes of Dainsey Hundred, in a place called Southminster, in the county of Essex, there suddenly appeared an infinite multitude of mice, which overwhelming the said marshes, did shear and gnaw the grass by the roots, spoiling and tainting the same with their venomous teeth, in such sort that the cattle which grazed thereon, were smitten with a murrein and died thereof, which vermin by policy of man could not be destroyed, till it came to pass that there flocked together all about the same marshes, such a number of owls as all the shire was not able to yield, whereby the marsh-holders were shortly delivered from the vexation of mice.'

Chronicles, John Stow.

Also on this day, opera was born, in 1607. Monteverdi's *Orfeo* was first performed for Carnival in Mantua, on February 24th, 1607, in the Palace of Duke Vincenzo Gonzaga I, with hand-painted décor and daring 'flying' machines. *L'Orfeo* may not have been quite the first opera but it mapped out a musical terrain that is still being followed 400 years later.

Backwinter

Backwinter is a fierce spell of winter weather that returns just when we are expecting spring to appear. In Thomas Nashe's *Summer's Last Will and Testament*, Backwinter, the son of winter, makes a roaring, surly, malevolent entrance into the pageant:

Would I could bark the sun out of the sky,
Turn moon and stars to frozen meteors
And make the ocean a dry land of ice;
With tempests of my breath turn up high trees,
On mountains heap up second mounts of snow,
Which melted into water, might fall down,
As fell the deluge on the former world.
I hate the air, the fire, the Spring, the year,
And whatsoe'er brings mankind any good.
Oh that my looks were lightning to blast fruits!
Would I with thunder presently might die,
So I might speak in thunder to slay men.
Earth, if I cannot injure thee enough,
I'll bite thee with my teeth, I'll scratch thee thus;
I'll beat down the partition with my heels,
Which as a mud-vault severs hell and thee.
Spirits, come up ! 'Tis I that knock for you,
One that envies the world far more than you.
Come up in millions; millions are too few
To execute the malice I intend.

A Winter Landscape by Esias van de Velde, 1623

Will Summer, Henry VIII's fool

Will Summer (in reality the jester to Henry VIII) in his fool's coat, who acts as a chorus to the pageant, explains Backwinter to the audience:

This Backwinter plays a railing part to no purpose; my small learning finds no reason for it, except as Backwinter or an after-winter is more raging-tempestuous and violent than the beginning of winter, so he brings him stamping and raging as if he were mad, when his father is a jolly, mild, quiet old man, and stands still and does nothing.

Also on this day, in 1598, *Henry IV Part One* was registered in the Stationers' Register, and Falstaff was immortalised in print.

Pirates
• • • • • • • • •

But ships are but boards, sailors but men: then there be land rats and water rats, water thieves and land thieves, I mean pirates, and then there is the peril of waters, winds and rocks.

The Merchant of Venice (Act 1 Scene 3)

'In the month of February, through sundry heinous complaints brought to the Queen's majesty and her council, of pirates that keep the narrow seas, doing many robberies, as also robbing the Earl of Worcester, it pleased her majesty to send one of her ships named the Swallow, under the charge of William Holstocke Esquire, controller of her Highness' ships, who had with him Gillian, the barque Garet, and the barque of Yarmouth, and 306 able mariners, gunners and soldiers in the said three ships, and one barque which scoured the narrow sea, from North Foreland as far Westward as Falmouth in Cornwall, and took twenty ships and barques of sundry nations, viz English, French and Flemmings, (but all pirates) and in fashion of war. He apprehended in those ships and barques to the number of 900 men of all nations, and sent them to Sandwich, Dover, Wight and Portsmouth (whereof three of them that had robbed the Earl of Worcester were shortly executed at Wight). Also the said William Holstocke did rescue and take from the above said pirates 15 other merchant ships laden with merchandises that were their prizes, and set at liberty the said 15 merchant ships and goods, which done he returned.'

Chronicles, John Stow

Pirates may make cheap pennyworths of their pillage

And purchase friends and give to courtezans,
Still revelling like lords till all be gone

Henry VI Part Two (Act 1 Scene 1)

Hamlet's ship is attacked by pirates on his way to England, an event which in the end saves his life (see October 11th), and in *Pericles*, Marina is kidnapped by 'roguing thieves' who serve 'the great pirate Valdes'. Leonine declares:

There's no hope she will return. I'll swear she's dead,
And thrown into the sea.

Pericles (Act 4 Scene 1)

Shakespeare mentions a number of notable pirates, all of whom have splendid names. There are Menecrates and Menas, with whom Pompey allies and holds Rome to ransom. These:

... famous pirates,
Make the sea serve them, which they ear and wound
With keels of every kind: many hot inroads
They make in Italy.

Antony and Cleopatra (Act 1 Scene 4)

And in *Measure for Measure*, the Provost proposes that, instead of cutting off Claudio's head, they cut off the head of 'a most notorious pirate' called Ragozine, who happens to have died of a cruel fever that morning in the prison. Then there is Bargulus, the strong Illyrian pirate mentioned in *Henry VI Part Two*. Antonio in *Twelfth Night* is accused by Orsino of being another Illyrian pirate, and salt-water thief; a charge which Antonio denies. Illyrian waters (the Adriatic) were notorious for pirates.

Horse Racing

In 1604, King James I is credited with introducing horseracing into Britain.

'Upon Wednesday 27th February, in the year above written, the high and mighty Prince James, by the Grace of God, King of Great Britain, France and Ireland, Defender of the Faith etc. did hunt the hare with his own hounds in our fields of Fordham and did kill hare at a place called Blacklands. And afterwards did take his repast in the said field at a bush near unto king's path.'

Fordham Parish Register Records, 1604

The fortunes of the little East Anglian market town of Newmarket were changed for ever when King James I decided to pursue two of his favourite pastimes, hunting and hawking, nearby.

Here, King James advises his son Prince Henry about horse riding:

'And amongst all unneccessary things that are lawful and expedient, I think exercises of the body most commendable to be used by a young prince, in such honest games and pastimes, as may further ability and maintain health. For albeit I grant it to be most requisite for a King to exercise his engine, which surely with idleness will rust and become blunt; yet certainly bodily exercises and games are very commendable, as well for banishing idleness (the mother of all vices) as for making his body able and durable for travel, which is very necessary for a King. But for this count I debar all rough and violent exercises, as the football, meeter for laming, than making able the users thereof. But the exercises I would have you use (although but moderately, not making a craft of them) are running, leaping, wrestling, fencing, dancing, and playing at the catch or tennis, archery, paille maille, and such like other pleasant field games. And the honourablest most commendable games that you can use, are on horseback, for it becometh a Prince best of any man. Use therefore to ride great and courageous horses: and specially use such games on horseback, as may teach you to handle your arms thereon, such as tilt, the ring, and low-riding for handling your sword. I cannot omit here the hunting, namely running with hounds; which is most honourable and noblest sort thereof.'

A Royal Gift, Basilikon Doron, 1599

In Shakespeare's erotic narrative poem *Venus and Adonis*, he describes, with almost unseemly relish, the sumptuous proportions of a fine stallion:

Look, when a painter would surpass the life,
In limning out a well-proportion'd steed,
His art with nature's workmanship at strife,
As if the dead the living should exceed;
So did this horse excel a common one
In shape, in courage, colour, pace and bone.

Round-hoof'd, short-jointed, fetlocks shag and long,
Broad breast, full eye, small head and nostril wide,
High crest, short ears, straight legs and passing strong,
Thin mane, thick tail, broad buttock, tender hide:
Look, what a horse should have he did not lack,
Save a proud rider on so proud a back.

Friendship

On this day in 1533, the French essayist Montaigne was born.

This extract is taken from his *Essay on Friendship* (referring to his friend Etienne de la Boétie).

'If I were pressed to say why I love him, I feel that my only reply could be: because it was he, because I was I.

'There is, beyond all my reasoning, and beyond all that I can specifically say, some inexplicable power of destiny that brought our union. We were looking for each other before we met, by reason of the reports we heard of each other, which made the impression greater on our emotions than mere reports reasonably should. I

Michel de Montaigne by Daniel Dumonstier

believe that this was brought about by some decree of Heaven. We embraced one another by name. At our first meeting, which happened by chance at a great feast and gathering in the city, we found ourselves so captivated, so familiar, so bound to one another, that from that time nothing was closer to either than each was to the other. He wrote an excellent Latin satire, which has been published, in which he excuses and explains the suddenness of our understanding, which so quickly grew to perfection. Having so short a time to live, and having begun so late, for we were both grown men and he some years the elder, it had no time to lose, and none in which to conform to the regular pattern of those mild friendships that require so many precautions in the form of long preliminary intercourse. Such a friendship has no model but itself, and can only be compared to itself. It was not one special consideration, nor two, nor three, nor four, nor a thousand; it was some mysterious quintessence of all this mixture which possessed itself of my will, and led it to plunge and lose itself in his; which possessed itself of his whole will, and led it, with a similar hunger and a like impulse, to plunge and lose itself in mine. I may truly say lose, for it left us with nothing that was our own, nothing that was either his or mine.'

My true love hath my heart and I have his,
But just exchange one for the other giv'n;
I hold his dear, and mine he cannot miss,
There never was a better bargain driv'n.

Arcadia, Sir Philip Sidney

To me, fair friend, you never can be old,
For as you were when first your eye I eyed,
Such seems your beauty still. Three winters cold
Have from the forests shook three summers' pride,
Three beauteous springs to yellow autumn turn'd
In process of the seasons have I seen,
Three April perfumes in three hot Junes burn'd,
Since first I saw you fresh, which yet are green.
Ah, yet doth beauty, like a dial-hand,
Steal from his figure and no pace perceived;
So your sweet hue, which methinks still doth stand,
Hath motion and mine eye may be deceived:
For fear of which, hear this, thou age unbred;
Ere you were born was beauty's summer dead.

Sonnet CIV

Job's Day: Leap Year's Day (An Unlucky Day!)

Job, from Les Très Riches Heures du Duc du Berry

What hath this day deserved? What hath it done
That it in golden letters should be set
Among the high tides of the calendar?
This day of shame, oppression, perjury:
Or if it must stand still, let wives with child
Pray that their burdens may not fall this day
Lest that their hopes prodigiously be crossed:
But on this day let seamen fear no wrack;
No bargains break that are not this day made;
This day all things begun come to ill end;
Yea, faith itself to hollow falsehood change.

King John (Act 3 Scene 1)

Elizabethan almanacs would list which days in the month were unlucky, and which were auspicious days. Leap Year's Day was known as Job's Day in Shakespeare's time, a very unlucky day. (1564 and 1600 were Leap Years.)

The Prophet Job cursed the day he was born; however, God, in his mercy, only allowed that day to happen once in four years.

After this, opened Job his mouth, and cursed his day. And Job spake and said,

Let the day perish wherein I was born, and the night in which it was said there is a man child conceived.

Let that day be darkness: let not God regard it from above, neither let the light shine upon it.

Let darkness and the shadow of death stain it: let a cloud dwell upon it, let the blackness of the day terrify it.

As for that night, let darkness seize upon it; let it not be joined unto the days of the year. Let it not come into the number of the months.

Lo, let that night be solitary, let no joyful voice come therein,

Let them curse it that curse the day, who are ready to raise up their mourning.

Let the stars of the twilight thereof be dark; let it look for night but have none; neither let us see the dawning of the day;

Because it shut not up the doors of my mother's womb, nor hid sorrow from my eyes.

Job, 3: 1–10

This was also the day that ladies were allowed to propose to gentlemen, and if the gentlemen refused, they had to give their spurned partner a pair of gloves on Easter Day.

... daffodils,
That come before the swallow dares, and take
The winds of March with beauty.
The Winter's Tale (Act 4 Scene 3)

Worse than the sun in March.
Henry IV Part One (Act 4 Scene 1)

'It is now March, and the Northern wind drieth up the southern dirt: the tender lips are now masked for fear of chapping, and the fair hands must not be ungloved: now riseth the sun a pretty step to his fair height, and St Valentine calls the birds together, where Nature is pleased in the variety of Love: the fishes and the frogs fall to their manner of generation, and the adder dies to bring forth her young: the Air is very sharp, but the sun is comfortable and the hay begins to lengthen: the forward gardens give the fine sallets and a Nosegay of violets is a present for a lady: Now beginneth Nature (as it were) to wake out of her sleep, and send the traveller to survey the walks of the world: the sucking rabbit is good for weak stomachs, and the diet of the rheum doth make a great cure: the farrier now is the horses' physician, and the fat dog feeds the falcon in the mew: The Tree begins to bud, and the grass to peep abroad, while the thrush and the blackbird make a charm in the young springs: the Milkmaid with her best beloved, talk away weariness to the Market: the Football now tryeth the legs of strength, and merry matches continue good fellowship: It is a time of much work and tedious to discourse of: but in all I find of it, I thus conclude in it: I hold it the servant of Nature, and the Schoolmaster of Art: the hope of labour, and the subject of reason. Farewell.'
Fantasticks, Nicholas Breton

'For March, there come violets, specially the single blue, which are the earliest; the yellow daffodil, the daisy, the almond-tree in blossom, the peach-tree in blossom, the cornelian-tree in blossom, sweet-briar.'
Of Gardens, Francis Bacon

'March, in a tawny dress with a fierce aspect, a helmet upon his head to show this month was dedicated to Mars, his father, the sign of Aries in his right hand, leaning upon a spade; in his left hand almond blossoms; upon his arm a basket of garden seeds.'
Emblems, Henry Peacham

St David's Day

I do believe your majesty takes no scorn
To wear a leek upon St Davy's day.
Henry V (Act 4 Scene 7)

Second only perhaps to Captain Fluellan, the most famous Welsh character in the canon of Shakespeare's plays has to be Owen Glendower in *Henry IV Part One*.

Glendower: *Give me leave*
To tell you once again that at my birth
The front of heaven was full of fiery shapes,
The goats ran from the mountains, and the herds
Were strangely clamorous to the frighted fields.
These signs have mark'd me extraordinary;
And all the courses of my life do show
I am not in the roll of common men.
Where is he living, clipp'd in with the sea
That chides the banks of England, Scotland, Wales,
Which calls me pupil, or hath read to me?
And bring him out that is but woman's son
Can trace me in the tedious ways of art
And hold me pace in deep experiments.
Hotspur: *I think there's no man speaks better Welsh.*
(Act 3 Scene 12)

In *A Hundred Merry Tales* is one which Shakespeare must have known when he wrote the spat between Parson Hugh Evans and Falstaff in *The Merry Wives of Windsor*:

'I find written among old gest, how God made Saint Peter porter of heaven, and that God of His goodness soon after His passion, suffered many men to come to the Kingdom of heaven with small deserving – at which time there was in heaven a great company of Welshmen, which with their cracking and babbling troubled all the others. Wherefore God said to Saint Peter that He was weary of them, and that he would fain have them out of heaven. To whom Saint Peter said: "Good Lord, I warrant you that shall be shortly done." Wherefore Saint Peter went out of heaven's gates and cried with a loud voice – "Cause bob!" – that is as much as to say "roasted cheese," which thing the Welshmen hearing, ran out of heaven a great pace. And when Saint Peter saw them all out, he suddenly went into heaven and locked the door and so sparred all the Welshmen out.'

St Chad's Day

Lenten Stuff: In Praise of the Red Herring

Thomas Nashe had written a comedy called *The Isle of Dogs*, with George Chapman and Ben Jonson, which caused such offence that a warrant was issued for their arrest. Nashe managed to escape prison and fled. He headed home for Norfolk by way of Lowestoft, and ended up in Great Yarmouth, where he penned his most extravagantly silly work. And as we are still in Lent, here is an extract from *Lenten Stuff*, Nashe's glorious eulogy to the Red Herring. Here he describes how to cook it:

'Now you must accept of it as the place serves, and, instead of comfits and sugar to strew him with, take a farthing of flour to white him over and wamble him in, and having no great pieces to discharge for his benvenue, or welcoming in, with this volley of Rhapsodies or small shot he must rest pacified, and so ad rem (to the thing itself), spur cut through thick and thin, and enter the triumphal chariot of the red herring:

'Of our appropriate glory of the red herring, no region twixt the poles arctic and antarctic may, can, or will rebate from us one scruple. On no coast like ours is it caught in such abundance, nowhere dressed in his right cue but under our horizon; hosted, roasted, and toasted here alone it is, and as well powdered and salted as any Dutchman would desire. If you articulate with me of the gain, or profit of it, without the which the newfanglest rarity (that nobody can boast of but ourselves), after three days of gazing is reversed over to children and babies to play with. Behold, it is everyman's money from the King to the courtier. Every householder or goodman Baltrop that keeps a family in pay casts for it as one of his standing provisions. The poorer sort make it three part of their sustenance; with it for his denier, the patchedest leather coated labourer may dine like a Spanish Duke, when the niggardliest mouse of beef will cost him sixpence. In the craft of catching or taking it, and smudging (smoking) it, (merchant and chapmanable as it should be), it sets a-work thousands, who live all the rest of the year gaily and well by what in some weeks they scratch up then... Carpenters, shipwrights, makers of lines, ropes and cables, dressers of hemp, spinners of thread and net-weavers it gives their handfuls to, sets up so many salt-houses to make salt, and salt upon salt; keeps in earnings the cooper and the brewer, the baker, and numbers of other people, to gill, wash and pack it, and carry it, and recarry it.'

St Chad is a Midlands saint. He was the first bishop of Mercia in the seventh century, and was buried at Lichfield. At once he was venerated as a saint, and a cult built up. The Bishop of Lichfield pleaded with Henry VIII to spare his shrine, which he did for a while, but then it was split up. Some of his relics were preserved by recusants. Four large bones, said to be his, are preserved in the Catholic Cathedral in Birmingham. Several churches and wells are dedicated to him, mostly in the Midlands area.

Also on this day, in 1619 Queen Anne died. She and King James had lived apart since 1606.

Jog On
••••••••

Why, this is like the mending of highways
In summer, where the ways are fair enough.
The Merchant of Venice (Act 5 Scene 1)

Kemp's Jig: Day Seven

'Upon Friday morning I set on towards Thetford, dancing that ten mile in three hours: for I left Bury somewhat after seven in the morning, and was at Thetford somewhat after ten that same forenoon. But indeed considering how I had been booted the other journeys before, and that all this way or the most of it was over a heath, it was no great wonder: for I fared like one that had escaped the stocks and tried the use of his legs to out-run the Constable: so light were my heels, that I counted the ten mile no better than a leap.

'At my entrance into Thetford,the noble gentleman Sir Edwin Rich, gave me entertainment in such bountiful and liberal sort, that I want fit words to express[it]: and to conclude liberally as he had begun, at my departure on Monday, his worship gave me five pound.

Kemp's Jig: Day Eight

'On Monday morning I danced to Rockland ere I rested, and coming to my Inn, where the Host was a very boon companion, I desir'd to see him: but in no case he would be spoken with, till he had shifted himself from his working days suit. Being armed at all points, from the cap to the codpiece, his black shoes shining, and made straight with copper buckles of the best, his garters in the fashion, and every garment fitting

Corremsquandam (to use his own word): he enters the Hall with his bonnet in his hand, began to cry out: "O Kemp dear Master Kemp: you are even as as as...", and so stammering, he began to study for a fit comparison, and I thank him at last he fitted me, for saith he, "Thou art even as welcome as the Queen's best grey-hound."

'After this dogged yet well-meaning salutation, the Carouses were called in: and my friendly Host of Rockland began with all this: blessing the hour upon his knees, that any of the Queen's Majesty's well-willers or friends would vouchsafe to come within his house: as if never any such had been within his doors before.

'Having rested me well, I began to take my course for Hingham, whether my honest Host of Rockland would needs be my guide: but good true fat-belly he had not followed me two fields, but he lies all along, and cries after me to come back and speak with him. I fulfilled his request: and coming to him, "Dancer," quoth he, "if thou dance a God's name, God speed thee: I cannot follow thee a foot farther, but adieu good dancer, God speed thee if thou dance a God's name."

'I having haste of my way, and he being able to keep no way, there we parted. Farewell he, he was a kind good fellow, a true Troyan: and it ever be my luck to meet him at more leisure, I'll make him full amends with a Cup full of Canary.

'Well after all these farewells I am sure to Hingham I found a foul way, as before I had done from Thetford to Rockland.'

❀

Also on this day, in 1591 Philip Henslowe records in his diary a performance of *Henry VI* at the Rose Theatre. It is possibly the first ever recorded performance of a play by Shakespeare.

Violets

....

... violets dim,
But sweeter than the lids of Juno's eyes
Or Cytherea's breath.
The Winter's Tale (Act 4 Scene 3)

In his *Herbal*, John Gerard describes many herbs and flowers, but he reserves his highest praise for the March Violet:

'March violets ... have a great prerogative above others, not only because the mind conceiveth a certain pleasure and recreation by smelling and handling those most odiferous of flowers, but also for that very many by these violets receive ornament and comely grace; for there be made of them garlands for the head, nosegays and posies, which are delightful to look on and pleasant to smell too, speaking nothing of their appropriate virtues; yea gardens themselves receive by these the greatest ornament of all, chiefest beauty, and most excellent grace, and the recreation of the mind which is taken hereby, cannot be but very good and honest; for flowers through their beauty, variety of colour, and exquisite form do bring to a liberal and gentle-manly mind, the remembrance of honesty, comeliness, and all kinds of virtues: for it would be an unseemly and filthy thing (as a certain wise man saith) for him that doth look upon and handle fair and beautiful things, to have his mind not fair, but filthy and deformed.'

The forward violet thus did I chide;
Sweet thief, whence did thou steal thy sweet that smells,
If not from my love's breath? The purple pride
Which on thy soft cheek for complexion dwells
In my love's veins thou have too grossly dy'd.
The lily I condemned for thy hand,
And buds of marjoram had stol'n thy hair;
The roses fearfully on thorns did stand,
One blushing shame, another white despair,
A third, nor red, nor white, had stol'n of both,
And to this robbery had annex'd thy breath;
But, for this theft, in pride of all his growth
A vengeful canker eat him up to death.
More flowers I noted, yet I none could see
But sweet or colour it had stolen from thee.
Sonnet XCIX

I had never quite appreciated how powerful the fragrance of violets in spring could be, until coming across a bank of March violets along an abandoned railway line in Stratford one bright morning. It is an effect captured by Orsino in the following lines:

That strain again – it had a dying fall,
O, it came o'er my ear like the sweet sound
That breathes upon a bank of violets,
Stealing, and giving odour.
Twelfth Night (Act 1 Scene 1)

Welcome, my son: Who are the violets now,
That strew the green lap of the new-come spring?
Richard II (Act 5 Scene 2)

Stratford-upon-Avon was once famous for its violets.

A Lenten Pie

Mercutio: *A bawd, a bawd, a bawd! So ho !*
Romeo: *What hast thou found?*
Mercutio: *No hare, sir, unless a hare, sir, in a lenten pie, that is something stale and hoar ere it be spent.*
[*sings*] *'An old hare hoar, and old hare hoar,*
Is very good meat in Lent,
But a hare that is hoar, is too much for a score,
When it hoars ere it be spent.'
Romeo and Juliet (Act 2 Scene 4)

Here is a contemporary recipe for such a Lenten Pie: 'Hash the flesh of as many hares, as you please, very small. Then beat them strongly in a Mortar into a Paste, which season duly with Pepper and Salt. Lard it thoroughly all over with great Lardons of Lard well rowled in Pepper and Salt. Put this into a straight earthen pot, to lie close in it. If you like Onions, you may put one or two quartered into the bottom of the Pot. Put store of Sweet-butter upon the meat, and upon that, some strong red Claret-wine. Cover the pot with a double strong brown paper, tied close about the mouth of it. Set it to bake with household bread (or in an oven, as a Venison pasty) for eight or ten hours. Then take out the pot, and the meat, and pour away all the Liquor, which let settle. Then take all the congealed butter and clarify it well. Put your meat again into the pot, put upon it your clarified butter, and as much more as is necesary. (And I believe the putting of Claret-wine to it now is better, and to omit it before). Bake it again, but a less while. Pour out all the Liquor, when it is baked, and clarify all the Butter again, and pour it upon the meat, and so let it cool; The Butter must be at least two or three fingers breadth over the meat.

The Closet Opened, Sir Kenelm Digby

Frog-spawn

Also at about this time the frogs are starting to produce spawn in meadow ponds all over Britain. Dr John Hall, Shakespeare's son-in-law, records the following in his case books:

'Robert Sartor of Stratford-upon-Avon fell into violent bleeding at the nose, which intermitted for four hours and returned again was stopped as followeth: I caused tents made of new cloth, often dipped in frog-spawn in March, and dried, to be put up his nostrils. And thus within half an hour the flux was stayed.'

Frog spawn was collected in the spring, and used to infuse these 'tents' or small rolls of cloth, as preparations for such things as nose bleeds, burns, inflammations and skin diseases.

Stratford Theatre Fire

Shakespeare's own theatre in London, the Globe, burned down in 1613 (see June 30th). On this day in 1926, the Shakespeare Memorial Theatre in Stratford-upon-Avon met with the same fate.

The Shakespeare Memorial Theatre goes up in flames, 1926

'In the early afternoon of a buffeting spring day, 6th March, 1926, a man employed at the theatre was cycling down Chapel Lane when he saw ahead of him a thin spiral of smoke from the roof. He rushed to the stage door; a choking smoke-cloud thrust him back, and everywhere he heard timber crackling. There was a wild rush to Waterside. Fire brigades from Evesham, Warwick, Solihull and Kenilworth hastened to aid the hard-pressed Stratford men. Volunteers on Waterside formed a human chain to save the treasures of the Picture Gallery and library, and thousands of books and pictures passed from hand to hand across the road to be dumped in a lecture room. Two men carried out an enormous marble bust, which it took seven men to get back. In a bitter wind people worked silently until not a book or a picture remained. It was obvious now that nothing could save the building: flames had spread on both sides of the fireproof curtain; the auditorium blazed like desert dry tinder; and when the fire reached the roof, a wind blowing across the theatre to the Avon, acted as a gigantic fan. Before five o'clock, in a tempest of sparks, the roof collapsed, and the flame turned the tower into a pillar of fire. People in Stratford streets had got on with their neglected shopping. Soon after twilight the tower swayed and crashed in ruin, and tongues and streamers of fire shot to fifty feet. By seven o'clock it was nearly over: the theatre of Benson and Charles Flower was in smouldering chaos.

Shakespeare's Country, J. C. Trewin

The previous spring, George Bernard Shaw, proposing the toast to the Immortal Memory of the Bard at the annual birthday luncheon, had described the old Memorial Theatre as 'an admirable building, adapted for every conceivable purpose – except that of a theatre'. After the fire he wrote a telegram to the theatre chairman, Archibald Flower, which read: **'Congratulations. It will be a tremendous advantage to have a proper modern building. There are a number of other theatres I should like to see burned down.'**

March Beer
• • • • • • • • • • • • •

March beer was a strong beer brewed in March, the first beer of the year.

Here William Harrison (in 1577) describes how his wife makes malt beer:

'But what have I to do with this matter, wherewith I am not acquainted? Nevertheless, sith I have taken occasion to speak of brewing, I will exemplify in such a proportion as I am best skilled in, because it is once in a month practised by my wife and her maid-servants, who proceed withal after this manner, as she hath oft informed me. Having therefore ground eight bushels of good malt upon our quern, she addeth unto it half a bushel of wheat meal, and so much of oats small ground, and so mixeth them with the malt that you cannot easily discern the one from the other; otherwise these latter would clunter, fall into lumps, and thereby become unprofitable.

'The first liquor (which is full eighty gallons, according to the proportion of our furnace) she maketh boiling hot, and then poureth it softly into the malt, where it resteth (but without stirring) until her second liquor be almost ready to boil. This done, she letteth her mash run till the malt be left without liquor, which she perceiveth by the stay and soft issue thereof; and by this time her second liquor in the furnace is ready to seethe, whereunto she addeth two pounds of the best English hops, and so letteth them seethe together by the space of two hours in summer or an hour and a half in winter, whereby it getteth an excellent colour, and continuance without any superfluous tartness.

'But, before she putteth her first woort into the furnace, she taketh out a vessel full, of eight or nine gallons, which she shutteth up close, and suffereth no air to come into it till it become yellow, and this she reserveth by itself unto further use, calling it brackwoort and, as she saith, it addeth also to the colour of the drink, whereby it yieldeth not unto amber or fine gold in hue unto the eye.

'...Finally, when she setteth her drink together, she addeth to her brackwoort half an ounce of arras, and half a quarter of an ounce of bayberries, finely powdered. Some, instead of arras and bays, add so much long pepper only, but, in her opinion and my liking, it is not so good as the first, and hereof we make three hogsheads of good beer, such as is meet for poor men as I am to live withal. For my twenty shillings I have ten score gallons of beer or more.'

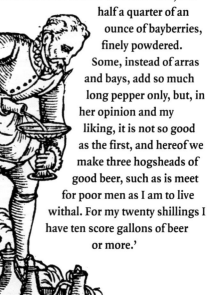

Daffodils
. . . .

When daffodils begin to peer,
With heigh! the doxy over the dale,
Why, then comes in the sweet o' the year;
For the red blood reigns in the winter's pale.
The Winter's Tale (Act 4 Scene 2)

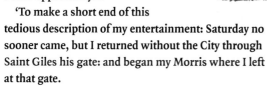

Kemp Delays the Finale of his Nine Days' Wonder

'From Barford bridge I danced to Norwich: but coming within sight of the City, perceiving so great a throng of people still crowding about me, was advised to stay my Morris a little above Saint Giles his gate, where I took my gelding, and so rid into the City, procrastinating my merry Morris dance through the City till better opportunity...

'To make a short end of this tedious description of my entertainment: Saturday no sooner came, but I returned without the City through Saint Giles his gate: and began my Morris where I left at that gate.

'Passing the gate, Wifflers made me a way through the throng of the people, which pressed so mightily upon me: with great labour I got thorough that narrow peaze into the open market place. Where on the cross stood the City Waits, which not a little refreshed my weariness. Such Waits, few Cities in our Realm have the like, none better. Who, besides their excellency in wind instruments, their rare cunning on the Viol, and Violin: their voices be admirable, every one of them able to serve in any Cathedral Church in Christendom for Choristers.

'Passing by the Market place, the press still increasing by the number of boys, girls, men and women, thronging more and more before me to see the end. It was the mischance of a homely maid, that belike was but newly crept into the fashion of long waisted petticoats tied with points, and coming unluckily in my way, as I was fetching a leap, it fell out that I set my foot on her skirts: the point breaking, off fell her petticoat from her waist, but as chance was, though her smock were coarse, it was cleanly: yet the poor wench was so ashamed (the rather for that she could hardly recover her coat again from unruly boys), that looking before like one that had the green sickness, now had she her cheeks all coloured with scarlet.

'I went towards the Mayor's, and deceived the people, by leaping over the Church-yard wall at St Johns, getting so into Mr Mayor's gates a nearer way: (but at last I found it the further way about: being forced on the Tuesday following to renew my former dance, because George Sprat, my over-seer, having lost me in the throng, would not be deposed that I had danced it, since he saw me not). But now I return again to my jump, the measure of which is to be seen in the Guild-hall at Norwich, where my buskins, that I then wore, and danced in from London thither, stand equally divided, nailed on the wall. The Mayor gave me five pound in Elizabeth angels.'

March Hares

As mad as a march hare.

The Two Noble Kinsmen (Act 3 Scene 5)

Hares are said to behave oddly in March, boxing their rivals away from potential mates. Shakespeare gets inside the mind of a terrified hunted hare in his poem, *Venus and Adonis*. Here is his description of the 'dew-bedabbled wretch', Poor Wat:

And when thou hast on foot the purblind hare,
Mark the poor wretch, to overshoot his troubles
How he outruns the winds, and with what care
He cranks and crosses with a thousand doubles:
The many musits through the which he goes
Are like a labyrinth to amaze his foes.

Sometime he runs among a flock of sheep,
To make the cunning hounds mistake their smell,
And sometime where earth-delving conies keep,
To stop the loud pursuers in their yell,
And sometime sorteth with a herd of deer;
Danger deviseth shifts; wit waits on fear:

For there his smell with others being mingled,
The hot scent-snuffing hounds are driven to doubt,
Ceasing their clamorous cry till they have singled
With much ado the cold fault cleanly out;
Then do they spend their mouths: Echo replies,
As if another chase were in the skies.

By this, poor Wat, far off upon a hill,
Stands on his hinder legs with listening ear,
To hearken if his foes pursue him still:
Anon their loud alarums he doth hear;
And now his grief may be compared well
To one sore sick that hears the passing-bell.

Then shalt thou see the dew-bedabbled wretch
Turn, and return, indenting with the way;
Each envious briar his weary legs doth scratch,
Each shadow makes him stop, each murmur stay:
For misery is trodden on by many,
And being low never reliev'd by any.

After the parade of the seasons in Spenser's *The Faerie Queen* comes the procession of the months led by March riding on Aries, the Ram, and ready to sow the land:

These, marching softly, thus in order went,
And after them, the Months all riding came;
First, sturdy March with brows full sternly bent,
And armed strongly, rode upon a Ram,
The same which over Hellespontus swam:
Yet in his hand a spade he also hent,
And in a bag all sorts of seeds ysame,
Which on the earth he strowed as he went,
And filled her womb with fruitful hope of nourishment.

Mutabilitie Cantos, VII: XXXII

Props
......

I will draw a bill of properties such as our play wants.
A Midsummer Night's Dream (Act 1 Scene 2)

The following intriguing list comes from Philip Henslowe's diary:
The inventory taken of all the properties for my Lord Admiral's Men, the 10th of March 1598
Item: 1 rock,1 cage,1 tomb,1 Hell-mouth
Item: 1 tomb for Guido, 1 tomb for Dido, 1 bedstead
Item: 8 lances, 1 pair of stairs for Phaeton
Item: 2 steeples, and 1 chime of bells, and 1 beacon
Item: 1 globe, and 1 golden sceptre; 3 clubs
Item: 2 marchpanes, and the city of Rome
Item: 1 golden fleece, 2 rackets, 1 bay-tree
Item: 1 wooden canopy, old Mahomet's head
Item: 1 lion skin; 1 bear skin; and Phaeton's limbs, and
    Phaeton's chariot; and Argus' head
Item: Neptune fork and garland
Item: 8 vizards, Tamburlaine's bridle, 1 wooden
    mattock
Item: Cupid's bow and quiver; the cloth of the sun
    and moon
Item: 1 boar's head, and Cerberus' three heads
Item: 1 caduceus; 2 moss banks, and 1 snake
Item: 2 fans of feathers; Belin Dun's stable; 1 tree of
    golden apples; Tantalus' tree; 9 iron targets
Item: Mercury's wings; Tasso picture; 1 Helmet with a
    dragon; 1 shield with 3 lions: 1 elm bowl
Item: 1 lion; 2 lion heads; 1 great horse with his legs;
    1 sackbut
Item: 1 black dog
Item: 1 cauldron for the Jew.

There are clearly several properties used in plays by Christopher Marlowe: the tomb for Dido, Queen of Carthage, the cauldron Barabbas falls into at the end of *The Jew of Malta*, and the bridle with which Tamburlaine forced the several kings, 'the pampered jades of Asia', to draw his chariot, and possibly the

cage in which he imprisoned Bajazeth. Might the city of Rome be from *Faustus*? But who said they had no scenery then? There are three prop trees mentioned, a bay tree, a tree with golden apples and Tantalus' tree, as well as two moss banks, a rock and two steeples.

There must have been a play in the repertoire about the fatal attempt of Phaeton to control his father's chariot, 'wanting the manage of unruly jades', which clearly climaxed with the appearance of his severed limbs. And there is quite a menagerie: a snake, a black dog, a three-headed Cerberus, a bear skin, a lion skin and head, a boar's head, and particularly intriguing is the '1 great horse with his legs'. Was that some kind of pantomime horse, or something more sophisticated ?

Another insight into the stagecraft of the time comes in *Othello*:
Are there no stones in heaven
But what serve for thunder?
(Act 5 Scene 2)
Othello refers to the prop stones rattled in a wooden box in the roof, to create the sound of thunder.

Also on this day in 1613, Shakespeare bought an apartment in Blackfriars; his first London property.

Cats

······

Care killed a cat.

Much Ado About Nothing (Act 5 Scene 1)

Cats in Shakespeare don't have a great time. Benedick in *Much Ado About Nothing* declares that if he were ever to love a woman, his friends can, ' hang me up in a bottle like a cat and shoot at me'. This refers to the cruel practice of using live cats for target practice. In *Macbeth*, Lady Macbeth castigates her husband for his cowardice, saying he is like the poor cat in the adage 'letting I dare not wait upon I would'. The adage describes a cat that wants the fish, but does not want to get its feet wet. And the disgraced Parolles in *All's Well That Ends Well* is described by the old courtier Lafeu as 'a musk cat that has fallen in the fish pond of my lady's displeasure'.

If I might alter kind,
What think you I would be ?
Nor fish, not fowl, nor flea,
Nor frog, nor squirrel on a tree.

The fish, the hook, the fowl
The limed twig doth catch;
The flea the finger, and the frog
The buzzard doth dispatch.

The squirrel thinking naught,
That featly cracks the nut,
The greedy goshawk wanting prey
In dread of death doth put.

But scorning all these kinds,
I would become a cat.
To combat with the creeping mouse
And scratch the screeching rat.

I would be present aye
And at my lady's call,
To guard her from the fearful mouse
In parlour and in hall.

In kitchen for his life
He should not show his head;
The pear in poke should lie untouched
When she were gone to bed.

The mouse should stand in fear,
So should the squeaking rat:
All this would I do
If I were converted to a cat.

The Lover whose mistress feared a mouse, declareth that he would become a cat, if he might have his desire, George Turberville

Joan Flower, who was executed for being a witch on this day in 1611, claimed that she had a familiar, who did her bidding for her – her cat, Rutterkin. The first witch in *Macbeth* calls on her feline familiar, Grey Malkin.

Also on this day in 1574, Shakespeare's second brother, Richard, was christened. Will was nearly ten.

St Gregory's Day

Spare meadow at Gregory, marshes at pasque
For fear of dry summer no longer time ask.
Then hedge them and ditch them, bestow thereon pence,
Corn, meadow, and pasture ask always good fence.
Five Hundred Good Points of Husbandry, Thomas Tusser

On this day the English antiquary and folklorist John Aubrey, was born. He is perhaps most famous for his *Brief Lives*, a collection of memoirs of the great men and women of the age he had just missed, being born the year that King James I died and his son Charles I came to the throne. As an historian Aubrey is unreliable, as a storyteller he is irresistible. Aubrey frequently gets his facts wrong. He tells us that William Shakespeare's father was a butcher, and that Ben Jonson killed Christopher Marlowe. He is often scurrilous, and perhaps too fond of a dirty story. His gossipy account of Mary Herbert, Countess of Pembroke (sister of Sidney, and mother to Shakespeare's patron), is worthy of the rumours about Catherine the Great:

'She was "very salacious", and she had a contrivance that in the Spring of the year, when the stallions were to leap the mares, they were to be brought before such a part of the house, where she had a vidette (*a hole to peep out at*) to look on them and please herself with their sport; and she would act the like sport herself with her stallions.'

Aubrey tells less damaging tales of Sir Walter Raleigh: 'He loved a wench well; and one time getting one of the maids of Honour up against a tree in a wood, who seemed at first boarding to be something fearful of her honour, and modest, she cried, "Sweet Sir Walter, what do you me ask ? Will you undo me? Nay Sweet Sir Walter! Sweet Sir Walter! Sir Walter!" At last, as the danger and the pleasure at the same time grew higher, she cried in the ecstasy, "Swisser Swatter Swisser Swatter !"'

But sometimes Aubrey relates some gossip which sounds as though it might be suspiciously accurate. For example, he says of the relationship between playwrights Francis Beaumont and John Fletcher that 'they lived together on the Bankside, not far from the Playhouse, both bachelors; lay together'. Now, I don't believe that he's talking about their sharing a bed as Morecambe and Wise did on their television show. He goes on to say they shared the services of a

The portrait of John Fletcher by an unknown artist was recently purchased for the nation by the National Portrait Gallery

maid, and wore the same clothes and cloak. And, perhaps more interestingly, that it was Beaumont's job in their writing partnership 'to lop the overflowings of Mr Fletcher's luxuriant fancy and flowing wit.'

Exit Burbage

Astronomers and star gazers this year
Write but of four eclipses: five appear
Death interposing Burbage - and their staying
Hath made a visible eclipse of playing.

On the death of that great master in his art and quality, painting
and playing: Richard Burbage, by Thomas Middleton

A portrait of a man, probably Richard Burbage,
by an unknown artist, 1619

On this day, March 13th, 1609, Richard Burbage died at the age of 50 (a few days after Queen Anne). True to form, the leading actor of the King's Men upstaged royalty even in death. His funeral was a huge public event. Several poems were written in his honour, mourning the loss of England's greatest actor and all the brilliant characters who died with him.

Imagine being Richard Burbage, and having these parts written for you: Richard III when you are 23, Hamlet when you are 30, Othello at 34, and King Lear at 36 or 37. And those are just the Shakespeare roles we know that Burbage played. Ben Jonson has one or two for you as well. There's Volpone, and Subtle in *The Alchemist*, and Sejanus. Webster writes a cracking role in *The Duchess of Malfi*, Ferdinand (you have to turn into a werewolf in that one), and Marston's got a great lead called Malevole in *The Malcontent* lined up. And there's Old Heironimo in Kyd's *The Spanish Tragedy* as well.

Here is an account of his acting ability which may have been written by the playwright John Webster: **'Whatsoever is commendable to the grave orator, is most exquisitely perfect in him; for by a full and significant action of body, he charms our attention; sit in a full theatre, and you will think you see so many lines drawn from the circumference of so many ears, whiles the actor is in the centre.**

'He doth not strive to make Nature monstrous, she is often seen in the same scene with him, but neither on stilts nor crutches; and for his voice it is not lower than the prompter; not louder than the foil or target. By his actions he fortifies moral precepts with examples; for what we see him personate we think truly done before us.'

An Excellent Actor, from Thomas Overbury's Characters

Here is a famous anecdote about Burbage and Shakespeare:
'Upon a time when Burbage played Richard III, there was a citizen grew so far in liking him, that before she went from the play, she appointed him to come that night unto her by the name of Richard III. Shakespeare, overhearing their conclusion, went before, was entertained, and at his game ere Burbage came. Then message being brought that Richard III was at the door, Shakespeare caused return to be made that William the Conqueror was before Richard III.'

from The Diary of John Manningham of Middle Temple (1602)

Of the Breeding of All Sorts of Horses

Dauphin: *When I bestride him I soar, I am a hawk: he trots the air; the earth sings when he touches it; the basest horn of his hoof is more musical than the pipe of Hermes.*
Orleans: *He's of the colour of the nutmeg.*
Dauphin: *And of the heat of the ginger.*
Henry V (Act 3 Scene 7)

'For the choice of a good Stallion and which is best in our Kingdom, opinion swayeth so far that I can hardly give well-received Directions. Yet surely if you will be ruled by the Truth of experience, the best Stallion to beget horses for the Wars is the *Courser*, the *Jennet*, or the *Turks*; the best for coursing and running is the *Barbary*; the best for hunting is the *Bastard Courser* begot of the *English*; the best for the Coach is the *Flemish*; and the best for travel or burden is the *English*; and the best for ease is the *Irish hobby*.

'For the choice of Mares, you shall greatly respect their shapes and mettles, especially that they be beautifully fore-handed, for they give much goodness to their Foals. For their Kinds any of the races before spoken of is very good, or any of them mixt with our true English Races, as *Bastard-Courser Mare*, *Bastard-Jennet*, *Bastard-Turk*, *Barbary*, etc.

'The best time to put your Stallion and Mares together is in the middle of March if you have any grass, as you should have great care for that purpose. One foal falling in March is worth two falling in May, because he possesseth as it were two winters in a year and is thereby so hardened that (almost) nothing can after impair him.

'To know whether your Mare hold to the Horse or no, there be diverse ways, of which the best is by offering her the Horse again at the next increase of the Moon, which if she willingly receive, it is a sign she held not before, but if she refuse, it is most certain she is sped.

'If you have any advantage given you by friendship or otherwise whereby you may have a Mare at the present well covered, only yours is not yet ready for the Horse, you shall in this case, to provoke lust in her, give her to drink good store of clarified honey and new milk mixt together, and then with a brush of nettles all to nettle her privy parts and then immediately offer her to the Horse.'
From *The Compleat Horseman* by Gervase Markham (1614)

Gervase Markham was such a prolific writer, on so many topics, that he often repeated himself. So much so that in 1617 his booksellers made him promise not to produce any more books on certain subjects.

The Ides of March
·······················

Caesar: *The Ides of March are come.*
Soothsayer: *Aye, Caesar, but not gone.*
Julius Caesar (Act 3 Scene 1)

The coronation of King James I in July 1603 had had
to be rushed through because of an outbreak of
plague in London, and the celebrations were
postponed until the following year. Why the Privy
Council chose the inauspicious Ides of March to
mount the King's triumphal procession is unclear,
but it took place on this day in 1604.

James, not as at ease as Queen Elizabeth had been
with pomp and ceremony, rode on a white jennet
under a canopy held by eight of his Gentlemen of the
Privy Chamber. Queen Anne followed behind in a
carriage. They paraded though seven great arches
from the Tower to Whitehall.

The first arch at Fenchurch was devised by Ben
Jonson. It was covered with a curtain of silk painted
like a thick cloud, which was drawn up as the King
approached. Called the Londinium Arch, it was
fantastically decorated with the City of London
carved in miniature, and had two chambers for
musicians, and niches for live actors, dressed as
various characters. There was Genius Orbis, dressed
in purple, and a personification of the River Thames,
dressed in a mantle of sea green with a crown of
sedge and water lilies, who welcomed the new King
to the city.

In Gracious Street, the second arch was erected by
the city's Italian merchants, while the arch near the
Royal Exchange at Cornhill was built by Dutch
merchants, and sported seventeen children
representing each of the provinces of the Low
Countries.

The next three arches were designed by Thomas
Dekker; the Nova Felix Arabia arch in Cheapside
boasted Fame dressed in golden wings, with a robe
painted with eyes and tongues and a trumpet in her

The New World Arch in Fleet Street

hand; the Garden of Plenty Arch, garnished with fruit
and flowers, housed Peace and Plenty, and nine little
boys from St Paul's representing the Muses; and then
the New World Arch in Fleet Street had a huge globe
with Fortune standing on it, and Envy below,
'unhandsomely attired in black' with snakes in
her hair.

The seventh and last arch, at Temple Bar, was
Jonson's responsibility again, as was a final tableau
in the Strand, bedecked with a rainbow, and two
seventy-foot pyramids. By the last arch, however, as
yet another classical figure stepped forward to
address the new monarch, James had had enough.
Dekker tells us that 'a great part of the speeches were
left unspoken'. Apparently irritated by the crowds the
King cried out, 'God's wounds, I will pull down my
breeches and they shall also see my arse!'

Fishing

Here comes the trout that must be caught with tickling.
Twelfth Night (Act 2 Scene 5)

On this day the angling season opens on certain river fish. Shakespeare knew his freshwater fish well enough to make jokes about their appearance, for instance a carrier (in *Henry IV, Part One*) complains of a wayside inn in Rochester:
I think this be the most villainous house in all London road for fleas: I am stung like a tench.
(*Act 2 Scene 1*)

The tench has spots on its scales, said to resemble flea bites. Today the anglers whiling away a sunny day along the Seven Meadows stretch of the Avon at Stratford still fish for tench, as well as chub, roach and barbell.

Here is Michael Drayton on the abundance of river fish available in Shakespeare's day:
The Barbell, than which fish, a braver doth not swim,
Nor greater for the ford within my spacious brim,
Nor (newly taken) more the curious taste doth please;
The Greyling, whose great spawn is big as any peas:
The Perch with pricking fins, against the Pike prepared...
The Trout by Nature marked with many a crimson spot,
As though she curious were in him above the rest,
As of fresh water fish, did note him for the best;
The Roach, whose common kind to every flood doth fall;
The Chub (whose neater name) which some a Chevin call,
Food for the tyrant Pike (most being in his power)
Who for their numerous store he most doth them devour.

The lusty Salmon then, from Neptune's watr'y realm,
When as his season serves, stemming his tideful stream,
Then being in his kind, in me his pleasure takes
(For whom the fisher then all other game forsakes)
Which bending then himself in fashion of a ring,
Above the forced weirs, himself doth nimbly fling,
And often when the net hath dragged him safe to land,
Is seen by natural force to 'scape the murderer's hand,
Whose grain doth lie in flakes, with fatness interlarded,
Of many a liquorish lip, that highly is regarded.
Poly-Olbion, Book 26

Mrs Overdone: But what's his offence ?
Pompey: Groping for trouts in a peculiar river.
Measure for Measure (Act 1 Scene 2)

St Patrick's Day
· · · · · · · · · · · · · · · · ·

Horatio: *There's no offence, my lord.*
Hamlet: *Yes, by Saint Patrick, but there is, Horatio
And much offence too!*
Hamlet (Act 1 Scene 5)

St Patrick is here invoked by Hamlet as the keeper of Purgatory (from whence his father's ghost has just emerged), rather than in Patrick's more familiar role as the patron saint of Ireland.

Here, the English traveller and writer, Fynes Moryson, describes the diet and dress of the wild Irish. Moryson had served as personal secretary under Lord Mountjoy in Ireland during the attempts to suppress Tyrone's Rebellion.

'The wild, I may say mere Irish, inhabiting many and large provinces, are barbarous and most filthy in their diet. They skum the seething pot with a handful of straw, and strain the milk taken from the cow through a like handful of straw, none of the cleanest, and so cleanse, or rather defile, the pot and milk. They devour great morsels of beef unsalted, and they eat commonly swine's flesh, seldom mutton, and all these pieces of flesh, as also the entrails of beasts unwashed, they seeth in a hollow tree, lapped in a raw cow's hide, and so set over the fire, and therewith swallow whole lumps of filthy

butter. Yea, (which is more contrary to nature) they will feed on horses dying of themselves, not only upon small want of flesh, but even for pleasure. For I remember an accident in the army, when the Lord Mountjoy, the Lord Deputy, riding to take the air out of the camp, found the buttocks of dead horses cut off, and suspecting that some soldiers had eaten that flesh out of necessity, being defrauded of the victuals allowed them, commanded the men to be searched out, among whom a common soldier, and that of the English-Irish, not of the mere Irish, being brought to the Lord Deputy, and asked why he had eaten the flesh of dead horses, thus freely answered, "Your Lordship may please to eat pheasant and partridge, and much good do it you that best likes your taste, and I hope it is lawful for me without offence to eat this flesh which likes me better than beef."
Whereupon the Lord Deputy gave the soldier a piece of gold to drink in Usquebagh for better digestion, and so dismissed him.

'It may truly be said of them that they wander slovenly and naked, and lodge in the same house with their beasts. I say slovenly, because they seldom put off a shirt till it be worn: and these shirts in our memory before the last Rebellion were made of some twenty or thirty ells, folded in wrinkles, and coloured with saffron to avoid lowsiness, incident to the wearing of foul linen. And let no man wonder, that they are lowsey, for never any barbarous people were found in all kinds more slovenly than they are, and nothing is more common among them, than for the men to lie upon the women's laps upon green hills, till they kill their lice, with a nimbleness, proper to that Nation. Their said breeches are so close, as they expose to full view, not only the noble but the shameful parts, yea, they stuff their shirts about their privy parts, to expose them more to the view.'
An Itinerary, Fynes Moryson

St Edward's Day
····················

A very forward March-chick.
Much Ado About Nothing (Act 1 Scene 3)

The Crown Imperial is the flower dedicated to St Edward, but as we always have hyacinths in the rehearsal room at this time of year, here is the story of their origin.

Just as Jupiter had placed Ganymede in the firmament as Aquarius, so Phoebus Apollo (who accidentally killed his beloved boy in a deadly game of discus), immortalised the Spartan youth, Hyacinth as that most fragrant of spring flowers. Ovid tells the story in *Metamorphoses*, 'As watery Pisces giveth place to Aries':

They stripped themselves and nointed them with oil of
*   Oyfle fat,*
And fell to throwing of a sledge that was right huge and flat.
First Phoebus, peysing it, did throw it from him with
*   such strength,*
As that the weight drove down the clouds in flying. And
*   at length*
It fell upon substantial ground, where plainly it did show
As well the cunning of the force of him that did it throw.
Immediately upon desire himself the sport to try
The Spartan lad made haste to take up unadvisedly
The sledge before it still did lie. But as he was in hand
To catch it, it rebounding up against the hardened land,
Did hit him full upon the face. The God himself did look
As pale as did the lad, and up his swounding body took.

Now culls he him, now wipes he from the wound the
*   blood away,*
Another while his fading life he strives with herbs to stay.
'Thou fad'st away, my Hyacinth, defrauded of thy prime
Of youth' (quoth Phoebus) 'and I see thy wound my
*   heinous crime.*
Both in my mind and in my mouth, thou evermore shalt be.
My Viol strucken with my hand, my songs shall sound
*   of thee,*

And in a new made flower thou shalt with letters represent
Our sighings...'
While Phoebus thus did prophesy, behold the blood of him
Which dyed the grass, ceased blood to be, and up there
*   sprang a trim*
And goodly flower, more orient than the Purple cloth ingrain.

The flower of the hyacinth is said to have the Greek letters 'ai' inscribed on the petals, in remembrance of the sighs of Apollo for his beautiful boy.

If of thy mortal goods thou art bereft,
And from thy slender store
Two loaves alone to thee are left,
Sell one and from the dole,
Buy Hyacinths to feed the soul.
The Gulistan of Saadi, Sheikh Muslih-uddin Saadi Shirazi, 1270

The Burning of Bishop Hooper

It is an heretic that makes the fire,
Not she which burns in't.
The Winter's Tale (Act 2 Scene 3)

Here is John Foxe's account of the agonisingly slow burning of his friend, John Hooper, Bishop of Gloucester. The guard had delivered to Bishop Hooper three bladders filled with gunpowder to place between his legs and under each arm, before he was bound to the stake with a hoop of iron:

'Then commandment was given that the fire should be kindled. But there were put to it no fewer green faggots than two horses could carry upon their backs, so it kindled not speedily, and was a pretty while before it caught. At length it burned about him, but the wind having full strength at that place, and being a lowering cold morning, it blew the flame from him, so that he was little more than touched by the fire.

'Within a space after, a few dry faggots were brought, and a new fire kindled with faggots, (for there were no more reeds) and those burned at the nether parts, but had small power above, because of the wind, saving that it burnt his hair and scorched his skin a little. In the time of which fire, even as at the first flame, he prayed, saying mildly, and not very loud, but as one without pain, "O Jesus, Son of David, have mercy upon me, and receive my soul!" After the second fire was spent, he wiped both his eyes with his hands, and beholding the people, he said with an indifferent, loud voice, "For God's love, good people, let me have more fire!" and all this while his nether parts did burn; but the faggots were so few that the flame only singed his upper parts.

'The third fire was kindled within a while after, which was more extreme than the other two. And then the bladders of gunpowder broke, but this did him little good as they were so misplaced, and the wind had such power. In this fire he prayed with a loud voice, "Lord Jesus, have mercy upon me! Lord Jesus, receive my spirit!" And these were the last words he was heard to utter. But when he was black in the mouth, and his tongue so swollen that he could not speak, yet his lips went until they were shrunk to the gums: and he knocked his breast with his hands until one of his arms fell off, and then knocked still with the other, while the fat, water, and blood dropped out at his fingers' ends, until by renewing the fire, his strength was gone, and his hand clave fast in knocking to the iron upon his breast. Then immediately bowing forwards, he yielded up his spirit.

Thus was he three quarters of an hour or more in the fire.'

Foxe's Book of Martyrs

Foxe's Book of Martyrs

On this day in 1563, the year before Shakespeare was born, John Foxe published his monumental work, popularly known as *Foxe's Book of Martyrs*. In the front pages, he published a *Kalender* recording the names of the martyrs who were executed on that day. It stands as an alternative litany of saints. 'Not such saints as the Pope makes,' Foxe writes, 'or which are mentioned in *The Legend of the Saints* or in such fabulous books; but... true martyrs of Christ.'

Two hundred of the days marked in this Kalender are dedicated to the men and women who were executed as part of Bloody Mary's persecution during the previous decade, from 1555 to 1558, when nearly three hundred Protestants were led to the stake for their faith.

The Convocation of Bishops decreed that Foxe's Martyrology should stand in every cathedral in the land, where, chained to a lectern, it could be read by the general public, alongside the Bible. It profoundly influenced early Protestant sentiment, and remained popular among the Puritans, and later in America with the Evangelical Anglican congregation until the end of the nineteenth century. (Inside the cover of my own copy is a worn label from the British Protestant Institute, Great Homer Street, awarding the book as a prize in the Men's Bible Class, in 1899.)

John Foxe lived near Stratford for a while. He had been forced to resign as a fellow of Magdalen College in 1547 because of his faith, and was offered refuge by Sir Thomas Lucy, as tutor to his children at Charlecote House. During his stay, he married a girl from Coventry called Agnes Randall. He fled with her to Basle when Mary came to the throne, and only returned to England under Elizabeth. He was buried at St Giles, Cripplegate in London, in 1587.

Also on this day in 1414, King Henry IV died in Jerusalem. He had always imagined that he would die on crusade in the Holy Land. In fact he died in the Jerusalem Chamber in Westminster Abbey, thus fulfilling his own prophesy. It is thought he died of leprosy. Later, Sir Thomas More is said to have written his Appeal to the General Council in the Jerusalem Chamber, when imprisoned under the wardenship of the last abbot.

King Henry: *Doth any name particular belong
Unto the lodging where I first did swound?*
Warwick: *'Tis called Jerusalem, my noble lord.*
King Henry: *Laud be to God! Even there my life
must end.
It hath been prophesied to me many years
I should not die but in Jerusalem
Which vainly I supposed the Holy Land.
But bear me to that chamber; there I'll lie:
In that Jerusalem shall Harry die.*
Henry IV Part Two (Act 4 Scene 5)

The First Day of Spring

...Welcome hither,
As is the Spring to the earth.
The Winter's Tale (Act 5 Scene 1)

It was a lover and his lass,
With a hey, and a ho, and a hey nonino,
That o'er the green corn-field did pass
In the spring time, the only pretty ring time,
When birds do sing, hey ding a ding, ding.
Sweet lovers love the spring.

Between the acres of the rye,
With a hey, and a ho, and a hey nonino,
These pretty country folks would lie,
In the spring time, the only pretty ring time,
When birds do sing, hey ding a ding, ding.
Sweet lovers love the spring.

This carol they began that hour,
With a hey, and a ho, and a hey nonino,
How that a life was but a flower,
In the spring time, the only pretty ring time,
When birds do sing, hey ding a ding, ding.
Sweet lovers love the spring.

And therefore take the present time,
With a hey, and a ho, and a hey nonino,
For love is crowned with the prime,
In the spring time, the only pretty ring time,
When birds do sing, hey ding a ding, ding.
Sweet lovers love the spring.
As You Like It (Act 5 Scene 3)

In sooth thou wast in very gracious fooling last night when
thou spokest of Pigrogromitus of the Vapians passing the
equinoctial of Queubus : 'twas very good in faith. I gave thee
sixpence for thy leman. Hadst it?'
Twelfth Night (Act 2 Scene 3)

Equinox literally means *equal night*. On the spring and
autumn equinoxes, day and night are the same
length. Since the early Egyptians built the Sphinx to
face directly towards the rising sun on the day of the
vernal equinox, this moment has been celebrated
ritually by succeeding civilisations.

The Christian church observed Easter on the
Sunday after the first full moon on
or after the day of the vernal
equinox. But because the date
varies slightly from year to
year (the various phases of
the moon only repeat exactly
every 19 years), the
church decided to plump
for March 21st as the official
ecclesiastical vernal
equinox. Watch out for
the next full moon, the
Paschal Moon, and
Easter will fall on the
following Sunday.

And today, therefore, is
the first day of spring.

Mid-Lent Sunday
• • • • • • • • • • • • • • • •

I'll to thee a Simnel bring
Gainst thou go a mothering
So that when she blesseth thee
Half that blessing thou'll give me.
To Dianame: A Ceremony in Gloucester, Robert Herrick

Mid-Lent Sunday happened round about this date. It became traditional on this day for servants and apprentices to visit their mothers, and hence it became known as Mothering Sunday. One of the traditions associated with this day was to celebrate with some excellent furmety. Furmety (sometimes called frumenty) was a pottage or porridge made of whole grains of wheat first boiled plump and soft, and then boiled in milk, sweetened and spiced.

The Simnel that Herrick refers to above is a kind of cake with a layer of almond paste baked into the middle. It was also known as mothering cake, as maidservants would bake it to take to their mothers on Mid-Lent Sunday. One legend suggests that the pretender to the throne, Lambert Simnel, invented the recipe when he was forced to work in Henry VII's kitchens.

Also on this day in 1594, the Protestant Henri of Navarre, declaring that ' Paris is worth a mass', converted to Catholicism, and entered Paris as King Henri IV of France.

Though a King of Navarre appears in *Love's Labour's Lost*, he bears little resemblance to his namesake.

Le Bon Roi Henri, as he is still known in France, was one of the country's most popular rulers ever. He proceeded to ensure that religious liberties were guaranteed in his country, by enacting the Edict of Nantes in 1598. He insisted that, 'God willing, every

working man in my kingdom will have a chicken in the pot every Sunday at least.' Never before had a French monarch even considered the importance of a chicken to his subjects, nor would any other until after the French Revolution.

He added the Grande Galerie to the palace of the Louvre, and invited hundreds of artists and craftsmen to live and work on the building's lower floors, a tradition which lasted for two centuries until Napoleon abolished it. Henri was stabbed to death in his coach in 1610, by a fanatical Catholic called François Ravaillac. His daughter, Henrietta Maria, born just six months before her father's assassination, was to become the wife of King Charles I of England.

Henri's statue stands at the end of the Pont Neuf on the Ile de la Cité in Paris.

Moll Cutpurse: A Life of Frolic Freedom
•••

On this day in 1614, Moll Cutpurse, the famous Roaring Girl, got married.

'The Amazon of Bankside... She moves among rowdies and profligates without suffering any contamination; she has the thews of a giant and the gentleness of a child. Secure in her armed and iron maidenhood, and defying the breath of scandal, she daffs the world aside and chooses a life of frolic freedom.'
From The Works of Thomas Middleton edited by A.H.Bullen, 1885

It might be thought rather surprising that the Amazon of Bankside, who dressed in men's clothes, should have wanted to get hitched. Her husband was Lewknor Martin, son of Gervase Markham, the writer, but the whole thing was thought to be a scam. It did, however, allow her some protection from the charges frequently brought against her.

This extraordinary woman had been born to a shoemaker sometime in the 1580s. Her real name was Mary Frith. She liked to wear a doublet and baggy breeches in public, and would swear like a sailor and smoke a pipe. She came to prominence in the early 1600s and must have been fairly notorious by the time Middleton and Dekker wrote a play about her in 1611 called *The Roaring Girl*.

That year she also appeared on the stage of the Fortune Theatre, in a sort of stand-up routine including a saucy number or two. However, she was arrested on Christmas Day that year, accused of prostitution, and had to do penance for 'evil living' at St Paul's Cross the following February.

'She wept bitterly and seemed very pentinent, but it is since doubted she was maudlin drunk, being discovered to have tippled of three-quarters of sack.'
John Chamberlain in a letter to Dudley Carlton

The Roaring Girle. OR Moll Cut-Purse.
As it hath lately beene Acted on the Fortune-stage by the Prince his Players.
Written by T. Middleton and T. Dekkar.
My case is alter'd, I must worke for my living.
Printed at London for Thomas Archer, and are to be sold at his shop in Popes head-pallace, neere the Royall. Exchange. 1611.

By the 1620s Moll was working as a pimp, and by the 1640s was confined in Bethlehem Hospital, where she was treated for insanity. There are many myths and stories about Moll Cutpurse, of her escapes from the gallows, for instance, or that she robbed General Fairfax and shot him in the arm during the Civil War. She died of dropsy in 1659 on Fleet Street.

Our Lady's Eve: Death of Good Queen Bess

A lass unparallel'd.
Antony and Cleopatra (Act 5 Scene 2)

On this day in 1603 Queen Elizabeth died at Richmond.

'Here was some whispering that her brain was somewhat distempered, but there was no such matter, only she held an obstinate silence for the most part; and because she had persuasion that if she once lay down she should never rise, could not be gotten to bed in a whole week till three days before her death. So that after three weeks' languishing, she departed the 24 of this present, being Our Lady's Eve, between two and three in the morning.

'She made no will, nor gave anything away, so that they which come after shall find a well-stored jewel house and a rich wardrobe of more than 2000 gowns with all things else answerable.'

John Chamberlain, letter

'This morning about 3 at clock her majesty departed this life, mildly like a lamb, easily like a ripe apple from the tree...

'About 10 at clock the counsel and diverse noblemen, having been a while in consultation, proclaimed James VI, King of Scots, the King of England, France, and Ireland, beginning at Whitehall gates, where Sir Robert Cecil read the proclamation, which he carried in his hand and after read it again in Cheapside. The gates at Ludgate and portcullis were shut and down, by the Lord Mayor's command, who was there present, with aldermen. There was a diligent watch and ward kept at every gate and street, day and night, by householders, to prevent garboils: which God be thanked were more feared then perceived.'

Diary of John Manningham

'Thursday the 23rd of March, about two o'clock in the morning, deceased Queen Elizabeth at her manor of Richmond in Surrey, being then aged 70 years, and had reigned 44 years 5 months and odd days. Whose corpse was privily conveyed to Whitehall and there remained till 28th April and then buried at Westminster... Embalmed, laid in lead, covered with purple velvet, laid on a chariot, drawn by four horses trapped in black velvet, the lively picture of her whole body in her parliament robes with a crown on her head, and a sceptre in her hand, lying on the corpse, was attended on by all the nobility, honourable of estate, the worshipful officers, and servants of the household, all in black, gentlemen of the Chapel, and Choir of the College, all in rich copes, singing, was conveyed from Whitehall to the Collegiate Church of St Peter, called Westminster, and there entered in the vault of her grandfather, Henry the Seventh, in his most beautiful Chapel, and there were estimated, mourners in black, about the number of 1600 persons.'

Fugger Newsletter (see page 109)

The Ermine portrait, attributed to William Segar

Lady Day: The First Day of the Year

And the angel came in unto her and said, 'Hail, thou that art highly favoured, the Lord is with thee: blessed art thou among women.'
Luke 1:26 – 38

Lady Day is the Feast of the Annunciation, which celebrates the Incarnation of Christ in the womb of his mother, the Virgin Mary. Lady Day is followed in exactly nine months' time by Christmas Day, the day of Christ's birth. So for centuries, New Year's Day, the day of the saviour's conception, was celebrated on March 25th. And in England, since a synod held at Worcester in 1240, all servile work was forbidden.

It may seem very odd to us now that in Shakespeare's day the year began on March 25th. So for instance, this day (the day Shakespeare dictated his revised will), Tuesday March 25th, 1616, followed Monday March 24th, 1615. The last day of the Sixteenth Century was March 24th, 1600, followed by the first day of the seventeenth century on March 25th, 1601.

Julius Caesar had set January 1st as the first day of the year in 46 BC. But various countries chose different dates to start their official new year. It was not until the rule of Pope Gregory XIII that Europe standardized January 1st as New Year's Day in 1583. England did not follow suit.

And even more oddly, England was out of synch with most of the rest of Europe in terms of dating the rest of the year. When the Pope celebrated mass on Christmas Day, December 25th, 1583, in Rome, it was only December 15th in London. Why was England ten days behind almost everyone else?

Pope Gregory XIII had achieved a massive bureaucratic feat. He had corrected time. He forced through, in the entire Catholic world under his control, a sweeping reform of the old calendar created by Julius Caesar: the Julian Calendar.

The new Gregorian calendar removed ten days from October 1583. October was chosen because it was the month with the fewest Holy Days. Thus, the calendar year was realigned with the astronomical year, which had become out of synch.

England was about to follow suit. Dr John Dee had set out his proposals for a changed calendar, and the Queen's Council seemed set to accept them, when the plans were scuppered by the Archbishop of Canterbury and his bishops, who would not have anything to do with an initiative which had been instigated by Rome. As a result, England did not adopt the new Gregorian calendar until 1752, when eleven days were finally removed so that Wednesday September 2nd was followed by Thursday September 14th. Many people objected and there were riots where mobs shouted, 'Give us back our eleven days!'

In some years, Easter falls on Lady Day. In England these years are regarded as darkly ominous. It occurred in 1554, when Queen Mary married Philip of Spain, and in 1649 when Charles I lost his head. We still retain one last vestige of Lady Day's position as first day of the year, as the UK Tax Year still begins on April 6th (which is Lady Day old-style, i.e. ten days later).

The Highwayman's Hamlet and the First Theatre Knight

A face cut worse than Gamaliel Ratsey.

Ben Jonson, *The Alchemist* (Act 1 Scene 1)

A highwayman was hanged this day in 1605 in Bedford. His name was Gamaliel Ratsey.

He held up a troop of players in Norfolk, and advised one to go to London and challenge Burbage to play Hamlet for a wager. Here is the account from a pamphlet published in 1605:

'Gamaliel Ratsey, travelling up and down the country, came by chance into an inn, where that night there harboured a company of Players: and Ratsey, framing himself into a humour of merriment, caused one or two of the chiefest of them to be sent for up into his chamber. "I pray you," quoth Ratsey, "let me hear your music, for I have often gone to plays more for music sake than for action. For some of you, not content to do well, but striving to over-do and go beyond yourselves, oftentimes mar all, yet your poets take great pains to make your parts fit for your mouths, though you gape never so wide."

'Well, music was played, and that night passed over with such singing, dancing, and revelling, as if my Lord Prodigal had been there in his ruins of excess and superfluity. In the morning Ratsey made the Players taste of his bounty, and so departed.

'But having learned which way they travelled, he (being very well horsed, and mounted upon his black gelding) soon overtook them. And when they saw it was the gentleman who had been so liberal with them the night before, they began to do him much courtesy, and to greet his late kindness with many thanks. But that was not the matter which he aimed at: therefore he roundly told them, they were deceived in him, he was not the man they took him for.

'"I am a soldier," sayeth he, "and one that for means have ventured my fortunes abroad, and now for money am driven to hazard them at home. I am not to be played upon by Players: therefore be short, deliver me your money." He had them leave off their cringing and compliments and their apish tricks, and dispatch: which they did, for fear of the worst, seeing to beg was bootless. And having made a desperate tender of their stock into Ratsey's hands, he had them play for more.

'"And for you, Sirra," says he to the chiefest of them, "thou hast a good presence upon the stage, methinks thou darkenest thy merit by playing in the country. Get thee to London, for if one man were dead they will have great need of such a man as thou art. There would be none, in my opinion, fitter than thyself to play his part. My conceit is such of thee, that I durst venture all the money in my purse on thy head, to play Hamlet with him for a wager."

'"Sir, I thank you," quoth the player, "for this good counsel. I have heard indeed of some that have gone to London very meanly, and have come in time to be exceedingly wealthy."

'"And in this presage and prophetical humour of mine," says Ratsey, "kneel down. Rise up, Sir Simon two shares and a half: Thou art now one of my knights, and the first knight that was ever a player in England."'

Such a Pother

On this day in 1599, Queen Elizabeth sent the Earl of Essex on the Irish Campaign. Shakespeare imagined the reception he would receive on his return. How wrong he would be:

How London doth pour out her citizens
The mayor and all his brethren in best sort,
Like to the senators of the antique Rome,
With the plebeians swarming at their heels
Go forth and fetch their conquering Ceasar in
As by a lower but loving likelihood,
Were now the general of our gracious empress,-
As in good time he may, - from Ireland coming,
Bringing rebellion broached on his sword,
How many would the peaceful city quit
To welcome him!'

Henry V (Act 5 Chorus)

And here is another crowd, described by the cynical tribune Junius Brutus, clamouring to see the heroic return of Coriolanus to Rome:

All tongues speak of him, and the bleared sights
Are spectacled to see him: your prattling nurse
Into a rapture lets her baby cry

While she chats him: the kitchen malkin pins
Her richest lockram 'bout her reechy neck,
Clambering the walls to eye him: stalls, bulks, windows,
Are smothered up, leads fill'd, and ridges hors'd
With variable complexions, all agreeing
In earnestness to see him: seld-shown flamens
Do press among the familiar throng, and puff
To win a vulgar station: our veil'd dames
Commit the war of white and damask in
Their nicely-gawded cheeks to the wanton spoil
Of Phoebus' burning kisses: such a pother
As if that whatsoever god that leads him
Were slily crept into his human powers,
And gave him graceful posture.

Coriolanus (Act 2 Scene 1)

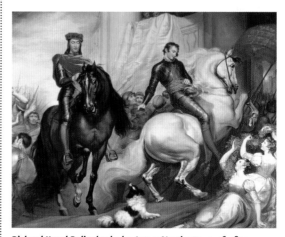

Richard II and Bolingbroke by James Northcote, 1746-1831

In Richard II, Bolingbroke's triumphal entry into London is described in Act 5, Scene 2. When he makes his way to his coronation, he makes a point of riding the deposed King Richard's own horse, the roan Barbary.

Also on this day, in 1625, King James died at Theobald's Palace.

Passion Week: The Eternal Struggle of the Seasons

This day would have fallen in Passion Week in the year Shakespeare was born.

Passion Week began with Palm Sunday. The Sunday before was called Care Sunday, on which, says Barnabe Googe (in his translation of *The Popish Kingdom*), folk made straw dummies of Death, or of Summer and Winter, and celebrated the eternal struggle of the seasons:

The boys with ropes of straw doth frame an ugly
　　monster here
And call him Death, who from the town with proud and
　　solemn cheer,
To hills and valleys they convey, and villages thereby,
From whence they straggling do return, well
　　beaten commonly.
Thus children also bear, with spears, their cracknels
　　round about,
And two they have, whereof the one is called Summer stout,
Apparelled all in green and dressed in youthful fine array;
The other Winter clad in moss, with hair all hoare and grey:
These two together fight, of which the palm doth Summer get,
From whence to meat they go, and all with wine their
　　whistles wet.

Stow in his *Survey of London* describes the following intriguing ritual which also took place this week: **'In the week before Easter had ye great shows made for the fetching in of a twisted tree or Wyth, as they termed it, out of the woods into the King's house, and the like into every man's house of honour or worship.'**

The Wyth, or withy tree, was a willow tree brought in to represent the palm with which Christ was welcomed into Jerusalem.

In 1548, Stow tells us: **'This year the ceremony of bringing palms into the church was left off, and not used as before.'** Just as candles were no longer blessed on Candlemas, and ashes no longer used to anoint the congregation on Ash Wednesday, palms were abandoned on Palm Sunday.

St Paul's Cathedral once had a great censer, like the one still used today at the Cathedral of Santiago de Compostela in Northern Spain, which would be swung through the nave, filling the air with incense in tremendous sweeps on special Holy Days. It too, inevitably, did not survive the Reformation of the English Church.

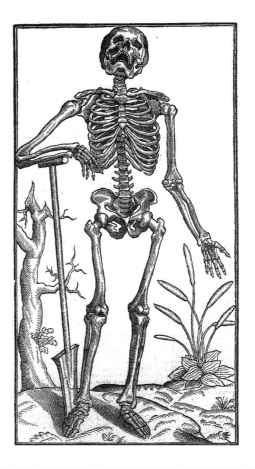

Holy Week Continued with Maundy Thursday and Good Friday

St George and the Dragon

In the sixteenth century, on Holy Thursday, Stratford held its annual pageant of St George and the Dragon. There are wardens' accounts for payments for dressing the dragon, and for the supply of gunpowder and 24 bells. The sight of gallant St George charging a jangling dragon, which emitted fireworks and smoke as they processed through the town streets, must have been a very exciting spectacle. It was banned in 1547, although revived under Queen Mary, just as the painting of St George spearing the dragon in the Guild Chapel was whitewashed out.

Shakespeare's Ring

Man with a ring by Werner van den Valckert, 1617

March 1818
My Dear Keats,
I shall go mad ! In a field at Stratford-upon-Avon, that belonged to Shakespeare, they have found a gold ring and seal, with the initials W.S. and a true lover's knot between. If this is not Shakespeare, who is it ? – A true lover's knot! I saw an impression of it today, and am to have one as soon as possible: as sure as you breathe, and that he was the first of beings, the seal belonged to him.
O Lord !
B.R.Haydon

And Keats writes back:
Teignmouth, Sunday Morning.
My Dear Haydon,
In sooth, I hope you are not too sanguine about that seal, in sooth I hope it is not a Brummagem, in double sooth I hope it is his, and in triple sooth I hope I shall have an impression.

Sir Henry Wotton

Sir Henry Wotton by an unknown artist

Today was the birthday of Sir Henry Wotton. He was born in Boughton Malherbe (or Bocton) in Kent in 1568. The famous Ambassador to Venice is still quoted for his 'merry definition of an ambassador', which got him into trouble with James I: 'An Ambassador is an honest man sent to lie abroad for the good of his country.'

He was also a poet and here is his poem,
The Character of a Happy Life:
How happy is he born and taught
That serveth not another's will;
Whose armour is his honest thought,
And simple truth his utmost skill!

Whose passions not his masters are;
Whose soul is still prepared for death,
Untied unto the world by care
Of public fame or private breath;
Who envies none that chance doth raise,

Nor vice; who never understood
How deepest wounds are given by praise;
Nor rules of state, but rules of good;

Who hath his life from rumours freed;
Whose conscience is his strong retreat;
Whose state can neither flatterers feed,
Nor ruin make oppressors great;

Who God doth late and early pray
More of His grace than gifts to lend;
And entertains the harmless day
With a religious book or friend;

This man is freed from servile bands
Of hope to rise or fear to fall:
Lord of himself, though not of lands,
And having nothing, yet hath all.

A Russian Eastertide described by Antony Jenkinson: 'They have an order at Easter which they always observe, and it is this: every year against Easter, to dye or colour red with brazell a great number of eggs, of which every man and woman giveth one unto the priest of their parish upon Easter Day in the morning. And moreover the common people used to carry in their hands one of their red eggs, not only upon Easter Day but also three or four days after, and gentlemen and gentlewomen have eggs gilded which they carry in like manner. They use it as they say for a great love, and in token of the resurrection, whereof they rejoice. For when two friends meet during the Easter holy days they come and take one another by the hand: the one of them sayeth, the Lord or Christ is risen, the other answereth, it is so of a truth, and then they kiss and exchange their eggs both men and women, continuing in kissing four days together.'

John Donne's Dreadful Vision

As virtuous men pass mildly away,
And whisper to their souls to go,
Whilst some of their sad friends do say,
'The breath goes now,' and some say, 'No.'
A Valediction Forbidding Mourning, John Donne

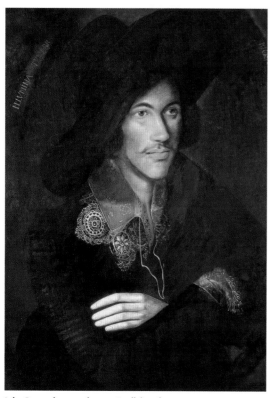

John Donne by an unknown English artist

Izaak Walton, in his *Life of John Donne*, says that Donne gave these verses to his wife around 1610, when he had to leave with Sir Robert Drewry and Lord Hay on a visit to the French King, Henri IV. She was pregnant at the time, and not well enough to accompany her husband to Paris.

'Two days after their arrival there, Mr Donne was left alone in that room, in which Sir Robert, and he, and some other friends, had dined together. To this place Sir Robert returned within half an hour; and as he left so he found, Mr Donne alone; but in such an ecstasy, and so altered as to his looks, as amazed Sir Robert to behold him; insomuch that he earnestly desired Mr Donne to declare what had befallen him in the short time of his absence. To which Mr Donne was not able to make a present answer: but after a long and perplexed pause, did at last say, "I have seen a dreadful vision since I saw you: I have seen my dear wife pass twice by me through this room, with her hair hanging about her shoulders, and a dead child in her arms: this I have seen since I saw you." To which Sir Robert replied, "Sure, Sir, you have slept since I saw you; and this is the result of some melancholy dream, which I desire you to forget, for you are now awake." To which Mr Donne's reply was: "I cannot be surer that I now live, that I have not slept since I saw you: and am as sure, that at her second appearing, she stopped, and looked me in the face, and vanished."

'Rest and sleep had not altered Mr Donne's opinion the next day: for he then affirmed this vision with a more deliberate, and so confirmed a confidence, that he inclined Sir Robert to a faint belief that the vision was true, for he immediately sent a servant to Drewry-house with a charge to hasten back, and bring him word, whether Mrs Donne were alive; and if alive, in what condition she was as to her health. The twelfth day the messenger returned with this account – That he found and left Mrs Donne very sad, and sick in her bed; and that after a long and dangerous labour, she had been delivered of a dead child. And, upon examination, the abortion proved to be the same day, and about the very hour, that Mr Donne affirmed he saw her pass by him in his chamber.'

John Donne died on this day in 1631.

The uncertain glory of an April day.

The Two Gentlemen of Verona (Act 1 Scene 3)

Well-apparel'd April on the heel
Of limping winter treads.

Romeo and Juliet (Act 1 Scene 2)

'It is now April, and the Nightingale begins to tune her throat against May: the sunny showers perfume the air, and the bees begin to go abroad for honey: the Dew, as in pearls, hangs upon the tops of the grass, while the turtles sit billing upon the little green boughs: the Trout begins to play in the brooks, and the salmon leaves the sea, to play in the fresh waters: the garden banks are full of gay flowers, and the thorn and the plum send forth their fair blossoms: the March Colt begins to play, and the cosset lamb is learned to butt. The Poets now make their studies in the woods, and the youth of the country make ready for the Morris-dance; the little fishes lie nibbling at the bait, and the porpoise plays in the pride of the tide: the Shepherd's pipe entertains the Princess of Arcadia, and the healthful soldier hath a pleasant march. The Lark and the Lamb look up at the Sun, and the labourer is abroad by the dawning of the day: Sheep's eyes in lamb's heads, tell kind hearts of strange tales, while faith

and troth make the true lover's knot: the aged hairs find a fresh life and the youthful cheeks are as red as a cherry: It were a world to set down the worth of this month: but in sum, I thus conclude, I hold it the Heavens' blessing and the earth's comfort. Farewell.'

Fantasticks, Nicholas Breton

'**In April follow the double white violet, the wallflower, the stock-gillyflower, the cowslip, flower-deluces, and lilies of all natures; rosemary flowers, the tulippa, the double peony, the pale daffodil, the French honeysuckle; the cherry tree in blossom, the damson and plum-trees in blossom, the white-thorn in leaf, the lilac-tree.**'

Of Gardens, Francis Bacon

'April as a young man in green with a garland of myrtle and hawthorn buds; in one hand primroses and violets, in the other the sign of Taurus.'

Emblems, Henry Peacham

All Fools' Day

The heaving of my lungs provokes me to ridiculous smiling.

Love's Labour's Lost (Act 3 Scene 1)

Dick Tarleton Makes the Queen Laugh

Here is a description of how the clown, Dick Tarleton, and his little dog could cheer up Queen Elizabeth, or 'un-dumpish' her, as he vividly describes it:

'When the Queen was serious (I dare not say sullen) and out of good humour, he could un-dumpish her at his pleasure. Her highest favourites would in some cases go to

Tarleton before they would go to the Queen as he was their usher to prepare their advantageous access unto her. He told the Queen more of her faults than most of her chaplains and cured her melancholy better than all of her physicians.

'How Tarleton played the God Luz with a flitch of bacon at his back, and how the Queen bade them take away the knave for making her to laugh so excessively, as he fought against her little dog, Perrico de Faldas, with his sword and long staff, and bade the Queen take off her mastie; and what my Lord Sussex and Tarleton said to one another. The three things that make a woman lovely.'

Fuller's Worthies

Henry Peacham said Dick Tarleton only had to thrust his head out of the curtain to:
Set all the multitude in such a laughter
They could not hold for scarce an hour after.
from 'To Sir Ninian Ouzel' in Thalia's Banquet

In *The Two Gentlemen of Verona* Shakespeare may have written the clown Launce with his dog Crab in memory of Tarleton, and is perhaps also remembering him in the character of Yorick, the King's jester, whose skull Hamlet contemplates:
Alas, poor Yorick! I knew him, Horatio: a fellow of infinite jest, of most excellent fancy: he hath borne me on his back a thousand times; and now, how abhorred in my imagination it is! my gorge rises at it. Here hung those lips that I have kissed I know not how oft. Where be your gibes now? Your gambols? your songs? your flashes of merriment, that were wont to set the table on a roar? Not one now, to mock your own grinning? quite chap-fallen? Now get you to my lady's chamber, and tell her, let her paint an inch thick, to this favour she must come; make her laugh at that.

Hamlet (Act 5 Scene 1)

Ironically, King James I's fool Archie was buried on this very day in 1672.

Easter

Herrings, herrings white and red
Ten a penny, Lent's dead
Rise Dame and give a Negg
Or else a piece of bacon
One for Peter, two for Paul
Three for Jack-a-Lents all
Away, Lent, away.

Quoted by John Aubrey in *Brief Lives*

Today would have been Easter Day in the year Shakespeare was born, 1564. (Easter can range from roughly March 22nd to April 25th.)

At midnight straight, not tarrying till the daylight doth
  appear,
Some gets in flesh, and glutton-like they feed upon
  their cheer.
They roast their flesh, and custards great, and eggs and
  radish store,
And trifles, clotted cream, and cheese and whatsoever more.
And to their wonted life they fall, and bid the rest adieu.
Go now and laugh the Jews to scorn, and all the Turks
  that be,
For Faith, religion, laws and life, and their idolatry.

The Popish Kingdom, translated by Barnabe Googe

Easter Fashions

Didst thou not fall out with a tailor for wearing his new doublet before Easter?

Romeo and Juliet (Act 3 Scene 1)

Mercutio bates Benvolio about his quick temper. To wear a new doublet before Easter (during the penitential period of Lent) might be regarded as inappropriate. New fashions apparently came out at Easter, and it was considered very unlucky not to wear at least one item of new clothing to church on Easter Day; a custom that evolved into the fashion for Easter bonnets.

Easter Customs: Lifting

In Warwickshire and some other counties, the odd custom of 'lifting' was practised. On Easter Monday the men lift the women, and on Easter Tuesday the women lift or heave the men. The process was performed by two 'lusty' men or women, joining their hands across each other's wrists: then, making the person to be heaved sit down on their arms, they lifted them several yards across the street.

The custom may have represented some distant idea of the raising up of Christ at the Resurrection. (See Hocktide festivities on April 10th.)

Easter Day

'It is now Easter, and Jack of Lent is turned out of doors. The Holy Feast is kept for the Faithful, and a known Jew has no place among Christians. The Earth now begins to paint her upper garments and the spirit of youth is inclined to mirth... The minstrel calls the maid from her dinner, and the lover's eyes do troll the tennis balls. There is mirth and joy when there is health and liberty ... I conclude it is a day of much delightfulness: the sun's dancing day and the Earth's holiday. Farewell.'

Fantasticks, Nicholas Breton

Washington Irving and Mrs Ormsby

On this day in 1783, Washington Irving was born. The American author, famous for such stories as *The Legend of Sleepy Hollow*, here describes his pilgrimage to Stratford-upon-Avon, where he meets the eccentric Mrs Ormsby at the Birthplace:

'I had come to Stratford on a poetical pilgrimage. My first visit was to the house where Shakespeare was born, and where, according to tradition, he was brought up to his father's craft of wool-combing. It is a small mean-looking edifice of wood and plaster, a true nestling-place of genius, which seems to delight in hatching its offspring in by-corners. The walls of its squalid chambers are covered with names and inscriptions in every language by pilgrims of all nations, ranks, and conditions, from the prince to the peasant, and present a simple but striking instance of the spontaneous and universal homage of mankind to the great poet of Nature.

'The house is shown by a garrulous old lady in a frosty red face, lighted up by a cold blue, anxious eye, and garnished with artificial locks of flaxen hair curling from under an exceedingly dirty cap. She was peculiarly assiduous in exhibiting the relics with which this, like all other celebrated shrines, abounds. There was the shattered stock of the very matchlock with which Shakespeare shot the deer on his poaching exploits. There, too, was his tobacco-box, which proves that he was a rival smoker of Sir Walter Raleigh; the sword also with which he played Hamlet; and the identical lantern with which Friar Laurence discovered Romeo and Juliet at the tomb. There was an ample supply also of Shakespeare's mulberry tree, which seems to have as extraordinary powers of self-multiplication as the wood of the true cross, of which there is enough extant to build a ship of the line.

'The most favourite object of curiosity, however, is Shakespeare's chair. It stands in a chimney-nook of a small gloomy chamber just behind what was his father's shop. In this chair it is the custom of every one that visits the house to sit: whether this be done with the hope of imbibing any of the inspiration of the bard I am at a loss to say; I merely mention the fact, and mine hostess privately assured me that, though built of solid oak, such was the fervent zeal of devotees the chair had to be new bottomed at least once in three years.

'There is nothing like resolute good-humoured credulity in these matters, and on this occasion I went even so far as willingly to believe the claims of mine hostess to a lineal descent from the poet, when, unluckily for my faith, she put into my hands a play of her own composition, which set all belief in her own consanguinity at defiance.'

Sketches, Washington Irving

Hero or Pirate?

I'll put a girdle round about the earth
In forty minutes.

  A Midsummer Night's Dream (Act 2 Scene 1)

Sir Francis Drake by Nicholas Hilliard, 1581

On this day in 1581 Francis Drake was knighted at Deptford on board his ship the *Golden Hinde*, after sailing around the world. Puck might boast that he could circumnavigate the earth in forty minutes. It took Drake nearly three years.

'The Queen dined at Deptford, and there after dinner entered the ship wherein Captain Drake had sailed about the world and being there, a bridge (that her majesty came over) broke, being on the same more than 200 persons, and no hurt done by the same, and

then she did make Captain Francis Drake knight in his ship.'

  Chronicles, John Stow

A somewhat different view of Drake is expressed in the following newsletters from the correspondents of the House of Fugger, the famous bankers of Augsburg:

Cologne, October 1580
Our Antwerp correspondent assures us of the return of the English Captain Drake, who is a pirate and has been away for three years. In India, which belongs to the King of Spain, he has stolen two millions in cash, has passed through the Straits of Magellan and come back home. If this is true many pirates and adventurers will follow him.

Antwerp, November 1580
On the report that four English ships have been confiscated in Spain, the Queen of England has had four Spanish ships confiscated in Plymouth. It is believed that Spain is holding up the ships because of Captain Drake, who arrived in London a few weeks ago with a quantity of bullion. A year ago he attacked the ships on their way from New Spain, and the King of Spain demands that he be sentenced.

Antwerp, December 1580
Again news from London is confirmed that Drake, the English pirate, has presented the Queen with several horses laden with silver and gold from the booty which he got two years ago off the Peru ships. This Drake is said to be proposing to make a raid on the Peru ships and to try his luck afresh.

An Elizabethan Sweeney Todd
....

Murder most foul as in the best it is.
Hamlet (Act 1 Scene 5)

In the short Elizabethan novel Thomas of Reading by Thomas Deloney (published in 1600), the main plot is a murder, and the victim is the eponymous hero. Thomas falls prey to an unscrupulous pair who run an inn called the Crane, at Colnbrook (or Colebrooke), but which has been identified as The Ostrich.

'Thomas of Reading, having many occasions to come to London, it chanced on a time, that his Host and Hostess of Colebrooke, who through covetousness had murdered many of the guests, and having everytime he came thither great store of his money to lay up, appointed him to be the next fat pig that should be killed: For it is to be understood, that when they plotted the murder of any man, this was always their term, the man to his wife, and the woman to her husband: "Wife, there is now a fat pig to be had, if you want one."

'Whereupon she would answer thus, "I pray you put him in the hogsty till tomorrow."

'This was when any man came thither alone without others in his company, and they saw he had great store of money.

'This man should then be laid in a chamber right over the kitchen, which was a fair chamber, and better set out than any other in the house: the best bedstead therein, though it were little and low, yet was it most cunningly carved, and fair to the eye, the feet whereof were fast nailed to the chamber floor, in such sort, that it could not in any wise fall. The bed [mattress] that lay therein was fast sewed to the sides of the bedstead: Moreover, that part of the chamber whereon the bed and bedstead stood, was made in such sort, that by pulling out two iron pins below in the kitchen, it was to be let down and taken up by a drawbridge, or in manner of a trap door: moreover in the kitchen, directly under the place where this should fall, was a mighty great cauldron, wherein they used to seethe their liquor, when they went to brewing. Now, the men appointed for slaughter, were laid into this bed, and in the dead time of the night, when they were sound asleep, by plucking out the aforesaid iron pins, down would the man fall out of his bed, into the boiling cauldron, and all the clothes that were upon him: where being suddenly scalded and drowned, he was never able to cry or speak a word.'

Earthquakes

Nurse: *'Tis since the earthquake now eleven years.*
Romeo and Juliet (Act I Scene 3)

Diseased nature oftentimes breaks forth
In strange eruptions; oft the teeming earth
Is with a kind of colic pinch'd and vex'd
By the imprisoning of unruly wind
Within her womb; which, for enlargement striving,
Shakes the old beldam earth and topples down
Steeples and moss-grown towers.
Henry IV Part One (Act 3 Scene 1)

On this day in 1580, an earthquake damaged
St Paul's.

Though severe earthquakes in the South of England
are rare, the Dover Straits earthquake of April 6th,
1580 appears to have been the largest in the recorded
history of England. The earthquake, which occurred
about 6 o'clock in the evening, is well described in
contemporary documents, such as this:
'The sixth of April being Wednesday in Easter week
about six oclock in the evening, a sudden
earthquake happened at London and
generally throughout England, by
violence whereof, the great clock
bell at Westminster stroke against
the hammer, as divers clocks and
bells against their hammers and
clappers both in the city and
country did the like. In
London a piece of the Temple
church fell down. In the late
dissolved church of the
Greyfriars now called
Christ's Church, in the
sermon time, a stone falling
from the top killed a young
man out of hand, and one

other stone so bruised a maiden his fellow servant,
both to one master, that she lived but four days.
Divers others were sore bruised running out of the
church. Some stones fell from the Church of St Paul's
in London, and some from the Church of St Peter at
Westminster. Divers chimneys with shaking lost their
tops, and the ships in the river of Thames and on the
seas, were seen to totter. This earthquake continued
about London not passing one minute of an hour, but
in East Kent, and on the sea coast thereabout, it was
felt three times to wit at 6,9,11 of the clock.'
Chronicles, John Stow

Also on this day: the John Stow Commemoration.
Every year, at St Andrew Undershaft in London, the
great chronicler of Shakespeare's London is
remembered. A new quill is placed in the hand of
Stow's bust in the church by the Lord Mayor.

Stow's Survey of London

It is a miracle that the Great Fire of London spared St Andrew Undershaft, and in it the monument to John Stow, the man who more than any other tells us what London was like before the terrible conflagration which destroyed so many of the buildings of Shakespeare's time.

Here, for example, in his *Survey of London*, Stow describes Smithfield, now the meat market:

'**Without one of the gates is a plain field, both in name and deed (*Smooth Field*, Smithfield), where every Friday, unless it be a solemn bidden holy day, is a notable show of horses to be sold; earls, barons, knights, and citizens repair thither to see or to buy; there you may of pleasure see amblers pacing it delicately; there you may see trotters fit for men of arms, stitting more hardly; there you may have notable young horses not yet broke; there you may have strong steeds, well limbed geldings, whom the buyers do especially regard for pace and swiftness; the boys which ride these horses do sometime run races for wagers, with a desire of hope or victory. In another part of that field are to be sold all implements of husbandry, as also fat swine, milch kine, sheep and oxen; there also stand mares and horses fit for ploughs and teams, with their young colts by them. At this city merchant strangers of all nations have their quays and wharfs; the Arabians sent gold; the Sabians spice and frankincense; the Scythian armour, Babylon oil, Indian purple garments, Egypt precious stones, Norway and Russia amber and sables and the Frenchman wine.'**

And here he is on the old stews of Southwark:

'**Next to the bank was sometime the Bordello or Stews, a place so called of certain stew-houses privileged there, for the repair of incontinent men, or the like women. These allowed stew-houses had signs on their fronts, towards the Thames, not hanged out but painted on the walls, as the Boar's Head, the Cross Keys, the Gun, the Castle, the Crane, the Cardinal's Hat, the Bell, the Swan etc. I have heard of ancient men, of good credit, report that these single women were forbidden the rites of the church so long as they continued that sinful life, and were excluded from Christian burial, if they were not reconciled before their death. And therefore there was a plot of ground called the Single Woman's Churchyard, appointed for them far from the parish church.'**

Famous Visitors to the Tomb of the 'Mighty Wizard'

On this day in 1828, Sir Walter Scott paid his respects at Shakespeare's grave:

'We visited the tomb of the mighty wizard. It is in the bad taste of James the First's reign; but what a magic does the locality possess! There are stately monuments of forgotten families; but when you have seen Shakespeare's what care we for the rest. All around is Shakespeare's exclusive property.'

Washington Irving also wrote about his pilgrimage to the tomb:

'From the birthplace of Shakespeare a few paces brought me to his grave. He lies buried in the chancel of the parish church, a large and venerable pile, mouldering with age, but richly ornamented. It stands on the banks of the Avon on an embowered point, and separated by adjoining gardens from the suburbs of the town. Its situation is quiet and retired; the river runs murmuring at the foot of the churchyard, and the elms which grow upon its banks droop their branches into its clear bosom. An avenue of limes, the boughs of which are curiously interlaced, so as to form in summer an arched way of foliage, leads up from the gate of the yard to the church-porch.

'The tomb of Shakespeare is in the chancel. The place is solemn and sepulchral. A flat stone marks the spot where the bard is buried. There are four lines inscribed on it, said to have been written by himself, and which have in them something extremely awful. If they are indeed his own, they show that solicitude about the quiet of the grave which seems natural to fine sensibilities and thoughtful minds.

'A few years since, as some labourers were digging to make an adjoining vault, the earth caved in, so as to leave a vacant space almost like an arch, through which one might have reached into his grave. No one, however, presumed to meddle with his remains so awfully guarded by a malediction; and lest any of the

Walter Scott at Shakespeare's Tomb, attributed to David Roberts

idle or the curious or any collector of relics should be tempted to commit depredations, the old sexton kept watch over the place for two days, until the vault was finished and the aperture closed again. He told me that he had made bold to look in at the hole, but could see neither coffin nor bones – nothing but dust. It was something, I thought, to have seen the dust of Shakespeare.

'As I trod the sounding pavement there was something intense and thrilling in the idea that in very truth the remains of Shakespeare were mouldering beneath my feet. It was a long time before I could prevail upon myself to leave the place; and as I passed through the churchyard I plucked a branch from one of the yew-trees.'

Francis Bacon

On this day in 1626, Francis Bacon died after trying to freeze a chicken.

John Aubrey's account:
'Mr Hobbes told me that the cause of his Lordship's death was trying an experiment; viz. as he was taking his air in a coach with Dr Witherborne (a Scotchman, Physician to the King) towards Highgate, snow lay on the ground, and it came into my Lordship's thoughts, why flesh might not be preserved in snow, as in salt. They were resolved they would try the experiment presently. They alighted out of the coach and went into a poor woman's house at the bottom of Highgate Hill, and bought a hen, and made the woman exenterate it, and then stuffed the body with snow and my Lord did help to do it himself. The snow so chilled him that he immediately fell so extremely ill, that he could not return to his lodging but went to the Earl of Arundel's House at Highgate, where they put him into a good bed warmed with a pan, but it was a damp bed that had not been lain in in about a year before, which gave him such a cold that in 2 or 3 days as I remember Mr Hobbes told me, he died of suffocation.
  'This October (1681) it rang all over St Albans that Sir Harbottle Grimston, Master of the Rolls, had removed the coffin of this most renowned Lord Chancellor to make room for his own to lie in in the vault there at St Michael's church.'

Aubrey is ambivalent about Bacon's character:
'He was a (in Greek) pederast. His Ganymedes and Favourites took bribes; but his Lordship always gave judgement according as was just and good.'

Of Bacon's extravagance he writes:
'When his Lordship was at his Country-house at Gorhambury, St Albans seemed as if the Court were there, so nobly did he live. His servants had liveries with his crest (a boar); his watermen were more employed by Gentlemen than any other, even the King's...None of his servants durst appear before him without Spanish leather boots; for he would smell the neat's leather, which offended him.'

And then:
'He had a delicate, lively, hazel eye; Dr Harvey told me it was like the eye of a viper.'

❖

Also on this day in 1413, Henry V was crowned.

Hocktide

The Hock Tuesday Play was performed before Queen Elizabeth at Kenilworth Castle in 1575:

'And that there might be nothing wanting that these parts could afford, hither came the Coventry men, and acted the ancient play, long since used in that city, called Hocks' Tuesday, setting forth the destruction of the Danes in King Ethelred's time, with which the Queen was so pleas'd, that she gave them a brace of bucks, and five marks in money, to bear the charges of a feast.'

Letter from Robert Laneham

On April 23rd, 1016 (exactly six hundred years before William Shakespeare died), the Saxon king we know as Ethelred the Unready breathed his last. Ethelred was not a lucky man. According to William of Malmesbury, he had defecated in the baptismal font at his christening, leading St Dunstan to prophesy that the English monarchy would be overthrown during his reign.

For four years at the end of the first millennium the Vikings had attacked Ethelred's realm. He was advised that these raids were supported by the Danish settlers living in England, and one day in 1002 he launched a pogrom against them.

The Old Coventry play of Hock Tuesday, which apparently so delighted the queen, told the story of that massacre.

Shakespeare may have had a hand in writing a play about Ethelred's son, *Edmund Ironside*.

In England today, the tradition of celebrating Hocktide has pretty much died out, and survives only in Hungerford in Berkshire.

Traditionally Hocktide festivities consisted of a practice called Binding: the men of the parish would tie up the women, demanding a kiss for their release. The next day the women would tie up the men and demand a similar payment before setting them free.

It seems not unlike the lifting customs described at Easter above. The monies collected would then be donated to the parish funds.

The origins of the name Hocktide are unknown.

Men are April when they woo, December when they wed: maids are May when they are maids but the sky changes when they are wives.

As You Like It (Act 4 Scene 1)

On this day in Shakespeare's time, the Sun arrived in Taurus. In Spenser's parade of the months, April enters riding on the back of a bull, as once Europa did with lusty Jove 'when he would play the noble beast in love':

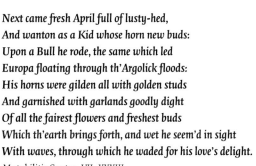

Next came fresh April full of lusty-hed,
And wanton as a Kid whose horn new buds:
Upon a Bull he rode, the same which led
Europa floating through th'Argolick floods:
His horns were gilden all with golden studs
And garnished with garlands goodly dight
Of all the fairest flowers and freshest buds
Which th'earth brings forth, and wet he seem'd in sight
With waves, through which he waded for his love's delight.

Mutabilitie Cantos, VII: XXXIII

Birth of the Anti-Christ, 1592

There dwelt a man in Babylon, lady, lady.
Twelfth Night (Act 2 Scene 3)

'This week a news-letter has been circulated here which is said to have been written by the Grand Master of Malta and divers other Christian princes. This news-letter reports that in a certain province of Babylon there has been born to a woman of evil repute a child, whose father is unknown. This child is reported to be covered with cat's hair and to be a dreadful sight. It began to talk eight days after its birth and to walk after a month. It is said to have intimated that it is the Son of God. At its birth the sun grew dark at midday and on the previous night a mighty flame of fire appeared above its house. Many mountains opened and on one of these there was seen a column covered with Hebrew script reading 'This is the hour of my birth!' On the next day there fell from Heaven a goodly quantity of manna and precious stones; at other places howsoever, snakes and other horrible creatures. When the child was questioned as to the meaning of this it made answer: that the precious stones stand for the supreme delight of those who will keep his commandments, the snakes for the martyrdom and castigation of the

disobedient. Adoration of the infant has already begun because it has performed great miracles, awakening the dead and making the blind to see and the lame to walk. The populace is being encouraged by a bare foot friar, who alleges that this is the true Son of God. For the sake of brevity I must omit further reports which do not sound credible. It is said that the Rabbis have come to the conclusion that this is the Child of Perdition, the Anti-Christ.'
Fugger Newsletter, from Venice, April 1592

And here in another sensational Fugger Newsletter, in August 1592, an apocalyptic apparition appears in the sky over Vienna: 'These days at 10 o'clock at night a most alarming wonder has manifested itself in the skies. The firmament was rent asunder and through this gap one could distinguish chariots and armies, riders with yellow, white, red and black standards, moving as though to do battle against each other. This awesome and unusual vision continued from ten at night till about two of the morning, and was witnessed with alarm and dismay by many honest and trustworthy people. The significance thereof is known but to Almighty God, who may graciously prevent the shedding of innocent blood.'

The New Union Jack

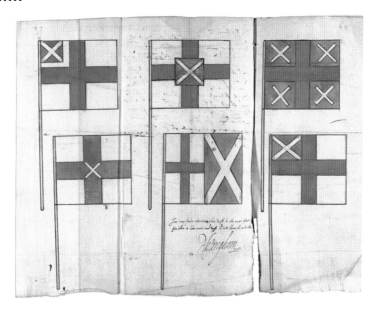

Unwind your bloody flag.
Henry V (Act 1 Scene 2)

On this day in 1606, the Union Jack was created.

A Royal Proclamation for a new Union flag stated:
'From henceforth all our subjects of this Isle and Kingdom of Great Britain and the members thereof, shall bear in their maintoppe the red cross, commonly called St George's cross, and the white cross, commonly called St Andrew's cross, joined together according to a form made by our heralds, and sent by us to our admiral to be published by our said subjects... Wherefore we will and command all our subjects to be conformable and obedient to this our order, and that from henceforth they do not use to bear their flags in any other sort as they will answer the contrary at their peril.

'Given at our palace of Westminster the twelfth day of April, in the fourth year of our reign of Great Britain, France and Ireland etc...'

King James commissioned the Earl of Nottingham to design the first 'Flag of the great Union', and marry the two flags of England and Scotland.

The Earl said of his design:
'In my poor opinion, this will be the most fittest for this is like man and wife without blemish one to other.'

The Union Jack in its present form (since 1801) is described officially thus:
'The Union flag shall be Azure, the Crosses Saltire of St Andrew and St Patrick, Quarterly per saltire, countercharged Argent and Gules, the latter fimbriated of the second, surmounted by the cross of St George of the third, fimbriated as the Saltire.'

A 'Saltire' is a diagonal cross, and 'fimbriation' is a narrow white border, to distinguish between two colours laid together.

Football Banned

You base football player!
King Lear (Act 1 Scene 4)

Mass football matches played in the streets were so popular in London in the reign of Edward II that shopkeepers called on the King to outlaw the game in the city. Thus on this day in 1314 football was banned by law. The following decree contains the first ever reference to football:

'For as much as there is great noise in the city caused by hustling over large footballs in the fields of the public, from which many evils might arise (which God forbid): we command and forbid on behalf of the King, on pain of imprisonment, such game to be used in the city in the future.'

The ban didn't work, and several other kings tried to ban the game too, including Edward III, Richard II, and Henry IV. Oliver Cromwell did manage briefly to get football banned, but it started up again after the Restoration, when its popularity only increased.

Mass football received its most hysterical criticism from the rabidly puritanical Phillip Stubbes:

'For as concerning football playing, I protest unto you it may be called a friendly kind of fight, than a play or recreation; a bloody and murdering practice, than a fellowly sport or pastime. For doth not everyone lie in wait for his adversary, seeking to overthrow him and pitch him on his nose, though it be upon hard stones? Sometimes their necks are broken, sometimes their legs, sometimes their arms, sometimes their noses gush out with blood, sometimes their eyes start out.

'But whoever scapeth away the best, goeth not scot-free, but is either fore wounded, crazed, and bruised so as he dieth of it, or else scapeth very hardly, and no marvel for they have the sleights to meet one betwixt two, to dash him against the heart with their elbows, to hit him under the ribs with their griped fists, and with their knees to catch him upon the hip, and to pitch him upon the neck with a hundred such murdering devices: and hereof groweth envy, malice, rancour, choler, hatred, displeasure, enmity and whatnot else, and sometimes fighting, brawling, contention, quarrel-picking, murder, homicide, and great effusion of blood, as experience daily teacheth. Is this murdering play now an excercise for the sabbath day?'

Also on this day, albeit several centuries later, Virginia Woolf writes in her diary in 1930, about reading Shakespeare:

'I read Shakespeare directly I have finished writing, when my mind is agape and red and hot. Then it is astonishing. I never yet knew how amazing his stretch and speed, and word coining power is, until I felt it utterly outpace and outrace my own, seeming to start equal, and then I see him draw ahead and do things I could not in my wildest tumult and utmost press of mind imagine... Why then should anyone else attempt to write? This is not writing at all. Indeed I should say that Shakespeare surpasses literature altogether, if I knew what I meant.'

Torture in the Tower

On this day in 1597, the Lancashire-born Jesuit priest, John Gerard, was horribly tortured in the Tower of London.

'We went to the torture room in a kind of procession, the attendants walking ahead with lighted candles. The chamber was underground and dark, particularly near the entrance. It was a vast place and every device and instrument of human torture was there. They pointed out some of them to me and said I would try them all. Then they asked me again whether I would confess.

'"I cannot," I said. I fell on my knees for a moment's prayer. Then they took me to a big upright pillar, one of the wooden posts which held the roof of this huge underground chamber. Driven into the top of it were iron staples for supporting heavy weights. Then they put my wrists into iron gauntlets and ordered me to climb two or three wicker steps.

'My arms were then lifted up and an iron bar was passed through the rings of one gauntlet, then through the staple and rings to the second gauntlet. This done, they fastened the bar with a pin to prevent it from slipping, and then, removing the wicker steps one by one from under my feet, they left me hanging by my hands and arms fastened above my head. The tips of my toes, however, still touched the ground, and they had to dig the earth away from under them.

They had hung me up from the highest staple in the pillar and could not raise me any higher, without driving in another staple. Hanging like this I began to pray. The gentlemen standing around me asked me whether I was willing to confess now.

'"I cannot and I will not," I answered. But I could hardly utter the words, such a gripping pain came over me. It was worst in my chest and belly, my hands and arms. All the blood in my body seemed to rush up into my arms and hands and I thought that blood was oozing from the ends of my fingers and the pores of my skin. But it was only a sensation caused by my flesh swelling above the irons holding them.

'The pain was so intense that I thought I could not possibly endure it, and added to it, I had an interior temptation. Yet I did not feel any inclination or wish to give them the information they wanted. The Lord saw my weakness with the eyes of His mercy, and did not permit me to be tempted beyond my strength. With the temptation He sent me relief. Seeing my agony and the struggle going on in my mind, He gave me this most merciful thought: the utmost and worst they can do is to kill you, and you have often wanted to give your life for your Lord God. The Lord God sees all you are enduring – He can do all things. You are in God's keeping.'

The Autobiography of John Gerard

Mermaids

• • • • • • • • • • • •

I'll stop mine ears against the mermaid's song.
Comedy of Errors (Act 3 Scene 2)

Here's another ballad of a fish, that appeared upon the coast on Wednesday the four-score of April, forty thousand fathom above water, and sung this ballad against the hard hearts of maids; it was thought she was a woman and was turned into a cold fish for she would not exchange flesh with one that loved her: the ballad is very pitiful and as true.
The Winter's Tale
(Act 4 Scene 4)

Richard Whitbourne was haunted for twelve years by the sight of a strange creature which appeared one morning in the freezing waters off Newfoundland. His

account, written in 1622, is so rational, so lacking in sensational detail, that you begin to wonder what he could have seen:

'Now also I will not omit to relate something of a strange creature that I first saw there in the year 1610, in the morning early as I was standing by the waterside, in the harbour of Saint John's, which I espied very swiftly to come swimming towards me, looking cheerfully, as it had been a woman, by the face, eyes and nose, mouth, chin and ears, neck and forehead: It seemed to be so beautiful, and in those parts so well proportioned, having round about the head, all blue streaks, resembling hair, down to the neck (but certainly it was hair) for I beheld it long, and another of my company also, yet living, that was not then far from me, and seeing the same then coming so swiftly towards me, I stepped back, for it

was come within the length of a long pike. Which when this strange creature saw that I went from it, it presently thereupon dived a little under water, and did swim to the place where before I landed; whereby I beheld the shoulders and back down to the middle, to be as square, white and smooth as the back of a man, and from the middle to the hinder part, pointing in proportion like a broad hooked Arrow; how it was proportioned in the forepart from the neck to the shoulders, I know not; but the same came shortly after unto a boat, wherein one William Hawkridge, (then my servant was, that had been since a Captain in a Ship to the East Indies, and is lately there employed again by Sir Thomas Smith, in the like voyage); and the same Creature did put both his hands upon the side of the boat, and did strive to come in to him and the others then in the said boat: whereat they were afraid; and one of them struck it a full blow on the head; whereat it fell off from them: and afterwards it came to two other boats in the harbour; the men in them, for fear fled to land: This (I suppose) was a mermaid.
Discourse and Discovery of Newfoundland, Richard Whitbourne, 1622

⚙

Also on this day in 1569, Shakespeare's sister Joan was baptized. She married a hatter called William Hart, who died just eight days before her brother. Joan was the only one of William's sisters to survive childhood. She outlived her brother by thirty years.

Charles' Wain

First carrier (with a lanthorn in his hand):
*Heigh-ho! an't be not four by the day I'll be
hanged: Charles' Wain is over the new chimney
and yet our horse not packed! What, ostler!*
Henry IV Part One (Act 2 Scene 1)

The month of April is the best time to view
Charles' Wain, at about 9 o'clock in the
evening. Charles' Wain is said to be named
after King Charlemagne. But if you are not
aware of this particular constellation, you
may know it better as the Plough, or
perhaps the Big Dipper.

These seven stars are the brightest in
Ursa Major, the Great Bear, a distinct
grouping mentioned in the Bible, and in
many cultures from time immemorial. The
Bible refers to it as 'the seven stars' (Amos,
5:8), though some translations have 'Big
Dipper' explicitly, and some translations of
that verse refer to the Pleiades, which also
has seven stars visible to the naked eye.
*He is wise in heart and mighty in Strength...
Which commandeth the sun, and it riseth not; and
    sealeth up the stars.
Which maketh Arcturus, Orion, and Pleiades, and
    the chambers of the south.*
Job, 9: 4–9

And later:
*Canst thou bind the sweet influences of Pleiades,
or loose the bands of Orion? Canst thou bring forth
Mazzaroth in his season? Or canst thou guide Arcturus with
his sons? Knowest thou the ordinances of Heaven?*
Job, 38: 31–3

The Pleiades' high visibility in the night sky has
guaranteed it a special place in many cultures, both
ancient and modern. In Greek mythology, they
represented the Seven Sisters. To the Celts, the
Pleiades were associated with mourning and with
funerals, since at that time in history, on the cross-
quarter day between the autumn equinox and the
winter solstice, which was a festival devoted to the
remembrance of the dead, the cluster rose in the
eastern sky as the sun's light faded in the evening.

The Entry of Spring

In *Summer's Last Will and Testament*, written in the late-summer of 1592, Thomas Nashe paraded the seasons in a satirical pageant for Archbishop Whitgift and his friends at his house in Croydon. Here is the entry of Spring:

(Enter Ver with his train, over laid with suits of green moss, representing short grass, singing.)

Spring, the sweet spring, is the year's pleasant king,
Then blooms each thing, then maids dance in a ring;
Cold doth not sting, the pretty birds do sing,
Cuckoo, jug jug, pu we, to witta woo.

The palm and may make country houses gay,
Lambs frisk and play, the shepherds pipe all day
And we hear aye birds tune this merry lay,
Cuckoo, jug jug, pu we, to witta woo.

The fields breathe sweet, the daisies kiss our feet,
Young lovers meet, old wives a-sunning sit;
In every street these tunes our ears do greet,
Cuckoo, jug jug, pu we, to witta woo.
Spring, the sweet spring.

The refrain, 'Cuckoo, jug jug, pu we, to witta woo' represents the calls of the cuckoo, the nightingale, the lapwing (or peewit) and the tawny owl.

In the epilogue of the pageant, we hear that the youths who took part **'have bestowed great labour in sewing leaves and grass and straw, and moss upon cast-suits [cast-off clothes]'** and therefore deserve the audience's warm applause: **'You may do well to warm your hands with clapping, before you go to bed, and send them to the tavern with merry hearts.'**

A History of Four-Footed Beasts

Edward Topsell published his *A History of Four-Footed Beasts* in 1607. He was Perpetual Curate of St Botolph's, Aldersgate. Here are three extracts:

The Medicinal properties of Mouse dung:
'The dung of Mice being steeped or washed in rain water, doth ease and refresh the swelling of women's dugs in their time of delivery. The dung of a Mouse being given in any drink or liquor to one that is troubled with the disease called the Colic and stone to drink, will in very short space of time cure him of the same. There is an excellent remedy arising from Mouse-dung against the sciatica or hip-gout which is this: To take nine grains of a mouse's dung mixed or mingled with half a pint of wine, and given to the party grieved upon a bench or foot stool to drink, so that he drink it standing upon that foot which paineth him even at the Sun-rising; and having drunk it to leap down, and afterward let him leap three times, and let him do this but three days toegther, and he shall have present help and remedy of his disease.

'The urine of a mouse is of such strong force, that if it shall but touch any part of a man's body, it will eat up his very bones.'

For Blindness:
'For the pain and blindness in the eye, by reason of any skins, webs, or nails, this is an approved medicine; take the head of a black cat, which hath not a spot of another colour in it, and burn it to powder in an earthen pot leaded or glazed within, then take this powder and through a quill blow it thrice a day into the eye, and if in the night time any heat do thereby annoy thee, take two leaves of an oak wet in cold water and bind them to the eye, and so shall all pain fly away, and blindness depart although it hath oppressed thee a whole year: and this medicine is approved by many physicians both elder and latter.'

Topsell explodes the myth that beavers bite off their own testicles.
'It hath been an opinion of some, that when a beaver is hunted and is in danger to be taken, he biteth off his own stones, knowing that for them only his life is sought; but this is most false. They likewise affirm, that when it is hunted (having formerly bitten off his stones) that he standeth upright and sheweth the hunters that he hath none of them, and therefore his death cannot profit them, by means whereof they are averted and seek for another.'

A Little Jaunt to Stratford

Stratford-upon-Avon became a tourist destination in the mid-eighteenth century. On this day in 1928, J.B.Priestley publishes *Apes and Angels*. Here is an extract from that book about his visit to the town:

'And it was a lovely morning; spring in blue and gold; not the smallest pocket-handkerchief of cloud in the whole sky. Not only did I agree to visit Stratford-upon-Avon but I also helped to take down the hood and the screens of the car, for apparently the moment had arrived for it to be converted into an open summery affair. Is there anything more terrifying to a person with sense and sensibility than a day's pleasure, what some people call a "little jaunt"?

'The official literary business with its documents of birth, marriage and death, its museum and antique shop airs, its array of beds and pens and desks and chairs, its visitors' books and picture postcards and glib custodians, is simply so much solemn nonsense... I hope Shakespeare knows all about it, that he is keeping an immortal eye on his birthplace. How he must enjoy the fun! I can hear him roaring with laughter. I can see him bringing other immortals (probably Cervantes among them, for if those two are not hand-in-glove then there is no friendship among the shades) to see the local branch of the Midland Bank, which tries to look Elizabethan and romantic, and even has some scenes from the plays drearily depicted round its walls. He will show them how everything in the place is conscientiously thatched and beamed. He will watch us paying our shillings in this place and that to gape at an array of articles that really have nothing to do with him, rooms full of Garrick and Hathaway relics.

'And there was one moment, the other afternoon, when I did really feel I was treading upon his own ground. It was when we were in the gardens of New Place, very brave in the spring sunlight. You could have played the outdoor scene from *Twelfth Night* in

them without disturbing a leaf. There was the very sward for Viola and Sir Andrew. Down that paved path Olivia would come, like a great white peacock. Against that bank of flowers the figure of Maria would be seen flitting like a starling. The little knot garden alone was worth the journey and nearer to Shakespeare than all the documents and chairs and monuments. It was a patterned blaze of tulips, the Elizabethan gentlefolk among flowers. The white ones, full open and very majestic, were the great ladies in their ruffs; and the multi-coloured ones, in all their bravery of crimson and yellow, were the gentlemen in doublet and striped hose. The little crazy-paved paths added a touch of pride and fantasy and cross-gartering, as if Malvolio had once passed that way. And then to crown all, there were tiny rows of sweet-smelling English herbs, thyme and sage and marjoram, and misty odorous borders of lavender. I remember that when we left the garden to see the place where Shakespeare was buried, it didn't seem to matter much. Why should it, when we had just seen the place where he was still alive?'

Priestley eventually moved to Stratford and lived in a house which he had seen from the top of a bus during his chronicled journey around Britain in the 1930s. It was called Kissing Tree House, in Alveston, and he died there in 1984 aged 90.

Simon Forman sees Macbeth

Let us ... on your imaginary forces work.
Chorus to Henry V

On this day the notorious physician and astrologer Simon Forman saw *Macbeth* at the Globe Theatre. His playbook includes some of the first eyewitness accounts of Shakespeare's plays.

'At the Globe, 1610, the 20 of April, Saturday, there was to be observed, first, how Macbeth and Banquo, two noble men of Scotland, riding through a wood, there stood before them three women fairies or nymphs, and saluted Macbeth, saying three times unto him, "Hail, Macbeth, King of Codon; for thou shall be a king, but shall beget no kings," etc. Then said Banquo, "What all to Macbeth, and nothing to me?" "Yes," said the nymphs, "hail to thee, Banquo, thou shall beget kings, yet be no king." And so they departed and came to the country of Scotland to Duncan, King of Scots, and it was in the days of Edward the Confessor. And Duncan had them both kindly welcome, and made Macbeth forthwith Prince of Northumberland, and sent him home to his own castle, and appointed Macbeth to provide for him, for he would sup with him the next day at night, and did so.

'And Macbeth contrived to kill Duncan and through the persuasion of his wife did that night murder the King in his own castle, being his guest; and there were many prodigies seen that night and the day before. And when Macbeth had murdered the King, the blood on his hands could not be washed off by any means, nor from his wife's hands, which handled the bloody daggers in hiding them, which by means they became both much amazed and affronted. The murder being known, Duncan's two sons fled, the one to England, the other to Wales, to save themselves. They being fled, they were supposed guilty of the murder of their father, which was nothing so.

'Then was Macbeth crowned King; and then he, for fear of Banquo, his old companion, that he should beget kings but be no king himself, he contrived the death of Banquo, and caused him to be murdered on his way as he rode. The next night, being at supper with his noble men whom he had to bid to a feast, to the which also Banquo should have come, he began to speak of noble Banquo, and to wish that he were there. And as he did thus, standing up to drink a carouse to him, the ghost of Banquo came and sat down in his chair behind him. And he, turning about to sit down again, saw the ghost of Banquo, which fronted him so, that he fell into a great passion of fear and fury, uttering many words about his murder, by which, when they heard that Banquo was murdered, they suspected Macbeth. Then MackDove fled to England to the King's son, and soon they raised an army and came to Scotland, and at Dunstonanse overthrew Macbeth. In the meantime, while MackDove was in England, Macbeth slew MackDove's wife and children, and after in the battle MackDove slew Macbeth. Observe also how Macbeth's queen did rise in the night in her sleep, and walked and talked and confessed all, and the doctor noted her words.'

On exactly the same day the following year, Forman saw a play called *Richard II*. But it is clearly not Shakespeare's version, and includes events from the Peasants' Revolt.

Cuckoos

The cuckoo sings in April,
The cuckoo sings in May,
The cuckoo sings in part of June
And then she flies away.
Traditional

The cuckoo is regarded as the harbinger of spring, so it is perhaps a little odd that it waits a whole month before making its first appearance, or at any rate before letting itself be heard. It is popularly believed that the cuckoo traditionally makes its first appearance by today.

At the end of *Love's Labour's Lost* in the debate between Spring (Ver) and Winter (Hiems), Spring 'is maintained' by the cuckoo:
When daisies pied and violets blue
And lady-smocks all silver-white
And cuckoo-buds of yellow hue
Do paint the meadows with delight,
The cuckoo then, on every tree
Mocks married men; for thus sings he:
'Cuckoo, cuckoo, cuckoo.'
O word of fear, unpleasing to a married ear.

When shepherds pipe on oaten straws
And merry larks are ploughmen's clocks,
And turtles tread, and rooks and daws,
And maidens bleach their summer smocks,
The cuckoo then, on every tree,
Mocks married men; for thus sings he:
'Cuckoo, cuckoo, cuckoo.'
O word of fear, unpleasing to a married ear.
Love's Labour's Lost, (Act 5 Scene 2)

In some parts of the country when the first cuckoo was heard, the workmen in the fields would leave work and make a holiday of the rest of the day, drinking cuckoo ale. To others, the cuckoo is the 'merriest songster of summer', and it is the summer she represents, not the spring, as here in the oldest sample of English secular music:
Summer is icumen in
Lhude sing Cuccu!
(Summer is a-coming in,
Loudly sing Cuckoo)

'Doctor Millward preaching at Paul's Cross, in the midst of a sermon, a cuckoo came flying over the pulpit (a thing I never saw or heard of before) and very lewdly called and cried out with open mouth.'
John Chamberlain, April 30th, 1605

The Queen of the Fairies Blesses Windsor Castle

Mistress Quickly: About, about;
Search Windsor Castle, elves, within and out:
Strew good luck, ouphes, on every sacred room:
That it may stand till the perpetual doom,
In state as wholesome as in state 'tis fit,
Worthy the owner, and the owner it.
The several chairs of order look you scour
With juice of balm and every precious flower:
Each fair instalment, coat, and several crest,
With loyal blazon, evermore be blest!
And nightly, meadow-fairies, look you sing,
Like to the Garter's compass, in a ring:
The expressure that it bears, green let it be,
More fertile-fresh than all the field to see;
And 'Honi soit qui mal y pense' write
In emerald tufts, flowers purple, blue and white;
Let sapphire, pearl and rich embroidery,
Buckled below fair knighthood's bending knee:
Fairies use flowers for their charactery.
Away; disperse: but till 'tis one o'clock,
Our dance of custom round about the oak
Of Herne the hunter, let us not forget.
The Merry Wives of Windsor (Act 5 Scene 5)

Tomorrow is St George's Day, and on this day in 1597 a great Garter Feast was held at Windsor, for the investiture of the new Garter Knights. One of them that year was Henry Carey, the Lord Chamberlain and Shakespeare's patron. Shakespeare was probably himself therefore in attendance with his men, dressed in 'blue coats faced with orange-coloured taffety, with orange coloured feathers in their hats'. At this feast, it is thought a masque written by Shakespeare might have been performed, in which the Fairy Queen herself appeared. It later found its way into The Merry Wives of Windsor.

Here Mrs Quickly, dressed as the Queen of the Fairies, herself instructs the elves, ouphes and fairies in their tasks for the night, to scatter Windsor Castle with good luck for the coming celebrations:

In 1599, the Earl of Essex held a Garter Feast immediately after his arrival in Ireland. This rivalled the Garter Feast he had himself attended at the age of twenty in Utrecht, held by the Earl of Leicester in 1586. Essex's feast was a legendary, extravagant affair, designed to irritate the monarch who was paying for it.

St George's Day: Shakespeare's Birthday
....

He will weep you, an't were a man born in April.
Troilus and Cressida (Act 1 Scene 2)

Shakespeare's birth was registered in Holy Trinty Church in 1564. He was baptized on April 25th (it is assumed he was born two days before), which means he was born under Taurus:

Sir Andrew: *Shall we set about some revels ?*
Sir Toby: *What shall we do else ? Were we not born under Taurus?*
Sir Andrew: *Taurus! that's sides and heart.*
Sir Toby: *No, sir, it is legs and thighs. Let me see thee caper. Ha! Higher: ha-ha! excellent!*
Twelfth Night (Act 1 Scene 3)

In fact, Toby Belch is wrong. The members of the body associated with Taurus are actually the neck and throat, according to Elizabethan astrologers. The sides and heart come under Leo, along with the stomach, back, breast and ribs. If Toby and Andrew were born under Taurus, as Shakespeare was, they would be referring to the Taurean influence over the neck, throat and wens! Perhaps such a display of ignorance suggests that Shakespeare didn't pay much attention to all that kind of thing. As Edmund says of himself in King Lear, Shakespeare should have been that he was 'had the maidenliest star in the firmament twinkled' on his birth.

In one pamphlet published in 1598, called *A Brief and Most Easy Introduction to the Astrological Judgements of the Stars*, listed under the natures and complexions associated with Taurus, the author suggests 'Earthy, cold, and dry, melancholy, feminine, nocturnal, meridional, fixed, oblique', as well as 'having voice, fruitful, and luxurious'. But if Shakespeare was a typical Taurean, the positive traits listed on his astrological coffee cup might also have included being disciplined, hard-working, prudent, artistic, romantic, sensual, strong, shy, organized, cautious, tenacious, patient, resourceful, careful, dependable, honest and having a good sense of humour. On the other hand his negative characteristics might also include being stubborn, hyper-sensitive, resentful, moody, aggressive, ultra-conservative, possessive, insecure, materialistic, lazy and over-conscientious. And he might find an ideal career in banking, building, acting, or being a vet. He might tend to like time to ponder, but would hate disruption, anything synthetic, or being indoors.

It is perhaps worth pointing out in figuring Shakespeare's nativity charts that he was also born in the Chinese Year of the Rat, which would suggest that he was a perfectionist, a good communicator, quick-witted, chose his friends carefully, and could suss out his enemies early in the game. He was shrewd and knew how to amass wealth, was potentially miserly, and could be quick-tempered, nervous, edgy, and a downright nag.

The rat is the first animal in the zodiacal cycle, and was thought to be ambitious, suspicious and power-hungry. But those born under the rat could be imaginative, charming, but over-critical. So they could be writers, publicists or critics. Whether Shakespeare was a playwright by spherical predominance or not, one thing is sure: like Beatrice, a star danced at his nativity and under that was he born.

Shakespeare Reviews his Career

Don Marquis created a series of poems based on the friendship of two unlikely mates: archy, a cockroach with the soul of a poet, and mehitabel, an alley cat who claims she was Cleopatra in another life. Marquis, a writer for the *Evening Sun and Mail* in New York, introduced archy into his column in 1916. Here is an extract from a poem from his 1927 collection *archy and mehitabel*. It is a parody of e e cummings, hence the lack of capital letters or punctuation. Pete the parrot, who used to belong to the fellow who ran the Mermaid Tavern, tells archy about what a disappointed man bill was, poor mutt.

After two or three pints of sack and sherries, bill goes on to explain:
*i live a hell of a life i do
the manager hands me some mouldy old
manuscript and says
bill here s a plot for you
this is the third of the month
by the tenth I want a good
script out of this that we
can start rehearsals on
not too big a cast
and not too much of your
damned poetry either
you know your old
familiar line of hokum
they eat up that falstaff stuff
of yours ring him in again
and give them a good ghost
or two and remember we gotta
have something dick burbage can get
his teeth into and be sure
and stick in a speech
somewhere the queen will take
for a personal compliment and if
you get in a line or two somewhere
about the honest english yeoman*

*it s always good stuff
and it s a pretty good stunt
bill to have the heavy villain
a moor or a dago or a jew
or something like that and say
i want another comic welshman in this
but I don't need to tell
you bill you know this game
just some of your ordinary
hokum and maybe you could
kill a kid or two a prince
or something they like
a little pathos along with
the dirt now you better see burbage
tonight and see what he wants
in that part oh says bill
to think i am
debasing my talents with junk
like that oh god what I wanted
was to be a poet
and write sonnet serials
like a gentleman should*

archy and mehitabel, Don Marquis

St Mark's Day (and Last Possible Date for Easter)

According to the parish register in Holy Trinity Church, Shakespeare was both baptized and buried on this day.

In 1662, early in the Restoration, John Ward, then Vicar of Holy Trinity, jotted in his diary that Shakespeare had died of a fever. He had heard that Shakespeare, Michael Drayton and Ben Jonson 'had a merry meeting and it seems drank too hard for Shakespeare died of a fever there contracted'. He also confides in his journal, 'Remember to peruse Shakespeare's plays, and be versed in them, that I may not be ignorant in the matter.' How many subsequent Vicars of Holy Trinity have made similar mental notes?

⧗

This is St Mark's Day, and it was regarded as a Holy Day, on which work was forbidden. Here is what happened to an ale-wife who ignored that prohibition:

'In the year of our Lord 1589, I being as then but a boy, do remember that an ale-wife, making no exception of days, would needs brew upon St Mark's Day; but lo, the marvellous work of God! Whiles she was thus labouring, the top of the chimney took fire; and, before it could be quenched, her house was quite burnt. Surely a gentle warning to them that violate and profane forbidden days.'
The Golden Grove, William Vaughan

Another superstition associated with St Mark's Day is described in the anonymous poem below:

'Tis now, replied the village belle,
St Mark's mysterious Eve,
And all that old tradition's tell
I tremblingly believe;
How, when the midnight signal tolls,
Along the churchyard green,
A mournful train of sentenced souls,
In winding sheets are seen.
The ghosts of all whom death shall doom
Within the coming year
In pale procession walk the gloom,
Amid the silence drear.

The custom, on St Mark's Eve, of seeing the ghosts of those who will die in the coming year prompts the question as to whether anyone ever witnessed a spectral haunting by the Sweet Swan of Avon himself. Surely none has ever been recorded. Or has it?

The Three Witches and Hecate in *Macbeth* by John Boydell

Delia Bacon

The famous malediction inscribed on Shakespeare's grave (see December 5th) warns anyone foolhardy enough to disturb the stones that a curse will light upon them. This curse may already have had its effect. The ill-advised would-be tomb raider was a genteel lady from Ohio.

Delia Bacon is best known for her work on Shakespearean authorship. Delia intended to prove that the plays attributed to William Shakespeare were written by a coterie of men, including her namesake, Francis Bacon, along with Sir Walter Raleigh and Edmund Spenser, for the purpose of inculcating a philosophic system, for which they felt they themselves could not afford to assume the responsibility. She wrote *The Philosophy of the Plays of Shakespeare Unfolded* (1857), for which she spent several years in study in England, where she was befriended by Thomas Carlyle and Nathaniel

Hawthorne. She spent one night alone in Holy Trinity Church, contemplating opening the grave, despite its gruesome warning.

'**I had a dark lantern like Guy Fawkes, and some other articles which might have been considered suspicious if the police had come upon us. I was alone there till ten o'clock. All the long drawn aisle was in utter darkness. I heard a creaking in it, a cautious step, repeatedly, and I knew that the clerk was there and watching me. I had made a promise to the clerk that I would not do the least thing for which he could be called in question and though I went far enough to see that the examination I had proposed to make could be made, leaving all exactly as I found it, it could not be made at the time, nor under those conditions. I did not feel at liberty to make it, for fear I might violate the trust this man had reposed in me, and if I were not wholly and immediately successful I should have run the risk of losing any chance of continuing my research.**'

What scared Delia Bacon off her quest? Was it Shakespeare's ghost or the dreadful curse? Later, Miss Bacon came to believe that she was no longer Delia Bacon but the Holy Ghost, and was surrounded by devils. A nephew arrived and managed to get her back to America, where she was committed to an asylum. She died in 1859.

The less famous inscription on Shakespeare's tomb monument reads:
Stay, passenger, why goest thou by so fast?
Read if thou canst, whom envious death hath placed
Within this monument Shakespeare; with whom
Quick nature did; whose name doth deck this tomb,
Far more than cost: since all, that he hath writ,
Leaves living art, but page to serve his writ.

Kingfishers
• • • • • • • • • • • • •

Expect St Martin's summer, halcyon days!
Henry VI Part One (Act 1 Scene 2)

'A little bird called the King's
fisher, being hanged up in the air
by the neck, his neb or bill, will be
always direct or straight against
the wind.'
Tenth Book of Notable Things, T. Lupton

The halcyon was the kingfisher. In
classical mythology she built her
nest upon the waves, and
therefore halcyon days were days
of calm. But here the image is
rather more mundane and cruel, for kingfishers were
used as weather vanes. A dead bird would be hung by
its neck, or tail feathers and as it turned in the
breeze, its beak would, like a weather vane, point in
the direction of the wind.

   Kingfishers can be seen flashing up and down the
Avon at this time of year. Surprisingly tiny, they
really do seem to catch fire, as Gerard Manley
Hopkins wrote. They are usually laying their
eggs by late-March, and the clutches tend to
hatch out in April, so the parent birds are kept
very busy streaking backwards and forwards
with minnows, sticklebacks and tadpoles.
Once the chicks have emerged from the nest
their parents only feed them for a few days before
chasing them out of the territory and starting on the
next batch.

In *King Lear*, Kent rails at Regan's steward
Oswald, and all 'such smiling rogues' that:
turn their halcyon beaks
With every gale and vary of their masters,
Knowing naught (like dogs) but following.
King Lear (Act 2 Scene 2)

But now how stands the wind?
Into what corner peers my halcyon's bill?
The Jew of Malta, Christopher Marlowe *(Act 1 Scene 1)*

🐚

Ye may simper, blush and smile,
And perfume the air awhile ;
But, sweet things, ye must be gone,
Fruit, ye know, is coming on ;
Then, ah ! then, where is your grace,
When as cherries come in place.
To Cherry Blossoms, Robert Herrick

An Elizabethan Visits the Pyramids

That handkerchief did an Egyptian to my mother give ... And it was dyed in mummy.
Othello (Act 3 Scene 4)

On this day in 1586, John Sandys visited Giza.

'The eight and twentieth of April, 1586, I went to see the Pyramids and Momia. The Momia are thousands of embalmed bodies, which were buried thousands of years past in a sandy cave, at which there seemeth to have been some city in times past. We were let down by ropes, as into a well, with wax candles burning in our hands, and so walked upon the bodies of all sorts and sizes, some great and small, and some embalmed in little earthen pots. These are set at the feet of the greater bodies. They gave no noisome smell at all, but are like pitch, being broken. For I broke off all the parts of the bodies to see how the flesh was turned to drug, and brought home divers heads, hands, arms, and feet for a show. We brought also 600 pounds for the Turkey Company in pieces; and brought into England in the Hercules, together with a whole body. They are lapped in above a hundred double of cloth, which rotting and peeling off, you may see the skin, flesh, fingers, and nails firm, only altered black. One little hand I brought into England, to show, and presented it to my brother, who gave the same to a doctor in Oxford.

'But let us now return to the pyramids... the greatest of them is ascended by 255 steps, each step above three feet high, of a breadth proportionable. From the top is discerned the country, with her beloved Nile, the mummies and many huge pyramids afar off, each of which, were this away, might be reputed wonderful. Descending on the east side, they approached the entrance, into which they went with a light in everyman's hand: a narrow and dreadful passage, stooping or creeping, as down the steep of a hill 100 foot, the descent still continuing, but few daring to venture further...

'Master Sandys saith they ascended by like uneasy passage about a hundred and twenty feet; and thence passing through a long irksome entry, they came to a little room with a compassed roof of polished marble. From thence they climbed 120 feet higher, at the top entering a goodly room twenty foot wide and forty foot long, the roof of a marvellous height, the stones of well wrought Theban marble. At the upper end is a tomb of stone, uncovered and empty, breast-high, sounding like a bell, more probably supposed the builder's sepulchre. Not far hence is that Sphynx, a huge colossus, with the head of a maid and body of a lion, the face disfigured by time, or the moors' superstition, detesting images.'
Purchas, His Pilgrimes, Samuel Purchas

John Sandys brought back six hundred pounds of mummified flesh from the Egyptian pyramids for sale to the apothecaries of London. This substance, known simply as 'mummy', was thought to have medicinal value, and sold for a high price.

The Runaway Elephants

On this day in 1591, Ralph Fitch returned to England from his travels in the east. During his visit to the court of the Moghul Emperor, Akbar the Great, he had watched the famous elephant fights. During one such fight, between the Emperor's elephant Hawa'i and his opponent Ran Bagha, the animals suddenly ran amok. The following account is taken from a life of Akbar written after his death:

'Among the events of this time was the occasion that His Majesty himself mounted the elephant Hawa'i and engaged in a fight.

'The elephant Hawa'i was a mighty animal and reckoned among the most special of elephants. In choler, passion, fierceness and wickedness he was a match for the world. Strong and experienced drivers, who had spent a long life in riding similar elephants, mounted him with difficulty.

'So when the Ataga Khan saw that His Majesty was bent upon the combat, he at once obeyed and, out of respect, seemed to compose his agitatation. His lion-hearted master calmly proceeded with this terrifying pursuit, until the elephant Hawa'i (by divine fortune, and the strength of some hidden arm), gained victory over its opponent. Ran Bagha let fall the strong cable of steadfastness and turned to flee. Hawa'i looked neither behind nor before, and disregarding heights and hollows, went like the wind in pursuit of the fugitive elephant. His Majesty, a rock of firmness, continued to sit steadily and to watch the ways of destiny. After running a long way, the elephants came to the edge of the River Jumna and to the head of the great bridge of boats.

'Ran Bagha in his confusion fled on to the pontoon bridge, and Hawa'i with the tiger of fortune's jungle on his back, came up behind him. Owing to the great weight of those two mountain-forms, the pontoons were sometimes submerged and sometimes lifted up out of the water. The royal servants flung themselves

Akbar the Great riding the elephant Hawa'i, 1561

into the river on both sides of the bridge and went on swimming until the elephants crossed the whole of the bridge and got onto the other side. At this time when the spectators were looking at the wonderful affair, the Khedive of the age, in a moment, restrained Hawa'i, who was like a fire in disposition, and like the wind in swiftness. Ran Bagha ran off, carrying his life with him. New life too came to the world and distraught hearts were composed.'

May Eve

May Eve was the night to spend in the woods, in order (as Lysander says in *A Midsummer Night's Dream*) 'to do observance to a morn of May'. Here is a Puritan reaction to these heathen practices:

'Against May, Whitsunday, or other time, all the young men and maids, old men and wives, run gadding over night to the woods, groves, hills and mountains, where they spend all the night in pleasant pastimes; and in the morning they return, bringing with them birch and branches of trees, to deck their assemblies withal. And no marvel, for there is a great Lord present among them as superintendant over their pastimes and sports, namely Satan, prince of Hell. But the chiefest jewel they bring thence is their Maypole, which they bring home with great veneration as thus. They have twenty or forty yoke of oxen, every oxen having a sweet nosegay of flowers placed on the tip of his horns, and these oxen draw home this maypole (this stinking idol rather) which is covered all over with flowers and herbs, bound round about with strings from top to bottom and sometime painted with variable colours, with two or three hundred men, women and children following it with great devotion. And thus being reared up with handkerchiefs and flags hovering on the top, they strew the ground round about, bind green boughs about it, set up summer halls, bowers and arbours hard by it; And they fall to dance about it like as the heathen people did at the dedication of the idols whereof this is a perfect pattern, or rather the thing itself.

'I have heard it credibly reported (and that viva voce) by men of great gravity and reputation, that of forty, three score or a hundred maids going to the wood over night, there have scarcely the third part of them returned home again undefiled. These be the fruits which these cursed pastimes bring forth.'

Anatomy of Abuses, Phillip Stubbes

From you I have been absent in the spring,
When proud-pied April, dressed in all her trim,
Hath put a spirit of youth in everything,
That heavy Saturn laughed and leaped with him.
Yet nor the lays of birds, nor the sweet smell
Of different flowers in odour and in hue,
Could make me any summer's story tell,
Or from their proud lap pluck them where they grew:
Nor did I wonder at the lily's white,
Nor praise the deep vermilion in the rose;
They were but sweet, but figures of delight,
Drawn after you, you pattern of all those.
Yet seemed it winter still, and, you away,
As with your shadow, I with these did play.
Sonnet XCVIII

As full of spirit as the month of May
And gorgeous as the sun at midsummer.

Henry IV Part One (Act 4 Scene 1)

Love, whose month is ever May.

Love's Labours Lost (Act 4 Scene 3)

As flush as May.

Hamlet (Act 3 Scene 3)

'It is now May, and the sweetness of the air refresheth every spirit: the sunny beams give forth fair blossoms, and the dripping clouds water Flora's great garden: the male deer puts out the velvet head, and the pagged doe is near her fawning: The Spar-hawk now is drawn out of the mew, and the fowler makes ready his whistle for the quail: the Lark sets the morning watch and the evening, the nightingale: the Barges, like bowers, keep the streams of the sweet rivers, and the mackerel with the shad are taken prisoners with the sea: the tall young oak is cut down for the maypole: the Scythe and the sickle are the mowers furniture, and the fair weather makes the labourer merry; the Physician now prescribes the cold whey and the Apothecary gathers the dew for a medicine: Butter and Sage make the wholesome breakfast, but fresh cheese and cream are meat for a dainty mouth: and the strawberry and the peascod want no price in the market: the chicken and the duck are fattened for the market, and many a gosling never lives to be a goose. It is the month wherein Nature hath her fill of mirth, and the senses are filled with delights. I conclude, it is from the Heavens a grace, and to Earth a gladness. Farewell.'

Fantasticks, Nicholas Breton

'In May and June come pinks of all sorts, specially the blush pink; roses of all kinds, except the musk, which comes later; honeysuckles, strawberries, bugloss, columbine; the French marigold, flos Africanus; cherry trees in fruit, figs in fruit, rasps, vine-flowers, lavender in flowers, the sweet satyrian, with the white flower; herba muscaria, lilium convallium, the apple-tree in blossom.'

Of Gardens, Francis Bacon

'May must be drawn with a sweet and amiable countenance, clad in a robe of white and green, embroidered with daffodilles, hawthorn and blewbottles. Upon his head a garland of white, damask and red roses; in one hand a lute; upon the forefinger of the other a nightingale with the sign of Gemini.'

Emblems, Henry Peacham

May Day & The Feast of St Philip and St Jacob

Get up, get up for shame, the blooming morn
Upon her wings presents the god unshorn.
See how Aurora throws her fair
Fresh-quilted colours through the air.
Corinna's Going a-Maying, Robert Herrick

In Shakespeare and Fletcher's *The Two Noble Kinsmen*, the pedantic schoolmaster, Master Gerald, has rehearsed the villagers in a May Day entertainment. There is a May Lord and a May Lady, a He-fool and a She-fool, a Moor, and a Babion (or baboon: 'with long tail and eke long tool'). They will perform before the Duke Theseus and his bride Hippolyta (these characters are revived from *A Midsummer Night's Dream*). But the rehearsal isn't going terribly well, and the schoolmaster cries plaintively, 'What tediosity and dis-insanity is there among ye.' (It's a line every director needs on a bad rehearsal day.)

He instructs the company that on an agreed signal, when the Duke rides by on his hunting expedition, they will all rush out from their hiding places, and dance a morris.
1st Countryman: *And sweetly will we do it, Master Gerald.*
2nd Countryman: *Draw up the company. Where's the taborer?*
3rd Countryman: *Why, Timothy!*

Taborer: *Here, my mad boys, have at ye!*
School teacher: *But, I say, where's these women?*
3rd Countryman: *Here's Friz and Maudlin,*
2nd Countryman: *And little Luce with the white legs, and bouncing Barbary.*
1st Countryman: *And freckled Nell, that never failed her master.*
School teacher: *Where be your ribbons, maids? Swim with your bodies*
And carry it sweetly and deliverly,
And now and then a favour and a frisk.
Nell: *Let us alone, sir.*
School teacher: *Where's the rest of the music?*
3rd Countryman: *Dispersed, as you commanded.*
Schoolmaster: *Couple then*
And see what's wanting. Where's the babion?
My friend, carry your tail without offence
Or scandal to the ladies; and be sure
You tumble with audacity and manhood,
And, when you bark, do it with judgement.
Babion: *Yes, sir.*

But when he realises that Cicely the seamstress's daughter has not turned up, the school teacher throws his hands in the air, declaring the whole venture to be 'a woeful and a piteous nullity'.

An Actor on Tour

Joan Alleyn by an unknown artist, 1596

On this day in 1593, the actor Edward Alleyn wrote a letter to his wife, from Bristol while on tour:

'My good sweet mouse, I commend me heartily to you, and to my father, my mother, and my sister Bess, hoping in God, though the sickness be around you, yet by his mercy it may escape your house, which by the grace of God it shall. Therefore use this course: keep your house fair and clean (which I know you will) and every evening throw water before your door and in your backside, and have in your windows good store of rue and herb of grace, and withal the grace of God, which must be obtained by prayers; and by so doing, no doubt but the lord will mercifully defend you.

'Now good mouse, I have no news to send you but this, that we have all our health, for which the lord be praised. I received your letter at Bristol, by Richard Cowley, for the which I thank you. I have sent you by this bearer, Thomas Pope's kinsman, my white waistcoat, because it is a trouble to me to carry it: receive it with this letter, and lay it up for me till I come. If you send any more letters, send to me by the carriers of Shrewsbury, or to West Chester or to York, to be kept till my Lord Strange's players come. And thus sweetheart, with my hearty commendations of all our friends, I cease. From Bristol this Wednesday, after St James' Day, being ready to begin the play of Harry of Cornwall. Mouse, do my hearty commend to Mr Griggs, his wife and all his household, and to my sister Phillips.

Your loving husband, E. Alleyn

Then he added a heartfelt postscript:

Mouse, you send me no news of anything. You should send me of your domestical matters, such things as happen at home, as how your distilled water proves, or this and that, or anything, what you will. And Jug I pray you, let my orange tawny stockings of woollen be dyed a very good black against I come home, to wear in the winter. You sent me not a word of my garden, but next time you will; but remember this in any case, that all that bed which was parsley, in the month of September you sow it with spinach, for then is the time. I would do it myself but we shall not come home till All Hallowtide. And so sweet mouse, farewell, and brook our long journey with patience.

Richard Cowley and Thomas Pope were fellow stage players. John Griggs was a carpenter and playhouse builder.

Nightingales

Philomel with melody
Sing in our sweet Lullaby
Lulla, lulla, lullaby, Lulla, lulla, lullaby,
Never harm, nor spell nor charm
Come our lovely lady nigh,
So good night with lullaby.
A Midsummer Night's Dream (Act 2 Scene 2)

On the first full moon in May, it is said, nightingales arrive in England.

Izaak Walton writes that the bird: 'breathes such sweet loud music out of her little instrumental throat that it might make mankind to think miracles had not ceased'.

The sad story of Philomel is told by Ovid in his *Metamorphoses*. Tereus, the King of Thrace, rapes and imprisons poor Philomel and has her tongue cut out so that she cannot tell her tale. She manages to convey what happened to her sister, Procne, in a tapestry. They unite to take revenge upon Tereus, by killing his son and serving him to his father for dinner. Tereus is about to slay them when they are both turned into birds by divine intervention. Philomel is changed into a nightingale, Procne into a swallow. Tereus himself, according to Aristophanes' version of the story, is metamorphosed into a hoopoe.

❀

Our love was new and then but in the spring
When I was wont to greet it with my lays,
As Philomel in summer's front doth sing
And stops her pipe in growth of riper days;
Not that the summer is less pleasant now
Than when her mournful hymns did hush the night,
But that wild music burthens ev'ry bough
And sweets grown common lose their dear delight.
Therefore like her I sometime hold my tongue,
Because I would not dull you with my song.
Sonnet CII

In a gracious letter to Queen Elizabeth, the Sultana Baffo (wife to the Ottoman Sultan, Murad) wrote: 'I send your majesty so honourable and sweet a salutation of peace, that all the flock of Nightingales with their melody cannot attain to the like, much less this simple letter of mine.'

Murder and New Place

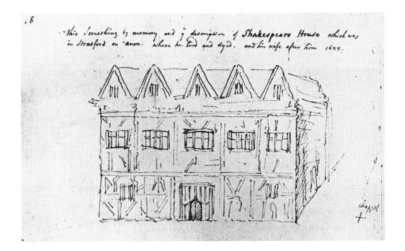

On this day in 1597, Shakespeare bought New Place in Chapel Lane opposite the Guild Chapel. It was the second-biggest house in Stratford and it cost him £60. The previous owner of the house was murdered two months later.

He was a man called William Underhill. He sold New Place that May, and in July of that same year he was dead. His 19-year-old son, Fulke, was executed for the crime. In 1602, a commission was appointed 'to obtain an account of the possessions of Fulke Underhill of Fillongley, co Warwick, felon, who had taken the life of his father, William Underhill by poison'. It was only then that Underhill's other son, Hercules, who came of age in 1602, was able to complete the transfer of the deeds of New Place to Shakespeare.

Perhaps Shakespeare was thinking of the effects of William Underhill's poisoning when he was writing *Hamlet*. Here the father's ghost tells his son how he died:

Upon my secure hour thy uncle stole,
With juice of cursed hebona in a vial,
And in the porches of my ears did pour
The leperous distilment; whose effect

Holds such an enmity with blood of man
That swift as quicksilver it courses through
The natural gates and alleys of the body,
And with a sudden vigour it doth posset
And curd, like eager droppings into milk,
The thin and wholesome blood. So did it mine;
And a most instant tetter bark'd about,
Most lazar-like with vile and loathsome crust
All my smooth body.
Hamlet (Act 1 Scene 5)

Shakespeare is said to have written the epitaph for a cousin of Underhill's who died young:
As dreams do slide, as bubbles rise and fall
As flowers do fade and flourish in an hour,
As smoke doth rise and vapours vanish all,
Beyond the wit or reach of human power,
As summer's heat doth parch the withered grass
Such is our stay, so life of man doth pass.

Shakespeare lived in New Place until his death, when his daughter, Susanna, moved in from Hall's Croft, with her husband, Dr John Hall, and their six-year-old daughter, Elizabeth.

Shakespeare's Mulberry Tree

More matter for a May morning.
Twelfth Night (Act 3 Scene 4)

David Garrick as Steward of the Shakespeare Jubilee by Benjamin Van der Gucht, 1769

In May 1742, David Garrick came to visit the shrine of his beloved Shakespeare. New Place was at that time owned by Sir Hugh Clopton. He was a descendant of the original owner, who had built 'a pretty house of brick and timber' next to the Guild Chapel during the reign of Henry VIII. Shakespeare's granddaughter Elizabeth had lived in the house until her death in 1670, and the house had remained empty for five years, returning by coincidence to the Clopton family. The present Sir Hugh had 'beautified' the house in 1702. His modernization would have made the house unrecognizable to Shakespeare. In the garden, however, stood a large mulberry tree. Sir Hugh insisted that this was the very tree that

Shakespeare had planted. David Garrick and indeed the whole town believed him.

When Sir Hugh died in 1751, the house was bought by a clergyman called the Reverend Francis Gastrell. But, as a contemporary Stratford historian put it, Gastrell 'felt no sort of pride or pleasure in this charming retirement, no consciousness of his being possessed of the sacred ground which the Muses had consecrated to the memory of their favourite poet'.

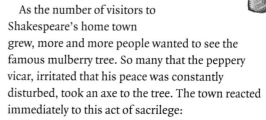

As the number of visitors to Shakespeare's home town grew, more and more people wanted to see the famous mulberry tree. So many that the peppery vicar, irritated that his peace was constantly disturbed, took an axe to the tree. The town reacted immediately to this act of sacrilege:

'After the first astonishment was over, a general Fury seized them all, and vengeance was the Word! They gathered together, surrounded the house, reviewed the fallen Tree, and vowed to sacrifice the offender, to the immortal memory of the Planter! In short, such a spirit was on foot, that the clergyman, after consulting with his friends, and skulking from place to place was persuaded to quit the Town, where he would never have been permitted to abide in Peace – and where all the Inhabitants have most religiously resolved never to suffer any one of the same name to dwell amongst them.'
Benjamin Victor, 1771

A quick check through the Stratford phone book today – there are no Gastrells listed - suggests that this is still the case.

Mulberries

And Thisbe, tarrying in mulberry shade.
A Midsummer Night's Dream (Act 5 Scene 1)

Shakespeare derives the rude mechanicals play of
Pyramus and Thisbe from Golding's translation of
Ovid's *Metamorphoses*. The story explains the colour
of the mulberry.

And when he had bewept and kissed the garment that
*   he knew,*
'Receive thou my blood too,' quoth he, and therewithal
*   he drew*
His sword, the which among his guts he thrust, and
*   by and by*
Did draw it from the bleeding wound begining for to die,
And cast himself upon his back, the blood did spin on high
As when a conduit pipe is cracked the water bursting out
Does shoot itself a great way off and pierce the air about.
The leaves that were upon the tree, besprinkled with
*   his blood*
Were dyed black. The root also bestained as it stood,
A deep dark purple colour straight upon the berries cast.
Anon scarce ridded of her fear with which she was aghast,
For doubt of disappointing him comes Thisbe forth
*   in haste,*
And for her lover looks about, rejoicing for to tell
How hardly she had scaped that night the danger
*   that befell.*
And as she knew right well the place and fashion of the tree
(As which she saw so late before); even so when she did see
The colour of the berries turned, she was uncertain whether
It were the tree at which they both agreed to meet together.

Thisbe finds her lover dead and curses the
mulberry tree:
... And thou unhappy tree
Which shroudest now the corpse of one, and shalt anon
*   through me*
Shroud two, of this same slaughter hold the sicker signs
*   for aye,*

Black be the colour of thy fruit and mourning like alway,
Such as the murder of us twain shall ever more bewray.
Her prayer with the Gods and with their parents took effect.
For when the fruit is thoroughly ripe, the berry is bespecked
With colour tending unto black.
Ovid's Metamorphoses (Book Four), *translated by*
Arthur Golding

Customers at the Dirty Duck in Stratford have often,
like Thisbe, cursed the mulberry tree which stands
on the terrace in front of the pub. When it is in fruit,
the berries tend to drop suddenly from above,
staining anything they fall upon with dark purple
splatters.

Now humble as the ripest mulberry
That will not hold the handling.
Coriolanus (Act 3 Scene 2)

Rogation Sunday: Beating the Bounds

That every man might keep his own possessions,
Our fathers used, in reverent processions
(With zealous prayers and with praiseful cheer)
To walk their parish limits once a year,
And well known marks (which sacrilegious hands
Now cut or break) so bordered out their lands,
That everyone distinctly knew his own,
And many brawls now rife were then unknown.

Emblems, George Withers

Rogation Sunday was originally so called because of the words in the gospel for the day: 'Whatever you ask the Father in my name, he will give to you.' The Latin for 'to ask' is 'rogare'.

In Rogation week it was the custom by the seventeenth century to go round the bounds or limits of the parish, when the minister, accompanied by his church wardens and parishioners, would invoke a blessing on the fruits of the earth, and pray for the rights and properties of the parish. George Herbert, himself a country parson, in the 1630s commended the practice, not only for the just preservation of the parish boundaries, but for the social occasion it afforded, walking with one's neighbours and reconciling differences, if there were any, and also for distributing largesse to the poor.

   The church had adapted the old Roman festival of 'Terminalia', or 'Boundaries'. The lines of demarcation between the parishes were not always clear, especially where there were open field systems. During the beating of the bounds, boys were bumped on boundary stones, or pitched into briars and ditches, or chucked in the pond to make sure they never forgot those boundaries. The Victorians made it more civilized by beating objects rather than people.

The boundaries were often marked out by certain trees under which the Gospel would be read. Herrick refers to them in the following poem:

Dearest, bury me
Under that Holy-Oak or Gospel tree,
Where (though thou see'st not) thou may'st think upon
Me, when thou yearly go'st Procession.

To Anthea, Robert Herrick

These trees were called Gospel Oaks.

We know there was a Gospel Bush in Stratford, as the town clerk, Thomas Greene, recorded in his diary a conversation between Shakespeare and his son-in-law, John Hall, talking about the controversial proposed enclosure of common land in the Welcombe Hills, in which he said, referring to trenching and hedging, that 'they assured him they would go no further than to Gospel Bush'.

Ben Jonson's Best Piece of Poetry

'When the King came in England, at that time the pest was in London, he (Jonson) being in the country at Sir Robert Cotton's house with old Camden, he saw in a vision his eldest son (then a child and at London), appear unto him with ye mark of a bloody cross on his forehead as if it had been cut with a sword, at which amazed he prayed unto God, and in the morning he came to Mr Camden's chamber to tell him, who persuaded him it was but an apprehension of his fantasy at which he should not be dejected. In the meantime, come a letter from his wife of the death of the boy in the plague. He appeared to him, he said, of a manly shape and of the growth that he thinks he shall be at the resurrection.'

Hawthornden's Conversations

Homo Bulla: A Boy Blowing Bubbles by Bartolomeus van der Helst, c.1665

Farewell, thou child of my right hand, and joy;
My sin was too much hope of thee, lov'd boy.
Seven years thou wert lent to me, and I thee pay,
Exacted by thy fate, on the just day.
O, could I lose all father, now. For why
Will man lament the state he should envy?
To have so soon 'scaped world's and flesh's rage,
And, if no other misery, yet age?
Rest in soft peace, and, ask'd, say here doth lie
Ben Jonson his best piece of poetry.
For whose sake, hence-forth, all his vows be such,
As what he loves may never like too much.

Ben Jonson

In Spenser's *The Faerie Queene*, the parade of months reaches May. She enters supported on the shoulders of Gemini, the heavenly twins. The sun would have entered the house of Gemini ten days earlier in Shakespeare's day, in just a few days' time:

Then came fair May, the fairest maid on ground,
Decked all with dainties of her season's pride,
And throwing flowers out of her lap around:
Upon two brethren's shoulders she did ride,
The twins of Leda; which on either side
Supported her like to their sovereign Queen.
Lord! how all creatures laughed, when her they spied,
And leapt and danced as they had ravished been!
And Cupid self about her fluttered all in green.

Mutabilitie Cantos, VII: XXXIV

Time's Glory

On this day in 1594, Shakespeare registered his second narrative poem, *The Rape of Lucrece*. Here is an extract:

Time's glory is to calm contending kings,
To unmask falsehood and bring truth to light,
To stamp the seal of time in aged things,
To wake the morn and sentinel the night,
To wrong the wronger till he render right,
To ruinate proud buildings with thy hours,
And smear with dust their glittering golden towers;

To fill with worm-holes stately monuments,
To feed oblivion with decay of things,
To blot old books and alter their contents,
To pluck the quills from ancient ravens' wings,
To dry the old oak's sap and cherish springs,
To spoil antiquities of hammer'd steel,
And turn the giddy round of Fortune's wheel;

To show the beldam daughters of her daughter,
To make the child a man, the man a child,
To slay the tiger that doth live by slaughter,
To tame the unicorn and lion wild,
To mock the subtle in themselves beguiled,
To cheer the ploughman with increaseful crops,
And waste huge stones with little water drops.

The Darling Buds of May

Shall I compare thee to a summer's day?
Thou art more lovely and more temperate:
Rough winds do shake the darling buds of May,
And summer's lease hath all too short a date:
Sometime too hot the eye of heaven shines,
And often is his gold complexion dimm'd;
And every fair from fair sometime declines,
By chance or nature's changing course untrimm'd;
But thy eternal summer shall not fade
Nor lose possession of that fair thou owest;
Nor shall Death brag thou wander'st in his shade,
When in eternal lines to time thou growest:
So long as men can breathe or eyes can see,
So long lives this and this gives life to thee.
Sonnet XVIII

Bluebells are in full and glorious haze in the English woodland about now. A walk in a bluebell wood is part of an English spring. Shakespeare refers to bluebells as harebells in this scene from *Cymbeline*, set in the Welsh Mountains:

Guiderius: *Why, he but sleeps:*
If he be gone, he'll make his grave a bed;
With female fairies will his tomb be
      haunted,
And worms will not come to thee.
Arvarigus: *With fairest flowers*
Whilst summer lasts and I live here,
      Fidele,
I'll sweeten thy sad grave: thou
      shalt not lack
The flower that's like thy
face, pale primrose, nor
The azured harebell, like thy
      veins, no, nor
The leaf of eglantine, whom not to
      slander,
Out-sweeten'd not thy breath...
Cymbeline (Act 4 Scene 2)

Simon Forman saw *Cymbeline* at the *Globe* in 1611. Here he tries to recall the complicated storyline:

'Remember also the story of Cymbeline, King of England...How Lucius came with a great army of soldiers, who landed at Milford Haven, and after were vanquished by Cymbeline, and Lucius taken prisoner. All by means of three outlaws: of which two of them were the sons of Cymbeline, stolen from him when they were but two years old by an old man whom Cymbeline banished. He kept them as his own sons twenty years with him in a cave. And how one of them slew Cloten, the Queen's son, going to Milford Haven to seek the love of Imogen, the King's daughter, whom he had banished also for loving his daughter... And after Imogen, who had turned herself into man's apparel and fled to meet her love at Milford Haven and chanced to fall on the cave in the woods where her two brothers were. How by eating a sleeping dram they thought she had been dead, and laid her in the woods, the body of Cloten by her, in her love's apparel that he left behind him. And how she was found by Lucius, etc...'

Ascension Day

Is this Ascension-day? Did not the prophet
Say that before Ascension-day at noon
My crown I should give off? Even so I have:
I did suppose it should be on constraint;
But heaven be thanked, it is but voluntary.

King John (Act 5 Scene 1)

King John has been told by a prophet called Peter of Pomfret that he will deliver up his crown on Ascension Day, for which news he promises to hang him.

Today was the feast of the Ascension in the year of Shakespeare's birth. Ascension celebrates Our Lord's ascent into heaven. It falls on a Thursday, forty days after Easter. There is a tiny fragment of medieval stained glass in Holy Trinity Church, Stratford, which escaped the blitz of the Reformation when the other windows in the church were smashed. It is high up in the topmost lights of one of the windows nearest the altar, on the south side of the chancel, and it shows Christ's feet disappearing into the clouds, as if he himself is escaping the iconoclasts.

Dandelions and Buttercups

On this day in 1906, Edith Holden wrote in her famous diary (later to be known as *The Country Diary of an Edwardian Lady*) of a trip she made to Stratford-upon-Avon. She lived in Olton, then a small village in Warwickshire, about 20 miles north of Stratford, and now swallowed up in the urban sprawl of South Birmingham:

'Walked to Shottery across the meadows. On the way I gathered hawthorn blossom from the hedges, and saw fields yellow with buttercups and banks of blue speedwell. The dandelions were a wonderful sight along the railway cutting.'

Follow Edith's footsteps today, a hundred years later, along what is now a cycle way, and you will find the meadows just as full of dandelions, buttercups and speedwell as she reported them to be in 1906. Dandelions were known as 'golden lads' in Shakespeare's day, and when they turned into dandelion clocks were called 'chimney sweepers'. As thus in the dirge in *Cymbeline*: 'Golden lads and girls all must as chimney sweepers come to dust.' And buttercups were often referred to as Mary buds.

It's a sad irony that Edith Holden's passion should also have brought about her death in 1920. She was reaching to gather some chestnut buds with an umbrella, one March evening in a backwater of the River Thames near Kew Gardens Walk, when, Ophelia-like, 'clambering on the pendent boughs' at the water's edge, she fell into the 'weeping brook' and drowned. Edith was 46.

The summer's flower is to the summer sweet,
Though to itself it only live and die,
But if that flower some base infection meet,
The basest weed outbraves its dignity:
For sweetest things turn sourest by their deeds;
Lilies that fester smell far worse than weeds.

Sonnet XCIV

Whitsuntide Ale Festivals

Morris dancers at Richmond Palace, Flemish School, 1620

Methinks I play as I have seen them do
In Whitsun Pastorals.
The Winter's Tale (Act 4 Scene 3)

Ten days after the Feast of the Ascension comes Whit Sunday, also known as Pentecost, which is celebrated on the Sunday which falls on the 50th day after Easter. Pentecost comes from a Greek word meaning 'fiftieth', which means Whitsuntide could fall on any day between the 10th of May and the 10th of June.

Pentecost marks the inspiration of the Holy Spirit, who descended in tongues of flame on the Apostles in the upper room. But Whitsuntide was also identified with one of the summer pagan festivals that pre-dated Christianity.

In Gloucestershire they still roll cheeses at Whit, as they did in Shakespeare's day.

In *Henry V*, the Dauphin proposes war on the English thus:
And let us do it with no show of fear
No, with no more than if we heard that England
Were busied with a Whitsun morris dance.
Henry V (Act 2 Scene 4)

Whitsun was also celebrated with pastorals and the 'Whitsun-ale', a festival where the drink flowed freely. In the prologue to *Pericles*, Gower refers to these events:
To sing a song that old was sung,
From ashes ancient Gower is come;
Assuming man's infirmities,
To glad your ear, and please your eyes.
It hath been sung at festivals,
On ember-eves and holy-ales.

Ember days happened four times a year and were three days in the week set aside for fasting and prayer; once during Lent, now after Pentecost, then again in September after Holy Rood Day, and again during Advent after the feast of St Lucy.

Fasting days and Emberings be
Lent, Whitsun, Holyrood, and Lucie.

The word 'ember' derives from an Anglo-Saxon word relating to the annual cycle of the year.

Artist in Residence

Just after World War II, the painter Laura Knight stayed for several seasons in Stratford-upon-Avon, as what we would now call an artist-in-residence. Apart from spending time in the wings, or in the dressing rooms, trying to capture Paul Scofield preparing to play Hamlet in 1948, she would sketch, draw and paint in some of the other departments of the theatre.

'For the first year at Stratford I concentrated my work on the old wardrobe opposite the theatre; the contents of this building, still only half reorganized after the war, was a goldmine for me. Here I found activity in the employment of needle and thread on dummy actor and actresses; cutting, pinning and fitting; the floor strewn with odd lengths of material, scissors and velvet of considerable antiquity, these superb pieces of colour, cutting and workmanship, in spite of their moth-chewed fur trimmings, were historical – worn long ago by performers of fame.

'I remember the opening of Irving's own wardrobe trunk. He had been proud of his shapely feet as was evident from the contents of his box; many were the remains, mostly only the soles, of elaborately coloured and tooled footwear on which some sort of beastie had feasted.

'In the foreground of one picture I then painted was a rich purple and gold cloak for Pericles to wear; but before I had time to say, "Don't touch", every actor who came in to be fitted had swung round the dummy on which it was draped, changing all its folds – finally, I had to work all Sunday when the workshop was empty. I believe I did some of my best work in that wardrobe, before it was eventually put into perfect order. One of these paintings, of an old yellow silk dress hung on a dummy, is in Worcester Permanent Art Gallery. Another was of girls at work adjusting odd pieces worn by former actors, found in a prop basket containing all sorts of scraps including ostrich feathers of great beauty. But perhaps my favourite, hung in the Royal Academy as "Jester", was of the man in charge of all headwear, dressed in fool's cap and gown.'

Yellow Dress by Dame Laura Knight, 1948

The Magic of a Line, The Autobiography of Laura Knight

The Jacobean Olympic Games

Mr Robert's Dover's Olimpick Games upon the Cotswold Hills

Page: *I am glad to see you, good Master Slender.*
Slender: *How does your fallow greyhound, sir?*
I heard say he was outrun on Cotsall.
Page: *It could not be judged, sir.*
Slender: *You'll not confess, you'll not confess.*
The Merry Wives of Windsor (Act 1 Scene 1)

The Cotswold Games on Dover's Hill overlooking the Vale of Evesham, above the town of Chipping Campden, Gloucestershire, were first organized in 1612. However, greyhound racing and coursing had long been held there, as witnessed by the extract from The Merry Wives of Windsor, above. The Games were originally a protest by a local attorney, Robert

Dover, against the growing Puritanism of the day. The games were held on Thursday and Friday of Whit-Week, or the week of Whitsuntide, which would normally fall around the middle of May to the middle of June. They continued for many years until about the time of Dover's death, and have been since revived.

The games were quite a spectacle in their day. Robert Dover presided over the games on horseback, dressed ceremonially in a coat, hat, feather and ruff that originally belonged to the king. Horses and men were abundantly decorated with yellow ribbons (Dover's colour), and he was duly honoured by all as king of their sports for a number of years. Tents were erected for the gentry, who came in great numbers from far and wide, and refreshments were supplied in abundance. Tables stood in the open air, or cloths were spread on the ground, for the common folk.

On Cotswold Hills there meets
A greater troop of gallants than Rome's streets
E'er saw in Pompey's triumphs! beauties too,
More than Diana's bevy of nymphs could show
On their great hunting days.
None ever hungry from these games come home,
Or ever make plaint of viands or of room;
He all the rank at night so brave dismisses,
With ribands of his favour and with blisses.
The Annals of Dover, Annalia Dubrensia

Watching Shakespeare

Merrily, merrily shall I live now,
Under the blossom that hangs on the bough.
The Tempest (Act 5 Scene 1)

On this day in 1611 Simon Forman sees *The Winter's Tale* at the Globe:

'Observe there how Leontes, the king of Sicilia, was overcome with jealousy of his wife with the king of Bohemia, his friend, that came to see him. How he contrived his death, and would have had his cupbearer to have poisoned him: who have the king of Bohemia warning thereof and fled with him to Bohemia.

'Remember also how he sent to the oracle of Apollo, and the answer of Apollo – that she was guiltless and that the King was jealous, etc.; and how, except the child was found again that was lost, the King should die without issue. For the child was carried into Bohemia and there laid in a forest and brought up by a shepherd. The King of Bohemia's son married that wench. And how they fled into Sicilia to Leontes. The shepherd, having shown the letter of the nobleman by whom Leontes sent away that child and the jewels found about her, she was known to be Leontes' daughter, and was then sixteen years old.

'Remember also the rogue that came in all tattered like Coll Pixie; how he feigned him sick and to have been robbed of all that he had. How he cozened the poor man of all his money. And, after, came to the sheep-shearing with a pedlar's pack and there cozened them again of all their money. How he changed apparel with the King of Bohemia's son, and then how he turned courtier, etc. Beware of trusting feigned beggars or fawning fellows.'

Simon Forman's Diary, May 15th, 1611

Adonis' Flower: The Chequered Daffodil

In his *Herbal*, John Gerard writes of the Turkey or Ginny-hen Flower:

'It hath been called Fritillaria, of the table or board upon which men play Chess, which square checkers, the flower doth very much resemble... In English we may call it Turkey-Hen or Ginny-hen flower, and also Chequered Daffodil.'

Gerard is surely describing the snake's head fritillary of the kind that spring up in the water meadows behind Magdalen College, Oxford, in May. Their delicate intricacy is quite astonishing; as Gerard writes:

'Nature or rather the Creator of all things, hath kept a very wonderful order, surpassing (as in all other things) the curiousest painting that Art can set down.'

This flower must have been in Shakespeare's mind when, at the end of his great erotic narrative poem *Venus and Adonis*, he describes the flower that springs up from the blood of the mortally wounded Adonis:

By this the boy that by her side lay kill'd
Was melted like a vapour from her sight.
And in his blood that on the ground lay spill'd
A purple flower sprung up chequer'd with white.

The Language and Virtue of Flowers

Ophelia: There's rosemary, that's for remembrance; pray, love, remember: and there is pansies. That's for thoughts.
Laertes: A document in madness, thoughts and remembrance fitted.
Ophelia: There's fennel for you, and columbines: there's rue for you; and here's some for me: we may call it herb-of-grace o' Sundays. O, you must wear your rue with a difference. There's a daisy: I would give you some violets, but they withered all when my father died: they say he made a good end.

Hamlet (Act 4 Scene 5)

John Gerard informs us in his *Herbal* that: **'The distilled water of the flowers of rosemary being drunk morning and evening first and last, taketh away the stench of the mouth and breath and maketh it very sweet. The Arabians do write that rosemary comforteth the brain, the memory, the inward senses and restoreth speech unto them that are possessed with the dumb palsy. The flowers made up into plates with sugar and eaten, comfort the heart, and make it merry, quicken the spirits and make them more lively.'**

Of violets, the symbol for faithfulness, he says: **'The flowers are good for all inflammations, especially of the sides and lungs; they take away the hoarseness of the chest, the ruggedness of the windpipe and the jaws, and take away thirst.'**

Fennel, according to Gerard, **'is so well known among us, that it were but lost labour to describe the same. The powder of the seed of fennel drunk for certain days** together fasting preserveth the eye-sight'; while columbines, he says, are **'used especially to deck the gardens of the curious, garlands and houses'.**

'Rue hath a very strong and rank smell and a biting taste,' he writes, and assures us that **'the juice of rue made hot in the rind of a pomegranate and dropped into the ears, takes away the pain thereof'.**

Gerard lists the virtues of the daisy thus: **'The leaves stamped, take away bruises and swellings proceeding of some stroke, if they be stamped and laid thereon; whereupon it was called in old time bruisewort. The juice of the leaves and roots sniffed up into the nostrils purgeth the head mightily and helpeth the megrim.'**

But then Gerard continues: **'The same given to little dogs with milk, keepeth them from growing great.'**

Shakespeare Becomes a King's Man

Polonius: The best actors in the world, either for tragedy, comedy, history, pastoral, pastoral-comical, historical-pastoral, tragical-historical, tragical-comical-historical-pastoral, scene individable, or poem unlimited: Seneca cannot be too heavy, nor Plautus too light. For the law of writ and the liberty, these are the only men.

Hamlet (Act 2 Scene 2)

On this day in 1603, King James I issued a warrant for letters patent authorizing:

'William Shakespeare... and the rest of their Associates freely to use and exercise the Art and faculty of playing Comedies, Tragedies, Histories, Interludes, Morals, Pastorals, Stageplays, and such others like as they have already studied or hereafter shall use or study as well for the recreation of our loving Subjects as for our Solace and pleasure when we shall think good to see them during our pleasure...'

The players are to be given special privileges, and another Royal Patent instructs:

'all justices, mayors, other officers, and loving subjects to allow them such former Courtesies as hath been given to men of their place and quality and also what further favour you shall show to these our Servants for our sake, for such favour we shall take kindly at your hand.'

Shakespeare's Company, until that point under the patronage of the Lord Chamberlain, became the King's Men. And for the carrying out of their new duties, according to an account in the records of the Master of the Wardrobe, they were to be issued with scarlet cloth for new outfits, to accompany the new King on his Royal Procession through London.

Shakespeare's attitude to this honour might be revealed in the question which opens Sonnet CXXV:
Were't aught to me I bore the canopy,
With my extern the outward honouring,
Or laid great bases for eternity,
Which proves more short than waste or ruining?

Clopton Bridge

As through an arch the violent roaring tide,
Outruns the eye that doth behold his haste,
Yet in the eddy boundeth in his pride
Back to the strait that forced him on so fast
In rage sent out, recall'd in rage, being past.

The Rape of Lucrece

Caroline Spurgeon's classic work *Shakespeare's Imagery* was first published in 1935. For the most part, she deals with her subject with thorough and dispassionate precision, except for one moment, where Miss Spurgeon turns detective in 1930s Stratford and meets an ancestor of Shakespeare's printer:

'I feel as sure as I can be of anything that these many pictures drawn by Shakespeare of the movement and behaviour of a river in flood are all boyhood memories of the Avon at Stratford. This, I believe, is peculiarly true when he compares the movement of the waters to the emotions and passions of men.

'I had an interesting confirmation of this belief on one visit to Stratford recently, when I made the acquaintance of Captain William Jaggard, the owner of the old print and book shop in Sheep Street and descendant of the William Jaggard, who in 1599 and 1612 printed and published *The Passionate Pilgrim*, and from whose press, in 1623, the First Folio was issued.

'I was telling Captain Jaggard that I was very anxious to see the river in flood, and particularly to stand on old Clopton bridge and watch the movement of the current, as Shakespeare often referred to it. "Oh Yes!" he said, "and you should stand on the eighteenth arch of the bridge (the one nearest the London side), for when the river is in flood, the force of the current under the adjoining arches combined with the curved shape of the bank onto which it is driven, produces the most curious effect. I have often stood there and watched the current being forced beneath the narrow Tudor arch onto the right bank at

an angle which produces a swirling eddy, so that the water is then forced back through the arch equally swiftly and in an exactly contrary direction to that in which it has come. I have," he added, "sometimes hardly been able to believe my eyes when I have seen sticks or straws, which I have just noticed swirled on the flood downward through the arch, being brought back again just as swiftly in the opposite direction and against the flood weight."

'Captain Jaggard, as he said this, was at the further end of his shop, searching among its piled-up masses of books and papers for some prints to show me, and his voice, coming thus somewhat muffled from the distance, gave me the most curious thrill and start, as if it were a voice from the dead. For here was a present day Stratfordian describing to me in prose, exactly what a Stratford man had thus set down in verse nearly three hundred and fifty years ago.'

Sir Hugh Clopton's late-fifteenth-century bridge spans the Avon just upstream from the Theatre. There are only fourteen arches visible; four of them carry the approach road from the town, and are now completely hidden.

Larks
• • • • • •

Hark, hark! the lark at heaven's gate sings,
And Phoebus 'gins arise,
His steeds to water at those springs
On chaliced flowers that lies;
And winking Mary-buds begin
To ope their golden eyes:
With every thing that pretty is,
My lady sweet, arise:
Arise, arise!
Cymbeline (Act2 Scene 3)

In the play, the dull clot, Cloten, serenades Imogen with this song of the lark ascending. Skylarks, the 'ploughmen's clocks', are now in full song, and the chaliced, golden eyes of the buttercups or Mary-buds fill the meadows.

The lark, Shelley's 'Blithe Spirit', was also highly regarded as a tasty delicacy in Shakespeare's day. In fact, the trade in larks continued right the way through the Victorian period and was only banned as recently as 1931. The land 'where larks fall ready roasted from the skies' was a sixteenth-century version of the land of milk and honey.

The glorious, delicate exuberance of the lark's song, high in the early-summer sky, inspires the most melancholy of spirits, as here in one of the sonnets:

When, in disgrace with fortune and men's eyes,
I all alone beweep my outcast state
And trouble deaf heaven with my bootless cries
And look upon myself and curse my fate,
Wishing me like to one more rich in hope,
Featured like him, like him with friends possess'd,
Desiring this man's art and that man's scope,
With what I most enjoy contented least;
Yet in these thoughts myself almost despising,
Haply I think on thee, and then my state,
Like to the lark at break of day arising
From sullen earth, sings hymns at heaven's gate;
For thy sweet love remember'd such wealth brings
That then I scorn to change my state with kings.
Sonnet XXIX

Also on this day in 1603, the Globe was closed for nearly a year, until April 9th, 1604 because of the plague.

Shakespeare's Lost Play

On this day in 1613, the Privy Council authorized payment to the King's Men of £20 for a season of plays at court, including a play called *Cardenn*.

Cardenn was performed before the ambassador of the Duke of Savoy again on July 9th. It was not included in the First Folio in 1623 (neither is The *Two Noble Kinsmen*), but in 1653, the publisher Humphrey Moseley applies to the Stationers' Register to publish numerous plays, including *The History of Cardenio* by Mr Fletcher and Shakespeare, which suggests that a manuscript was still in existence at that point.

In 1612, the first translation of Cervantes' *Don Quixote* by Thomas Shelton had appeared in English. It contains the story of Cardenio, a young man driven mad when he believes the woman he loves has been stolen by his friend and has married him. The false friend has already raped a young farmer's daughter, who dresses as a boy and, in pursuit of her honour, follows him. All the distressed lovers end up among the shepherds in the mountains of the Sierra Morena, where everything is resolved. The play has overtones of *The Two Gentlemen of Verona*, and certainly of *Cymbeline*. John Fletcher, having written *All is True* and *The Two Noble Kinsmen* with Shakespeare, embarked on *Cardenio* as their third collaboration.

In 1727, Lewis Theobold claimed to have been given a copy of this manuscript by John Downes, the bookkeeper of the Drury Lane Theatre, and he presented an adaptation of this lost play, which he called *Double Falsehood*, or *The Distressed Lovers*, at Drury Lane. It ran very successfully for thirteen performances over the next few months.

Theobold was a struggling writer. He had earned a degree of success and money by penning hugely popular pantomimes for John Rich at Lincoln's Inn Fields. But he thought of himself as better than that.

The previous year, perhaps in a bid to establish his credentials, he made the mistake of criticizing Alexander Pope for his edition of Shakespeare, in which Pope corrects the Bard's bad rhymes or errant metre. Pope considered Theobold an upstart, and savaged him as the chief Dunce of his vicious satire, *The Dunciad*. Theobold became a laughing stock. When he finally published his own complete works of Shakespeare, he himself left out *Cardenio*. Did such a manuscript exist? Indeed, Theobold claimed there was more than one in his possession. An article in a magazine of 1777 suggested that it was 'treasured up' in the museum of the Covent Garden Playhouse. If that is true then it went up in flames with the theatre in 1808.

Theobold had, however, published his *Double Falsehood* in 1727. It is perhaps as close as we are going to get to Shakespeare's lost play.

Also on this day in 1608 *Antony and Cleopatra* and *Pericles* were entered in the Stationers' Register, but not published. On the same day in 1609, the *Sonnets* were also registered.

The Ceremony of Lilies and Roses

I'll throw thy body in another room
And triumph Henry in thy day of doom.
Henry VI Part Three (Act 5 Scene 6)

Richard III, from The Trevelyon Miscellany, 1608

On this day in 1471 King Henry VI, held prisoner in the Tower of London, was murdered. Shakespeare attributed his death to Crook-back Gloucester, soon to become King Richard III. But, whoever was responsible for the crime, certainly the saintly king was killed while at his prayers in the Oratory in the Wakefield Tower, between eleven and twelve o'clock on the night of May 21st .

Every year on this day, the Ceremony of Lilies and Roses takes place in the room where Henry is supposed to have died. Henry VI founded both Eton College and King's College, Cambridge. Delegates from both institutions place flowers on the spot of the murder – lilies from Eton and roses from King's.

Though still very simple, the Ceremony of the Lilies and Roses has over the years acquired a certain formality. The Provost of Eton, the Provost of King's and the Chaplain of the Tower are conducted by the Resident Governor and Keeper of the Jewel House, with an escort of Yeoman Warders, from Queen's House to the Wakefield Tower. The Chaplain conducts the short service and the lilies and roses are ceremoniously laid: to lie until dusk on the next day as token that King Henry's memory is evergreen in the two Colleges which are perhaps his most enduring monument.

The ceremony was observed even during World War II, when The Tower of London was a restricted area and the Wakefield Tower itself was hit by a German bomb.

But with the word the time will bring on summer,
When briars shall have leaves as well as thorns,
And be as sharp as sweet.
All's Well That Ends Well (Act 4 Scene 4)

The silent war of lilies and of roses
Which Tarquin view'd in her fair face's field.
The Rape of Lucrece (lines 71 – 72)

'Here on this Molehill Will I Sit Me Down'

Henry VI at Towton by William Dyce, 1855–60

On this day in 1465 King Henry VI was captured in the Wars of the Roses. In Shakespeare's version of events, the gentle King sits on a molehill and meditates on the cares of state:

O God! methinks it were a happy life,
To be no better than a homely swain;
To sit upon a hill, as I do now,
To carve out dials quaintly, point by point,
Thereby to see the minutes how they run,
How many make the hour full complete;
How many hours bring about the day;
How many days will finish up the year;
How many years a mortal man may live.
When this is known, then to divide the times:
So many hours must I tend my flock;
So many hours must I take my rest;
So many hours must I contemplate;
So many hours must I sport myself;
So many days my ewes have been with young;
So many weeks ere the poor fools will ean:
So many years ere I shall shear the fleece:
So minutes, hours, days, months, and years,
Pass'd over to the end they were created,
Would bring white hairs unto a quiet grave.
Ah, what a life were this! how sweet! how lovely!
Gives not the hawthorn-bush a sweeter shade
To shepherds looking on their silly sheep,
Than doth a rich embroider'd canopy
To kings that fear their subjects' treachery?
O, yes, it doth; a thousand-fold it doth.
And to conclude, the shepherd's homely curds,
His cold thin drink out of his leather bottle.
His wonted sleep under a fresh tree's shade,
All which secure and sweetly he enjoys,
Is far beyond a prince's delicates,
His viands sparkling in a golden cup,
His body couched in a curious bed,
When care, mistrust, and treason wait on him.
King Henry VI Part Three (Act 2 Scene 5)

Moles
·······

... The blind mole casts
Copp'd hills towards heaven, to tell the earth is throng'd
By man's oppression; and the poor worm doth die for't.
Pericles (Act 1 Scene 1)

And still on the subject of moles, here is Edward Topsell on molehills:
'Before any rain and change of weather these silly beasts heave up the earth more abundantly than at other times; and in Thessaly (as Varro sayeth) a whole town was once undermined by moles. With the skins of moles are purses made for the rough and soft hair, and also the black russet colour is very delectable.'

Well said, old mole! Canst work i' th'earth so fast?
A worthy pioneer.
Hamlet (Act 1 Scene 5)

How to get rid of moles:
'The Grecians did destroy and drive away their moles by this invention, they took a great nut, wherein they included Chaff, Brimstone, and Wax, then they did stop all the breathing places of the moles, except one at the mouth, wherein they set this device on fire, so as the smoke was driven inward, wherewithal they filled the hole and the place of their walks, and so stopping it, the moles were either killed or driven away.

'Also Paramus showeth another means to drive away and take moles: If you take white Hellebore, and the rinds of white Mercury instead of Hemlock, and dry them and beat them to a powder, afterwards sift them and mix them with meal, and with milk beaten with the white of an egg, and so make it into little morsels or balls, and lay them in the mole hole and passages, it will kill them if they eat thereof, as they will certainly do.

'And to conclude, by setting an earthen pot in the earth and Brimstone burning therein, it will certainly drive them for ever from that place. Unto which I may add a superstitious conceit of an obscure author, who writeth that if you whet a mowing scythe in a field or meadow, upon the feast of Christ's nativity (commonly called Christmas Day), all the moles that are within hearing thereof, will certainly forever forsake that field, meadow or garden.'

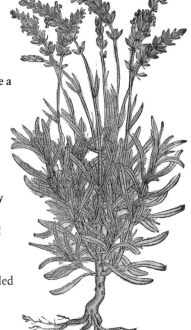

And among the many medicinal properties of moles, Topsell notes the following:
'Whosoever shall take a mole and hold her in his right hand until she die, shall have such excellent virtue therein, that he shall ease the pain of a woman's breasts only by touching them.'
The History of Four-Footed Beasts, Edward Topsell

Moles were often called 'mowdewarps' in Shakespeare's day.

Up to London for a Shopping Spree

In the Elizabethan novel *Thomas of Reading*, a group of Clothiers' wives arrange to meet up for a spot of shopping and sight-seeing in the capital. The author, Thomas Deloney, was a silk weaver from Norwich by trade, and drew his inspiration from the ordinary people he knew.

So here are Simon's wife of Southampton, Sutton's wife of Salisbury, Grey's wife of Gloucester and Fitzallen's wife of Worcester out on the town:

'Now when they were brought into Cheapside, there with great wonder they beheld the shops of the Goldsmiths; and on the other side, the wealthy Mercers, whose shops shined with all sorts of coloured silks: in Watling Street they viewed the great number of drapers: in Saint Martin's shoemakers: at Saint Nicholas church, the flesh shambles: at the end of the old Change, the fishmongers: in Candleweeke Street the

Book and Picture Shop by Salomon de Bray, 1628

weavers: then came into the Jews' Street, where all the Jews did inhabit: then came they into Blackwell Hall, where the country Clothiers did use to meet.

'Afterwards they proceeded, and came to St Paul's church, whose steeple was so high, that it seemed to pierce the clouds, and the top whereof, was a great and mighty weathercock, of clean silver, the which notwithstanding seemed as small as a sparrow to men's eyes, it stood so exceeding high, the which goodly weathercock was afterwards stolen away, by a cunning cripple, who found means one night to climb up to the top of the steeple, and took it down: with the which, and a great sum of money which he had got together by begging in his lifetime, he builded a gate on the Northside of the City, which to this day is called Cripplegate.

'From thence they went to the Tower of London, which was builded by Julius Caesar, who was Emperor of Rome. And there they beheld salt and wine, which had lain there ever since the Romans invaded this land, which was many years before our Saviour Christ was born, the wine was grown so thick, that it might have been cut like a jelly. And in that place also they saw the money that was made of leather, which in ancient time went current amongst the people.'

From *Thomas of Reading (or The Six Worthy Yeomen of the West)*, Thomas Deloney

St Urban's Day

In May get a weed hook, a crotch and a glove
And weed out such weeds, as the corn doth not love.

The May-weed doth burn, and the thistle doth fret;
The fitches pull downward both rye and the wheat:
The brake and cockel, be noisome too much;
Yet like unto boodle, no weed there is such.

From *Five Hundred Good Points of Husbandry*, Thomas Tusser

Churching

A month after Shakespeare's baptism, his mother Mary Arden would have been 'churched', at Holy Trinity.

This was the ceremony which allowed women back into church after they had given birth, and had undergone a period in which they were regarded as unclean. Mothers were thus never able to attend the baptism of their own children. The gossips, or godparents, stood in their place. The ritual was accompanied by a feast to mark the occasion.

In *Thomas of Reading*, Deloney describes one such churching feast, and the gossip of the women as they come together to celebrate the event:

'Sutton's wife of Salisbury, which had lately been delivered of a son, against her going to Church, prepared great cheer; at what time Simon's wife of Southampton came thither, and so at this churching did divers other Clothiers' wives, only to make merry at the Churching Feast: and whilst these dames sat at the Table, Crab, Weasel and Wren, waited on the board, and as the old proverb speaketh, "Many women: many words", so fell it out at that time: for there was such prattling that it passed: some talked of their husbands' frowardness, some showed their maids' sluttishness, othersome deciphered the costliness of their garments, some told many tales of their neighbours: and to be brief, there was none of them but would have talked for the whole day.'

Put on thy holy filletings, and so
To the temple with the sober midwife go,
Attending thus, in a most solemn wise,
By those who serve the childbed mysteries.
Burn first the incense; next, whenas thou seest
The candid stole thrown o'er the pious priest,
With reverend curtsies come, and to him bring
Thy fee (and not decurted) offering.
All rites well ended, with fair auspice come
(As to the breaking of a bride-cake) home
Where ceremonious Hymen shall for thee
Provide a second epithalamy.

Julia's Churching, Robert Herrick

St Urban is invoked against storms and lightning.

Shakespeare's First Child Baptized

Mark how one string, sweet husband to another,
Strikes each in each by mutual ordering;
Resembling sire and child and happy mother,
Who, all in one, one pleasing note do sing.
Sonnet VIII

On this day in 1583, Shakespeare's first child, Susanna, was baptized, just six months after the wedding of her parents. There has been much speculation as to whether this implies that William was forced to marry Anne (eight years his senior) because he had got her pregnant. But it is equally possible that, once the couple were betrothed, they couldn't wait until the wedding day in November, and conceived their first daughter in some glorious moonlit midsummer meadow, the previous July.

Just before her twenty-third birthday, Susanna was fined for failing to receive communion on Easter Day in 1606. It was dangerous to be named as a recusant Catholic six months after the Gunpowder Plot, in which Catholic fundamentalist terrorists had attempted to annihilate the King and his Parliament. But if Susanna's recusancy marks her out as a follower of the Old Faith, then she was not alone in Stratford. William Clopton, who had died in 1592, lies next to his wife Anne in the north aisle of the nave of Holy Trinity, in alabaster effigy, and he was a Catholic recusant.

Alderman Thomas Barber was the host of the Bear Inn at the bottom of Bridge Street for more than half a century. Known as Barber of the Bear, he was made Bailiff of this ultra-Protestant borough of Stratford three times. But even he was suspected of recusancy because both his first and his second wives were Roman Catholics.

Bridge Street used to have a row of houses running down the centre called Middle Row, and here, in the Shambles, another Alderman, Rafe Cawdrey, the butcher, was a Catholic. His wife and daughters were recusants and his son was a fugitive Jesuit priest. And the woollen draper in Henley Street, George Whateley, paid secret annuities to his two brothers, who were also fugitive Catholic priests. His fellow woollen-draper, George Badger, was also 'obstinate on the Catholic side', as was the tailor in Wood Street, William Hiccocks.

The wealthy Thomas Reynolds, father of Shakespeare's friend William Reynolds (to whom he left a gold memorial ring in his will), had the largest household in Stratford – 22 people, including servants. He and his wife were stout Roman Catholics and paid their monthly fines for recusancy. One day in 1604 a Jesuit priest ran for his life along Chapel Street disguised in green round hose and high-heeled shoes. He fell in the mud, threatened to overthrow a boy in his path and finally found refuge in Reynolds' house near the church.

It is perhaps significant that a year after Susanna Shakespeare was named as a recusant, she married a well-respected Puritan, Dr John Hall.

Just eight months later she gave birth to Shakespeare's first grandchild, Elizabeth. So, like her mother, Susanna conceived her first child before her wedding day too.

Stratford-under-Avon

Therefore the winds, piping to us in vain
As in revenge, have sucked up from the sea
Contagious fogs, which falling in the land,
Hath every pelting river made so proud
That they have overborne their continents.
A Midsummer Night's Dream (Act 2 Scene 1)

In 1932, a month after the new Shakespeare
Memorial Theatre opened in Stratford, a huge flood
occurred. Here is the graphic account from the
Stratford Herald, on this day, Friday May 27th in 1932:

'From late on Sunday to the afternoon of Monday
Stratford-upon-Avon became Stratford-under-Avon.
    'The river rose 13ft., exceeding by two inches the

Stratford's New Shakespeare Memorial Theatre in 1932

height of the Avon in the great flood of 1801, but
falling five inches short of the high watermark
reached during the famous "century" flood which
occurred on December 31st 1900 – January 1st 1901
and which is still vividly remembered by many
Stratford people.

'Local people saw the rare spectacle of the Avon
carrying away the carcasses of a horse, some cows
and some sheep. Scores of houses, shops, hotels and
other premises were invaded by the irresistible
torrent.

'The new Shakespeare Memorial Theatre was
surrounded by water and for some time was
inaccessible except by boat. The safety of the building
was the thought uppermost in many minds.
Fortunately it stood the test and escaped with only a
leakage into the bay of one of the rolling stages.

'The most spectacular result of the spate of water,
and one that grimly indicated its overwhelming force,
was the sweeping away of Mr C. M. Collins' 70ft
boathouse off its foundation. The massive structure
crashed into Clopton bridge where it has since
remained, wedged under the iron footbridge.

'If this was the most spectacular, the adventure of a
Luddington man and his wife was certainly the most
thrilling event of Stratford's great flood. For four
hours they were marooned in trees above the swirling
torrent, and were rescued only through the heroic
efforts carried on partly after nightfall.'

❄

You can still see the mark of the height of the flood
on the wall of one of the houses on Waterside. It also
shows the high watermarks of other floods,
including the 1900/1901 deluge referred to above. On
April 10th, 1998, another high flood cut off the
theatre. Ironically the productions playing at that
time were *The Merchant of Venice* and *The Tempest.*

Angels
• • • • • • • •

Angels and ministers of grace defend us!
Hamlet (Act 1 Scene 4)

On this day in 1583, Dr John Dee, the great Elizabethan philosopher-magician, was visited by angels.

He and his skryer, Edward Kelly (E.K.) had been summoning up archangels by the use of a crystal globe at his house in Mortlake. Many had appeared, including Uriel and Gabriel himself. Dee recorded the visitations in his extraordinary diary. On this day he wrote of the appearance in his room of a strange little girl:

'Tuesday... As I and E.K. sat discoursing, suddenly there seemed to come out of my oratory a spiritual creature, like a pretty girl of seven or nine years of age, attired on her head with her hair rolled up before and hanging down very long behind, with a gown of changeable green and red, and with a train.

'She seemed to play up and down, child-like, and seemed to go in and out behind my books, lying on heaps: and as she should ever go between them, the books seemed to give place sufficiently, distinguishing one heap from the other as she passed between them. And so I considered a while the divers reports E.K. made unto me of this pretty maiden, and I said: "Whose maiden are you?"

She: Whose man are you?
Dee: I am the servant of God, both by my bound duty, and also (I hope) by his adoption.
Voice: You shall be beaten if you tell
She: Am I not a fine maiden? Give me leave to play in your house, my mother told me she would come and dwell here.
She went up and down with most lively gesture of a young girl, playing by herself, and divers times another did speak to her from the corner of my study by a great perspective glass, but none was seen beside herself.

Dee: Tell me who you are?
She: I am a poor little maiden, Madimi. I am the last but one of my mother's children. I have a little baby-child at home.
Dee: Where is your home?
Madimi: I dare not tell you where I dwell, I shall be beaten.

The diary accounts of these angelic visitations are astonishing to read. Dee's skryer, Kelly, who describes everything he sees to his master, must have been a very brilliant manipulator indeed. Dee, a highly regarded philosopher and astrologer, was no fool. He was frequently consulted by Queen Elizabeth and many others.

Dee is thought to have been one of the inspirations for Prospero in *The Tempest*.

An English Empress of Muscovy

The barbarous Scythian,
Or he that makes his generation messes
To gorge his appetite.
King Lear (Act 1 Scene 1)

Ivan the Terrible of Russia wanted to marry Queen Elizabeth. He was, according to Jerome Horsey (who spent some time in Russia in Elizabeth's reign), 'a right Scythian, full of ready wisdom, cruel, bloody, merciless'.

Horsey wrote that the Tsar consulted an English magician, **'to know his likelihood of success if he should be a suitor for the hand of the Queen. And though he was much disheartened, not only that he had two wives living and that many kings, and great princes had been suitors to her majesty and could not prevail, yet he magnified himself his person, his wisdom, greatness, riches above all other princes and said he would have a try, and presently put his last wife into a nunnery.'**

Elizabeth declined his generous offer of marriage, but suggested, diplomatically, that he might like to consider one of her ladies in waiting. She proposed that he present his suit to one Lady Mary Hastings instead. Finally, after several further attempts to put the Russians off altogether, an embassy from Moscow arrived in London to see Lady Mary and carry news of her beauty back to the Tsar.

Elizabeth tried once again to hedge, by suggesting that, before Ivan's ambassador could see her, Lady Mary needed time to recover from an illness which had left her face somewhat pock-marked. However, the interview finally took place in the garden of York House. Ivan's ambassador, Pissemski, trusted with the job of wooing Lady Mary by proxy, was according to Horsey, a **'noble, grave, wise and trusty gentleman'.** When he saw her Ladyship and her ladies, he fell prostrate at her feet and then,

'rose, and ran back from her, his face still towards her; she and the rest admiring at his manner. Said, by an interpreter, it did suffice him to behold the angel he hoped should be his master's spouse; and commended her angelical countenance, state and admirable beauty.'
Lady Mary Hastings was known ever afterwards to her close friends in court as *the Empress of Muscovy.*

It may be that this famous encounter was in Shakespeare's mind when he was writing the scene in *Love's Labour's Lost* where the King of Navarre, Berowne and their friends dress as Russians to woo the Princess of France and her ladies.

Princess: *But what, but what; come they to visit us?*
Boyet: *They do, they do; and are apparell'd thus,*
Like Muscovites, or Russians as I guess.
Love's Labour's Lost (Act 5 Scene 2)

Marlowe Murdered

A great reckoning in a little room.

As You Like It (Act 3 Scene 3)

On this day in 1593, Christopher Marlowe was murdered in Deptford.

On May 11th, the Privy Council had ordered the arrest of those responsible for the appearance of some libellous tracts, posted around town. The following day Thomas Kyd (author of *The Spanish Tragedy*) was arrested and his lodgings were searched. Some heretical tracts were found, which, Kyd confessed under torture, belonged to his former room-mate, Christopher Marlowe, thus implicating his friend as a heretic and atheist. Within the week, Marlowe's arrest was ordered. He was caught at the house of Thomas Walsingham, cousin of Sir Francis Walsingham, Elizabeth's spy-master. On May 20th, Marlowe appeared before the Council and was accused of heresy. He was told to attend their presence daily. A week later, an informer named Robert Baines delivered a report on Marlowe to the Privy Council, accusing him of certain libels, of promoting atheism and making various heretical statements, such as claiming that the world was older than 6,000 years and that Jesus and his disciple, John, were lovers. The report ended with the recommendation that Marlowe's 'mouth should be stopped'.

Three days later, on May 30th, Marlowe was stabbed above the right eye by Ingram Frizer in

A 1585 portrait discovered in Corpus Christi College, Cambridge, in 1953 and believed to be of the 21-year-old Christopher Marlowe

Eleanor Bull's lodging house in Deptford, a London suburb. He died immediately. Robert Poley and Nick Skeres, the two 'witnesses' to the crime, were both veteran spies and provocateurs. They claimed it was the result of a fight over the tavern bill. However, Marlowe had been a sometime spy for the crown, and he may have been murdered as a result of his clandestine activities.

Thomas Kyd was a broken man. He never wrote again and died the following year.

In tribute to the subversive spirit and anarchic wit of Christopher Marlowe, here is one of my favourite extracts from his work. It is an example of what Ben Jonson called Marlowe's 'mighty line', as Tamburlaine the Great promises, with his weapons of mass destruction, to 'persist a terror to the world':

I will with engines never exercised,
Conquer, sack and utterly consume
Your cities and your golden palaces,
And with the flames that beat against the clouds
Incense the heavens and make the stars to melt,
As if they were the tears of Mahomet
For hot consumption of their country's pride;
And till by vision or by speech I hear
Immortal Jove say 'Cease my Tamburlaine',
I will persist a terror to the world.

Tamburlaine the Great, Part Two (Act 4 Scene 1)

Hero and Leander
• • • • • • • • • • • • • • • • • • • •

This extract, from Marlowe's epic poem *Hero and Leander*, shows the poet in lighter vein, as the god Neptune delights in the beauty of Leander's body while he tries to swim the Hellespont to meet his love Hero:

With that he stripped him to the ivory skin
And crying, 'Love I come', leapt lively in.
Whereat the sapphire visaged god grew proud,
And made his capering triton sound aloud,
Imagining that Ganymede, displeased,
Had left the heavens; therefore on him seized.
Leander strived, the waves about him wound,
And pulled him to the bottom, where the ground
Was strewed with pearl and in low coral groves
Sweet singing mermaids sported with their loves...
The lusty god embraced him, called him love,
And swore he never should return to Jove.
But when he knew it was not Ganymede,
For under water he was almost dead,
He heaved him up, and looking on his face,

Beat down the bold waves with his triple mace...
Leander being up, began to swim,
And looking back saw Neptune follow him;
Whereat aghast the poor soul 'gan to cry,
'O let me visit Hero ere I die.'
The god put Helle's bracelet on his arm
And swore the sea should never do him harm.
He clapped his plump cheeks, with his tresses played,
And wantonly, his love bewrayed.
He watched his arms, and as they opened wide,
At every stroke, betwixt them he would slide,
And steal a kiss, and turn about and dance,
And as he turned, cast many a lustful glance,
And threw him gaudy toys to please his eye,
And dive into the water, and there pry
Upon his breast, his thighs, and every limb,
And up again, and close behind him swim,
And talk of love. Leander made reply
'You are deceived, I am no woman, I.'
Thereat smiled Neptune...

He was but as the cuckoo is in June,
Heard, not regarded.

Henry IV Part One (Act 3 Scene 2)

The breeze upon her, like a cow in June.

Antony and Cleopatra (Act 3 Scene 10)

Here's flowers for you;
Hot lavender, mints, savoury, marjoram;
The marigold, that goes to bed wi' the sun
And with him rises weeping: these are flowers
Of middle summer, and I think they are given
To men of middle age.

The Winter's Tale (Act 4 Scene 4)

'It is now June and the hay makers are mustered to
make an army for the field, where not always in
order, they march under the bag and the bottle,
when bewixt the fork and the rake there is seen
great force of arms: Now doth the broad oak
comfort the weary labourer, while under his shady
bows he sits singing to his bread and cheese: the
haycock is the poor man's lodging, and the fresh
river is his gracious neighbour: Now the falcon and
the tassell try their wings at the partridge, and the
fat buck fills the empty pasty: the trees are all in
their rich array: but the seely sheep is turned out of

his coat: the Roses and sweet herbs put the distiller
to his cunning, while the green apples on the tree
are ready for the great bellied wines: Now begins
the Hare to gather up her heels and the fox begins
to look about him, for fear of the Hound: the Hook
and the sickle are making ready for harvest: the
Meadow grounds gape for the rain, and the corn in
the ear begins to harden: the little lads make pipes
of the straw, and they that cannot dance will still be
hopping: the Air now groweth somewhat warm,
and the cool winds are very comfortable: the Sailor
now makes merry passage, and the nimble Footman runs with pleasure: In brief, I thus conclude, I
hold it a sweet season, the senses perfume, and the
spirits comfort. Farewell.'

Fantasticks, Nicholas Breton

'June in a mantle of dark grass green; upon his head a
garland of bents, king-cups and maiden's hair; in his
left hand an angle, with a box of cantharides, in his
right the sign of cancer; upon his arm a basket of
fruits of the season.'

Emblems, Henry Peacham

Sheep Shearing

'Sheep are shorn once a year, in the haymonth, and the heaviest rams weigh from forty to sixty pounds, yielding however only four to six pounds of wool. The best rams fetch five to ten franks a head. A pelt or the wool about one frank.'

Journal, Thomas Platter, 1599

Wash sheep (for the better) where water doth run,
And let him go cleanly, and dry in the sun:
Then shear him and spare not, at two days an end,
The sooner the better, his corps will amend.

Reward not thy sheep (when ye take his great coat),
With twitches and patches as broad as a groat;
Let not such ungentleness happen to thine,
Lest fly with her gentils*, do make it to pine.

June's Husbandry, Thomas Tusser

*Gentils are maggots

At shearing of sheep, which they do keep,
Good lord! What sport is than.
What great good cheer,
What ale and beer,
Is set to every man.
With beef and with bacon,
In wooden brown platters, good store,
They fall to their meat, and merrily eat:
They call for no sauce therefore.

16th Century Ballad

In *The Winter's Tale*, the young shepherd charged with buying spices for his sister, gives a lively account of the sheep-shearing feast to come:

Let me see: Every 'leven wether tods; every tod yields pound and odd shillings: fifteen hundred shorn – what comes the wool to? I cannot do it without compters. Let me see... what am I to buy for our sheep-shearing feast? 'Three pound of sugar; five pound of currants; rice' – what will this sister of mine do with rice? But my father hath made her mistress of the feast, and she lays it on. She hath made me four-and-twenty nosegays for the shearers, three-man song-men all, and very good ones; but they are most of them means and bases; but one puritan amongst them and he sings psalms to hornpipes. I must have saffron to colour the warden pies; mace – dates, – none; that's out of my note; nutmegs seven; a race or two of ginger, – but that I may beg; – four pounds of prunes, and as many raisins o' the sun.

(Act 4 Scene 2)

First American Shakespeare

Thrice happy the nation that Shakespeare has charmed,
More happy the bosoms his genius has warmed;
Ye children of nature, of fashion and whim,
He painted you all, all join to praise him.

Ode to Shakespeare, David Garrick

On this day, in 1752, a company of English actors arrived at Yorktown, Virginia, on board the *Charming Sally*. Led by Lewis Hallam, they gave the first professional performance of a Shakespeare play in the United States of America.

They should have presented their work first in New York, but the man they sent ahead with the cash to make the arrangements absconded with the money, having first financed his own amateur performances as Othello and Richard III, at a make-shift theatre in Nassau Street.

Nevertheless, Hallam, his wife and a company of ten other adults and three children opened their season in Williamsburg with *The Merchant of Venice* on September 15th ; and continued to present their repertoire of two dozen plays for another eleven months. There were six or eight Shakespeares, including the Colley Cibber adaptation of *Richard III* (with the snappy line, 'Off with his head! So much for Buckingham', which even Olivier retained in the film) and the Garrick version of *Romeo and Juliet* (where Juliet wakes up before Romeo dies and they play a scene together). There were standards by Farquhar, Congreve and Gay, as well as stirring stuff like Joseph Addison's *Cato*, Rowe's *The Fair Penitent*, and Nathaniel Lee's *Theodosius*.

Lewis Hallam's company did tour to New York eventually, and indeed built a theatre there, before continuing on to Philadelphia and Charleston, South Carolina, and then leaving for the West Indies, in 1755. Hallam died in Jamaica the following year.

Who were these English actors? Certainly not the cream of British acting talent. Lewis' brother, William, had run the New Wells Theatre in Leman Street (near the present Wilton's Music Hall), but it seems had been forced out of business. Hallam has a distinct air of Vincent Crummles, the 'provincial celebrity' in Dickens' *Nicholas Nickleby*, who finally leaves with his little company for America.

'The talented Vincent Crummles, long favourably known to fame as a country manager and actor of no ordinary pretension, is about to cross the Atlantic on a histrionic expedition,' reads the paragraph Crummles himself has placed 'among the varieties' in the paper. 'Crummles is certain to succeed.' And, to some extent, Lewis Hallam did too.

Lion Baiting at the Tower of London
·······································

On this day in 1605, King James and his family went to the Tower of London, to see the lions.

'This afternoon his majesty, being accompanied with divers noblemen and many knights came to the Lions' Tower. Then Mr Ralph Gill, keeper of the lions, was commanded that his servants should put forth into the walk the male and female breeder, but the lions would not go out until they were forced out with burning links, when they stood looking with amazement. Then there were two racks of mutton thrown down to them, which they straightway ate. Then a lusty cock was cast down, which they killed and sucked his blood; and then another live cock which they likewise killed, but sucked not.

'After that the king caused a live lamb to be easily let down by a rope, but the lions stood in their place and only beheld the lamb. But the lamb rose up and went towards the lions, who very gently looked upon him and smelled on him without sign of any further hurt. Then the lamb was softly drawn up again in as good plight as he was set down.

'Then they caused these lions to be put into their den, and another lion to be brought forth and two lusty mastiffs at a by-door to be let unto him.

These flew upon him, and perceiving the lion's neck to be defended by hair they sought only to bite him by the face. Then was a third dog let in, as fierce as either let in, a branded dog, that took the lion by the face and turned him upon his back; but the lion spoiled them all.'

On another occasion, on the June 23rd, 1609, the royal family watched a bear which had killed a child, a horse and six strong mastiffs.

'Then were divers other lions put into that place, one after another; but they showed no more sport nor valour than the first, and every of them, so soon as they espied the trap doors open, ran hastily into their dens. Lastly, there were put forth together the two young lusty lions which were bred in that yard, and were now grown great. These at first began to march proudly towards the bear, which the bear perceiving came hastily out of a corner to meet them; but both lion and lioness skipped up and down, and fearfully fled from the bear; and so these, like the former lions, not willing to endure any fight, sought the next way into their den.'

Tower of London Records

It is reported that Prince Henry became angry with his father for throwing beagles to the lions.

Thomas Nashe and the Bonfire of Books

And art made tongue-tied by authority.
Sonnet LXVI

On this day in 1599, at Stationers' Hall, a huge bonfire of books was set alight.

Stationers' Hall was the official record office where published works and approved plays had to be registered. The list of banned books was compiled and issued by John Whitgift, Archbishop of Canterbury, and Richard Bancroft, the Bishop of London. Their clampdown included any unlicensed plays and histories, Christopher Marlowe's translations of Ovid's erotic *Elegies*, and satires by both Thomas Middleton and John Marston. But the severest penalty landed on Thomas Nashe, who saw the destruction of his entire output. All his pamphlets and books were to 'be taken wheresoever they may be found' and destroyed. None of his works 'shall ever be printed hereafter'.

Nashe's career was over, and he was dead within two years. Here is an epitaph to him:

Let all his faults sleep with his mournful chest,
And there for ever with his ashes rest.
His style was witty, though it had some gall,
Some things he might have mended, so may all.
Yet this I say, that for a mother wit,
Few men have ever seen the like of it.
The Three Parnassus Plays, Anonymous

Nashe was described as 'a fellow ... whose muse was armed with a gag-tooth and his pen possessed with Hercules' furies'.

His satire could be devastatingly vicious, but hilariously funny too. Here is his account of a Merchant's wife:

'**In another corner, Mistress Minx, a Merchant's wife, that will eat no cherries, forsooth, but when they are at twenty shillings to the pound, that looks as simperingly as if she were besmeared, and jets it as gingerly as if she were dancing the canaries. She is so finical in her speech, as though she spoke nothing but what she had first sewed over before in her samplers, and the puling accent of her voice is like a feigned treble, or one's voice that interprets to the puppets.'**
Pierce Penniless

Then again Nashe could also write sublimely, of poetry for example:

'**Poetry is the honey of all flowers, the quintessence of all sciences, the marrow of wit, and the very phrase of angels.'**

A June Wedding

Honour, riches, marriage blessing,
Long continuance, and increasing,
Hourly joys be still upon you,
Juno sings her blessings on you.
The Tempest (Act 4 Scene 1)

On this day in 1607, Susanna, Shakespeare's elder daughter, married Dr John Hall in Holy Trinity Church in Stratford-upon-Avon. She was the first of Anne and William's two girls to get married.

The Two Noble Kinsmen, written with John Fletcher, opens with the wedding of Duke Theseus and Hippolyta. A stage direction reads:
Enter Hymen with a Torch burning: a Boy in a white Robe before, singing and strewing Flowers: After Hymen, a Nymph, encompassed in her Tresses, bearing a wheaten Garland. Then Theseus between two other Nymphs with wheaten Chaplets on their heads. Then Hippolyta the Bride, led by Pirithous, and another holding a Garland over her head (her Tresses likewise hanging). After her Emilia holding up her Train.

(Act 1 Scene 1)

The Song: (Music)
Roses their sharp spines being gone,
Not royal in their smells alone,
But in their hew.
Maiden Pinks, of odour faint,
Dasies smell-less, yet most quaint
And sweet Thyme true.

Primrose first born child of Ver,
Merry Spring time's Harbinger,
With hare bells dim.
Oxlips, in their Cradles growing,
Marigolds, on death beds blowing,
Lark's-heels trim. (Strew Flowers.)
All dear nature's children sweet,
Lie fore Bride and Bridegroom's feet,
Blessing their sense.
Not an angel of the air,
Bird melodious, or bird fair,
Is absent hence.

The Crow, the slandrous Cuckoo, nor
The boding Raven, nor Chough hoar
Nor chattering Pie,
May on our Bridehouse perch or sing,
Or with them any discord bring,
But from it fly.

A Visit to Cape Town

Wouter Schouten's drawing of Table Bay in 1658

What have we here ? A man or a fish?
The Tempest (Act 2 Scene 2)

Roe was taken to visit Robben Island, then known as Penguin Island, and noted its peculiar flightless inhabitants in his journal:
'**On Penguin there is a fowl so called that goes upright, his wings without feathers hanging down like sleeves, faced with white; they fly not, but walk in paths and keep their divisions and quarters orderly; they are a strange fowl, or rather a miscellaneous creature of beast, bird and fish, but most of bird, confuting that definition of a man to be animall bipes implumae ("that unfeathered two legged thing") which is nearer to a description of this creature.**'
Journal, Sir Thomas Roe, 1615

In 1615, Sir Thomas Roe travelled to India to become Britain's first ambassador to the Moghul court. He sailed around Africa on the *Red Dragon* with Captain William Keeling, the Shakespeare fan (see September 5th). On the morning of this day, before rounding the Cape of Good Hope, the fleet anchored in Table Bay, or Soldania Bay as it was then called.

On shore, on the site of present-day Cape Town, they were greeted by a group of Khoi San herdsmen. The headman spoke English. His name was Corey, and he had previously been kidnapped by English merchants and taken to London, in order to learn the language and act as an interpreter.

The English traveller Thomas Herbert depicts herdsmen bartering for sheep with copper in Table Bay, 1627

Execution of Dr Lopez

I am a Jew. Hath not a Jew eyes? Hath not a Jew hands,
organs, dimensions, senses, affections, passions?
The Merchant of Venice (Act 3 Scene 1)

On this day in 1594, Dr Lopez, the Jewish physician
to Queen Elizabeth, was executed for treason:
'For the poisoning of Her Highness, this miscreant,
perjured, murdering traitor and Jewish doctor hath
been provided a dearer traitor than Judas himself.
This plot and practise, more
wicked, dangerous and
detestable than all the former.

'He was her majesty's servant
sworn, graced and advanced with
many seemly and great favours
and rewards, used in special
place of credit, and trust,
permitted to have often access to
Her Highness' person, and so not
feared nor suspected, specially by
her majesty, whose gracious
nature and princely magnanimity
is such as her heart was never
touched with fear of her most
potent and capital enemies, much
less with suspicion or doubt of
any of her own servants.'
Prosecution of Lopez in the Queen's Bench Trial

According to Henslowe's diary, Marlowe's play The
Jew of Malta was revived four times that June, and
twice in July. Perhaps they were cashing in on the
surge of anti-semitism caused by the trial of Lopez.
Thomas Nashe is probably guilty of the same trend to
exploit the undercurrent of anti-semitism which
pervaded Elizabethan society. Witness the relish with
which he describes the torture of the Jew, Zadoch, in
this particularly nasty chapter from The Unfortunate
Traveller published in 1594, the same year as Dr Lopez

was put to death.
'To the execution place he was brought, where first
and foremost he was stripped: then on a sharp iron
stake fastened in the ground he had his fundament
pitched, which stake ran up along into the body like a
spit. A great bonfire they made round about him,
wherewith his flesh was roasted not burned; and ever
as with the heat his skin blistered, the fire was drawn
aside and they basted him with a mixture of aqua
fortis, alum water, and mercury
sublimatum, which smarted to
the very soul of him and
searched him to his marrow.
Then did they scourge his back
parts so blistered and blasted
with burning whips of red-hot
wires. His head they nointed
over with pitch and tar and so
inflamed it. To his privy
members they tied streaming
fireworks. The skin from the
crest of the shoulder, as also
from his elbows, his huckle
bones, his knees, his ankles,
they plucked and gnawed off
with sparkling pincers. His
breast and his belly with seal
skins they grated over, which as fast as they grated
and rawed, one stood over and laved with smith's
cindery water and aqua vitae. His nails they half
raised up, and then underpropped them with sharp
pricks, like a tailor's shop window half-open on a
holiday. Every one of his fingers they rent up to the
wrist; his toes they brake off by the roots, and let them
still hang by a little skin. In conclusion, they had a
small oil fire, such as men blow light bubbles of glass
with, and beginning at his feet, they let him
lingeringly burn up limb by limb, till his heart was
consumed, and then he died.'

Tourist Sights in London

Let us satisfy our eyes
With the memorials and the things of fame
That do renown this city.
Twelfth Night (Act 3 Scene 3)

Henry Peacham mentions, in the following poem, some of the tourist attractions on display in London and elsewhere in the early 1600s:

Why do the rude vulgar so hastily post in a madness
To gaze at trifles, and toys not worthy the viewing?
And think them happy when may be showed for a penny
The Fleet street mandrakes, that heavenly motion of Eltham,
Westminster monuments, and Guildhall huge Corinaeus,
That horn of Windsor (of a unicorn likely),
The cave of Merlin, the skirts of old Tom a Lincoln,
King John's sword at Linne, with the cup the fraternity
   drink in,
The tomb of Beauchamp and the sword of Sir Guy a Warwick;
The great long dutchman, and roaring Margret of Barwick,
The mummied Princes, and Caesar's wine yet in Dover,
Saint James his ginney hens, the cassaway moreover,
The beaver in the park (strange beast as any man saw)
Down shearing willows with teeth as sharp as a hand-saw.
The lance of John of Gaunt, and Brandon's still in the Tower;
The fall of Nineveh, which Norwich built in an hour.
King Henry's slip shoes, the sword of valiant Edward,
The Coventry boar's shield, and fireworks seen but to
bedward.
Drake's ship at Deptford, King Richard's bed stead
   in Leicester,
The Whitehall whale bones, the silver basin in Chester
The line-caught dog-fish, the wolf and Harry the Lion,
Hunks of the Bear Garden to be feared, if he be nigh on.
All these are nothing, were a thousand more to be scanned,
Coryate, unto thy shoes so artificially tanned:
That through thick and thin made thee so famous a trotter.
Henry Peacham's Prefix to Thomas Coryate's Crudities, 1611

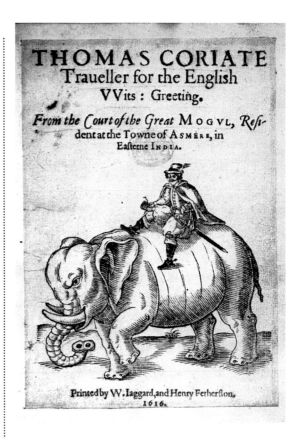

THOMAS CORIATE
Traueller for the English
VVits : Greeting.

From the *Court of the Great* MOGVL, *Resi-*
dent at the Towne of ASMERE, in
Easterne INDIA.

Printed by W. Iaggard, and Henry Fetherston.
1616.

The long-striding 'trotter' Thomas Coryate had written an account of his walk across the Continent (see June 21st), and hung up his worn shoes in Odcombe church.

In 1610 the Prince of Württemberg visited at least one of the tourist attractions mentioned above, the Perpetual Motion at Eltham:
'His excellency went to Eltham Park to see the perpetual motion; the inventor's name was Cornelius Trebel, a native of Alkamaar, a very fair and handsome man, and of very gentle manners, altogether different from such-like characters; we also saw three virginals which played of themselves.'

The King's Men Visit Stratford

On this day in 1622, Shakespeare's old company visited Stratford, and were paid not to perform:
'Six years after he died, and in the year before John Hemmings and Henry Condell edited the First Folio, the King's Men, Shakespeare's old colleagues, were on tour in the Midlands: Leicester 8th June; Coventry 9th June. They came over to Stratford, probably to see the tomb maker of Southwark's coloured bust in Holy Trinity. The council hastily forbade them to perform, but remembered at the same time that these were the King's Players, with special licence "freely to exercise the art and faculty of playing comedies, tragedies, histories, Enterludes, Moralls, pastorelles, stage-plays... and such other like". Some compensation was advisable. Hence the serio-comic note in the accounts of the borough chamberlain of Stratford. It reads with obstinate simplicity: "To the King's players for not playing in the hall. 6s." No more; and nothing more importantly theatrical occurred in Stratford for over 120 years.'
Shakespeare's Country, J.C. Trewin

The Stratford Town Council was controlled by a strict Puritan majority. When Shakespeare was a boy, however, we know that acting companies, including the Queen's Men, toured to Stratford, and performed there. Here, Thomas Nashe describes a performance by that company, in a country town, and mocks the pomposity of a local Justice of the Peace:
'Amongst other choleric wise justices, there was one, that having a play presented before him and his township by Tarleton and the rest of his fellows, Her Majesty's servants, and they were now entering into their first merriment, as they call it, the people began exceedingly to laugh when Tarleton first peeped out his head. Whereat the justice, not a little moved, and seeing with his becks and nods he could not make them cease, he went with his staff and beat them round about unmercifully on the bare pates, in that

they being but farmers and poor country hinds, would presume to laugh at the Queen's Men, and make no more account of her cloth in his presence.'
Pierce Penniless, Thomas Nashe

Summer flies
As summer flies are in the shambles
that quicken even with blowing
Othello (Act 4 Scene 2)

These summer flies have blown me full of maggot ostentation.
Love's Labour's Lost (Act 5 Scene 2)

The Emperor of Russia Crowned

On this day in 1584, 'the solemn and magnificent coronation of Pheodor Ivanowich, Emperor of Russia, was observed by Master Jerome Horsey, gentleman':

'In the morning the dead emperor (Ivan the Terrible) was laid in the church of Michael the Archangel into a hewn sepulchre, very richly decked with vestures fit for such a purpose. The time of mourning after being expired, the day of solemnizing of this coronation was come being upon the 10th day of June; and that day being Sunday, him being of the age of 25 years: at which time master Jerome Horsey was orderly sent for, and placed in a fit room to see all the solemnity.

'In the midst thereof was a chair of majesty placed,

The Murder of the Tsarevich in 1591

his robes then changed, and most rich and invaluable garments put on him: being placed in this Princely seat, his nobility standing round about him in their degrees, his imperial crown was set upon his head by the metropolitan, his sceptre globe in his right hand, his sword of justice in his left of great richness: his six crowns also by which he holdeth his kingdoms were set before him, and the Lord Boris was placed at his right hand.

'Thus at last the Emperor came to the great church door, and the people cried, "God Save the Emperor Pheodor Ivanowich of all Russia."

'There was a bridge made of 150 fathoms in length three manner of ways, three foot above the ground and two fathom broad, for him to go from one church to the other, from the press of the people which were in number infinite, and some at that time were pressed to death with the throng. As the Emperor returned out of the churches, they were spread under foot with cloth of gold, the porches of the churches with red velvet, the bridges with scarlet, and stammel cloth from one church to another: and as soon as the Emperor was passed by, the cloth of gold, velvet and scarlet was cut and taken of those that could come by it, every man desirous to have a piece, to reserve as a monument.

'The Lord Boris was sumptuously dressed and richly attired, with his garments decked with great orient pearls, beset with all sorts of precious stones. He was made chief counsellor of the Emperor, and had charge of his person.

'And so the Emperor accompanied with all his princes and nobles, at the least 50 thousand horse, departed through the city to his palace. This royal coronation would ask much time and many leaves of paper to be described particularly as it was performed: it shall suffice to understand that the like magnificence was never seen in Russia.'

Jerome Horsey in Hakluyt's Voyages, Vol, 1

St Barnabas' Day: 'Barnaby Garlands'

Barnaby bright, Barnaby bright
Light all day and light all night.
Traditional Rhyme

Saskia as Flora by Rembrandt Van Rijn, 1634

St Barnabas' Day coincided with the Summer
Solstice, in the days before the Gregorian
reformation of the Julian calendar, as it fell 11 days
later.

So-called 'Barnaby Garlands' of roses, pink ragged
robin, yellow star thistle, and sweet woodruff were
brought in to houses and churches on this day to
decorate both the church itself and the clergymen,
who would wear chaplets of roses while officiating.

John Gerard describes these garlands:

'The flowers of woodruff are of a white colour and a
very sweet smell: as is the rest of the herb, which
being made up into garlands and hanged up in the
houses in the heat of Summer, doth very well
attemper the air, cool and make fresh the place, to the
delight and comfort of such as are therein.'
Gerard's Herbal

When Saint Barnaby bright smiles night and day
Poor ragged robin blossom in the hay.
Traditional Rhyme

The ragged robin is dedicated to St Barnabas:
because it is said to bloom on this day, when the
cuckoo is in full song. The flower's Latin name,
'flos-cuculi', means 'cuckoo flower'.

Today is also Ben Jonson's birthday. He was born
in 1572.

Menenius' description of himself (below) rather
fits Ben Jonson:

I am known to be a humourous patrician, and one that loves
a cup of hot wine with not a drop
of allaying Tiber in't; ... one that
converses more with the buttock
of the night than with the
forehead of the morning; what I
think I utter and spend my malice
in my breath.
Coriolanus (Act 2 Scene 1)

The Blackbird

The ousel cock so black of hue
With orange tawny bill
The throstle with his note so true
The wren with little quill.

A Midsummer Night's Dream (Act 3 Scene 1)

Bottom finds himself lost and abandoned by his workmates in the middle of the dark midsummer forest. To cheer himself up he sings about the ordinary song birds of his acquaintance, a sweet little ditty which perfectly captures the essence of each bird.

The ousel cock, or blackbird, has a bright orange or 'crocus-coloured bill' (as Thomas Hardy once described it). The throstle, or song thrush, sings beautifully ('the jocund throstle' the poet Michael Drayton called it) and Jenny Wren is farthing tiny.

The size of the wren is used elsewhere by Shakespeare. Lady Macduff protests that, no matter how weak and insignificant she may be against the tyranny of Macbeth, she will fight to protect her children:

The wren, the most diminutive of birds will fight,
(Her young ones in her nest), against the eagle.

Macbeth (Act 4 Scene 2)

The blackbird and the wren are the most abundant and widespread of all British birds. It is surely the blackbird Matthew Arnold is thinking of when he describes 'some wet, bird haunted English lawn'.

Both the blackbird and the thrush were commonly eaten in Shakespeare's day. The price for a dozen blackbirds to bake in a pie varied from ten pence in 1575 to one shilling in 1633, while there are references to the eating of thrushes that go back to Homer.

Justice Silence, when asked by Justice Shallow how his daughter Ellen is, replies darkly: **'Alas! a black ousel, cousin Shallow.'**

Henry IV Part Two (Act 3 Scene 2)

After May has made her appearance in Spenser's parade of months in the *Mutabilitie* cantos of *The Faerie Queen*, jolly June, like an actor, makes his theatrical entrance riding the crab of Cancer. The sun would have been about to enter Cancer at this time in Shakespeare's day:

And after her, came jolly June, arrayed
All in green leaves, as he a Player were;
Yet in his time, he wrought as well as played,
That by his plough-irons mote right well appear:
Upon a Crab he rode, that him did bear
With crooked crawling steps an uncouth pace,
And backward yode, as Bargemen wont to fare
Bending their force contrary to their face,
Like that ungracious crew which feigns demurest grace.

Mutabilitie Cantos, VII: XXXV

Willem Barents Writes His own Epitaph

Like an icicle on a Dutchman's beard.

Twelfth Night (Act 3 Scene 2)

In 1871, a party of Norwegian seal hunters rowed ashore to the barren island of Novaya Zemlya in the Arctic Ocean. In the ruins of an abandoned wooden shack, they discovered the detritus of a shipwrecked expedition which had been forced to spend the winter there in the frozen wastes. A later visitor also found a letter. It was almost three centuries old, and was dated this day, June 13th, 1597.

Detail from a painting by Gerrit de Veer, 1596

It was written by the Dutch explorer, Willem Barents from Friesland, who had been commissioned to discover the north-east passage to China (Cathay) and the Indies, and had set out with two ships in 1596. This was Barents' third voyage.

In the first attempt they had encountered a polar bear, which had tried to climb on board. They decided to capture it and take it back to Holland, but once chained, it started to rampage and had to be

shot. Then they came across a herd of 200 walruses, but only managed to get a few tusks. Icebergs forced them to return home.

The following year, on the next attempt, two of the crew were killed by a polar bear. They were still unable to find a route. The third expedition split up after a disagreement, and Barents found himself trapped with his sixteen-man crew, as the pack ice started to split up their ship. They built a hut of driftwood and the ship's timbers, and were still living in it the following June, waiting for the weather to clear and the ice to melt.

This is when Barents wrote his letter. The English translation of Gerrit de Veer's account of the voyage was registered for publication also on this day, June 13th, in the following year, 1598:

'Then Barents wrote a letter which he put into a musket charge and hanged it up in the chimney, showing how we came out of Holland to sail to the Kingdom of China, and what had happened to us being there on land, with all our crosses, that if any man chanced to come thither, they might know what had happened unto us, and how we had been forced in our extremity to make that house and had dwelt ten months therein.'

Barents and the survivors then took to the sea in two small boats. Seven days out, Barents died while studying his maps and charts. Twelve of the crew made it back to Holland. Barents gave his name to the Barents Sea.

Corpus Christi
· · · · · · · · · · · · · · · ·

This feast day takes place on the Thursday following Trinity Sunday and commemorates Christ's institution of the Blessed Sacrament of the Holy Eucharist. On this day, the York Corpus Christi play was performed. Actually, the Corpus Christi play is a cycle of mystery plays and the York version is by far the most extensive, having 52 plays. They were banned in the 1570s.

Trees

In *All is True*, Queen Katherine of Aragon calls for her maid to take up her lute and sing to her to relieve her sorrows:

Orpheus with his lute made trees
And the mountain tops that freeze,
Bow themselves when he did sing;
To his music plants and flowers
Ever sprung; as sun and showers
There had made a lasting spring.

Everything that heard him play
Even the billows of the sea
Hung their heads, and then lay be.
In sweet music is such art
Killing care and grief of heart
Fall asleep, or hearing die.

(Act 3 Scene 1)

Here Ovid lists the trees that crowd themselves into a shade to cool the Thracian poet:

As soon as that this Poet born of Gods, in that same place
Sat down and touched his tuned strings, a shadow
*   came apace.*
There wanted neither Chaon's Tree, nor yet the trees to which
Fresh Phaeton's sisters turned were, nor Beech, nor Holm,
*   nor Wych,*
Nor gentle Asp, nor wyveless Bay, nor lofty Chestnut tree.

Nor Hazel spalt, nor Ash whereof the shafts of spears may be.
Not knotless Fir, nor cheerful Plane, nor Maple flecked grain.
Nor Lot, nor Sallow which delights by water to remain.
Nor slender twigged Tamarisk, nor Box aye green of hue.
Nor Fig trees loaden with their fruit of colours brown
*   and blue.*
Nor double coloured myrtle trees. Moreover thither came
The writhing ivy and the vine that runs upon a frame,
Elms clad with vines, and Ashes wild, and Pitch trees black
*   as coal,*
And Palmtrees lithe which in reward of conquest men
*   do bear,*
And Pineapple with tufted top and harsh and pricking hair.

Metamorphoses, (Book Ten, lines 95-110), translated by
Arthur Golding

Sumptuary Laws

For the apparel oft proclaims the man.
Hamlet (Act 1 Scene 3)

In Greenwich on this day in 1574, Queen Elizabeth brought the 'Statutes of Apparel' into force. Elizabethan Sumptuary Laws dictated what colour and fabric individuals were allowed to own and wear, an easy and immediate way to identify rank and privilege. They were intended to limit expenditure on clothes and of course to maintain the social structure of the Elizabethan class system.

'The excess of apparel and the superfluity of unnecessary foreign wares thereto belonging now of late years is grown to such an extremity that the manifest decay of the whole realm generally is like to follow, but also particularly the wasting and undoing of a great number of young gentlemen, who, allured by the vain show of those things, do not only consume themselves, their goods, and lands which their parents left unto them, but also run into such debts and shifts as they cannot live out of danger of laws without attempting unlawful acts, whereby they are not any ways serviceable to their country as otherwise they might be.

'Wherefore her majesty willeth and straightly commandeth all manner of persons within 12 days after the publication of this present proclamation to reform their apparel upon pain of her highness's indignation.'

Here are a few examples of these restrictions:

'None shall wear in his apparel: Any silk of the colour of purple, cloth of gold tissued, but only the King, Queen, King's mother, children, brethren, and sisters, uncles and aunts; and except dukes, marquises, and earls, who may wear the same in doublets, jerkins, linings of cloaks, gowns, and hose; and those of the Garter, purple in mantles only.

'Woollen cloth made out of the realm, but in caps only; velvet, crimson, or scarlet; embroidery or tailor's work having gold or silver or pearl therein: except dukes, marquises, earls, viscounts, barons, and knights being companions of the Garter, or any person being of the Privy Council. And caps, hats, hatbands, garters, or boot hose trimmed with gold or silver or pearl; silk nether stocks; enamelled chains, buttons, aglets: except men of the degrees above mentioned.

'Silk other than satin, damask, taffeta, camlet, in doublets; and sarcanet, camlet, or taffeta in facing of gowns and cloaks, and in coats, jackets, jerkins, coifs, purses being not of the colour scarlet, crimson, or blue; except men of the degrees and persons above mentioned.

'None shall wear spurs, swords, rapiers, daggers, skeans, wood knives, or hangers, buckles or girdles, gilt, silvered or damasked: nor in their trappings or harness of their horse any studs, buckles, nor stirrups, nor other garniture gilt, silvered, or damasked; nor any velvet in saddles or horse trappers: except knights and barons' sons, and others of higher degree or place.'

The Statutes of Apparel, 1574

The Sumptuary Laws on Women's Apparel

At the top of the social scale, very particular restrictions were put on some of the costliest fabrics:

※ None shall wear: Any cloth of gold, tissue: except duchesses, marquises, and countesses in their gowns, kirtles, partlets, and sleeves; cloth of gold, silver, tinselled satin, silk, or cloth mixed or embroidered with gold or silver or pearl, saving silk mixed with gold or silver in linings of cowls, partlets, and sleeves: except all degrees above viscountesses, and baronesses, and other personages of like degrees in their kirtles and sleeves.

And there were other restrictions :

※ None shall wear: Crimson or carnation velvet below the wives of knights of the Garter and of the Privy Council, the ladies and gentlewomen of the privy chamber and bedchamber, and maids of honour.

※ None shall wear any velvet in gowns below the wives of barons' sons, or of knights; or velvet in kirtles; below the wives of those that may dispend £100 by the year and so valued in the subsidy book.

※ None shall wear any velvet in their petticoats: except wives of barons, knights of the order, or councillors' ladies, and gentlewomen of the privy chamber and bedchamber, and the maids of honour.

※ None shall wear velvet in any cloak or safeguard: except the wives of barons, knights of the order, or councillors' ladies and gentlewomen of the privy chamber and bedchamber, and maids of honour, and the degrees above them.

And the instructions on who could wear which fur were very particular:

※ None shall wear fur of sables: except duchesses, marquises, and countesses in their gowns, kirtles, partlets, and sleeves;

※ None shall wear fur of black genets, or lucerns (black fur); below the wives of knights of the Garter and of the Privy Council, the ladies and gentlewomen of the privy chamber and bedchamber, and maids of honour.

※ None shall wear any furs of leopards, above the wives of barons' sons, or of knights.

※ None shall wear fur whereof the kind groweth not within the Queen's dominions, except foins, grey genets, bodge, and wolf: below the wives of those that may dispend £100 by the year and so valued in the subsidy book.

At my school, denim was referred to as the forbidden fabric. It may be surprising to note that Shakespeare mentions this tough cheap cotton cloth in *The Two Noble Kinsmen* when the schoolmaster chastizes his troop: *You most coarse frieze capacities, ye jean judgments.*

Ugglesome Monsters

... Hell and Night
Must bring this monstrous birth to the world's light.
Othello (Act 1 Scene 3)

On this day in 1580 according to John Stow's *Chronicles*, '**in the parish of Blansdon in Yorkshire, after a great tempest of lightning and thunder, a woman of four score years old named Alice Perin, was delivered of a hideous monster, whose head was like unto a sallet [a light helmet], the forepart of his body like a man, but having eight legs, not one like another, and a tail of half a yard long.'**

And then, three months later, on September 23rd: 'at Fennistanton in Huntingdonshire, one Agnes, wife to William Linsey, was delivered of an ugly strange monster, with a face black, mouth and eyes like a lion, and both male and female.'

A Strange Metamorphosis

'Myself travelling on a time by Vitry in France, happened to see a man, whom the Bishop of Soissons had in confirmation, named Germane, whom all the inhabitants thereabouts have both known and seen to be a woman-child, and until she was two and twenty years of age, called him by the name of Marie. He was when I saw him, of good years, and had a long beard, and was yet unmarried. He saith, that upon a time, leaping and straining himself, to overleap another, he wot not how, but where before he was a woman, he suddenly felt the instrument of a man to come out of him; and to this day the maidens of that town and country have a song in use, by which they warn one another, when they are leaping, not to strain themselves overmuch, or open their legs too wide, for fear they should be turned to boys, as Marie Germane was.'

From Montaigne's essay 'Of the Force of Imagination', translated by John Florio

'Hath He not caused wonderful eclipses in the sun and moon, with most dreadful conjunctions of stars and planets, as the like this thousand year have not been heard of? Have we not seen comets, blazing stars, fiery drakes, men fighting in the air, most fearfully to behold? Hath not Dame Nature herself denied unto us her operation in sending forth abortives, untimely births, ugglesome monsters and fearful misshapen creatures both in man and beast? And yet we are nothing amended: alas what shall become of us?'

The Anatomy of Abuses, Phillip Stubbes

A Rowsey, Ragged Rabblement of Rakehells

Rembrandt etching, Haarlem, 1630

Thomas Harman, in his *A Caveat for Common Cursitors*, 1566, gives his readers an alliterative example of the kind of language they might expect to hear from the thieves and vagabonds roaming the streets in his day: **'Here I set before the good reader the lewd lousy language of these loitering lusks and lazy lorels'**; and he presents an example of the **'unknown tongue'** used by **'these bold, beastly, bawdy beggars, and vain vagabonds'** or as he says elsewhere, **'this rowsey, ragged rabblement of rakehells… with their peevish, pelting and picking practices.'**

Upright man: **Bene lightmans to thy quarroms! Why, hast thou any lour in thy bung to booze?**
Good morrow to thy body! Why, hast thou any money in thy purse to drink ?

Rogue: **But a flag, a win, and make.**
But a groat, a penny and a halfpenny.

Upright man: **Why where is the ken that hath the bene booze?**
Where is the house that has good drink ?

Rogue: **A bene-mort hereby at the sign of the prancer. Tour ye, yonder is the ken. Dup the jigger and maund that is bene-ship.**
A goodwife hereby at the sign of the horse. See you yonder is the house. Open the door and ask for the best.

Upright man: **Maund of that mort what bene peck is in her ken.**
Ask of that wife what good meat she hath in the house.

Rogue: **She hath a cockling-cheat, a grunting-cheat, ruff-peck, cassan, and poplar of yarrum.**
She hath a hen, a pig, bacon, cheese, and milk porridge.

Upright man: **Yonder dwelleth a queer cuffin. It were bene-ship to mill him.**
Yonder dwelleth a hoggish and churlish man. It were very well to rob him.

Rogue: **Now bing we a waste to the highpad; the ruffmans is by.**
Nay let us go hence to the Highway; the woods is at hand.

Upright man: **So we may happen on the harmans, and cly the jerk, or to the queer-ken and scour queer camp-rings, and so to trining on the chats.**
So we may chance to sit in the stocks, either to be whipped, either had to the prison-house, and there be shackled with bolts and fetters, and then hang on the gallows.

Rogue: **Gerry gan! the ruffian cly thee!**
A turd in thy mouth, the Devil take thee.

Simple Time

Smell like Bucklersbury in simple time.

The Merry Wives of Windsor (Act 3 Scene 3)

Bucklersbury was the street in London where all the apothecaries worked, and simple time was about this time of year, when all the blossoms and herbs were brought in from the fields to be made into potions. Stow says: **'The whole street called Bucklersbury on both sides throughout is possessed of grocers and apothecaries towards the west end thereof.'**

Apothecaries all belonged to the Grocers' Guild.

Romeo: I do remember an apothecary,—
And hereabouts he dwells,—which late I noted
In tatter'd weeds, with overwhelming brows,
Culling of simples; meagre were his looks,
Sharp misery had worn him to the bones:
And in his needy shop a tortoise hung,
An alligator stuff'd, and other skins
Of ill-shaped fishes; and about his shelves
A beggarly account of empty boxes,
Green earthen pots, bladders and musty seeds,
Remnants of packthread and old cakes of roses,
Were thinly scatter'd, to make up a show.

Romeo and Juliet (Act 5 Scene 1)

Here Michael Drayton describes the herbs collected by a hermit in his native Warwickshire:

In those so sundry herbs which there in plenty grow;
Whose sundry strange effects he only seeks to know.
And in a little maund, being made of osiers small,
Which serveth him to do full many a thing withal,
He very choicely his simples got abroad.
Here finds he on an oak, rheum purging Polipode;
And in some open place that to the sun doth lie,
He Fumitory gets, and Eye-bright for the eye:
The Yarrow wherewithal he stops the wound-made gore:
The healing Tustan then and Plantan for a sore.
And hard by them again he holy Vervain finds,
Which he about his head that hath a megrim binds.
The wonder working Dill, he gets not far from these,
Which curious women use in many a nice disease.
For them that are with newts or snakes or adders stung,
He seeketh out an herb that's called Adders tong;
Of these most helpful herbs, yet we tell but a few,
To those unnumbered sorts of simples here that grew.

Poly-Olbion

The lime avenue in Holy Trinity churchyard is fragrant with blossom now.

A Grand Shakespeare Ball

On this day, the Tuesday of the week of King George V's coronation in 1911, a great fancy dress ball was held at the Royal Albert Hall. The theme was Shakespeare.

'One of the most beautiful and enjoyable entertainments of the Coronation season. The decorations of the hall itself, the beauty of the costumes, the rhythm of the moving figures in the great quadrilles, the colours, the lights, the gaiety, all produced an effect of brilliance and splendour.'

George Bernard Shaw contributed a witty sketch for the Souvenir Programme, and G. K. Chesterton (although not actually present at the ball), imagined the scene:

'All his plays are one huge Fancy Dress Ball. If there was one thing he loved it was the picturesquely incongruous, I might say even the picturesquely incompatible. And whatever contrasts or collisions occurred in all that million-coloured kaleidoscope of humanity at the Albert Hall, where cardinals must have talked with "savage man", and senators argued with elves, it is doubtful whether the deep note of a romantic diversity was anywhere more strongly struck than it is in those quiet sylvan scenes where the stiff and gaudy motley of Touchstone is relieved against the shaggy woods and shepherds, or the bristly head of Bottom rises among fairies against the moon.'

Mrs George Cornwallis-West, chairman of the committee, arrived as the Countess Olivia; Lady Alington as Cleopatra; the actress Violet Vanbrugh appeared as a ferocious Lady Macbeth; while the nineteen-year-old Vita Sackville-West chose to come as Katharina, brandishing a bull whip. The tickets

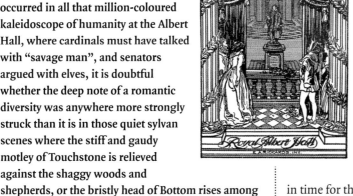

insisted that, *'The gentlemen must wear Shakespearian costumes or Venetian cloaks'*, but some clearly felt a little uncomfortable in tights:

'That night in June, Elizabethan England was loosed upon Kensington, but the mystery of memory reveals only a blur of magnificence, and if I am allowed to say so, splendour without gaiety. We were all too self conscious to be gay.'

There were special Shakespeare Quadrilles, a lavish banquet, while a pageant of Queen Elizabeth, (with her court presented by the direct descendants of the characters they played) proved a highlight of the evening.

The ball was **'graced by the stately presence of the world's regality'**, a host of Imperial, Royal and Serene Highnesses: from Crown Princes to Dowager Duchesses, Russian Archdukes, and Grand Dukes, Spanish Infantes, Indian Maharajahs, and the Sultan of Perak. **'Future ages may produce spectacles very striking, very beautiful. But this age has shot its bolt. And whatever the future may conceal of splendour and beauty, it will certainly not outdo this.'**

The patriotic ambition of the organising committee was to raise funds for a publicly endowed Shakespeare National Memorial Theatre, to be built in the capital, in time for the tercentenary of the Bard's death in 1916.

The Souvenir programme concluded by hoping all the guests would dance together again at the Tercentenary Ball. But by then the Great War had engulfed Europe, and the drive to create a Shakespeare National Memorial Theatre was put on hold.

Thomas Coryate Walks to Venice
·····································

On this day in 1608, on a Friday afternoon, Thomas Coryate arrived in Venice. He had walked all the way from his home in Odcombe in Somerset. He calculated he had travelled 952 miles, and accomplished the distance from Calais in just five weeks.

'For therehence may you see the whole model and form of the city, a sight that doth in my opinion surpass all the shows under the cope of heaven. There you may behold all their sumptuous Palaces adorned with admirable variety of beautiful pillars: the Church of St Mark which is but a little way therehence distant, with the Duke's [Doge's] stately Palace adjoining unto it, being one of the principal wonders of the Christian world, the lofty Rialto, the Piazza of Saint Stephen. Also many fair gardens; together with their little islands bordering about the city wonderfully frequented. Whatsoever thou art that meanest to see Venice, in any case forget not to go up to the top of St Mark's tower before thou comest out of the city. For it will cost thee but a gazet, which is not fully an English penny.'

Coryate's Crudities

And here is Coryate on gondolas:
'None of them are open above, but fairly covered, first with a pretty kind of arch or vault in the gondola; then with fair black cloth which is turned up at both ends of the boat, to the end that if a passenger meaneth to be private, he may draw down the same, and after row so secretly that no man can see him: in the inside are benches finely covered with black

leather, and are very neatly garnished with fine linen cloth, the edge whereof is laced with bone lace. The ends are beautified with two pretty and ingenious devices, in the form of a dolphin's tail, with fins very artificially represented. The watermen that row, never sit as ours do in London, but always stand, and in my opinion they are as swift as our rowers about London. Of these gondolas they say there are ten thousand about the city.'

And here he is on the city's famous courtesans:
'You seem to enter into the paradise of Venus. For their fairest rooms are most glorious and glittering to behold. As for herself she comes to thee decked like the queen and goddess of Love. For thou shalt see her decked with many chains of gold and orient pearl, divers gold rings beautified with diamonds and other costly stones, jewels in both her ears of great worth. A gown of damask with a deep gold fringe, her petticoat or red chamlet edged with rich gold fringe, stockings of carnation silk, her breath and whole body, the more to enamour thee, most fragrantly perfumed. Moreover she will endeavour to enchant thee partly with her melodious notes that she warbles out upon her lute, and partly with that heart-tempting harmony of her voice. She may minister unto thee the stronger temptations to come to her lure. She will show thee her chambers of recreation where thou shalt see all manner of pleasing objects... and generally all her bedding sweetly perfumed.'

Coryate insists however that he did not avail himself of the courtesan's charms.

Titania's Flowery Bed

I know a bank where the wild thyme blows
Where oxlips and the nodding violet grows
Quite o'er canopied with luscious woodbine,
With sweet musk roses and with eglantine
There sleeps Titania some hour of the night
Lulled in these flowers with dances and delight,
And there the snake throws her enamell'd skin
Weed wide enough to wrap a fairy in.

A Midsummer Night's Dream (Act 2 Scene 1)

As Midsummer approaches, consider the flowers which Shakespeare chooses to decorate Titania's bower.

Wild thyme certainly is in full bloom in June on the chalky hillsides of the Chilterns and could well have been growing there at the time of Shakespeare's journey from Stratford to London. Nature writer Richard Mabey points out the flowers' resinous heady odour.

However the oxlips and nodding violets are way out of season by Midsummer. Musk roses would have produced a potent and delicious scent to perfume the queen of the fairies' bower, and eglantine, or the sweet briar rose, has leaves which when crushed smell of apples. They were used as breath fresheners by the Elizabethans.

Far from having a lulling soporific effect, the combined scents of this sensuous bower would rather provoke Titania into a heightened state of arousal.

Yet mark'd I where the bolt of Cupid fell:
It fell upon a little western flower,
Before milk-white, now purple with love's wound,
And maidens call it love-in-idleness.

A Midsummer Night's Dream (Act 2 Scene 1)

Richard Mabey also records that the shape of the tiny wild pansy, the love-in-idleness used by Oberon to squeeze into the lovers' eyes, was thought to look like two lovers with a third in between them.

Though decoctions of flowers were frequently made there is no such reference to a love potion being made from the wild pansy. That all came from Shakespeare's imagination.

Midsummer's Eve or St John's Eve

The nights in June are the shortest of the year. In Trevelyon's *Miscellany*, he gives an accurate account of precisely how short. The long summer's day stretched to sixteen hours and twenty-four minutes, while the brief dark hours of night only lasted seven hours and thirty-six minutes.

'The sun setteth,' he writes, **'at twelve minutes past eight, but twilight may last until twenty four minutes past ten. The Day breaketh,'** he continues, **'at thirty six minutes past one, with the sun then rising at forty seven minutes past three.'** This suggests that the actual hours of darkness only last a mere three hours and twelve minutes, which is just a little longer than the stage running time of *A Midsummer Night's Dream*.

If ye will with Mab find grace,
Set each platter in his place;
Rake the fire up, and get
Water in, ere sun be set.
Wash your pails and cleanse your dairies;
Sluts are loathsome to the fairies;
Sweep your house, who doth not so,
Mab will pinch her by the toe.
The Fairies, Robert Herrick

Midsummer was regarded as a portal in the year between this world and the world of the fairies. And from now until St Peter's Day, fairies were particularly active. Care had to be taken to protect the cradles of new-born infants, or they would be stolen by fairies and replaced with changeling children:

Oberon is passing fell and wrath,
Because that she as her attendant hath
A lovely boy, stol'n from an Indian King,
She never had so sweet a changeling.
A Midsummer Night's Dream (Act 2 Scene 1)

Fairies were thought to be fascinated by human children, and given the opportunity would steal them and leave a substitute in the child's place. The changeling might be just a piece of wood, but the parents would see it as their own offspring, and treat it as such. Changelings could be identified by birthmarks, or by their exceptional intelligence. Simple charms, such as a coat placed upside down or inside out on the cradle, were thought to ward them off.

At Midsummer in 1571, when Shakespeare was seven years old, the authorities in Stratford paid a glazier to smash out all the stained glass windows in the Guild Chapel, and replace them with clear glass.

St John's Day
••••••••••••••

The feast of St John the Baptist was celebrated on this day. It was fixed exactly six months before Christmas Eve, as St John heralded the birth of Christ.

Midsummer Fires and Flowers

Midsummer flowers or the Herbs of St John, such as Mugwort and Vervain, St John's Wort, Corn Marigold, Orpins, Yarrow and Dwarf Elder, played a special part in the festivities. They were wrought into garlands and hung on the doors of houses and byres to ward off evil spirits or were burned on the Midsummer fires of Johnsmas Eve to ward off disease.

Then doth the joyful feast of John the Baptist take his turn,
When bonfires great with lofty flames in every town
doth burn:
And young men round about with maids, do dance in
every street,
With garlands wrought of Motherwort, or else with
Vervain sweet,
And many other flowers fair, with Violets in their hands,
Whereas they all do fondly think, that whosoever stands,
And thorough the flowers beholds the flames, his eyes
shall feel no pain.
When thus till night they danced have, they through
the fire amain
With striving minds do run, and all their herbs they
cast therein,

And then with words devout and prayers, they
solemnly begin,
Desiring God that all their ills may there consumed be,
Whereby they think through all that year, from agues
to be free.
The Popish Kingdom, translated by Barnabe Googe

Later, the same poem mentions another custom – rolling a burning wheel down a steep hillside:
Some other get a rotten wheel, all worn and cast aside,
Which covered round about with straw, and tow, they
closely hide:
And carried to some mountain's top, being all with fire light,
They hurl it down with violence when dark appears
the night:
Resembling much the Sun, that from the heavens
down should fall,
A strange and monstrous sight it seems, and fearful to
them all,
But they suppose their mischiefs all are likewise thrown
to hell,
And that from harms and dangers now in safety here
they dwell.

Also on this day in 1604, Edward de Vere, Earl of Oxford, died. He is thought by some to be a contender for the authorship of Shakespeare's plays, although his death comes several years before at least a dozen of them were even written. Here, in tribute, is John Aubrey's famous anecdote about the Earl:
'This Earl of Oxford, making of his low obeisance to Queen Elizabeth, happened to let a fart, at which he was so abashed and ashamed that he went to travel, seven years. On his return the Queen welcomed him home, and said, "My Lord, I had forgot the fart."'
Brief Lives, John Aubrey

Dancing

Of any silver-sounding instrument,
Love makes them dance to those sweet
   murmurings
With busy skill and cunning excellent.
O that your feet those tunes would represent
With artificial motions to and fro,
That Love this art in every part might show!
Yet your fair soul, which came from heaven above
To rule this house (another heaven below),
With divers powers in harmony doth move;
And all the virtues that from her do flow
In a round measure, hand in hand do go.
Could I now see, as I conceive, this dance,
Wonder and love would cast me in a trance.

On this day in 1594, a *Poem of Dancing* was entered for copyright in the Stationers' Register.

Sir John Davies' poem *Orchestra*, which he himself described as 'This sudden, rash, half-capriole of my wit', describes the Dance of Life. Antinous, one of Penelope's suitors, tries to woo the Ithacan queen, by begging her to dance:

Love in the twinkling of your eyelids danceth,
Love danceth in your pulses and your veins,
Love, when you sew, your needle's point advanceth
And makes it dance a thousand curious strains
Of winding rounds, whereof the form remains,
To show that your fair hands can dance the hay,
Which your fine feet would learn as well as they.

And when your ivory fingers touch the strings

'Amorous, mixed, effeminate, lascivious, lust-exciting dancing is a dangerous incendiary of lust; an ordinary occasion of, a preparatory to, much whoredom, adultery, wantonness, and a diabolical, at least a pagan practice, misbeseeming all chaste, all sober Christians. I would our English nation would now at last consider that Pagan dancing, to God's, to Christ's dishonour, is religion's scandal, chastity's shipwreck, sin's advantage, and the eternal ruin of many precious souls.

'I would the dancing, wanton Herodiasses, the effeminate cinque-pace, coranto-frisking gallants of our age, together with our rustic hobbling satyrs, nymphs, and dancing fairies, who spend their strength, their time (especially Easter, Whitsun, Midsummer, and Christmas season) in such lewd, lascivious dancing, would not only abandon all such dancing themselves, but likewise withdraw their children, especially their daughters, from the dancing school.'

Histrio-Mastix: The Player's Scourge, William Prynne

The Worst Day of Mark Twain's Life

Mark Twain describes a visit to Stratford in late-June 1907, at the invitation of the redoubtable Marie Corelli, a romantic novelist who had retired there. Twain was visiting Oxford University, and Corelli had taken the opportunity to invite him to luncheon. Once Twain realized the round trip added at least a hundred miles to his journey he tried to decline:

Marie Corelli in her own gondola, *The Dream*, on the River Avon

'It hadn't the slightest effect; she was as hard as nails. I think there is no criminal in any jail with a heart so unmalleable, so unmeltable, so unfazeable, so flinty, so uncompromisingly hard as Marie Corelli's. I think one could hit it with a steel and draw sparks from it.

'She is about fifty years old but has no grey hairs; she is fat and shapeless; she has a gross animal face; she dresses for sixteen, and awkwardly and unsuccessfully and pathetically imitates the innocent graces and witcheries of that dearest and sweetest of all ages; and so her exterior matches her interior and harmonizes with it. With the result – as I think – that she is the most offensive sham, inside and out, that misrepresents and satirizes the human race today. I would willingly say more about her but it would be futile to try; all the adjectives seem so poor and feeble and flabby this morning...

'She received us at Stratford station with her carriage and was going to drive us to Shakespeare's church, but I cancelled that; she insisted, but I said that day's programme was generous enough in fatigues without adding another. She said there would be a crowd at the church to welcome me and they would be greatly disappointed, but I was loaded to the chin with animosity and childishly eager to be as unpleasant as possible.

'She said she had been purchasing the house which the founder of Harvard College had once lived in and was going to present it to America – another advertisement. She wanted to stop at that dwelling and show me over it. I said I didn't want to see the damned house. I didn't say it in those words but in that vicious spirit, and she understood; even her horses understood and were shocked, for I saw them shudder. As we drove by I saw that the house and the sidewalk were full of people – which meant that Marie had arranged for another speech. However we went by bowing in response to cheers, and presently reached Marie's house, a very attractive and commodious English home.

'I said I was exceedingly tired and would like to go immediately to a bed chamber and stretch out and get some rest, if only for fifteen minutes. She was voluble with tender sympathy and said I should have my desire at once; but deftly steered me into the drawing room and introduced me to her company.

'Toward the end of luncheon that implacable woman rose in her place, with a glass of champagne in her hand, and made a speech! With me for a text, of course. When she had finished I said, "I thank you very much" – and sat still. If I had made a speech, courtesy and custom would have required me to construct it out of thanks and compliments, and there was not a rag of that kind of material lurking anywhere in my system.

'We reached London at half past six in the evening in a pouring rain, and half an hour later I was in bed and tired to the very marrow. This was the most hateful day my seventy-two years have ever known.'

The First English Dictionary

A man of fire-new words.

Love's Labour's Lost (Act 1 Scene 1)

On this day in 1604, in Coventry, a defrocked priest called Robert Cowdray signed the dedicatory epistle to his book *A Table Alphabetical*. It was in fact the first English Dictionary, preceding Dr Johnson's by nearly 150 years.

Here are some choice entries:

Abecedarie the order of the Letters, or he that useth them

acetositie sharpness, or sourness

agglutinate to join together

amaritude bitterness

brachygraphie [gr] short writing

buggerie conjunction with one of the same kind, or of men with beasts

chambering lightness, and wanton behaviour in private places

duarchy the equal reign of two princes together.

driblets small debts

dulcifie sweeten

ebulliated boiled

emmot pissmire

exuclerate to make sore, to corrupt

floscles [fr] flowers

fuluide yellow

gnible bite

lingell shoemaker's thread

moosell to fetter

morigerous well mannered

nuncupatory telling or declaring anything

obnubilate to make dark

pellicles skins

pinguiditie fatness, or greasiness

queach thick heap

racha fie, a note of extreme anger, signified by the gesture of the person that speaketh it, to him that he speaketh to

smatterer somewhat learned, or having but a little skill

snipperings pairings

tapish [fr] lie down, hide itself

venuste fair, beautiful

zodiack [gr] a circle in the heaven, wherein be placed the 12 signs, and in which the Sun is moved

Shakespeare's Garden

The novelist E.F. Benson may have used Stratford-upon-Avon's Edwardian hostess, the gorgon Marie Corelli, as the model for Mrs Lucas (in his *Mapp and Lucia* series of novels). Here are two of his descriptions of Lucia's Shakespeare-inspired gardens:

'Perdita's garden requires a few words of explanation. It was a charming little square plot in front of the timbered façade of the Hurst, surrounded by yew-hedges and intersected with paths of crazy pavement, carefully smothered in stone-crop, which led to the Elizabethan sundial from Wardour Street in the centre. It was gay in spring with those flowers (and no others) on which Perdita doted. There were "violets dim", and primroses and daffodils, which came before the swallow dared and took the winds (usually of April) with beauty. But now in June the swallow had dared long ago, and when spring and the daffodils were over, Lucia always allowed Perdita's garden a wider, though still strictly Shakespearian scope. There was eglantine (Penzance briar) in full flower now, and honeysuckle and gillyflowers and plenty of pansies for thoughts, and yards of rue (more than usual this year), and so Perdita's garden was gay all the summer.'

Mapp and Lucia, E.F. Benson

'Here as was only right and proper, there was not a flower to be found save such as were mentioned in the plays of Shakespeare: indeed, it was called Shakespeare's garden, and the bed that ran below the windows of the dining room was Ophelia's border, for it consisted solely of those flowers which that distraught maiden had distributed to her friends when she should have been in a lunatic asylum. Mrs Lucas often reflected how lucky it was that such institutions were unknown in Elizabeth's day. Pansies naturally, formed the chief decoration (though there were some very flourishing plants of rue), and Mrs Lucas always wore a little bunch of them when in flower, to inspire her thoughts, and found them wonderfully efficacious. Round the sun dial, which was set in the middle of one of the squares of grass between which a path of broken paving-stones led to the front door, was a circular border, now in July, sadly vacant, for it harboured the spring flowers enumerated by Perdita, But the first day every year when Perdita's border put forth its earliest blossom was a delicious anniversary, and news of it spread like wildfire through Mrs Lucas's kingdom, and her subjects were very joyful, and came to salute the violet or daffodil, or whatever it was.'

Queen Lucia, E.F. Benson

The Feast of St Peter and St Paul

On this day, St Peter's Day, in 1613, Shakespeare's Globe burned down.

'Now, to let matters of state sleep, I will entertain you at the present with what happened this week at the Bank's side. The King's Players had a new play, called *All is True*, representing some principal pieces in the reign of Henry VIII, which was set forth with many extraordinary circumstances of pomp and majesty, even to the matting on the stage: the knights of the order with their Georges and garters, the guards with their embroidered coats, and the like – sufficient in truth within a while to make greatness very familiar if not ridiculous. Now King Henry making a masque at the Cardinal Wolsey's house, and certain chambers being shot off at his entry, some of the paper or other stuff wherewith one of them was stopped did light on the thatch, where being thought at first but an idle smoke, and their eyes more attentive on the show, it kindled inwardly and ran round like a train, consuming within less than an hour the whole house to the very grounds. This was the fatal period of that virtuous fabric wherein yet nothing did perish but wood and straw and a few forsaken cloaks. Only one man had his breeches set on fire that would perhaps have broiled him if he had not by the benefit of a provident wit put it out with bottle ale.'

Letter from Sir Henry Wotton to Sir Edmund Bacon, 2nd July, 1613

The Pitiful Burning of the Globe

This ballad was entered in the Stationers' Register on June 30th, 1613, and must have been written before the flames were even extinguished.

A Sonnet upon the pitiful burning of the Globe playhouse in London.

Now sit thee down Melpomene,
Wrapt in a sea-cole robe,
And tell the doleful tragedy,
That late was play'd at Globe:
For no man that can sing or say
Was scarred upon St Peter's Day.
Oh sorrow, pitiful sorrow, and yet all this is true!

All you that please to understand,
Come listen to my story,
To see Death with his rakeing brand
'Mongst such an auditory
Regarding neither Cardinal's might,
Nor yet the rugged face of Henry the eight.
Oh sorrow, pitiful sorrow, and yet all this is true!

This fearful fire began above,
A wonder strange and true,
And to the stage-house did remove,
As round as Taylor's clewe;
And burnt down both beam and snag,
And did not spare the silken flag.
Oh sorrow, pitiful sorrow, and yet all this is true!

Out run the Knights, out run the Lords,
And there was great ado,
Some lost their hats, and some their swords;
Then out run Burbage too:
The reprobates, though drunk on Monday,
Pray'd for the Fool, and Henry Condye.
Oh sorrow, pitiful sorrow, and yet all this is true!

The periwigs and drum heads fried,
Like to a butter firkin:
A woeful burning did betide
To many a good buff jerkin.
Then with swollen lips, like drunken Flemmings,
Distressed stood old stuttering Heminges.
Oh sorrow, pitiful sorrow, and yet all this is true!

No shower his rain did there down force
In all that sun-shine weather,
To save that great renowned house ;
Nor thou, O ale-house! neither.
Had it begun below, sans doubte,
Their wives for fear had pissed it out.
Oh sorrow, pitiful sorrow, and yet all this is true!

Be warned, you stage strutters all,
Least you again be catched,
And such a burning do befall,
As to them whose house was thatched:
Forbear your whoring, breeding biles,
And lay up that expense for tiles.
Oh sorrow, pitiful sorrow, and yet all this is true!

Go draw you a petition,
And do you not abhor it,
And get, with low submission,
A licence to beg for it ;
In churches, sans churchwarden's checks,
In Surrey and in Middlesex.
Oh sorrow, pitiful sorrow, and yet
All this is true!

On this day in 1614, exactly a year and day after the conflagration, a new Globe opened, with a tiled roof.

He makes a July's day short as December.

The Winter's Tale (Act 1 Scene 2)

As clear as founts in July.

All is True (Act 1 Scene 1)

A lover may bestride the gossamer
That idles in the wanton summer air.

Romeo and Juliet (Act 2 Scene 6)

'It is now July and the Sun is gotten up to his height, whose heat parcheth the earth and burns up the grass on the mountains. Now begins the cannon of heaven to rattle, and when the fire is put to the charge, it breaketh out among the clouds: the stones of congealed water cut off the ears of the corn: and the black storms affright the faint-hearted: the Stag and the Buck are now in pride of their time, and the hardness of their heads makes them fit for the Horner: Now hath the Spar-hawk the partridge in the foot, and the ferret doth tickle the cony in the borough. Now doth the farmer make ready his team, and the carter with his whip, hath no small pride in his whistle: Now do the reapers try their backs and their arms, and the lusty Youths pitch their sheaves into the Cart. The old Partridge calls her covey in the morning, and in the evening the Shepherd falls to folding in his flock: the Sparrows make a charm upon the reed bushes, till the fowler comes and takes them by the dozens: the Smelt now begins to be in season, and the Lamprey out of the river leaps into a pie: the Soldier now hath a hot march, and the Lawyer sweats in his lined gown; the pedlar now makes a long walk, and the Aqua vitae Bottle sets his face on a fiery heat: In sum, I thus conclude of it, I hold it a profitable season, the Labourer's gain, the rich man's wealth. Farewell.'

Fantasticks, Nicholas Breton

'July I would have drawn in a jacket of light yellow eating cherries, with his face and bosom sun burnt, on his head a wreath of centaury and wild thyme, a scythe on his shoulder and a bottle at his girdle, carrying the sign of Leo.'

Emblems, Henry Peacham

Loathsome Tobacco
• •

On this day, in 2007, smoking was banned in public places in the United Kingdom.

'Have you not reason then to be ashamed, and to forbear this filthy novelty, so basely grounded, so foolishly received and so grossly mistaken in the right use thereof? In your abuse thereof sinning against God, harming your selves both in persons and goods, and raking also thereby the marks and notes of vanity upon you: by the custom thereof making yourselves to be wondered at by all foreign civil Nations, and by all strangers that come among you, to be scorned and contemned. A custom loathsome to the eye, hateful to the nose, harmful to the brain, dangerous to the lungs, and in the black stinking fume thereof, nearest resembling the horrible Stygian smoke of the pit that is bottomless.'

Counterblast to Tobacco, King James I

'In the alehouses, tobacco, or a species of woundwort are also obtainable. The powder is lit in a small pipe. The smoke is sucked into the mouth and the saliva is allowed to run freely, after which a good draught of Spanish wine follows. This they regard as a curious medicine for defluctions, and as a pleasure, and the habit is so common with them, that they always carry the instrument on them and light up on all occasions, at the play, in the taverns or elsewhere, drinking as well as smoking together... and it makes them riotous and merry, and rather drowsy; just as if they were drunk, though the effect soon passes, and they use it so abundantly because of the pleasure it gives that their preachers cry out on them for their self-destruction, and I am told the inside of one man's veins after death was found to be covered in soot like a chimney.'

Travels in England, Thomas Platter, 1599

First, April, she with mellow showers
Opens the way for early flowers ;
Then after her comes smiling May,
In a more rich and sweet array;
Next enters June, and brings us more
Gems than those two that went before:
Then (lastly) July comes, and she
More wealth brings in than all those three.

The Succession of the Four Sweet Months, Robert Herrick

Time Flies

Elisabeth Scott is congratulated by HRH The Prince of Wales at the opening of the New Shakespeare Memorial Theatre, 1932

Men, like butterflies, show not their mealy wings, but to the summer.

Troilus and Cressida (Act 3 Scene 3)

Time Capsule

On this day in 1929, a time capsule was laid in the foundation stone for the new theatre in Stratford.

Lord Ampthill, the Most Worshipful Pro-Grand Master of the Masons, officially led the laying of the foundation stone of the new Shakespeare Memorial Theatre. The stone itself, from a quarry at nearby Edgehill, weighed over a ton. In its base was a specially designed cavity in which the time capsule was placed.

The glass casket contained newspapers of the day: *The Times*, the *Daily Telegraph*, the *Birmingham Post* and the *Stratford Herald*, as well as samples of all the coins of the realm. A copy of the Royal Charter of the Shakespeare Memorial Theatre and a souvenir programme for the ceremony were also placed in the casket.

Though the event was watched by 600 freemasons, and an enclosure full of people who had contributed to the rebuilding fund, actors or theatre practitioners were in very short supply. Sir Frank Benson was there, and Sir Barry Jackson, but few others.

Elisabeth Scott, the architect, was not only the first woman to design a prominent public building in the country, but was the first to be allowed the honour of participating in a Masonic ceremony when she handed Lord Ampthill a silver trowel. Then an ancient Egyptian maul (or mallet) was used to dedicate the stone and the building to commemorate the name of William Shakespeare and 'to be a temple of concord and conciliation among the nations of the world'.

In the rebuilding and redevelopment of the new Royal Shakespeare Theatre, eighty years later, the question was asked whether the time capsule would be opened. But it seems, as that part of the building would not be touched, the time capsule will remain for future generations to discover.

The Dog-days
·················

For now, these hot days, is the mad blood stirring.
Romeo and Juliet (Act 3 Scene 1)

Today is the first day of the Dog-days, which, according to The Book of Common Prayer (1552), end on August 17th. The Dog-days were named by the Romans '*caniculares dies*' (days of the dogs) after Sirius, the Dog Star, and originally they were the days when Sirius rose just before or at the same time as the Sun. The Dog Star is the brightest star beside the Sun.

Here are two of Shakespeare's lists of dogs. In the first, Macbeth is sneering at the murderers:
Ay, in the catalogue ye go for men;
As hounds and greyhounds, mongrels, spaniels, curs,
Shoughs, water-rugs and demi-wolves, are clept
All by the name of dogs: the valued file
Distinguishes the swift, the slow, the subtle,
The housekeeper, the hunter, every one
According to the gift which bounteous nature
Hath in him closed; whereby he does receive
Particular addition from the bill
That writes them all alike: and so of men.
Macbeth (Act 3 Scene 1)

And in this extract, Edgar, as Poor Tom, attempts to humour the mad King Lear:
King Lear: *The little dogs and all. Tray, Blanch and Sweetheart, see they bark at me.*
Edgar: *Tom will throw his head at them.*
Avaunt, you curs!
Be thy mouth or black or white,
Tooth that poisons if it bite;
Mastiff, greyhound, mongrel grim,
Hound or spaniel, brach or lym,
Bobtail tyke or trundle-tail;
Tom will make them weep and wail;
For, with throwing thus my head,
Dogs leap the hatch, and all are fled.
King Lear (Act 3 Scene 6)

Our Phoenix, Master William Byrd

Let the bird of loudest lay,
On the sole Arabian tree,
Herald sad and trumpet be,
To whose sound chaste wings obey.
The Phoenix and the Turtle

On this day in 1623, the great composer William Byrd died, aged 80, and was buried in an unmarked grave in the churchyard of Stondon Massey in Essex. In his Will and Testament he wrote:
'I pray that I may live and die a true and perfect member of the Holy Catholic Church without which I believe there is no salvation for me.'

Byrd managed to combine his Roman Catholic sympathies with his work in the court of the Protestant Queen Elizabeth I. Called the English

Detail from The Young Flute Player by Judith Leyster, 1635

Palestrina, William Byrd was the foremost composer of the Elizabethan age, writing madrigals and keyboard music as well as Latin and English church music. He was a member of the Chapel Royal, the sovereign's private religious establishment. Yet he remained throughout his life a dedicated Roman Catholic who was persecuted as a recusant but succeeded, through his art, in upholding the old faith.

  Byrd published three settings of the Mass Ordinary between 1592 and 1595, and in 1607 he published a collection of *Gradualia*, an elaborate year-long musical cycle. In the anti-Catholic frenzy following the 1605 Gunpowder Plot, the first volume of the *Gradualia* was banned in England under penalty of imprisonment, as indeed was all his Catholic music. Just before Byrd's death, Henry Peacham (in *The Complete Gentleman*) wrote:
'For motets and music of piety and devotion, as well for the honour of our nation as the merit of the man, I prefer above all our Phoenix, Master William Byrd.'

Some argue that it is Byrd who is referred to by Shakespeare in his enigmatic poem, *The Phoenix and the Turtle*, and that the poem is a secret Catholic eulogy for Anne Line and her husband Roger. Anne was executed at Tyburn for harbouring a priest in February 1601. The poem seems to take the allegorical form of a Catholic requiem for the couple. Anne Line was canonized as one of the Forty Martyrs of England and Wales in 1970.

As this is the Fourth of July, and American Independence Day, here is a quotation engraved on the American Fountain in the Market Square in Stratford-upon-Avon:
Ten thousand honours and blessings on the Bard
Who has gilded the dull realities of life with
     innocent illusions.
The Sketchbook of Geoffry Crayon, Washington Irving

The American Fountain was donated to the town in the year of Queen Victoria's Golden Jubilee in 1887, by an American journalist, publisher and philanthropist called George William Childs. The Victorian Gothic clock tower and fountain was unveiled by Sir Henry Irving and is surmounted by lions and eagles representing England and the United States.

Midsummer's Day (Old Style)

Here is John Aubrey, on why there are no more fairies these days:

'When I was a child (and so before the Civil Wars) the fashion was for old women and maids to tell fabulous stories at nighttimes of sprites and walking ghosts etc. This was derived down from mother to daughter, from the monkish balance which upheld holy church, for the divines say, "Deny Spirits, you are an atheist." When the wars came, and with them came liberty of conscience, and liberty of inquisition, the phantoms vanished. Now children fear no such things, having heard not of them; and are not checked with such fears.

'Our country people would talk much of Fairies. They swept up the hearth clean at night: and did set their shoes by the fire, and many times should find a threepence in one of them. Mistress Markey told me that her mother did use that custom and had as much money as made her a little silver cup of thirty shillings value. Elias Ashmole says there was in his time a Piper at Lichfield that did know what houses were fairy ground: and that the Piper had often times seen them.

'Before printing, Old Wives Tales were ingenious, and since printing came in fashion, till a little before the Civil Wars, the ordinary sort of people were not taught to read. Now a days books are common, and most of the poor people understand letters; and the many good books, and variety of turns of affairs, have put all the old fables out of doors: and the divine art of printing and gunpowder have frighted away Robin Goodfellow and the fairies.

'Civil Wars coming on have put out all these Rites, or customs quite out of fashion. Wars do not only extinguish Religion and Laws: but Superstition, and no Suffiman is a greater fugator of phantasmes than gunpowder.'

Miscellanies, John Aubrey

Perfumes

All the perfumes of Arabia will not sweeten this little hand.
Macbeth (Act 5 Scene 1)

Being entertained for perfumer, as I was smoking a musty room.
Much Ado about Nothing (Act 1 Scene 3)

Don John's troublemaking sidekick Borachio, employed in Leonato's house to fumigate the rooms, whips behind an arras and overhears Don Pedro's plan to woo Hero on Claudio's behalf. But what was a perfumer, and how would he 'smoke a musty room'?

Burton in his *Anatomy of Melancholy* tells us that:
'The smoke of Juniper is in great request with us at Oxford, to sweeten our chambers.'

And Trevelyon in his *Miscellany* has this little jingle for July:
Perfume thy house with savours sweet
But such as are for purpose meet
Abroad as thou in streets doest go
Defend thyself from stinks also.

Levinus Lemnius, a Dutch physician from Zeeland, also makes a note about how the English keep their houses cool in summer:
'The better to qualify and mitigate this heat, in sultry hot weather, it shall be very good to sprinkle on the pavements and cool the floors of our houses or chambers with springing water, and then to strew them over with sedge, and to trim up our parlours with green boughs, fresh herbs or vine leaves; which thing although in the Low Countries it be usually frequented, yet no nation more decently, more trimly nor more sightly than they do in England.'
Journal of Levinus Lemnius

A Perfume to Burn
'To make a good perfume to burn, take benjamin one ounce, storax, calamint two ounces, of mastic, white ambergris, of each one ounce, iroes, calamus aromaticus, cypress wood, of each half ounce, of camphor one scruple, labdanum one ounce: beat all these to powder, then take of sallow charcoal six ounces, of liquid storax two ounces, beat them all with aqua vitae, and then roll them into long round rolls.'
The English Housewife, Gervase Markham

In *Much Ado About Nothing*, Benedick's friends realize he is in love because he is wearing perfume:
Nay, 'a rubs himself with civet, can you smell him out by that?
Much Ado About Nothing (Act 3 Scene 2)

Civet was a musk produced from the civet cat, which was highly valued as a fragrance – the very uncleanly flux of a cat, derided by Touchstone. It was still used by Chanel until 1998, when it was replaced with a synthetic substitute.

Race Riots

The Arrest and Supplication of Sir Thomas More by Antoine Caron

On this day in 1535, Sir Thomas More was beheaded.

In a play about him, written by Shakespeare and a number of other hands, there is a speech in which More quells a group of May Day rioters intent on attacking the foreign immigrants, whom they think are flooding into the country, taking away their wives and their livelihoods. In the manuscript of the play in the British Library, this speech is in the handwriting of Shakespeare himself.

More: Look, what you do offend you cry upon,
That is the peace: not one of you here present,
Had there such fellows lived when you were babes
That could have topped the peace, as now you would,
The peace wherein till now you have grown up
Had been ta'en from you, and the bloody times
Could not have brought you to the state of men.
Alas poor things, what is it that you have got,
Although we grant you get the thing you seek?

Betts: Marry, the removing of the strangers, which cannot
choose but much advantage the poor handicrafts of the city.
More: Grant them removed, and grant that this your noise
Hath chid down all the majesty of England;
Imagine that you see the wretched strangers
Their babies at their backs and their poor luggage
Plodding to the ports and coasts for transportation,
And that you sit as kings in your desires
Authority quite silenced by your brawl,
And you in rough of your opinions clothed;
What have you got? I'll tell you: you had taught
How insolence and strong hand should prevail,
How order should be quelled; and by this pattern
Not one of you should live an aged man,
For other ruffians, as their fancies wrought,
With self same hand, self reasons, and self right,
Would shark on you, and men like ravenous fishes
Would feed on one another.
The Play of Sir Thomas More, Shakespeare and others
(Act 2 Scene 4)

King Philip of Spain Declared King of England

On this day in 1588 King Philip of Spain was declared King of England by the Pope.

Pius V had excommunicated Queen Elizabeth in a papal bull, called *Regnans in Excelsis*, issued in 1570. Then on this day in 1588, Pope Sixtus V renewed the excommunication, and, as witnessed by the correspondence below, declared Philip king in her place.

SIXTVS · V· PONT · MAX·

'There is war against England in the air, and nothing will come of attempts for peace, for His holiness the Pope has had a bull read publicly in the Chapel of the Vatican in the presence of my most gracious lord of Salzburg. Therein the Queen of England is declared to be dispossessed of her kingdom, her lands, and her subjects, being long since a condemned heretic. Her subjects, of whatever rank they be, are released from the vow whereby heretofore they have sworn her allegiance.

'The Pope also deprives her of all the titles she had held up to now, divests her of all honours and transfers them all to the King of Spain. On this account the latter is now to declare himself to be rightfully chosen and appointed King of England and Ireland and Protector of the Catholic faith in that country. He is to wage war upon the Queen and to endeavour to bring her lands and her people under his sway. His holiness has publicly proclaimed His Majesty King of Spain, England and Ireland, and will bestow this title upon him for all time, on condition, however that His Majesty when he obtain possession of these provinces pay tribute to the Holy Roman See with a certain yearly pension as is done on behalf of the Kingdom of Naples.

'In order that His Majesty should be able to do this with the greater ease, His holiness is granting him a million crowns for his assistance: half of it for the present putting to sea of the Armada, the other half whenever His Majesty's forces have set foot in England and captured an important harbour.'

Fugger Newsletter from Salzburg

Pope Sixtus V's excommunication is echoed in Cardinal Pandulph's 'fatwah' directed towards King John, in Shakespeare's play of that name:

Cardinal Pandulph: *Then, by the lawful power that I have,*
Thou shalt stand curs'd and excommunicate:
And blessed shall he be that doth revolt
From his allegiance to an heretic;
And meritorious shall that hand be call'd,
Canonized and worshipped as a saint,
That takes away by any secret course
Thy hateful life.

King John (Act 3 Scene 1)

Queen Elizabeth Visits Kenilworth Castle

On this day in 1575, Queen Elizabeth arrived at Kenilworth Castle (about a dozen miles from Stratford), to be entertained by Robert Dudley, the Earl of Leicester. He was keen to impress Elizabeth, and hoped to capture her hand in marriage. He organised several days of elaborate entertainment. The following is taken from George Gascoigne's account in *Princely Pleasures* of the Kenilworth festivities:

'Saturday: Her Majesty came hither (as I remember) on Saturday being the ninth of July past. On which day there met her on the way somewhat near the castle, Sibylla (being placed in an arbour, in the park near the highway), who prophesied unto her

Highness the prosperous reign that she should continue, according to the happy beginning of the same.

'Her Majesty passing on to the first gate, there stood on the leads and the battlements thereof, six trumpeters hugely advanced, much exceeding the common stature of men of this age, who had likewise huge and monstrous trumpets counterfeited, wherein they seemed to sound: and behind them were placed certain trumpeters who sounded indeed at her majesty's entry.

'And when her Majesty entered the gate, there stood Hercules for porter, who seeming to be amazed at such a presence, upon such a sudden, proffered to stay them. But yet at last being overcome by view of the rare beauty and princely countenance of her Majesty, yielded himself and his charge, presenting the keys unto her Highness.

'When her Majesty had entered the gate, and come into the base court, there came unto her a Lady attended with two nymphs, who came all over the pool, being so conveyed, that it seemed she had gone upon the water. This lady named herself the Lady of the Lake.

'Her Majesty proceeding towards the inner court, passed on a bridge, the which was railed in on both sides. And on the tops of the posts thereof were set sundry presents, and gifts of provision; as wine, corn, fruits, fishes, fowls, instruments of music, and weapons for martial defence. All of which were expounded upon by an actor clad as a poet.

'The speech being ended, she was received into the inner court with sweet music. And so alighting from her horse, the drums, fifes and trumpets sounded: wherewith she mounted the stairs and went to her lodging.'

Kenilworth: Day Two

Underwater Fireworks

'On the next day (being Sunday) there was nothing done until the evening, at which time there were fireworks showed upon the water, which were both strange and well executed; as sometimes passing under the water a long space, when all men had thought they had been quenched, they would rise and mount out of the water again, and burn very furiously until they were utterly consumed.'

Princely Pleasures, George Gascoigne

The following day, after returning from hunting (and being briefly waylaid by a wild man clad in ivy) the Queen witnesses a water pageant. Robert Laneham takes up the story of Monday's events:

'She was entertained with another show upon the water, in which appeared a person in the character of Arion, riding upon a dolphin twenty-four feet in length; and he sung an admirable song, accompanied with music performed by six musicians concealed in the belly of the fish. Her majesty, it appears, was much pleased with this exhibition.

'Harry Goldingham was to represent Arion upon the back of a dolphin; but finding his voice to be very hoarse and unpleasant when he came to perform his part, he tears off his disguise, and swears that he was none of Arion, not he, but even honest Harry Goldingham; which blunt discovery pleased the queen better than if it had gone through in the right way. Yet he could order his voice to an instrument exceedingly well.'

Letter by Robert Laneham

It's hard to resist the idea that John Shakespeare might just have ridden over from nearby Stratford with his 11-year-old son William, to witness this spectacular event. The Harry Goldingham anecdote is reminiscent of the rehearsal in *A Midsummer Night's Dream*:

Bottom: *Masters, you ought to consider with yourselves: to bring in a lion among ladies, is a most dreadful thing, for there is not a more fearful wild fowl than your lion living, and we ought to look to it.*

Snout: *Therefore another prologue must tell he is not a lion.*

Bottom: *Nay, you must name his name, and half his face must be seen through the lion's neck; and he himself must speak through saying thus or to the same defect 'Ladies, or Fair ladies, I would wish you', or 'I would request you', or 'I would entreat you, not to fear, not to tremble, my life for yours, if I come hither as a lion it were pity on my life: no I am no such thing: I am a man as other men are;' and there indeed let him name his name and tell them plainly he is Snug the joiner.*

A Midsummer Night's Dream (Act 3 Scene 1)

Also on this day in 1584 in Delft, Prince William the Silent became the first head of state to be assassinated with a handgun.

Hic Incepit Pestis

On this day in 1564, the plague claimed its first victim in Stratford. Shakespeare was 11 weeks old. 'Hic incepit pestis' ('Here the plague begins') was recorded alongside a burial entry in the parish register in Holy Trinity Church. Six years before, his sister Joan died of the plague just two months after her birth, and, just under a year before William was born, the family had buried another daughter, Margaret, aged only six months. A man just up the street from the Shakespeares lost four children by the end of that year.

When it petered out, having devastated the town, 200 people had died. The town population was then about 1,500; today just about half that number work for the RSC in Stratford, while the town's population is about 24,000 – sixteen times what it was in Shakespeare's day.

Also on this day in 1649, Shakespeare's first child, Susanna, died aged 66, widow to Dr John Hall. The inscription on her tomb in Holy Trinity describes her as:

Witty above her sex, but that's not all,
Wise to salvation was good Mistress Hall.
Something of Shakespeare was in that, but this
Wholy of him with whom she's now in bliss.
Then, Passenger, hast ne'er a tear,
To weep with her that wept with all;
That wept, yet set her self to cheer
Them up with comfort's cordial.
Her love shall live, her mercy spread,
When thou hast ne'er a tear to shed.

See August 17th for a tragic death that same year, just over a month after Susanna's funeral.

Polar Bear Baiting

From a letter written on this day in 1623:
'The Spanish ambassador is much delighted in bear baiting. He was the last week at Paris Garden where they showed him all the pleasure they could both with bull and bear and horse, besides Jackanapes, and then turned a white bear into the Thames where the dogs baited him swimming, which was the best sport of all.'

The search for novelty was clearly a feature at Paris Garden. The Duke of Najera had attended a bear baiting in 1544, and had noted with some delight:
'a pony with an ape fastened on its back. To see the animal kicking among the dogs, with the screams of the ape, beholding the curs hanging from the ears and neck of the pony, is very laughable.'

And Lupold von Wedel in 1584 described the hilarious finale:
'Right over the middle of the place a rose was fixed, this rose being set on fire by a rocket: suddenly lots of apples and pears fell out of it down upon the people standing below. Whilst the people were scrambling for the apples, some rockets were made to fall down upon them out of the rose, which caused a great fright but amused the spectators. After this, rockets and other fireworks came flying out of all corners, and that was the end.'

The Porter in *All is True* recalls:
These are the youths that thunder at a playhouse and fight for bitten apples, that no audience but the tribulation of Tower Hill or the limbs of Limehouse, their dear brothers, are able to endure.
All is True (Act 5 Scene 4)

King Christian IV of Denmark had presented James I with two polar bears on his visit to England in 1606. In *The Masque of Oberon*, performed at court that Christmastide, Prince Henry, as the Fairy King himself, arrived onto the stage in 'a chariot drawn by white bears'.

It is intriguing to wonder how Shakespeare's most famous stage direction: *Exit pursued by bear*, in *The Winter's Tale*, was actually realized on the *Globe* Stage. The actors had had bears on stage before. One of the most popular plays of Shakespeare's theatre was an unattributed play called *Mucedorus*, in which a bear appears chasing Amadine, the daughter of the King of Aragon, and her cowardly fiancé Segasto. The hero Mucedorus arrives to rescue Amadine, and kill the beast. Did they use a bearskin? Certainly Henslowe's inventory from the Rose next door in 1598 includes a bearskin (see March 10th) or did they borrow Harry Hunks, or Sackerson, or the old blind bear, from the adjacent bear pits? Or might the King's Men have had access to these spectacular white bears from Denmark? Especially if they were indeed 'house-trained' enough to have taken the stage at Whitehall.

Mucedorus was performed at Witney in Oxfordshire on February 3rd, 1654, by a troop of travelling players. A number of the audience were killed when the floor collapsed under the weight of the crowd. As with the collapse of the Paris Garden's stand in 1583, (see January 13th), the Puritan preachers considered the accident a sign of God's displeasure with play-acting and theatre.

Weasels

Night-wandering weasels shriek to see him there.
The Rape of Lucrece

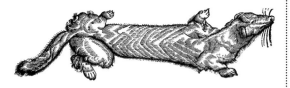

Edward Topsell on the odd behaviour of weasels:
'I do marvel how it came to pass, that a weasel was called an unhappy, unfortunate and unlucky beast among hunters, for they held opinion here in England, that if they meet with a weasel in the morning, they shall not speed well that day.

'They have knowledge like mice and rats to run out of houses before their downfall. They live in hatred of the serpent that hunteth mice, for by eating of rue they drive them out of the houses wherein they inhabit; and this is a wonderful work of God, that this silly beast should have the knowledge of the virtue of that herb, and not only arm herself with it, because it is hateful to serpents, and they in no wise in nature able to abide, but also by it to restore to life again her young ones after they are dead.

'There is a poison in weasels which destroyeth the cockatrice, for when the weasel findeth the cockatrice's hole or den, she layeth her poison in the mouth thereof, whereby two contrary natures meet and fight, and the lesser overcometh the greater.

'There is nothing in this beast more strange, than their conception and generation, for they do not engender and couple in their hinder parts, like other four-footed beasts, but at their ears and bring forth their young ones at their mouth, and for this cause Aristeas writeth , the Jews were forbidden to eat them for this their action was an emblem of folly and of foolish men which can keep no secrets, but a utter all that they hear (thus sayeth he).'

I can suck melancholy out of a song, as a weasel sucks eggs.
As You Like It (Act 2 Scene 5)

As the Sun would have entered the House of Leo on this day, in Shakespeare's time, here is Edmund Spenser's depiction of hot July, stripped naked and riding boldly on the lion's back. Spenser identifies the animal as the Nemean Lion, mentioned by Hamlet. The son of Amphytrion, Hercules, killed this beast in the first of his twelve labours and wore its impenetrable pelt as a cloak:

Then came hot July boiling like to fire,
That all his garments he had cast away:
Upon a Lion raging yet with ire
He boldly rode and made him to obey:
It was the beast that whilom did foray
The Nemaean forest, till th' Amphytrionide
Him slew, and with his hide did him array;
Behind his back a scythe, and by his side
Under his belt he bore a sickle circling wide.

Mutabilitie Cantos, VII: XXXV

St Revel's Day

Imports and Exports

Richard Hakluyt describes some of the plants, flowers and animals that have been imported into England in Shakespeare's day:

'In time of memory things have been brought in that were not here before, as the damask rose by Doctor Linaker, King Henry VII, and King Henry VIII's physician; the Turkey cocks and hens, about fifty years past, the Artichoke in the time of King Henry VIII; and of later time was procured out of Italy the musk rose plant, the plum called the Peridigwene and two kinds more by the Lord Crowell after his travel, and the Apricot by a French priest, one Wolfe, gardener to King Henry VIII; and now within these four years there have been brought into England from Vienna in Austria divers kinds of flowers called Tulips, and those and other procured thither a little before from Constantinople, by an excellent man called M. Carolus Clusius. And it is said that since we traded to Zante that the plant is also brought into this realm from thence.

'The Archbishop of Canterbury, Edmund Grindall, after he returned out of Germany, brought into this realm the plant of Tamarisk from thence, and this plant he hath so increased that there be here thousands of them; and many people have received great health by this plant; and if of such things brought in such care were had, then could not the first labour be lost. The seed of Tobacco hath been brought hither out of the West Indies, it groweth there, and with the herb, many have been eased of rheums etc.

'Each one of a great number of things were worthy of a journey to be made into Spain, Italy, Barbary, Egypt, Zante, Constantinople, the West Indies, and to divers other places near and further off than any of these, yet forasmuch as the poor are not able, and for that the rich settled at home in quiet will not, therefore we are to make suit to such as repair to foreign kingdoms, for other business, to have some care herein.'

Hakluyt's Voyages

As part of the export drive under Queen Elizabeth, Richard Hakluyt advises merchants what commodities to stow on board. They include:

'Karsies of all orient colours. Frizadoes, Motlies, Bristow friezes, Spanish blankets, Felts of divers colours. Tafetta hats. Deep caps for mariners, coloured in Stammel, whereof if ample vent may be found it would turn to an infinite commodity of the common people by knitting. Quilted caps of Levant tafetta for the night. Knit stocks of silk or jerzie yarn. Garters of silk of several kind. Girdles of Buff and all other leather with gilt and ungilt buckles. Spectacles of the common sort. Others of crystal trimmed with silver. Hour glasses, combs of box, ivory and horn, linen of divers sorts. Needles great and small of every kind. Buttons greater and smaller. Boxes with weights for gold and of every kind of the coin of gold, good and bad, to show that the people here use weight and measure, which is a certain show of wisdom and certain government settled here. Locks and keys and hinges and bolts, hasps etc.

'Take also a large map of London to make show of your city. And let the river be drawn full of ships of all sorts to make the more show of your great traffic in trade of merchandise.'

'Twas Tuesday Last, the fourteenth day of July,
Saint Revels day, the almanac will tell ye...
Penniless Pilgrimage, John Taylor

On this day in 1618, John Taylor, the so called 'Water Poet', a Thames Ferryman turned pamphleteer, set out to walk to Edinburgh on his *Penniless Pilgrimage*. He describes the journey in doggerel verse in a subsequent pamphlet. No other reference to St Revel has been found.

St Swithin's Day

Our Swithin then ensues, of him why ours I say,
Is that upon his feast, his dedicated day,
As it in Harvest haps, so ploughmen note thereby,
Th'ensuing forty days be either wet or dry.

Poly-Olbion (24th Song), Michael Drayton

The Wreck of the *Sea Adventure*

On this day in 1610, William Strachey, secretary to Sir Thomas Gates at Jamestown, Virginia, sent the following letter to an excellent lady. Although the letter was not published until 1625, Shakespeare may have read it when he was writing *The Tempest*. Strachey tells of 'a most dreadful Tempest (the manifold deaths whereof are here to the life described)'. Shakespeare was certainly prompted by the excitement caused by the disappearance at sea of Sir Thomas Gates, his safe return from Virginia in the autumn of 1610, and the subsequent publication of pamphlets describing the shipwreck in the Bermudas.

'Excellent Lady, know that upon Friday late in the evening, we brake our ground out of the Sound of Plymouth, our whole fleet then consisting of seven good ships, and two pinnaces all of which from the said second of June, unto the twenty three of July, kept in friendly consort together, not a whole watch at any time losing the sight each of other. We were within seven or eight days at the most of making Cape Henry upon the coast of Virginia.

'When on St James his day, being Monday (preparing for no less all the black night before) the clouds gathering thick upon us, and the winds singing, and whistling most unusually, a dreadful storm and hideous began to blow from out of the North-east, which swelling and roaring as it were by fits, some hours with more violence than others, at length did beat all light from heaven, which like a hell of darkness turned black upon us.

'For four and twenty hours the storm in a restless tumult had blown so exceedingly, as we could not apprehend in our imagination any possibility of greater violence, yet did we still find it, not only more terrible, but more constant; fury added to fury, and one storm urging a second more outrageous than the former.

'Prayers might well be in the heart and lips, but drowned in the outcries of the officers. Nothing heard that could give comfort, nothing seen that might encourage hope.

'Our sails wound up lay without their use. The sea swelled above the clouds and gave battle unto Heaven. It could not be said to rain, the waters like whole rivers, did flood in the air. The glut of water (as if throttling the wind ere while) was no sooner a little emptied and qualified, as the winds spake more loud, and grew more tumultuous and malignant. What shall I say? Wind and seas were mad, as fury and rage could make them. There was not a moment in which the sudden splitting or instant over-setting of the shop was not expected.

'Howbeit this was not all; it pleased God to bring a greater affliction yet upon us; for in the beginning of the storm we had received a mighty leak...'

St Elmo's Fire

I boarded the king's ship; now on the beak,
Now in the waist, the deck, in every cabin,
I flam'd amazement: sometime I'd divide
And burn in many places; on the topmast,
The yards and bowsprit, would I flame distinctly.

The Tempest (Act 1 Scene 2)

The Wreck of the *Sea Adventure* continued:

'Once so huge a sea brake upon the poop and quarter upon us, as it covered our ship from stern to stem like a garment or a vast cloud, it filled her brim full for a while within, from the hatches to the sparre deck.

'During all this time, the heavens looked so black upon us, that it was not possible the elevation of the Pole might be observed. Only upon the Thursday night Sir George Summers, being upon the watch, had an apparition of a little round light, like a faint star, trembling, and streaming along with a sparkling blaze, half the height upon the main mast, and shooting sometimes from shroud to shroud, and for three or four hours together, or rather more, half the night it kept with us; running sometimes along the main-yard to the very end and returning.

'The superstitious seamen make many constructions of this sea fire, which nevertheless is usual in storms... the Spaniards call it St Elmo, and have an authentic and miraculous legend for it.

'We unrigged our ship, threw over board much luggage, many a trunk and chest (in which I suffered no mean loss) and staved many a butt of beer, hogsheads of oil, cider, wine, and vinegar, and heaved away all our ordinance upon the starboard side and had now purpose to cut down the main mast, the more to lighten her. From Tuesday noon to Friday noon we bailed and pumped two thousand ton. It wanted little, but that there had been a general determination to have shut up hatches and commending our sinful souls to God, committed the ship to the mercy of the sea. Surely that night we must have done it, and that night had we then perished: but see the goodness and sweet introduction of better hope, by our merciful God given unto us. Sir George Summers, when no man dreamed of such happiness, had discovered and cried Land.'

Letter by William Strachey, wrecked on the Sea Adventure (1610)

Also on this day John White sketched the inhabitants of an Indian village.

Wine and Women Too!

In 1606, King Christian IV of Denmark, the King's brother-in-law, arrived for a month's visit.

Sir John Harrington provides an account of the revels, including a drunken masque:

'I came here a day or two before the Danish King, and, from the day he did come until this hour, I have been well nigh overwhelmed with carousal and sports of all kinds. The sports began each day, and in such manner and such sort, as well nigh persuaded me of Mahomet's paradise. We had women and indeed wine too, of such plenty as would have astonished each sober beholder. Our feasts were magnificent, and the two royal guests did most lovingly embrace each other at table. I think the Dane hath strangely wrought on our good English nobles; for those whom I could never get to taste good liquor, now follow the fashion and wallow in drunken delights. The ladies abandon their sobriety, and are seen to roll about in intoxication. In good sooth, the parliament did kindly to provide his Majesty so seasonably with money, for there hath been no lack of good living, shows, sights and banquetings from morn to eve.

'One day, a great feast was held, and after dinner, the representation of Solomon and his temple and the coming of the Queen of Sheba was made, or (I may better say) was meant to have been made, before their majesties, by device of the Earl of Salisbury and others. But alas! as all earthly things do fail to poor mortals in enjoyment, so did prove our presentment hereof.

'The lady who did play the Queen's part, did carry most precious gifts to both their majesties; but forgetting the steps arising to the canopy, over set her caskets into his Danish Majesty's lap, and fell at his feet, although I rather think it was in his face. Much was the hurry and confusion; cloths and napkins were at hand to make all clean.

'His Majesty then got up and would dance with the Queen of Sheba; but he fell down and humbled himself before her, and was carried to an inner chamber and was laid on a bed of state; which was not a little defiled with the presents of the Queen which had been bestowed on his garments; such as wine, cream, jelly, beverage, cakes, spices, and other good matters. The entertainment and show went forward, and most of the presenters went backward, or fell down; wine did so occupy their upper chambers.

'Now did appear in rich dress, Hope, Faith and Charity: Hope did assay to speak, but wine rendered her endeavours so feeble that she withdrew, and hoped the king would excuse her brevity: Faith was then all alone (for I am certain she was not joined with Good Works), and left the court in a staggering condition: Charity came to the King's feet, and seemed to cover the multitude of sins her sisters had committed; in some sort she made obeisance and brought gifts, but said she would return home again, as there was no gift which heaven had not given his Majesty. She then returned to Hope and Faith, who were both sick and spewing in the lower hall.'

Letter from Sir John Harrington

Danes
·······

The visit of the Danish King to England in 1606 may have provoked a number of jokes about their love of drink. In *Hamlet*, Shakespeare has the young prince rail at his countrymen's love of the bottle:

Hamlet: *The King doth wake tonight and takes his rouse,*
Keeps wassail, and the swaggering up-spring reels;
And as he drains his draught of Rhenish down,
The kettle-drum and trumpet thus bray out
The triumph of his pledge.
Horatio: *Is it a custom?*
Hamlet: *Ay marry, is't:*
But to my mind, – though I am native here
And to the manner born, – it is a custom
More honoured in the breach than in the observance.
This heavy-headed revel east and west
Makes us traduced of other nations;
They clepe us drunkards, and with swinish phrase
Soil our addition.

Hamlet (Act 1 Scene 4)

And here is an example of just that, as Thomas Nashe, in a nakedly racist attack on the Danes in general, soils their addition:

'The most gross and senseless proud dolts are the Danes, who stand so much upon their unwieldy burly-boned soldiery that they account of no man that hath not a battle axe at his girdle to hough dogs with, or wears not a cock's feather in a red thrummed hat like a cavalier. Briefly, he is the best fool and braggart under heaven. For besides nature hath lent him a face, like one of the four winds, and cheeks that sag like a woman's dugs over his chin bone, his apparel is so puffed up with bladders of taffaty, and his back like beef stuffed with parsley; so drawn out with ribbons and devices, and blistered with light sarsanet bastings, that you would think him nothing but a swarm of butterflies if you saw him far off. Thus he walks up and down in his majesty, taking a yard of ground at every step, and stamps on the earth so terrible, as if he meant to knock up a spirit, when, foul drunken bezzle, if an Englishman set his little finger on him, he falls like a hogs-trough that is set on one end. Therefore I am the more vehement against them, because they are an arrogant, ass-headed people, that naturally hate learning and all that love it. Yes, and for they would utterly root it out from among them, they would have withdrawn all rewards from the professors thereof. Not Barbary itself is half so barbarous as they are.'

Pierce Penniless, His Supplication to the Devil, Thomas Nashe

Christian IV, King of Denmark

Unicorns
••••••••••

Now I will believe that there are unicorns.

The Tempest (Act 3 Scene 3)

'We are now come to the history of a beast, whereof divers people in every age of the world have made great question, because of the rare virtues thereof; therefore it behoveth us to use some diligence in comparing together the several testimonies that are spoke of this beast, for the better satisfaction of such as are now alive, and clearing of the point for them that shall be born hereafter, whether there be a unicorn; for that is the main question to be resolved.

'But to the purpose, that there is such a beast, the Scripture itself witnesseth, for David thus speaketh in the 92nd Psalm, that is "My horn shall be lifted up like the horn of a unicorn." And do we think that David would compare the virtue of his kingdom, and the powerful redemption of the world to a thing that is not? Likewise in the prophesy of Esau (the 34th chap) and in many other places in scripture, whereby God himself must needs be traduced, if there be no unicorns in the world.

The History of Four-Footed Beasts, Edward Topsell

On this day, July 19th, 1577:

'And coming to those straits in July [1577] found them in manner shut up with a long Mure of ice, which sometime endangered their ships, especially on the nineteenth of that month. They found a dead fish, round like a porpoise, twelve foot long, having a horn of two yards, lacking two inches, growing out of the snout, wreathed and straight, like a wax taper and might be thought to be a sea unicorn. It was broken at the top wherein some sailors said they put spiders which presently died. It was reserved as a jewel by the Queen's commandment, in her Wardrobe of Robes, and is still at Windsor to be seen.

'In departing from thence the *Salamander*, one of their ships, being under both her courses and bonnets, happened to strike on a great whale with her full stem, with such a blow, that the ship stood still and neither stirred forward or backward. The whale thereat made a great and hideous noise and casting up his body and tail, presently sank under water. Within two days they found a whale dead, which they supposed was this which the *Salamander* had stricken.'

Purchas His Pilgrimes: Book Eight, Samuel Purchas

Roses
········

A Presumptious Woman

Blow like sweet roses in this summer air.
Love's Labour's Lost (Act 5 Scene 2)

In the Temple garden, Richard Plantagenet challenges those present to proclaim their allegiances in 'dumb significants'. Those on his side should 'from off this brier pluck a white rose with me'. And the Earl of Somerset responds by asking his party to 'pluck a red rose from off this thorn with me'.

   As the parties of York and Lancaster declare their sides, the Earl of Warwick predicts the dreadful outcome of the bloody Wars of the Roses:

... this brawl today,
Grown to this faction in the Temple garden,
Shall send between the red rose and the white
A thousand souls to death and deadly night.
Henry VI Part One (Act 2 Scene 4)

With sweet musk roses and with eglantine.
A Midsummer Night's Dream (Act 2 Scene 1)

Even so it was with me when I was young:
If ever we are nature's, these are ours; this thorn
Doth to our rose of youth rightly belong;
Our blood to us, this to our blood is born;
It is the show and seal of nature's truth,
Where love's strong passion is impress'd in youth:
By our remembrances of days foregone,
Such were our faults, or then we thought them none.
All's Well That Ends Well (Act 1 Scene 3)

See, my women!
Against the blown rose may they stop their nose
That kneel'd unto the buds.
Antony and Cleopatra (Act 3 Scene 13)

I have seen roses damasked red and white,
But no such roses see I in her cheeks.
Sonnet CXXX

When I have pluck'd the rose,
I cannot give it vital growth again.
It must needs wither: I'll smell it on the tree.
Othello (Act 5 Scene 2)

When he did frown, O, had she then gave over,
Such nectar from his lips she had not suck'd.
Foul words and frowns must not repel a lover;
What though the rose have prickles, yet 'tis pluck'd.
Venus and Adonis

Swans

All the water in the ocean,
Can never turn the swan's black legs to white,
Although she lave them hourly in the flood.
Titus Andronicus (Act 4 Scene 2)

Around about this date in the third full week of July, the ceremony of Swan Upping takes place on the Thames.

All swans on open waters in Britain are automatically the property of the crown. The only exception is that a certain number of swans on the River Thames have belonged to the London Guilds of the Vintners and the Dyers since the 1470s. Since Elizabethan times, these distinguished guilds have organized an annual Swan Voyage in the third week of July, when the young cygnets are reckoned to be about two months old. During this voyage the swans are 'upped' or lifted from the river to be examined for the beak marks which denote them as the company's swans.

In the days when the Vintners and the Dyers owned magnificent state barges this event was quite a celebration, with much feasting and ceremonial. Now it happens in rowing boats. Nevertheless the Queen's Swanherd, in royal red livery, with the company's Swan Marker join the voyage, and as they pass Windsor Castle they stand and salute 'Her Majesty the Queen, Seigneur of the Swans'.

I will play the swan
And die in music.
Othello (Act 5 Scene 2)

As Emilia, murdered by her husband, Iago, dies in the last Act of *Othello*, she recalls the willow song sung by Desdemona, and the famous myth that the mute swan suddenly finds its voice in death, perhaps most beautifully expressed in Orlando Gibbons' 1612 madrigal:

The silver swan, who living had no note,
When death approach'd, unlock'd her silent
throat;
Leaning her breast against the reedy
shore,
Thus sung her first and last,
and sung no more.
Farewell, all joys; O Death,
come close mine eyes;
More geese than swans
now live, more fools
than wise.
Othello (Act 5 Scene 2)

Roanoke Mysteriously Abandoned
••

On the Fourth Voyage of the Virginia Company in 1587, John White sought out the colony they had left there the previous year.

'The two and twentieth of July [1587] the Governor John White went aboard the pinnace accompanied with forty of his best men, intending to pass up to Roanoke forthwith, hoping there to find those fifteen Englishmen, which Sir Richard Greville had left there the year before, with whom he meant to have conference, concerning the state of the country, the

Savages, meaning after he had done so, to return again to the fleet, and pass along the coast to the Bay of Chesapeake.

'The same night at sunset we went aland on the island, in the place where our fifteen men were left, but we found none of them, nor any sign that they had been there, saving only we found the bones of one of those fifteen which the Savages had slain long before.

'The three and twentieth of July the Governor with divers of his company walked to the North end of the island, where Master Ralph Lane had his fort, with sundry necessary and decent dwelling houses, made by his men about it the year before, where we hoped to find some signs, or certain knowledge of our fifteen men. When we came thither, we found the fort raised down, but all the houses standing unhurt, saving that the nether rooms of them, and also of the fort, were overgrown with melons of divers sorts: so we returned to our company, without hope of ever seeing any of the fifteen men living.

'The same day order was given, that every man should be employed for the repairing of those houses, which we found standing, and also to make new cottages, for such as would need.

'The eight and twentieth, George Howe, one of our twelve assistants was slain by divers Savages, which were come over to Roanoke, either of purpose to espy our company, and what number we were, or else to hunt deer, whereof there are many in the Island. These Savages being secretly hidden among the reeds, espied our man wading in the water alone, almost naked, without any weapon, save only a small forked stick, catching crabs therewithal, and shot at him in the water, where they gave him sixteen wounds with their arrows, and after they had slain him with their wooden swords, they beat his head in pieces, and fled over the water to the main.'

The Fifth Voyage of Mr John White into the West Indies and Parts of America

'The Most Beautiful Book in the English Language'
••

In 1567, Arthur Golding dedicated the first edition of his translation of Ovid's *Metamorphoses* to Robert, Earl of Leicester. Ezra Pound called it 'the most beautiful book in the English Language'.

Daphne and Apollo by Antonio Pollaiuolo

This is the moment when the nymph Daphne prays to Jove to be rescued from the pursuit of the amorous Apollo. She is changed into a Laurel tree:

Howbeit he that did pursue of both the swifter went,
(As furthered by the feathered wings that Cupid had
    him lent),
So that he would not let her rest, but pressèd at her heel,
So near that, through her scattered hair, she might his
    breathing feel:
But when she saw her breath was gone, and strength began
    to fail,
The colour faded in her cheeks, and 'ginning for to quail
She looked to Penaeus' stream and said 'Now Father dear,
And, if yon stream have power of Gods, then help your
    daughter here.
O let the earth devour me quick, on which I seem too fair,
Or else this shape (which is my harm), by changing straight
    impair.'
This piteous prayer scarcely said; her sinews waxèd stark.
And therewithal about her breasts did grow a tender bark.
Her hair was turned into leaves, her arms in boughs
    did grow,
Her feet that were ere while so swift, now rooted were as slow.
Her crown became the top, and thus of that she erst had been,
Remainèd nothing in this earth but beauty fresh and green.
Which when that Phoebus did behold (affection so did move)
The tree to which his love was turned he could no less
    but love,
And as he softly laid his hand upon the tender plant,
Within the bark, yet over-grown, he felt her heart yet pant.
And in her arms embracing fast her boughs and branches
    lithe,
He proffered kisses to the tree, the tree did from him writhe.

Ovid's Metamorphoses (Book 1, lines 661 - 682), translated by
Arthur Golding

Salamon Pavy

It is probable that on this day in 1602, one of the leading boy actors of the Children of the Chapel died. He was buried the following day at St Mary Somerset. His name was Salamon or Salathiel Pavy. We know the names of perhaps a thousand players between 1590 and the closure of the theatres in 1642. Rarely do we get an insight into their talents. Pavy was lucky; he was immortalized by Ben Jonson in this sad little epitaph:

Weep with me all ye that read
This little story:
And know, for whom a tear you shed
Death's self is sorry.
'Twas a child, that so did thrive
In grace, and feature,
As Heaven and Nature seemed to strive
Which owned the creature.
Years he numbered scarce thirteen
When Fates turned cruel,
Yet three filled zodiacs had he been
The stage's jewel;
And did he act (what now we moan)
Old men so duly,
As, sooth, the Parcae* thought him one,
He played so truly.
So, by error, to his fate
They all consented;
But viewing him since (alas too late)
They have repented
And have sought (to give new birth)
In baths to steep him;
But, being so much too good for earth,
Heaven vows to keep him.

*Parcae: the Fates

Stratford Exorcist Hanged, Drawn and Quartered

Also on this day in 1586, Robert Dibdale was arrested and taken to prison in London. Dibdale was a Stratford man. He was born in Shottery in 1556, eight years Shakespeare's senior. He left Warwickshire for ever in 1575 to be ordained a Catholic priest in Rheims. He was later sent back to England as a missionary and became chaplain to a recusant family in Buckinghamshire. It was there that he conducted several exorcisms. *Three poor maids and two men*, records Fr Anthony Tyrell, were subjected to *conjurations, witchcrafts, sorceries and illusions*. Apparently in the course of the exorcism, Dibdale extracted out of the bowels of a man *a hooked pin, a piece of lead, and a shirt string, all fastened together*. He then proceeded to extract from the cheeks of the girls *a needle, a great blunt nail all rusty and a piece of a rusty knife*. Dibdale was, Tyrell reports, *a great deluder of the world*.

Whatever happened at those exorcisms in Buckinghamshire, the young Jesuit priest paid a heavy penalty. He was condemned for treason, and as John Stow reports, on the October 8th 1586, he was *drawn to Tyburn, and there hanged, disembowelled and quartered*. He has the dubious distinction of being the only Stratford man ever to have met his end in this way.

St James the Apostle
•••••••••••••••••••••

Down the Thames in a Brown Paper Boat

On this day in 1622, John Taylor set off down the Thames in a boat made of brown paper using two stockfish tied to canes as oars.

The trip to Queenborough, on the Isle of Sheppey in Kent, was about forty miles. He was accompanied on this stunt by a vintner friend called Roger ('Hodge') Bird. He described his madcap rowing feat in *In Praise of Hempseed* from which this is taken:

The year which I do call as others do
Full 1600, adding twenty two:
On that remarkable good day, Saint James,
I undertook a journey down the Thames.

The water to the paper being got,
In one half hour our boat began to rot.
In which extremity I thought it fit
To put in use a stratagem of wit,
Which was, eight bullocks bladders we had bought
Puffed stiffly full with wind, bound fast and taut,
Which on our boat within the tide we tied
One each side four upon the outward side.
The water still rose higher by degrees,
In three miles going, almost to our knees.
Our rotten bottom all to tatters fell,
And left our boat as bottomless as hell.

Yet such we feared the graves our end would be
Before we could the Town of Gravesend see :
Our boat drunk deeply with her dropsy thirst,
And quaft as if she would her bladders burst.
Thus did we drive, and drive the time away,
Till pitchy night had driven away the day.
The tossing billows made our boat to caper,
Our paper form scarce being form of paper,
The water four mile broad, no Oars, to row,
Night dark, and where we were we did not know.

And thus 'twixt doubt and fear, hope and despair
I fell to work, and Roger Bird to prayer.
And as the surges up and down did heave vs,
He cried most fervently, "Good Lord receive us".
I pray'd as much, but I did work and pray,
And he did all he could to pray and play.
Thus three hours darkeling I did puzzle and toil
Soused and well pickled, chafe and muzzle & moil,
Drench'd with the swassing waves and stewed in sweat
Scarce able with a cane our boat to set,
At last (by God's great mercy and his might)
The morning gan to chase away the night.
And as the morning more end more did clear,
The sight of Queenborough castle did appear.

The following day, and after further adventures, our foolhardy sailors arrived in Queenborough:

The Mayor of Queenborough in love affords
To entertain us, as we had been lords;
But Hodge and I were men of rank and note,
We to the Mayor gave our adventurous boat.
But whilst we at our dinners thus were merry,
The country people tore up our tattered wherry
In mammocks peacemeal, in a thousand scraps,
Wearing the relics in their hats and caps,
That never traitor's corpse could be more scattered
By greedy ravens than our poor boat was tattered.

In Praise of Hempseed, John Taylor

'Alas, Poor Yorick'

On this day in 1602 *Hamlet* was entered in the Stationers' Register.

❋

From my diary entry for July 26th, 2008, Courtyard Theatre, Stratford-upon-Avon:

'Third Preview of *Hamlet*. Tonight André was finally to play Yorick. Or that was the idea.

'In 1980, William Lockwood, the head of properties at the RSC, received a very strange parcel. It was a human skull. It belonged to André Tchaikowski, a pianist and composer, who had died of cancer in Oxford aged 46. He had bequeathed his skull in his will to the company to be used in a production of *Hamlet*, as Yorick. Apparently, the funeral directors handling André's cremation had baulked at removing his head, and permission had had to be sought from the Home Office. The head was removed and processed by medical staff at the hospital, but by the time William Lockwood received it, it still stank. Crusty, the Prop Shop dog, had gone berserk, and the skull had to be removed from the Delsey tissue box in which it had arrived, placed in a sprout bag and hung on a line outside for several months to dry out. And so far it has never been used. Roger Rees was painted for the poster of the 1984 production holding this skull, and Mark Rylance had used it in rehearsal in 1989, but André had never actually got on stage in performance. Tonight was to be his night.

'I had introduced the company to the skull on the first day of rehearsals, with the proposal that we used it in our production, not just so that we finally granted André his wish, but that the presence of a real skull would constantly remind us of the play's contemplation of mortality itself, which a prop skull, no matter how well made, would never quite provide. David Tennant, playing Hamlet, was eager to use it, and tonight was to be its first appearance. We were all excited at the prospect.

'Simon Ash the production manager approached me in the afternoon, his face the colour of his name. Unfortunately since a change in the law in 2005, a special licence was required from the Human Tissues Authority, and though one had been applied for, and acres of paperwork had been completed, it hadn't actually arrived, and, until it did, André would have to be consigned to his box in the Theatre Collection. I rang David Howells, our curator. He was apologetic, but proffered a temporary solution. As the objects in his care were part of a living theatre collection, he could offer me an alternative: another skull, but as this one was over a hundred years old, the HTA rules had no jurisdiction upon it. It was the skull Edmund Kean had used as Yorick when he played Hamlet in 1814. I accepted. The production photographs, taken that day, all show David staring into the empty eye sockets of Kean's skull.

'Luckily the licence soon arrived, at a cost of £250, and André, fresh from his make-up job in the props department (he had been too clean to have been lying in the earth for 'three and twenty years' and needed a little mud-pack applying), finally appeared on stage in front of the press for Monday's press call, and was used for the rest of the run.'

The Seven Sleepers
•••••••••••••••••••••

This day is marked as the feast day of the Seven Sleepers in Trevelyon's *Miscellany* of 1608.

Mentioned in Donne's poem *The Good Morrow*, the Seven Sleepers of Ephesus, persecuted for their Christianity under the Emperor Decius, slept in a cave for 100 years.

Here are seven thoughts on sleep by Mr W.S.

❋ **Helena:** *And sleep, that sometimes shuts up sorrow's eye,*
Steal me awhile from mine own company.
A Midsummer Night's Dream (Act 3 Scene 2)

❋ **Macbeth:** *Methought I heard a voice cry, 'Sleep no more! Macbeth does murder sleep.'*
Macbeth (Act 2 Scene 2)

❋ **Lady Macbeth:** *You lack the season of all natures: sleep.*
Macbeth (Act 3 Scene 4)

❋ **Iago:** *Not poppy nor mandragora*
Nor all the drowsy syrups of the world
Shall ever med'cine thee to that sweet sleep
Which thou owedst yesterday.
Othello (Act 3 Scene 3)

❋ **Hamlet:** *To die, to sleep, to sleep perchance to dream.*
Hamlet (Act 3 Scene 1)

❋ **King Henry IV:** *How many thousands of my poorest subjects*
Are at this hour asleep! O sleep, O gentle sleep,
Nature's soft nurse, how have I frighted thee,
That thou no more will weigh my eyelids down,
And steep my senses in forgetfulness?
Why rather, sleep, liest thou in smoky cribs,
Upon uneasy pallets stretching thee,
And hush'd with buzzing night-flies to thy slumber,
Than in the perfum'd chambers of the great,

Under the canopies of costly state,
And lull'd with sound of sweetest melody?
O thou dull god, why liest thou with the vile
In loathsome beds, and leav'st the kingly couch
A watch-case or a common 'larum-bell?
Wilt thou upon the high and giddy mast
Seal up the ship-boy's eyes, and rock his brains
In cradle of the rude imperious surge,
And in the visitation of the winds,
Who take the ruffian billows by the top,
Curling their monstrous heads, and hanging them
With deafing clamour in the slippery clouds,
That with the hurly, death itself awakes?
Canst thou, O partial sleep, give thy repose
To the wet sea-boy in an hour so rude;
And in the calmest and most stillest night,
With all appliances and means to boot,
Deny it to a king? Then, happy low, lie down!
Uneasy lies the head that wears a crown.
Henry IV Part Two (Act 3 Scene 1)

❋ **Player Queen:** *Sleep rock thy brain...*
Hamlet (Act 3 Scene 2)

The First Atlas of the British Isles Published

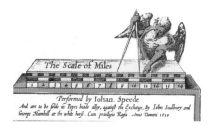

The Scale of Miles

Performed by Iohan. Speede.

And are to be solde in Popes heade alley, against the Exchange, By Iohn Sudbury and George Humbell at the white horse. Cum privilegio Regis Anno Domini 1610

On this day in 1629, the cartographer John Speed died and was buried in St Giles, Cripplegate.

In 1608, George Humble applied to the Stationers' Register for a Royal Licence for twenty-one years to print a book compiled by John Speed called *The Theatre of the Empire of Great Britayne with carts and maps* By 1611, it was ready, and was a great success. It had been a huge effort and a labour of love for Speed. He wrote of it:

'But by what fate I am forced still to go on, I know not unless it be the ardent affection and love to my native country; That this our Country and subject of History deserveth the love of her inhabitants, is witnessed even by foreign writers themselves, who have termed it the Court of Queen Ceres, the Granary of the Western World, the fortunate Island, the Paradise of pleasure and Garden of God...

'Where we from under our own vines without fear may behold the prints or endured miseries, sealed with the blood of those times, to the loss of their lives, and liberties; our selves hear not the sound of the Alarum in our Gates, nor the clattering of armour in our camps, whose swords are now turned into mattocks and spears into scythes.

'The Shires divisions into Lathes, Hundreds, Wapentakes and Cantreds according to their rateable, and accustomed manner I have separated, and under the same title that the record beareth, in their due places distinguished; wherein by the help of the Tables annexed, any City, Town, Borough, Hamlet, or place of note may readily be found, and whereby

safely may be affirmed that there is not any one kingdom in the world so exactly described.'

This royal throne of kings, this sceptred isle,
This earth of majesty, this seat of Mars,
This other Eden, demi paradise,
This fortress built by nature for herself
Against infection and the hand of war,
This happy breed of men, this little world,
This precious stone set in the silver sea
Which serves it in the office of a wall
Or as a moat defensive to a house
Against the envy of less happier lands,
This blessèd plot, this earth, this realm, this England.

Richard II (Act 2 Scene 1)

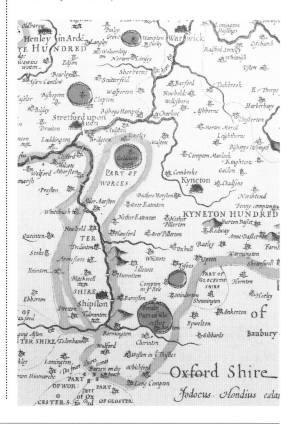

Defeat of the Spanish Armada
••••••••••••••••••••••••••••••••••••

On this day in 1588, the Spanish Armada was defeated.

Women on Board the Spanish Armada

'The last courier from Lisbon brings news of there having arrived a letter from London. Therefrom one learns of the preparations which are being made there. The people are reported to be unwilling to embark and it is presumed that the Catholics will join forces when the Armada arrives. It is also suspected that various lords will be their leaders.

'There were many women on board the Armada. The Duke ordered the captains to make a list of how many of them each had in his ship, and he requested them to bring the list to him in three or four days. It was found that there were somewhat more than six hundred. They were then not only put ashore again, but also removed from Lisbon. This was done after the soldiery had already come on board the ships. They were far from pleased on this account, but they were comforted with the report that there were comely wenches in England.'

Fugger Newsletter from Madrid

'The Armada of the King of Spain set sail from Portugal with one hundred and thirty-five ships, to wit: four galleasses from Naples, four galleons from Portugal, ten vessels with victuals, fourteen Venetian ships, among them several galleons. The remainder was made up of other large and small craft.

'The English sent forth against the Spanish Armada several burning ships, so that they were forced to cut their moorings and retire hastily. Each ship left two anchors behind and four of the largest galleasses were stranded and wrecked off Calais. The following day at eight o'clock, the two Armadas had a further encounter, heavily bombarding each other for eight hours. In this battle the Spanish lost four ships, namely two Portuguese galleasses, a vessel from Biscay and another. All four went to the bottom of the sea. The large Venetian craft remained behind off the coast of Flanders and were in great peril of going under. The inhabitants of Flushing took two of these ships, and a third was shipwrecked. One of them had on board the Colonel commanding the garrison of Seville. The Spaniards are said to have left one hundred and twenty ships, although others could only count one hundred and ten. The big galleon which the Duke of Florence had sent, was not to be seen anywhere after the battle.

'Hereafter the Armada made off and was pursued by the English for five days as far as Scotland. When they counted their men, they found they had already lost eight thousand, most of which had been killed or died of disease.'

Fugger Newsletter: Report from England received in Augsburg in November

What Happened at Roanoke

'On the Thirtieth of July, Master Stafford and twenty of our men passed by water to the island of Croatoan with Manteo, who had his mother, and many of his kindred dwelling in that island, of whom we hoped to understand some news of our fifteen men.

'We understood of them how that the 15 Englishmen left at Roanoke were suddenly set upon by 30 of the men of Secota, Aquascogoc and Dasamonguepeuk, in manner following. They conveyed themselves secretly behind the trees, near the houses where our men carelessly lived: and having perceived that of those fifteen they could see but eleven only, two of those savages appeared calling to them by friendly signs that two of their chiefest men should come unarmed to speak to them who seemed also to be unarmed. Wherefore two of the chiefest of our Englishmen went gladly to them: but whilst one of those Savages traitorously embraced one of our men, the other with his sword of wood, which he had secretly hidden under his mantle, struck him on the head and slew him, and presently the other eight and twenty savages showed themselves: the other Englishman perceiving this, fled to his company, whom the Savages pursued with their bow and arrows, so fast that the Englishman was forced to take the house wherein all their victual and weapons were: but the Savages forthwith set the same on fire: by means whereof our men were forced to take up such weapons as came first to hand, and without order to run forth among the Savages, with whom they skirmished above an hour.

'In this skirmish another of our men was shot into the mouth with an arrow, where he died, and also one of the Savages was shot into the side by one of our men, with a wild fire arrow, whereof he died presently. The place where they fought was of great advantage to the Savages, by means of the thick trees, behind which the Savages, through their nimbleness, defended themselves, and so offended our men with their arrows, that our men being some of them hurt, retired fighting to the water side, where their boat lay, with which they fled. By the time they rowed but a quarter of a mile, they espied their four fellows coming from a creek nearby, where they had been to fetch oysters. The four they received into their boat, leaving Roanoke, and landed on a little island where they remained a while, but afterward departed, whither as yet we know not.'

John White to Richard Hakluyt, 1587

There is an isolated island in Chesapeake Bay called Tangier Island. In the early days of the Virginia colonies, Captain John Smith stopped there in search of fresh water. Although it is only six miles from the Maryland Border, the island preserved its self-sufficiency and insularity for generations, and has attracted the attention of linguists because its people speak a unique dialect of American English, nearly unchanged since the days of its first occupation by English colonists. In other words, the islanders of Tangier Island may still speak Elizabethan English.

Lammas Eve

Juliet's birthday.

Nurse: How long is it now to Lammas tide?
Lady Capulet: A fortnight and odd days.
Nurse: Even or odd, of all the days in the year,
Come Lammas-eve at night shall she be fourteen.
Susan and she – God rest all Christian souls –
Were of an age. Well, Susan is with God;
She was too good for me. But as I said,
On Lammas Eve at night shall she be fourteen;
That shall she, marry. I remember it well.
'Tis since the earthquake now eleven years
And she was weaned, I never shall forget it,
Of all the days of the year upon that day
For I had then laid wormwood to my dug,
Sitting in the sun under the dovehouse wall
My Lord and you were then at Mantua,
Nay, I do bear a brain: but as I said,
When it did taste the wormwood on the nipple
Of my dug and felt it bitter, pretty fool,
To see it tetchy and fall out with the dug.

Romeo and Juliet (Act I Scene 3)

The silver-leafed Wormwood (*Artemisia absinthium*) is a bitter pungent herb, used in absinthe, as its Latin name suggests. It grows on waste ground, and is especially common in the West Midlands, so Shakespeare would have known it as a child. Presumably the Nurse had applied a little to her swollen dugs to ease the pain of her suckling charge, or perhaps to wean her off breast feeding, as the bitter taste of the wormwood makes the baby Juliet cry. John Gerard tells us that it was used to revive weary travellers and that people kept it about them so as not to get harmed by the sun. Perhaps that is why the Nurse, sitting in the sun, has used the herb.

Thomas Tusser recommends picking it now when it is in flower, and keeping it as a deterrent against fleas:

While Wormwood has seeds, get a bundle or twain,
To save against March, to make flea to refrain:
Where chamber is swept, and wormwood is strown,
No flea, for his life, dare abide to be known

July's Husbandry, Thomas Tusser

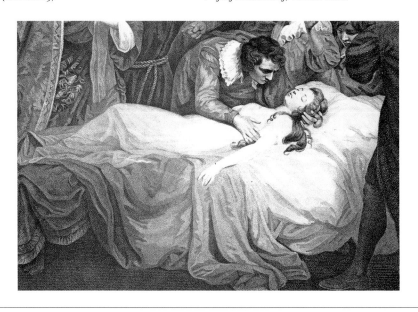

You sunburnt sickle men, of August weary
Come hither from the furrow and be merry
Make holiday ! Your rye-straw hats put on.
The Tempest (Act 4 Scene 1)

'August, in the form of a young man of a fierce and choleric aspect, in a flame coloured garment; upon his head a garland of wheat and rye, upon his arm a basket of ripe fruits, as pears, plums, apples, gooseberries, at his belt, a sickle bearing the sign of Virgo.'
Emblems, Henry Peacham

'It is now August, and the sun is somewhat towards his declination, yet such is his heat as hardeneth the soft clay, dries up the standing ponds, withereth the sappy leaves and scorches the skin of the naked : now begin the gleaners to follow the corn cart, and a little bread to a great deal of drink makes the travailers' dinner: the Melon and the cucumber is now in request: and the oil and vinegar give attendance to the sallet herbs: the Alehouse is more frequented than the Tavern, and a fresh river is more comfortable than a fiery furnace: the Bath is now much visited by diseased bodies, and in the fair rivers, swimming is a sweet exercise: the Bow and the Bowl pick many a purse, and the Cocks with their heels spurn away many a man's wealth: the Pipe and the Tabor is now lustily set on work, and the Lad and the Lass will have no lead on their heels: the new Wheat makes the Gossips cake, and the Bride Cup is carried above the heads of the whole parish: the Furmenty pot welcomes home the Harvest cart, and the Garland of flowers crowns the Captain of the Reapers. Oh, 'tis the merry time, wherein honest neighbours make good cheer, and God is glorified in his blessings on the earth. In sum, for that I find, I thus conclude, I hold it the world's welfare, and the earth's Warming pan. Farewell.'
Fantasticks, Nicholas Breton

Lammastide: Feast of First Fruits

Lammas, or Loaf Mass, was the feast of first fruits, when the first grain harvested could be made into loaves, and offered up in thanks for a good harvest. It signals the start of the harvest, and of harvest festivals.

Hunting Season Opens

Today the hunting season opens on fallow buck, and red deer stags, and on the hare.

Hunts are described in many of Shakespeare's plays. There was no ban in his day, except on the animals reserved specifically for the monarch to hunt.

Shakespeare describes the excitement, the anticipation and the sheer noise of the hunt with great familiarity. As he does here, for example, in *Titus Andronicus*:

Tamora: *Under their sweet shade, Aaron, let us sit,*
And, whilst the babbling echo mocks the hounds,
Replying shrilly to the well-tuned horns,
As if a double hunt were heard at once,
Let us sit down and mark their yellowing noise.

Titus Andronicus (Act 2 Scene 3)

And in Act Four of *A Midsummer Night's Dream* (Scene 1), Theseus and his Amazon Queen, Hippolyta, express their mutual appreciation of the sounds of the hunt:

Theseus: *We will, fair queen, up to the mountain's top,*
And mark the musical confusion
Of hounds and echo in conjunction.

Hippolyta: *I was with Hercules and Cadmus once,*
When in a wood of Crete they bay'd the bear
With hounds of Sparta: never did I hear
Such gallant chiding: for, besides the groves,
The skies, the fountains, every region near
Seem'd all one mutual cry: I never heard
So musical a discord, such sweet thunder.

Lammas was also a cross-quarter day. Lady Day, Midsummer, Michaelmas and Christmas were quarter days: the days on which servants were hired and rents were due. Cross-quarter days, which fell in between these quarter days, were Candlemas, May Day, Lammas, and All Hallows.

'Whiles Summer Days Do Last'

Cross-dressing at the French Court

On this day in 1589, King Henri III of France was stabbed to death by a fanatical monk:

'The Provost-Marshal led the monk to the King's chamber. But as there were several persons present, the monk demanded that the King might receive him alone. He led him into his cabinet and read various scripts which the monk handed to him. When the King had perused the letter he asked the monk if he had any more. The latter thereupon replied, "Yes" and in place of the script drew forth from his sleeve a short knife, the width of two fingers, which he thrust into the King's abdomen below the navel. He left it sticking in the wound. The King pulled it out himself and thus enlarged the wound. He then himself inflicted a stab upon the monk. At his calls for help several people came into the room, among them La Bastida who had helped to murder the late Guise, and he with his dagger slashed at the monk. Also one of the halberdiers thrust his halberd into the monk so that he was mortally wounded.'

Fugger Newsletter

King Henri III was an excessive, provocative monarch. In 1577, Catherine de Medici gave a ball for her favourite son, her 'precious eyes', in his park at Chenonceaux.

Agippa d'Aubigne, the French poet, soldier and satirist, describes the extravagant appearance of the king as he presided over this banquet, dressed as a woman. 'His hair roped with pearls was worn high in two arcs, under a little brimless Italian hat. His face was plastered with chalk and rouge, and his brow powdered 'like a wrinkled slut'. His bodice of black satin, cut à la espagnolle, was open; his chest bare; and his sleeves, slashed and braided, were caught here and there with pearls and emeralds. He wore diamonds in his ears, and his beard was dyed with violet powder. "So that at first glance", d'Aubigne

writes, "many had difficulty distinguishing whether they saw a lady-king or a man-queen".

The ladies of Henri's so-called *Flying Squadron*, the Mignons, waited at table, in dresses which left their breasts exposed, and their legs bare. After supper, a Saturnalia as debauched as any seen in Ancient Rome continued in the dark shadows, deep into the night.

Appearances such as this earned Henri the name 'Prince of Sodom'. The Spanish ambassador, Zuniga, wrote to King Philip II, 'With all of this he shows who he really is.'

The King of the Gypsies and the Devil's Arse

From the famous peak of Derby
And the Devil's Arse there hard by,
Where we yearly keep our musters
Thus the Egyptians throng in clusters.
Be not frighted by our fashion,
Though we seem a tattered nation,
We account our rags our riches
So our tricks exceed our stitches.
Give us bacon, rinds of walnuts
Shells of cockles and of small nuts
Ribbons, bells and saffroned linen,
All the world is ours to win in.
The Gypsies Metamorphosed, Ben Jonson

On this day in 1621 a masque called *The Gypsies Metamorphosed* was performed at Burleigh-on-the-Hill, in Rutlandshire, the country seat of George Villiers, 1st Duke of Buckingham. It was written by Ben Jonson, with music by Nicholas Lanier. It was the biggest popular hit of Jonson's masquing career.

The masque features none of the classical gods and goddesses. Instead, the characters are gypsies, who behave in stereotypical gypsy fashion: singing and dancing, telling fortunes, and picking pockets; until they metamorphose from their dark 'Ethiop' complexions to fair English ones, under the beneficent influence of King James and return all stolen goods to their proper owners. The Devil's Arse is a cavern in the Peak District of Derbyshire. It is so called because wind in the cave sounds like flatulence. It was a haven for bandits.

Cock Lorel would needs have the Devil his guest.
And bade him into the peak to dinner
Where never the fiend had such a feast
Provided him yet a the charge of a sinner
All which devoured, he then for a close
Did for a full draught of Derby Ale call
He heaved the huge vessel up to his nose,
And left not till he had drunk up all.
Then from the table he gave a start,
Where banquet and wine were nothing scarce,
All which he flirted away with a fart,
From whence it was called the Devil's Arse.
The Gypsies Metamorphosed, Ben Jonson

The Devil's Arse cavern is supposed to be the place where thieves' cant was created by a meeting between Cock Lorel, leader of the rogues, and the King of the Gypsies, 'to the end that their knaveries and villainies might not so easily be perceived and known'.

The Black Dog of Bungay

*All down the church in midst of fire, the hellish
    monster flew
And, passing onward to the quire, he many people slew.*
Contemporary pamphlet

On this day, a Sunday, in 1577, during a terrible thunderstorm, a spectral hound visited St Mary's Church in Bungay, Suffolk.

An account was published in a contemporary pamphlet:
'Immediately hereupon, there appeared (in a most horrible similitude and likeness), to the congregation then and there present, a dog as they might discern it, of a black colour; at the sight whereof (together with the fearful flashes of fire which were then seen), moved such admiration in the minds of the assembly, that they thought doomsday was already come.

'This black dog, or the devil in such a likeness (God knoweth all who worketh all) running all along down the body of the church with great swiftness and incredible haste, among the people, in a visible form and shape, passed between two persons, as they were kneeling upon their knees, and occupied in prayer as it seemed, wrung the necks of them both at one instant clean backward, in so much that even at a moment where they kneeled, they strangely died.

'There was at ye same time another wonder wrought; for the same black dog, still continuing and remaining in one and the self same shape, passing by another man of the congregation in the church, gave him such a gripe on the back, that therewith all he was presently drawn together and shrunk up, as it were a peace of leather scorched in a hot fire; or as the mouth of a purse or bag, drawn together with string. The man albeit he was in so strange a taking, died not, but as it is thought is yet alive: which thing is marvellous in the eyes of men, and offereth much matter of amazing the mind...

'The dog then reappeared a few miles away at a church, in Blythburgh...

'Placing himself upon a main baulk or beam, whereonsome ye Rood did stand, suddenly he gave a swinge down through ye church, and there also, as before, slew two men and a lad, and burned the hand of another person that was there among the rest of the company, of whom divers were blasted.'

Also on this day in 1600, *As You Like It* was entered in the Stationers' Register, but not printed.

St James' Day (Old Style)

A Yorkshire Tragedy

On this day in 1605, a father who murdered two of his children was pressed to death at York.

'Walter Calverly of Calverly in Yorkshire, Esquire, murdered two of his young children, stabbed his wife into the body, with full purpose to have murdered her, and instantly went from his house to have slain his youngest child at nurse, but was prevented. For which fact at his trial at York, he stood mute and was judged to be pressed to death, according to which judgement he was executed at the castle of York the 5th of August.'

Stow's Chronicles (1605)

On June 12th a pamphlet was printed detailing the murders. In July another appeared. And in August, after the execution, yet another, including details of Calverly's death. Then, cashing in on the sensational story, in a programme of four short plays in one evening, the Globe produced *The Yorkshire Tragedy*. Here is the scene where the father murders his first son:

[*Enters his little son with a top and scourge*]

Son: What ails you, father? Are you not well? I cannot scourge my top so long as you stand so: you take up all the room with your wide legs. Puh, you cannot make me afeared with this; I fear no vizards, nor bugbears.

[*Husband takes up the child by the skirts of his long coat in one hand and draws his dagger with the other*]

Husband: Up, sir, for hear, thou hast no inheritance left.

Son: Oh, what will you do, father? I am your white boy.

Husband: Thou shalt be my red boy. Take that. [*Strikes him*]

Son: Oh, you hurt me, father.

Husband: My eldest beggar! thou shalt not live to ask an usurer bread, to cry at a great man's gate, or follow, good your honour, by a coach; no, nor your brother, 'tis charity to brain you.

Son: How shall I learn now my head's broke?

Husband: Bleed, bleed rather than beg, beg! [*Stabs him*]
Be not thy name's disgrace:
Spurn thou thy fortunes first if thou be base:
Come view thy second brother. Fates,
My children's blood,
Shall spin into your faces, you shall see
How confidently we scorn beggars. [*Exit with his son.*]

The play used to be ascribed to Shakespeare but is now largely believed to be by Middleton.

O Rare Ben Jonson
·····················

On this day in 1637, Ben Jonson died, and was buried standing up in Westminster Abbey. The inscription on his grave stone, 'O Rare Ben Jonson', might be a stone carver's error, and should perhaps have read: 'Orare, Ben Jonson', an appeal in Latin to the passer-by to pray for his soul.

Drummond quotes a little verse that Jonson himself used to repeat:
So long as we may, let us enjoy this breath
For nought doth kill a man so soon as death.

In these lines, Francis Beaumont recalls the wit that enlivened the conversation at the Mermaid Tavern in the company of Ben Jonson, and the debt he owed him:

What things have we seen
Done at the Mermaid! Heard words that have been
So nimble, and so full of subtle flame,
As if that every one (from whence they came)
Had meant to put his whole wit in a jest,
And had resolved to live a fool the rest
Of his dull life;... and, when we were gone,
We left an air behind us; which alone
Was able to make the two next companies
(Right witty; though but downright fools) more wise!

When I remember this,... Fate once again,
Brings me to thee, who canst make smooth and plain
The way of knowledge for me, and then I
(Who have no good, but in thy company,)
Protest it will my greatest comfort be,
To acknowledge all I have, to flow from thee!
Ben, when these Scenes are perfect, we'll taste wine!
I'll drink thy Muse's health! thou shalt quaff mine!
Mr Francis Beaumont's Letter to Ben Jonson

And another uncredited anecdote seems worth recording in this context:
Master Ben Jonson and Master William Shakespeare being merry at a tavern, Master Jonson having begun this for his epitaph:
'Here lies Ben Jonson
That was once one...' .
He gives it to Master Shakespeare who presently writes:
'Who while he lived was a slow thing
And now, being dead, is a no thing.'

Also on this day in 1623, Anne Shakespeare (née Hathaway) died aged 67, shortly before the publication of the first complete edition of her husband's plays, known as the First Folio.

First Fruits

Table laid with cheese and fruit, Floris Van Dijck, 1615

'In August come plums of all sorts in fruit, pears, apricots, barberries, filberts, musk-melons, monkhoods of all colours.'

Of Gardens, Francis Bacon

There's pippins and cheese to come.

The Merry Wives of Windsor (Act 1 Scene 2)

'The best apples to make Cider, as Pearmains, Pippins, Golden-pippins, and the like. Codlings make the finest Cider of all. They must be ripe, when you make cider of them: and is in prime in the Summer Season, when no other Cider is good. But lasteth not long, not beyond the Autumn.'

The Closet Opened, Sir Kenelem Digby

In *Love's Labour's Lost*, Costard is named after a variety of apple, and (in Act 4 Scene 2) the schoolmaster Holofernes refers to an apple called a pomewater. The pomewater is now alas like the St Augustine's Orange, to be counted a lost breed of English apple.

(The) Pippin, which we hold of kernel fruits the king,
The Apple-orange; then the savoury russetting:
The Pearmain, which to France long ere to us was known,
Which fruiterers now have denizened our own.
The Renat: which though first it from the Pippin came,
Grown through his pureness nice, assumes that curious name,
Upon the Pippin stock, the Pippin being set;
As on the Gentle, when the Gentle doth beget
(Both by the sire and dame being anciently descended)
The issue born of them, his blood hath much amended.
The Sweeting, for whose sake the ploughboys oft make war:
The Wilding, Costard, then the well-known Pomewater,
That have their sundry names in sundry countries placed:
Unto whose dear increase the gardener spends his life,
With percer, wimble, saw, his mallet and his knife,
... And kills the slimy snail, the worm, the laboring ant,
Which many times annoy the graft and tender plant.

Poly-Olbion Song 18, Michael Drayton

I am withered like an old apple john.

Henry IV Part One (Act 3 Scene 3)

An apple john was an apple which matured about St John's Day and kept for two years. Hakluyt recommended them as provisioning for long sea voyages.

Harvest

In harvest-time, harvest folk, servants and all,
Should make, all together, good cheer in the hall,
And fill out the black bowl of blythe to their song,
And let them be merry all harvest time long.

Once ended thy harvest, let none be beguiled,
Please such as did help thee, man, woman, and child;
Thus doing, with alway, such help as they can,
Thou winnest the praise of the labouring man.

August's Husbandry, Thomas Tusser

The Watch and the Hooked Nose: Villainy in Enfield

In August 1586, Lord Burghley wrote the following to Francis Walsingham. The letter recalls 'the whole dissembly' of Dogberry's watch in *Much Ado About Nothing*, made up of Hugh Oatcake, George Seacoal and the like:

'As I came homeward from London, in my coach, I saw at every town's end the number of ten or twelve standing, with long staves, and until I came to Enfield I thought no other of them, but that they had stayed for avoiding of the rain, or to drink at some ale-house, for so they did stand under penthouses at ale-houses.

'But at Enfield, finding a dozen in a plump, when there was no rain, I bethought myself that they were appointed as watchmen, for the apprehension of such as are missing; and thereupon I called some of them to me apart, and asked them wherefore they stood there, and one of them answered:

'"To take three young men."

And demanding how they should know the persons, one answered with these words:

'"Marry my Lord, by intelligence of their favour."

'"What mean you by that?" quoth I.

'"Marry," said they, "one of the parties hath a hooked nose."

'"And have you," quoth I, "no other mark?"

'"No," sayeth they.

'And then I asked who appointed them; and they answered one Banks, a Head Constable, whom I willed to be sent to me.

'"Surely, sir, who so ever had the charge from you hath used the matter negligently; for these watchmen stand so openly in plumps, as no suspected person will come near them, and if they be better instructed but to find three persons by one of them having a hooked nose, they may miss thereof. And thus I thought good to advertise you, that the justices that had the charge as I think, may use the matter more circumspectly.'"

Sniggling for Eels

An eel is quick.

Love's Labour's Lost (Act 1 Scene 2)

Eels have always been fished in the Avon at Stratford. Back in the eleventh century (when the locals had names like Aelfric, Drogo, Grimulf, and Ordwig), the Domesday Book records a mill pond here which yielded 1,000 eels a year. Perhaps that pond belonged to the mill owned by the Lucy family. It used to stand on the river downstream of Clopton bridge, behind Holy Trinity Church. Today, an eel ladder spans the weir by Lucy's Mill, which is now a block of flats.

In early-summer, the eel ladder is patrolled by seagulls. They know that the young elvers are about to arrive, on their way upstream to their breeding grounds. In Shakespeare's day, there was a great deal of confusion as to where these eels actually spawned. Some suggested that eels were bred of a particular dew which fell on the banks of certain ponds in the months of May and June. The truth is much more extraordinary, for the eels which struggle up the eel ladder outside Lucy's Mill have travelled several thousand miles up the Gulf Stream from the wide Sargasso Sea where they hatched, by 'the still-vexed Bermoothes', in the Western Atlantic Ocean.

Shakespeare knew all about tickling for trout; perhaps he was also familiar with Izaak Walton's method for catching eels – 'Sniggling':

'In a warm day in summer I have taken many a good eel by sniggling, and have been much pleased with that sport. ... observing your time in a warm day, when the water is lowest, you may take a strong small hook, tied to a strong line, or a string about a yard long; and then into one of these holes, or between any boards about a mill, or under any great stone or plank or any place where you think an eel may hide or shelter herself, you may, with the help of a short stick, put in your bait, but leisurely, and as far as you may conveniently; and it is scarce to be doubted, but if there be an eel, within the sight of it, the eel will bite instantly and will gorge it; and you need not have any doubt to have him if you pull him not out of the hole too quickly, but pull him out by degrees.'

Izaak Walton was born in Stafford on this day in 1593. By the time he came of age, he had a little ironmonger's shop in London in Fleet Street, two doors west of Chancery Lane in the parish of St Dunstan's. But it is his fishing manual, which he wrote in his retirement, for which he is famous: *The Compleat Angler*.

Brave Talbot

The Pennant of the Earl of Shrewsbury, in the Talbot family colours

On this day, Lord Talbot was taken prisoner by the French, in the prequel Shakespeare wrote to the two *Henry VI* plays he had already written. It is one of the only times Shakespeare refers to a day by its date, rather than its feast day:

The tenth of August last this dreadful lord,
Retiring from the siege of Orleans,
Having full scarce six thousand in his troop,
By three and twenty thousand of the French
Was round encompassed and set upon.
No leisure had he to enrank his men;
He wanted pikes to set before his archers;
Instead whereof sharp stakes plucked out of hedges
They pitched in the ground confusedly,
To keep the horsemen off from breaking in.
More than three hours the fight continued;
Where valiant Talbot above human thought,
Enacted wonders with his sword and lance,
Hundreds he sent to hell and none durst stand him;
Here, there, and everywhere, enraged he flew:
The French exclaim'd the devil was in arms;
All the whole army gazed on him:
His soldiers spying his undaunted spirit

A Talbot! a Talbot! cried out amain
And rush'd into the bowels of the battle.
Hence grew the general wreck and massacre;
Enclosed were they with their enemies:
A base Walloon, to win the Dauphin's grace,
Thrust Talbot with a spear into his back,
Whom all France with their chief assembled strength
Durst not presume to look once in the face.
Henry VI Part One (Act 1 Scene 1)

Here, Thomas Nashe celebrates the playwright's use of the *English Chronicle* to provide heroic examples to 'these degenerate days of ours':
'**How would it have joyed brave Talbot, the terror of the French, to think that after he had lain two hundred years in his tomb, he should triumph again on the stage and have his bones new embalmed with the tears of ten thousand spectators at least (and several times), who, in the tragedian that represents his person, imagine they behold him fresh bleeding!**
  '**I will defend it against any cullion, or club-fisted usurer of them all, there is no immortality can be given to a man on earth like unto plays.**'
Pierce Penniless: His Supplication to the Devil, Thomas Nashe

Lammas Eve: Old Style

The following exchange from *The Winter's Tale* captures a father's joy in his young son:

Leontes: *Looking on the lines*
Of my boy's face, methoughts I did recoil
Twenty-three years, and saw myself unbreech'd,
In my green velvet coat, my dagger muzzled,
Lest it should bite its master, and so prove,
As ornaments oft do, too dangerous:
How like, methought, I then was to this kernel,
This squash, this gentleman. Mine honest friend,
Will you take eggs for money?
Mamillius: *No, my lord, I'll fight.*
Leontes: *You will! Why, happy man be's dole!*
My brother,
Are you so fond of your young prince as we
Do seem to be of ours?
Polixenes: *If at home, sir,*
He's all my exercise, my mirth, my matter,
Now my sworn friend and then mine enemy,
My parasite, my soldier, statesman, all:
He makes a July's day short as December,
And with his varying childness cures in me
Thoughts that would thick my blood.

The Winter's Tale (Act 1 Scene 2)

Shakespeare's 11-year-old son Hamnet, Judith's twin, died in Stratford and was buried on this day in 1596, in Holy Trinity Church.

King John may have been written (or re-written) and first produced in late-1596. The scenes depicting the death of the little boy Arthur and his mother's grief are particularly poignant.

Constance: *Grief fills the room up of my absent child,*
Lies in his bed, walks up and down with me,
Puts on his pretty looks, repeats his words
Remembers me of all his gracious parts,
Stuffs out his vacant garments with his form,
Then have I reason to be fond of grief.

King John (Act 3 Scene 4)

Shakespeare's Death Mask
· ·

'That summer I had the satisfaction of seeing the Kesselstadt "mask" supposed to be the one taken from Shakespeare's face after death, which was brought by Dr Becker, when with the Grand Duke of Hesse, to Windsor Castle. There is no satisfactory history regarding it, only conjecture, but it bears the most striking resemblance to what one hopes and wishes the poet to have looked like in life and in death. I never saw, not even in the cast of Napoleon's face after death, a finer featured or a more beautiful face, so serenely grand and so divinely calm, with a saddened look on it! I induced Dr Becker to allow this mask to be photographed by the Van der Weyde electric light in London, and I met him at the charming house of Mr W. Flower, at Stratford-on-Avon, when we were able to compare and measure the cast with the bust of Shakespeare over his grave; they tallied in a very remarkable manner.'

My Reminiscences, Lord Ronald Gower (1883)

Lord Ronald Gower was working on his statue of Shakespeare (which now stands outside the Theatre in Stratford) when the supposed 'death mask' of the bard arrived in the town. In 1775, a young German aristocrat called Franz Ludwig von Kesselstadt had returned from a study trip to England, with this mask of Shakespeare. It was then rediscovered by Dr Ludwig Becker,

librarian at the ducal palace at Darmstadt, in a rag shop at Mayence in 1849. He brought it with him to England, where it caused quite a stir.

The death mask appears in a rather fanciful picture painted three years after the mask's rediscovery, by Henry Wallis, now in the RSC Collection. It shows the sculptor, Gerard Johnson, putting the finishing touches to his carving of Shakespeare's funerary bust. Although Johnson had his workshop in Southwark, near the Globe, here he is on the banks of the Avon, and Holy Trinity Church can be seen in the background (although Shakespeare would not have known the church with its spire, which only arrived in the eighteenth century). A rather well-groomed Ben Jonson is holding the death mask for the sculptor to check the final details of his friend and fellow playwright's likeness.

The Kesselstadt Mask is now kept in Darmstadt. It had largely been dismissed as a fake, until recently. In 2006, a German professor at Mainz University claimed the mask is genuine. Apparently a process of detailed analysis has revealed a series of facial marks and idiosyncrasies that prove its authenticity. Not only that, but a bump over Shakespeare's left eye suggests a potentially fatal tumour, and a rare form of cancer which may after all have killed him.

Gower certainly used the likeness as inspiration for his statue of Shakespeare.

A Sculptor's Workshop, Stratford-upon-Avon, 1617, by Henry Wallis, 1830-1916

St Cassian's Day

Go bind thou up yon dangling apricocks
Which, like unruly children, make their sire
Stoop with oppression of
their prodigal weight;
Give some supportance to
the bending twigs.
Richard II (Act 3 Scene 4)

Here's a recipe for
August which uses
apricots, or apricocks
as they were often
called.It is for
Rattafia, or apricot
brandy:
Take a gallon of
brandy, put it into a
wide-mouthed glass;
then take 4 dozen of
Apricocks, pare them
& cut them into
quarters, & put them
to the brandy. Then
take the kernels out of
the stones & bruise
them a little & put

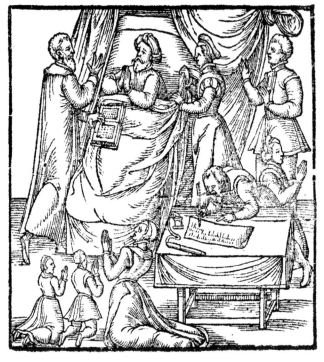

them to the brandy. Bladder down the glass & set it in
the sun for 14 days or 3 weeks according to the heat of
the weather. Then strain it off & put it into bottles for
use.
Receipt Book, Elinor Fettiplace

On this day in 1581, Alexander Hoghton made his
will:
'All my instruments belonging to musics, and all
manner of play clothes, if he be minded to keep and
do keep players; and if he will not keep and maintain
players, then it is my mind and will that Sir Thomas
Hesketh knight shall have the same instruments and
play clothes, and I
most heartily
require the said Sir
Thomas to be
friendly unto Foke
Gyllom and William
Shakeshafte, now
dwelling with me,
and either to take
them unto his
service, or else to
help them to some
good master.'
Could William
Shakeshafte be our
man?

As the sun moved
into the house of
Virgo on this day in
Shakespeare's time,
here is the sixth
entry in Edmund
Spenser's parade of
months. (August is the sixth month because the year
was dated from March.) August dressed in gold leads
in the lovely maiden Virgo:
The sixth was August, being rich arrayed
In garment all of gold down to the ground:
Yet rode he not, but led a lovely Maid
Forth by the lily hand, the which was crowned
With ears of corn, and full her hand was found;
That was the righteous Virgin, which of old
Lived here on earth, and plenty made abound;
But, after Wrong was loved and Justice sold,
She left th'unrighteous world and was to heaven extolled.
Mutabilitie Cantos, VII: XXXVII

Bookshops

O, let my books be then the eloquence
And dumb presagers of my speaking breast.
Sonnet XXIII

Where did you go to buy a copy of one of Shakespeare's plays in Jacobethan London? Your best bet was to start at the stations or bookstalls in St Paul's Churchyard, all of which had catchy shop signs.

The first of Shakespeare's plays to be published was the gore-fest *Titus Andronicus*. It was sold by Ed White and Tom Millington at their station just by the North door of St Paul's Cathedral, at the Sign of the Gun. It was sold in a quarto edition. Quarto merely refers to the number of sheets which could be got by folding a standard piece of paper. Fold once for folio (providing two sheets and thus four pages), twice for quarto (providing four sheets and eight pages), and three times for the small octavo editions (eight sheets and sixteen pages).

At the sign of the Swan, in Paul's Churchyard, one of Cuthbert Burby's stations, you could buy *Romeo and Juliet* and *Love's Labour's Lost*. Burby owned two other shops in his time, one in the Poultry, and one in Cornhill. Further along the Churchyard wall, at the Sign of the Angel, the history plays *Richard II, Richard III* and *Henry IV, Parts One* and *Two* were available at Andrew Wise's stall. Later, at the Tiger's Head (when Wise went into partnership with William Aspley), you might find a copy of *Much Ado About Nothing*.

If you had a taste for a bit more history then you would have to leave the Cathedral precincts and walk along to the Royal Exchange to the Sign of the Cat and Parrot, 'over against the Pope's Head Alley', where Thomas Pavier sold copies of *Henry V* and *Henry VI*. But if comedy was more your cup of tea, then *A Midsummer Night's Dream* was sold at the White Hart in Fleet Street, printed by Thomas Fisher, while *The Merry Wives of Windsor* was sold by John Busby in St Dunstan's Churchyard. Later, Busby joined up with Nat Butler at the Red Bull at St Augustine's Gate where they produced the quarto edition of *King Lear*.

Fifteen of Shakespeare's plays were published in these quarto editions in his lifetime, by seven or eight different printers and booksellers.

William Jaggard printed *The Passionate Pilgrim* at the Half Eagle and Key at the Barbican, but got into trouble with the Stationers' Company for publishing ten plays and attributing them all to Shakespeare, which he clearly considered a clever sales pitch.

Edmund Blount had applied for the right to print *Antony and Cleopatra*, but appears not to have done so. But when William Jaggard and his son Isaac formed a consortium to publish all Shakespeare's plays in a huge folio edition in 1623, the thousand copies printed were available from Blount's shop, the Black Bear in Paul's Churchyard.

But perhaps Shakespeare's most successful publishing venture was his first long narrative poem, *Venus and Adonis*. It was printed by his fellow Stratfordian, Richard Field, and sold by John Harrison at the sign of the Greyhound in the Churchyard. Harrison then sold the copyright to another Churchyard bookseller, William Leake, who took it through six more editions, available at his shop, the Holy Ghost.

Richard Field's own station, the Splayed Eagle in Wood Street, sold copies of Plutarch's *Parallel Lives of the Greeks and Romans*, in Sir Thomas North's translation. Raphael Holinshed's *Chronicles* were sold through the printer Henry Byneman's three outlets – the Black Boy, the Mermaid on Knight Rider Street, and the Three Wells. Perhaps the most successful printer in the country was Christopher Baker, who held the monopoly for printing the new *King James Bible*, as well as *The Book of Common Prayer* and all royal statutes and proclamations.

St Mary's Day

Saffron and Mustardseed

Pare saffron between the two St Mary days,
Or set, or go shift it, that knoweth the ways.
What year shall I do it, more profit to yield ?
The fourth in the garden, the third in the field.

Maids, mustard-seed gather, for being too ripe,
And weather it well, ere ye give it a stripe;
Then dress it and lay it in soller up sweet.
Lest foistiness make it for table unmeet.

August's Husbandry, Thomas Tusser

'It is reported from Saffron Walden that a pilgrim purposing to do good to his country, stole a head of saffron, and hid the same in his Palmers staff, which he had made hollow before of purpose, and so he brought thee root into this realm, with venture of his life. If the like love in this age were in our people that now become great travellers, many knowledges, and many trades, and many herbs and plants might be brought into this realm that might do the realm good.'

Hakluyt's Voyages

Holinshed, echoing Ovid's story of Hyacinth (see March 18th), reports:
'The saffron of England is the most excellent of all other. A certain young gentleman called Crocus went to play at quoits in the field with Mercury, and Mercury's quoit happened to hit him on the head, and ere long killed him, to the great discomfort of his friends. In the place where he bled, Saffron grew.'

In *The Winter's Tale*, Perdita wants saffron to colour the warden pies, for the Sheep Shearing feast. Saffron will give a hint of yellow to the delicious pear flans.

Mustardseed is one of the names given to Titania's fairies in *A Midsummer Night's Dream*. Perhaps the name suggests he is a sharp little chap. Bottom says to him:

Good Master Mustardseed, I know your patience well, that same cowardly oxbeef hath devoured many a gentleman of your house. I promise you, your kindred hath made my eyes water ere now. I desire you of more acquaintance good Master Mustardseed.

A Midsummer Night's Dream (Act 3 Scene 1)

Tewkesbury was famous for its mustard. Falstaff says of Prince Hal's friend Poins:
He a good wit! Hang him, baboon! His wit's as thick as Tewkesbury mustard.

Henry IV Part Two (Act 2 Scene 4)

Tewkesbury mustard was made by grinding the seeds into flour and combining it with finely grated horseradish. The mixture was sold in balls, which could then be mixed with vinegar or cider, and sometimes honey. These balls gave their name to balls of gunpowder, used as incendiary devices. In Gloucestershire, somebody with a sad or sour face was said to look as if they 'lived on Tewkesbury mustard'. And Banbury was once famous for its cheese (a particularly thin variety according to the insult Bardolph flings at Slender in *The Merry Wives of Windsor*):

Bardolph: *You Banbury cheese!*

The Merry Wives of Windsor (Act 1 Scene 1)

St Roch's Day
. . . .

On this day in 1955, *Titus Andronicus* became the last of all the Shakespeare plays (listed in the First Folio) to arrive in Stratford. The production, directed by Peter Brook, starred Laurence Olivier and Vivien Leigh.

Here is part of Ken Tynan's famous review:
'Mr Anthony Quayle plays the latter role (Aaron) with superbly corrupt flamboyance, and Miss Maxine Audley is a glittering Tamora. As Lavinia, Miss Vivien Leigh receives the news that she is about to be ravaged on her husband's corpse with little more than the mild annoyance of one who would have preferred foam rubber: otherwise the minor parts are played up to the hilt.

'Sir Laurence Olivier's Titus, even with one hand gone, is a five finger exercise transformed into an unforgettable concerto of grief. This is a performance that ushers us into the presence of one who is, pound for pound, the greatest actor alive. As usual, he raises one's hair with the risks he takes: Titus enters not as a beaming hero but as a battered veteran, stubborn, and shambling, long past caring about the people's cheers. A hundred campaigns have tanned his heart to leather, and from the cracking of that heart there issues terrible music, not untinged by madness. One hears great cries, which, like all of this great actor's effects, seem to have been dragged up from an ocean bed of fatigue. One recognized, though one had never heard it before, the noise made in its last extremity by the cornered human soul. We knew from his Hotspur and his Richard III that Sir Laurence could explode: now we know that he can suffer as well. All the grand unplayable parts after this, are open to him – Skelton's *Magnificence*, Ibsen's *Brand*, Goethe's *Faust* – anything, so long as we can see those lion eyes search for solace, that great jaw sag.'

Star-Crossed Lovers in Holy Trinity
In the chancel of Holy Trinity Church in Stratford is a monument which is overshadowed by the Bard, presiding next to it. In a double arch of garlanded black marble columns stare the alabaster demi-figures of a Cavalier gentleman and his bride-to-be, holding hands. Her other hand rests on a skull. She is Judith Combe, and her inscription reads:
'Here lieth the body of Judith Combe, daughter of William Combe, of Old Stratford, in ye county of Warwickshire, Esquire, who was to have married unto Richard Combe of Hemsted in ye county of Hartford, Esquire, had not Death prevented it, by depriving her of life, to ye extreme grief and sorrow of both their friends; but more especially of ye said Richard Combe, who, in testimony of his unfeigned love, hath erected this monument in her pious memory. She took her last leave of this life, the 17th day of August 1649, in ye arms of him who most entirely loved and was beloved of her, even to ye very death.'

St Roch, whose feast day it is today, was the patron saint of plague victims.

The Plague Bride

Judith Combe died on this day. Her story recalls Thomas Dekker's account of a doomed wedding: 'Behold, the sun had made haste and wakened the bridal morning. Now he's got up, and gaily attired to play the bridegroom, she likewise does as cunningly turn her self into a bride: kindred and friends are met together, sops and muscadine run sweating up and down till they drop again, to comfort their hearts, and because so many coffins pestered London Churches, that there was no room left for weddings, coaches are provided, and away rides all the train into the Country.

'On a Monday morning are the lusty lovers on their journey, and before noon are they alighted, entering (instead of an inn) for more state into a Church, where they no sooner appeared, but the Priest fell to his business, the holy knot was a tying, but he that should fasten it, coming to this, "In sickness and in health," there he stopped, for suddenly the bride took hold of, "in sickness", for "in health" all that stood by were in fear she should never be kept.

'The maiden-blush into which her cheeks were lately dyed, now began to loose colour: her voice (like a coward) would have shrunk away, but that her lover reaching her a hand, which he brought thither to give her (for he was not yet made a full husband) did with that touch somewhat revive her; on went they again so far, till they met with "For better, for worse", there was she worse than before, and had not the holy officer made haste, the ground on which she stood to be married might easily have been broken up for her burial.

'All ceremonies being finished, she was lead between two, not like a Bride, but rather like a Coarse, to her bed: that must now be the table, on which the wedding dinner is to be served up (being at this time, nothing but tears, and sighs, and lamentation) and Death is chief waiter, yet at length her weak heart wrestling with the pangs, gave them a fall, so that up she stood again, and in the fatal funeral Coach that carried her forth, was she brought back (as upon a bier) to the City: but see the malice of her enemy that had her in chase, upon the Wednesday following being overtaken, was her life overcome, Death rudely lay with her, and spoiled her of a maiden head in spite of her husband.

'Oh the sorrow that did round beset him! Now was his divination true, she was a wife, yet continued a maid: he was a husband and a widower, yet never knew his wife: she was his own, yet he had her not: she had him, yet never enjoyed him: here is a strange alteration, for the rosemary that was washed in sweet water to set out the Bridal, is now wet in tears to furnish her burial: the music that was heard to sound forth dances, can not now be heard for the ringing of bells: all the comfort that happened to either side being this, that he lost her, before she had time to be an ill wife, and she left him, ere he was able to be a bad husband.'

The Wonderful Year, Thomas Dekker

St Helena's Day

The celebrated actress, Helen Faucit, 'the Siddons of the age' (as she described herself), was granted the honour of opening the new Shakespeare Memorial Theatre in Stratford-upon-Avon. Although technically in retirement (she had played opposite Macready in the 1840s, and was now pushing sixty), she played the role of Beatrice in the first birthday performance on Wednesday April 23rd, 1879. She gave just that one performance, and was 'frequently and heartily applauded', said the *Stratford Herald*; so that 'at the close of the second act, nothing but her appearance before the curtain would satisfy the audience'.

That morning, Helen Faucit visited the church and was admitted within the altar rail, where she contemplated Shakespeare's image. 'The bust looks like a living friend, whom one would wish never to part with. There is no thought of death or separation about it,' she later wrote.

Two years after her death in 1898, her grieving husband, Sir Theodore Martin, wanted to create a memorial to his wife in Holy Trinity Church, and commissioned a marble relief of her. But some prominent Stratfordians objected. Sir Theodore was informed that the marble would not be appropriate, and the Theatre Picture Gallery got it instead.

However, he donated the dark green marble pulpit to the church. Around its sides, in white marble panels, stand the figures of various saints, but facing the congregation is the mother of Constantine, St Helena, who recovered the true cross upon which Christ was crucified. A number of people remarked on the elegance of the carved pulpit, though one commented that it was 'a most incongruous piece of church furniture'. But one or two even recognised Lady Martin in the face of St Helena.

Rush-bearing

One Sunday in August 1617, King James watched a rush-bearing ceremony in Lancashire, while on a visit to Hoghton Tower. Rush-bearing was a popular ceremony, as parishioners processed into their church, accompanied by a piper, with a harvest of new rushes to carpet the floor of the nave. Sometimes the rushes were tied with ribbons and garlanded with flowers to adorn the walls. In other parts of Lancashire, the rushes arrived in a specially decorated cart.

Rush-bearings still continue today, in Ambleside in the Lake District, for instance.

Also on this day in 1587, the first English child to be born in the New World was delivered. Her name was Virginia Dare. Her parents christened her after both the colony and their queen.

Actaeon's Hounds

As this is the height of the hunting season, and the dog-days are drawing to an end, here is the moment from Arthur Golding's translation of Ovid's *Metamorphoses* when the hunter Actaeon, having been turned into a stag by the goddess Diana (when he caught her bathing), is attacked by his own pack of hunting dogs. Golding translates the names of the hounds in very English fashion:

His hounds espied him where he was, and Blackfoot
    first of all,
And Stalker special good of scent began aloud to call.
This latter was a hound of Crete, the other was of Spart.
Then all the kennel fell in round, and every for his part,
Did follow freshly in the chase more swifter than the wind,
Spy, Eat-all, Scalecliff, three good hounds come all of
    Arcas kind,
Strong Bilbuck, currish Savage, Spring, and Hunter fresh
    of smell,
And Lightfoot, who to lead a chase did bear away the bell,
Fierce Woodman (hurt not long ago in hunting of a boar),
And Shepherd, wont to follow sheep and neat to field afore.
And Laund, a fell and eager bitch, that had a wolf to sire:

Another brach called Greedygut with two her pups by her.
And Ladon, gant as any Greewnd, a hound in Sycion bred,
Blab, Fleetwood, Patch whose flecked skin with sundry spots
    was spread,
Wight, Bowman, Royster, Beauty fair and whit as
    winters snow,
And tawny, full of dusky hairs that over all did grow,
And lusty Ruffler, passing all the res'due there in strength,
And Tempest, best of footmanship in holding out at length.
And Coal and Swift and little Wolf, as wight as any other,
Accompanied with a Cyprian hound that was his
    native brother,
And Snatch, amid whose forehead stood a star white
    as winter's snow,
The res'due being all as black and slick as any crow.
And shaggy Rug, with other twain that had a Sire of Crete,
And Dam of Sparta: T'one of them called Jollyboy, a great
And large flewd hound: the 'tother Chorle who ever
    gnorring went,
And Kingwood with a shrill loud mouth the which he
    freely spent,
With divers mo, whose names to tell it were but loss of time.
These fellows over hill and dale in hope of prey do climb.
Ovid's Metamorphoses (Book Three)

At Nonsuch Palace, Elizabeth had in her gardens a grove of Diana, with a natural spring which fell into a basin decorated with the story of Diana and Actaeon.

King James' 'Sweet Heart'

I think he only loves the world for him.
The Merchant of Venice (Act 2 Scene 8)

Today was the birthday of George Villiers. King James I had fallen in love with George while on a royal progress at Apethorpe. He swiftly made him a Gentleman of the Bedchamber, then created him Earl (later Duke) of Buckingham. Here, James defends his love for the 22-year-old before the Privy Council in 1614:

'I, James, am neither a God nor an angel, but a man like any other. Therefore I act like a man, and confess to loving those dear to me more than other men. You may be sure that I love the Earl of Buckingham more than anyone else, and more than you who are here assembled. I wish to speak in my own behalf, and not to have it thought a defect, for Jesus Christ did the same and therefore I cannot be blamed. Christ had his John and I have my George.'

Girolamo Lando, the Venetian ambassador, reported on the relationship he had observed between the King and Buckingham:
'In fact one might say the king himself, who has given him all his heart, will not eat, sup or remain an hour without him, and 'considers him his whole joy.'

Here is a letter from King James to Villiers:
My only sweet and dear child,
Notwithstanding of your desiring me not to write yesterday, yet had I written in the evening, if, at my coming out of the park, such a drowsiness had not come upon me as I was forced to sit and sleep in my chair half an hour. And yet I cannot content myself without sending you this present, praying God that I may have a joyful and comfortable meeting with you and that we may make at this Christmas a new marriage ever to be kept hereafter; for, God so love me, as I desire only to live in this world for your sake, and that I had rather live banished in any part of the earth with you than live a sorrowful widow's life without you. And so God bless you, my sweet child and wife, and grant that ye may ever be a comfort to your dear dad and master.

In the original of this letter, at the Bodleian Library in Oxford, James has scribbled out the word 'master' and inserted the word 'husband'.

Bees

Where the bee sucks there suck I
In the cowslip's bell I lie.
The Tempest (Act 5 Scene 1)

Cassius: Antony,
The posture of your blows are yet unknown;
But for your words, they rob the Hybla bees,
And leave them honeyless.
Antony: Not stingless too.
Brutus: O! yes, and soundless too;
For you have stol'n their buzzing, Antony.
And very wisely threat before you sting.
Julius Caesar (Act 5 Scene 1)

Beekeepers began gathering the honey crop at this time of the year, in preparation for St Bartholomew's Day, later this week. The Apostle Bartholomew (who was flayed alive) was regarded as patron saint of beekeepers. And St Bartholomew's Fair in London was famous for its honey-coated apples.

In All's Well That Ends Well, the old Courtier Lafeu calls Parolles 'a red-tailed Humble-bee', and in A Midsummer Night's Dream the transformed Bottom asks the Fairy Cobweb to kill him 'a red-hipped humble-bee on the top of a thistle', and bring him the honey bag.

All plants yeild honey as you see
To the Industrious Chymick Bee

Here is the Archbishop of Canterbury in Henry V, on the example bees can offer society:
... for so work the honey-bees,
Creatures that by a rule in nature teach
The act of order to a peopled kingdom.
They have a king and officers of sorts;
Where some, like magistrates, correct at home,
Others, like merchants, venture trade abroad,
Others, like soldiers, armed in their stings,
Make boot upon the summer's velvet buds,
Which pillage they with merry march bring home
To the tent-royal of their emperor;
Who, busied in his majesty, surveys
The singing masons building roofs of gold,
The civil citizens kneading up the honey,
The poor mechanic porters crowding in
Their heavy burdens at his narrow gate,
The sad-eyed justice, with his surly hum,
Delivering o'er to executors pale
The lazy yawning drone.
Henry V (Act 1 Scene 2)

St Philbert's Day, Bosworth Field

On this day in 1485, King Richard III faced the forces of Richmond at Bosworth Field:

Alarum: excursions.

Catesby: *Rescue, my Lord of Norfolk, rescue, rescue!*
The king enacts more wonders than a man,
Daring an opposite to every danger:
His horse is slain, and all on foot he fights,
Seeking for Richmond in the throat of death.
Rescue, fair lord, or else the day is lost!

Alarums. Enter King Richard III

Richard: *A horse! a horse! my kingdom for a horse!*
Catesby: *Withdraw, my lord; I'll help you to a horse.*
Richard: *Slave, I have set my life upon a cast,*
And I will stand the hazard of the die:
I think there be six Richmonds in the field;
Five have I slain to-day instead of him.
A horse! a horse! my kingdom for a horse!

Richard III (Act 5 Scene 4)

'This battle was fought at Bosworth in Leicestershire, the 22nd day of August in the year of our redemption 1485. The whole conflict endured little above two hours. King Richard as the fame went might have escaped and gotten save guard by flying. For when they which were next about his person saw and perceived (at the first joining of the battle) the soldiers faintly and courageously to set on their enemies, and not only that, but also that some withdrew themselves privily out of the press and departed, they began to suspect a fraud and to smell treason; and not only exhorted, but determinedly advised him to save himself by flight: and when the loss of the battle was imminent and apparent, they brought him a swift and light horse to convey him away.

'He which was not ignorant of the grudge and ill will that the common people bore towards him, casting away all hope of fortunate success and happy chance to come, answered (as men say) that on that day he would make an end of all battles or else finish his life. Such a great audacity and such a stout stomach reigned in his body, for surely he knew that to be the day in which it should be decided and determined whether he should peaceably obtain and enjoy his Kingdom during his life, or else utterly forego and be deprived of the same. He, being overcome, hastily closed his helmet, and entered fiercely into the hard battle. And so this miser at the very same point had like chance and fortune, as happeneth to such which in place of right, justice, and honesty (following their sensual appetite), love, use, and embrace mischief, tyranny and unthriftiness.'

From *The Union of the Two Noble Families of Lancaster and York*, Edward Hall, 1548

Hazelnuts are sometimes called Filberts, which are named after St Philbert, whose feast day in England was celebrated today.

Massacre at Paris on St Bartholomew's Eve (1572)

The Massacre at Paris by François Dubois, 1572

'Of the extraordinary happenings which took place in Paris, your Honour, without doubt, will already have heard through other channels. If no, then be it made known to you that the Admiral of France was on his way on horseback to court on the 22nd of this month. As he was reading a letter in the street, a musket was fired at him from a window. He was but hit in the arm yet stood in danger of his life.

'Whereupon it is said that the king evinced great zeal to probe into this matter. With this the admiral did not rest content, but is reported to have said, he knew well who was behind this, and would take revenge, were he to shed royal blood. So when the King's brother, the Duke of Anjou, and the Guises and others heard of this, they decided to make the first move and speedily dispose of the whole matter.

'On the night of the 23rd of this month they broke into the Admiral's house, murdered him in his bed, and then threw him out of the window. The same day they did likewise with all his kin, upon whom they could lay their hands. It is said that thirty people were thus murdered, among them the most noble of his following. This has been likened to the Sicilian Vespers, by which the Huguenots of this country had their wings well trimmed.

'This may in time cause great uproar, as it is more than probable that many a one at present regarded as harmless was party to this game.'

Fugger Newsletter from Amsterdam, 1572

At dawn of St Bartholomew's Day, the greatest religious massacre in European history began. Catholic bands roamed the streets of Paris killing any Huguenot they could find and setting fire to their houses. Over 3,000 men, women and children were slaughtered.

St Bartholomew's Day (or Bartlemas): Bartholomew Fair

Paul Hentzner (see September 12th) visited Bartholomew Fair in 1598:

'It is worthy of observation that every year upon Saint Bartholomew's Day, when the Fair is held, it is usual for the mayor, attended by the twelve principal aldermen, to walk into a neighbouring field dressed in a scarlet gown, and about his neck a golden chain. Upon their arrival at a place appointed for that purpose, where a tent is pitched, the mob begin to wrestle before them, two at a time. The conquerors receive rewards from the Mayor. After this is over, a parcel of live rabbits

are turned loose among the crowd, which boys chase with great noise.

'While we were at this show, one of our company, Tobias Salander, a Doctor of Physic, had his pocket picked of his purse with nine crowns, which without doubt was so cleverly taken from him by an Englishman who always kept very close to him, that the doctor did not in the least perceive it.'

Paul Hentzner's Travels in England (1598)

In the Induction to Ben Jonson's great play *Bartholomew Fair*, the old Stage Keeper comes on to explain the delay in starting the performance, and proceeds to give his own hilarious apology for what the audience are about to see. It's a great routine, full of backstage gossip, in-jokes, and self-deprecation, designed to get the audience onside. It displays comic rhythms that would be familiar to any stand-up comedian. There is a hint of Frankie Howerd about the character.

'Gentlemen, have a little patience, they are even upon coming instantly. He that should begin the play, Master Littlewit, has a stitch new fallen in his black silk stocking, it will be drawn up ere you can tell twenty.

'But for the whole play, will you have the truth on't ? (I am looking, lest the poet hear me, or his man Broome, behind the arras) it is like to be a very conceited scurvy one, in plain English. When it come to the Fair once, you were e'en as good go to Virginia for anything there is of Smithfield.

'He has not hit the humours, he does not know them: he has not conversed with the Bartholomew birds as they say; he has ne'er a sword and buckler man in his Fair; nor a little Davy to take toll of the bawds there, as in my time; nor a juggler with a well educated ape to come over the chain for the King of England, and back again for the Prince, and sit on his arse for the Pope and the King of Spain. None of these fine sights! Nothing! No: and some writer that I know had had but the penning of this matter, he would have made you such a jig-a-jog in the booths, you should have thought an earthquake had been at the Fair!

'He has kicked me three or four times around the tiring house, I thank him, for but offering to put in with my experience. I am an Ass! I ! and yet I kept the stage in Master Tarleton's time, I thank my stars. Ho! and had that man lived to have played in Bartholomew Fair!'

Galileo's Thrilling New Telescope

Galileo Galilei by Ottavio Leoni, 1624

On this day in 1609, Galileo demonstrated his first telescope to the Venetian State. He published his initial telescopic astronomical observations in March 1610 in a short treatise entitled *The Starry Messenger*:

'About ten months ago a report reached my ears that a certain Fleming had constructed a spyglass by means of which visible objects, though very distant from the eye of the observer, were distinctly seen as if nearby. [This] caused me to apply myself wholeheartedly to inquire into the means by which I might arrive at the invention of a similar instrument. This I did shortly afterwards, my basis being the theory of refraction.

'First I prepared a tube of lead, at the ends of which I fitted two glass lenses, both plane on one side while on the other side was one spherically convex and the other concave. Then placing my eye near the concave lens I perceived objects satisfactorily large and near,

for they appeared three times closer and nine times larger than when seen with the naked eye alone. Next I constructed another one, more accurate, which represented objects as enlarged more than sixty times. Finally, sparing neither labour nor expense, I succeeded in constructing for myself so excellent an instrument that objects seen by means of it appeared nearly one thousand times larger and over thirty times closer than when regarded with our natural vision.

'First I saw the moon from as near at hand as if it were scarcely two terrestrial radii away. After that I observed often with wondering delight both the planets and the fixed stars, and I saw these latter to be very crowded. Let us speak first of that surface of the moon which faces us. For greater clarity I distinguish two parts of this surface, a lighter and a darker; the lighter part seems to surround and to pervade the whole hemisphere, while the darker part discolours the moon's surface like a kind of cloud, and makes it appear covered with spots. Now those spots which are fairly dark and rather large are plain to everyone and have been seen throughout the ages. But there are other spots that have never been seen by anyone before me.

'From observations of these spots repeated many times I have been led to the opinion and conviction that the surface of the moon is not smooth, uniform, and precisely spherical as a great number of philosophers believe it to be, but is uneven, rough, and full of cavities and prominences, being not unlike the face of the earth...'

It should be said that, though Galileo Galilei is often credited with being the first person to look through a telescope and make drawings of the celestial objects he observed, recent research suggest that it was an Englishman, Thomas Harriot, who made the first attempt to map the surface of the moon in July 1609, several months before Galileo.

Battle of Crécy

On this day in 1346 the English forces of Edward III triumphed over the French at the Battle of Crécy. The battle features in the Elizabethan play *Edward III*, (newly 'canonized', and recognized to be at least in part by Shakespeare). Here the great English hero, Edward, the Black Prince, once again faces the French, this time at Poitiers:

Edward: At Crecy Field our clouds of warlike smoke
Chok'd up those French mouths and dissever'd them:
But now their multitudes of millions hide,
Masking as 'twere, the beauteous-burning sun;
Leaving no hope to us but sullen dark
And eyeless terror of all-ending night.

Audley: To die is all as common as to live:
The one ince-wise, the other holds in chase;
For, from the instant we begin to live,
We do pursue and hunt the time to die:
First bud we, then we blow, and after seed,
Then, presently, we fall; and, as a shade
Follows the body, so we follow death.
If, then, we hunt for death, why do we fear it?

If we fear it, why do we follow it?
If we do fear, how can we shun it?
If we do fear, with fear we do but aide
The thing we fear to seize on us the sooner:
If we fear not, then no resolved proffer
Can overthrow the limit of our fate;
For, whether ripe or rotten, drop we shall,
As we do draw the lottery of our doom.

Edward: Ah, good old man, a thousand thousand armours
These words of thine have buckled on my back:
Ah, what an idiot hast thou made of life,
To seek the thing it fears! and how disgraced
The imperial victory of murdering death,
Since all the lives his conquering arrows strike
Seek him, and he not them, to shame his glory!
I will not give a penny for a life,
Nor half a halfpenny to shun grim death,
Since for to live is but to seek to die,
And dying but beginning of new life.
Let come the hour when he that rules it will!
To live or die I hold indifferent.
Edward III Scene 12

A Town Called Shakespeare

On August 27th 1875, the founder of the Bank of California, William C. Ralston, went for a swim in San Francisco Bay and was drowned. He had invested heavily in a mining town in the Pyramid Mountains of New Mexico, which had been named Ralston in his honour. But the silver mines had proved disappointing, William Ralston faced financial ruin, and, in the Depression of 1875, his bank collapsed.

Ralston became a ghost town with one inhabitant until the arrival of two English brothers, William and John Boyle. Colonel William Boyle and his brother General John Boyle came to the Pyramid Mountains in the late-1870s. They had honoured their native country by forming the Shakespeare Mining Co. They began filing claims for many neglected mines near Ralston City.

They even changed the town's name to Shakespeare. The Main Street became Avon Avenue; and the hotel, built out of the old Confederate fort, became the Stratford Hotel. It is claimed that Billy the Kid, as a child, washed dishes in the kitchens.

The future of Shakespeare seemed to be secured when a spur line was sent up Avon Avenue to the mines at Valedon.

Shakespeare Threatened by Apaches

But the biggest threat to Shakespeare was the Apaches who were doing everything they could to get rid of the white settlers who had encroached upon their land.

The Shakespeare Guard was formed in the 1880s to protect the settlement from attacks. However, in 1883, influential residents Judge and Mrs McComas were killed by the Apache, and their son Charlie was kidnapped. Although the Guard offered a reward and attempted to track the Indians down, they were unsuccessful.

The Silver panic of 1893 turned Shakespeare into a ghost town once more.

Swallows

By late-August, swallows are already beginning to gather for their long journey south. They twitter around the Theatre roof in Stratford, as if queuing up on the telegraph lines waiting to leave. British swallows winter in South Africa, crossing the Pyrenees and the Sahara Desert.

Lord: *The swallow follows not summer more willingly than we, your Lordship.*
Timon: *Nor more willingly leaves winter.*
Timon of Athens (Act 3 Scene 6)

After his disastrous defeat at the Battle of Actium, Antony startles his soldiers by his rash decision to fight at sea once more. What will be the outcome?
Swallows have built
In Cleopatra's sails their nests: the augurers
Say they know not, they cannot tell; look grimly,
And dare not speak their knowledge. Antony
Is valiant, and dejected; and, by starts,
His fretted fortunes give him hope, and fear,
Of what he has, and has not.
Antony and Cleopatra (Act 4 Scene 12)

The Tinker and the Corpse (Part One) by Thomas Dekker

'A London citizen, escaping the plague in the capital, stops at a country pub.

The host ('a good fat burgher with a belly arching out like a beer barrel, which made his legs, that were thick and short, like two piles driven under London Bridge, to straddle half as wide as the top of Paul's'), spreads a table for the citizen, and leaves the room.

He returns only to find the gentleman has dropped dead:

'Whereupon the maids being raised, as if it had been a hue and cry, came hobbling into the room, like a flock of geese, and having upon search of the body given up this verdict, that the man was dead, and murdered by the Plague, Oh daggers to all their hearts that heard it !

'Away trudge the wenches. The gorbelly host that in many a year could not without grunting crawl over a threshold but two foot broad, leapt half a yard from the corpse, as nimbly as if his guts had been taken out by the hangman. Out of the house he wallowed presently, being followed with two or three dozen of napkins to dry up the lard, that ran so fast down to his heels, that all the way he went was more greasy than a kitchen-stuff-wife's basket.

'At length the town was raised. What is to be done in this strange alarum ? The whole village is in danger to lie at the mercy of God, and shall be bound to curse

none but him for it. They should do well therefore, to set fire to his house, before the plague scape out of it, lest it forage higher into the country, and knock them down, man, woman, and child, like oxen, whose blood, they all swear, shall be required at his hands.

'At those speeches my tender-hearted host fell down on his marybones, meaning to entreat his audience to be good to him. But they, fearing he had been peppered too, as well as the Londoner, tumbled one upon another, and were ready to break their necks for haste to be gone. Yet some of them, being more valiant than the rest, because they heard him roar out for some help very desperately stepped back, and with rakes and pitch forks lifted the gulch from the ground; concluding that whosoever would venture upon the dead man and bury him should have forty shillings out of the common town purse.

'This was proclaimed, but none durst appear to undertake the dreadful execution. And in that brave resolution, everyone with bag and baggage marched home, barricading their doors and windows with firbushes, fern, and bundles of straw, to keep out the pestilence at the stave's end.

'At last a tinker came sounding the town, mine host's house being the ancient watering place where he did use to cast anchor.'

The Tinker and the Corpse (Part Two)

'This excellent egregious tinker calls for his draught, being a double jug. It was filled for him, but before it came to his nose the lamentable tale of the Londoner was told, the chamber door where he lay, being thrust open with a long pole because none durst touch it with their hands, and the tinker bidden, if he had the heart, to go in and see if he knew him.

'The tinker, being not to know what virtue the medicine had which he held to his lips, poured it down his throat merrily, and crying trillil he feared no plagues, in he stepped, tossing the dead body to and fro, and was sorry he knew him not. Mine host, looking very ruefully on the tinker and thinking him a fit instrument to be played upon, offered him a crown out of his own purse if he would bury the party. A crown was a shrewd temptation to the tinker; many a hole might he stop before he could pick a crown of it. Yet being a subtle tinker, an angel he wanted to be his guide, and under ten shillings (by his ten bones) he would not put his finger into the fire.

'The whole parish had warning of this presently. Thirty shillings was saved by the bargain, and the town like to be saved too, therefore ten shillings was levied out of hand, put into a rag, which was tied to the end of a long pole and delivered (in sight of all the parish, who stood aloof stopping their noses) by the headborough's own self in proper person to the tinker, who with one hand received the money, and with the other, struck the board crying, "Hey, a fresh double pot." Which armor of proof being fitted to his body, up he hoists the Londoner on his back like a schoolboy, a shovel and pickaxe standing ready for him. And thus furnished, into a field some good distance from the town he bears his deadly load, and there throws it down, falling roundly to his tools, upon which the strong beer having set an edge, they quickly cut out a lodging in the earth for the citizen.

'But the tinker, knowing that worms need no apparel, saving only sheets, stripped him stark naked, but first dived nimbly into his pocket, to see what linings they had, assuring himself that a Londoner would not wander so far without silver. His hopes were of the right stamp, for from one of his pockets he drew a leathern bag with seven pounds in it. This music made the tinker's heart dance. He quickly tumbled his man into his grave, hid him over head and ears in dust, bound up his clothes in a bundle, and carrying that at the end of his staff on his shoulder, with the purse of seven pounds in his hands, back gain comes he through the town, crying aloud, "Have ye any more Londoners to bury, Hey down a down derry, have ye any more Londoners to bury?", the hobbinolls running away from him, as if he had been the dead citizen's ghost, and he marching away from them in all haste he could with that song still in his mouth.'

The Wonderful Year, Thomas Dekker

The Zodiac Ceiling

On this day in 1592, His Serene Highness, Frederick, Duke of Württemberg, Count Mumpelgart, visited the Cecils' family seat, Theobalds, in Hertfordshire, with its fabulous zodiac ceiling.

'On the morning of 30th of August his Highness proceeded towards London (from Cambridge) and on the way he went to see the magnificent palace of Theobalds, belonging to the Lord High Treasurer of England, which is reckoned one of the most beautiful houses in England, as in truth it is. First of all his Highness inspected the handsome and delightful hall which is so ornamental and artistic that its equal is not easily to be met with; for besides other embellishments in it, there is a very high rock, of all colours, made of real stones, out of which gushes a splendid fountain, that falls into a large circular bowl or basin, supported by two savages. This hall has no pillars; it is about sixty feet in length and upwards of thirty wide.

'The ceiling or upper floor is very artistically constructed: it contains the twelve signs of the zodiac, so that at night you can see distinctly the stars proper to each; on the same stage the sun performs its course, which is without doubt contrived by some concealed ingenious mechanism. On each side of the hall are six trees, having the natural bark so artfully joined, with birds' nests and leaves as well as fruit upon them, all managed in such a manner that you could not distinguish between the natural and these artificial trees; and as far as I could see there was no difference at all, for when the steward of the house opened the windows, which looked upon the beautiful pleasure garden, birds flew into the hall, perched themselves upon the trees and began to sing. In a word, this hall is so elegantly adorned with paintings and otherwise that it is right royal, and well worth the seeing.

'There are also many other spacious halls and fine galleries in this splendid palace, with very artistic paintings and correct landscapes of all the most important and remarkable towns in Christendom, as well as tables of inlaid-work and marble of various colours, all of the richest and most magnificent description.

'In another hall is depicted the kingdom of England, with all its cities, towns and villages, mountains and rivers; as also the armorial bearings and domains of every esquire, lord, knight and noble, who possess lands and retainers to whatever extent. In short, all the apartments and rooms are adorned with beautiful tapestries and the like to such a degree that no king need be ashamed to live here.'

A True and Faithful Narrative of the Excursion which His Serene Highness Frederick Duke of Württemberg, Count Mümpelgart made to the Far-Famed Kingdom of England, 1592

This last comment was prophetic. Cecil was eventually forced to give this remarkable house to King James in exchange for Hatfield House.

The Death of Henry V
• •

On this day in 1422, King Henry V died at Vincennes. Shakespeare's *Henry VI Part One* opens with his funeral in Westminster Abbey:

Bedford: *Hung be the heavens with black, yield day*
  to night!
Comets, importing change of times and states,
Brandish your crystal tresses in the sky,
And with them scourge the bad revolting stars
That have consented unto Henry's death!
King Henry the Fifth, too famous to live long!
England ne'er lost a king of so much worth.

Gloucester: *England ne'er had a king until his time.*
Virtue he had, deserving to command:
His brandish'd sword did blind men with his beams:
His arms spread wider than a dragon's wings;
His sparking eyes, replete with wrathful fire,
More dazzled and drove back his enemies
Than mid-day sun fierce bent against their faces.
What should I say ? His deeds exceed all speech:
He ne'er lift up his hand but conquered.

Exeter: *We mourn in black: why mourn we not in blood?*
Henry is dead and never shall revive:
Upon a wooden coffin we attend,
And death's dishonourable victory
We with our stately presence glorify,
Like captives bound to a triumphant car.
What! shall we curse the planets of mishap
That plotted thus our glory's overthrow?
Or shall we think the subtle-witted French
Conjurers and sorcerers, that afraid of him
By magic verses have contrived his end?

John Stow begins his account of Westminster Abbey where Henry V is buried in his *Survey of London* with a list of all the kings and queens crowned in this church: 'William, surnamed the Conqueror, and Matilde his wife were the first, and since them all the other kings and queens of this realm have been there crowned'. This still holds good, with the exception of King Edward VIII who was never crowned.

The *Survey* also contains a catalogue of all the monarchs who are buried in the Abbey church. Only a handful of the kings that Shakespeare wrote about are included. The first is Edward III. He lies alongside his wife Philippa of Hainault. King John ended up in Worcester Cathedral, as his son Prince Henry (who suddenly pops up unannounced in the last scene of that play) pronounces without further explanation:
At Worcester must his body be interr'd
For so he will'd it.

Henry IV, worn out by the age of 47, died in Westminster Abbey itself, in the Jerusalem Chamber (see March 20th above), but was buried under an alabaster effigy in Canterbury Cathedral, close to the shrine of Thomas à Becket, perhaps to assuage the guilt he felt for Richard II's deposition and murder. He was devoted to the cult of Becket and, at his coronation, he was even anointed with oil which he believed had been given to Becket by the Virgin Mary herself, and passed on to his father.

Richard II was murdered at Pontefract Castle in Yorkshire, and his body had been brought in a cart, with the face exposed so that every man could identify the corpse, to rest ingloriously at King's Langley in Hertfordshire. Henry IV's son, when he was crowned Henry V, and stood secure in his Lancastrian inheritance, had Richard's body brought to London to rest in the extravagant tomb Richard had built for himself and his wife Anne; 'with their images upon them', as Stow remarks, 'which cost more than 400 hundred marks for the gilding.'

For an account of the rest of Shakespeare's kings and where they are buried (see October 14th).

Earth's increase, foison plenty,
Barns and garners never empty,
Vines and clustering bunches growing,
Plants with goodly burthen bowing;
Spring come to you at the farthest
In the very end of harvest!
The Tempest (Act 4 Scene 1)

'It is now September, and the Sun begins to fall much from his height, the meadows are left bare by the mouths of hungry Cattle, and the Hogs are turned into the corn fields: the winds begin to knock the apples heads together on the trees, and the fallings are gathered to fill the pies for the Household: the Sailors fall to work to get afore the wind, and if they spy a storm it puts them to prayer: the Soldier now begins to shrug at the weather, and the Camp dissolved, the Companies are put to Garrison: the Lawyer now begins his Harvest and the client pays for his words by weight: the Inns now begin to provide for guests, and the night-eaters in the stable, pinch the traveller in his bed: paper, pen and ink are much in request, and the quarter sessions take order with the way-layers: Coals and wood make toward the chimney, and Ale and Sack are in account with good fellows: the Butcher now knocks down the great beeves, and the poulter's feathers make toward the upholsterer: Wallfleet oysters are the fish wives' wealth, and Pippins fine are the costermonger's rich merchandise: the flail and the fan fall to work in the barn, and the Corn market is full of the Bakers: the Porkets now are driven into the woods, and the home-fed pigs make pork for the market. In brief, I thus conclude of it, I hold it the Winter's forewarning and the Summer's farewell. Adieu.'
Fantasticks, Nicholas Breton

'In September come grapes, apples, poppies of all colours, peaches, melocotones, nectarines, cornelians, wardens, quinces.'
Of Gardens, Francis Bacon

'September with a merry cheerful countenance in a purple robe and a wreath of white and purple grapes upon his head; in his left hand a handful of millet, oats, and panicle, carrying a cornucopia of ripe peaches, pears, pomegranates and other fruits of the season, in his right hand the sign Libra. His purple robe sheweth how he reigneth like a king above the other months, abounding with plenty of things necessary for man's life.'
Emblems, Henry Peacham

Duck-hunting Season

The season opens on ducks, and geese, as well as on coot, moorhen and golden plover.

As wild geese that the creeping fowler eye,
Or russet-pated choughs, many in sort,
Rising and cawing at the gun's report
Sever themselves and madly sweep the sky...
A Midsummer Night's Dream (Act 3 Scene 2)

The Emperor's Birthday

On this day in 1617, Sir Thomas Roe witnessed the weighing of the Moghul Emperor Jahanghir on his birthday:

'The first of September was the king's birthday, and the solemnity of his weighing, to which I went, and was carried into a very large and beautiful garden, the square within all water, on the sides, trees and flowers, in the midst a pinnacle, where was prepared the seals, being hung in large tressels, and a cross beam plated on with gold thin: the scales of massy gold, the borders set with small stones, rubies and turkey, the chains of gold large and massy, but strengthened with silk cords.

'Here attended all the nobility all sitting about on carpets until the king came; who at last appeared clothed, or rather loaden with diamonds, rubies, pearls, and other precious vanities, so great, so glorious! his sword, target, throne to rest on, correspondent; his head, neck, breast, arms, above the elbows at the wrists, his fingers everyone with at least two or three rings; fettered with chains, or dyalled diamonds; rubies as great as walnuts, some greater, and pearls, such as mine eyes were amazed at.

'Suddenly he entered into the scales, sat like a woman on his legs, and there was put in against him, many bags to fit his weight, which were changed six times, and they say was silver, and that I understood his weight to be nine thousand rupias, which are almost one thousand pound sterling; after with gold and jewels and precious stones; then against cloth of gold, silk stuffs, linen, spices, and all sorts of goods. Lastly against meal, butter, corn, which is said to be given to the banian: but I saw it carefully carried in and none distributed. The scale he sat in by one side, he gazed on me, and turned me his stones and wealth, and smiled, but spake nothing, for my interpreter could not be admitted in.

'After he was weighed, he ascended his throne, and had basins of nuts, almonds, fruits, spices, of all sort, made in thin silver, which he cast about, and his great men scrambled prostrate upon their bellies, which seeing I did not, he reached me one basin almost full and poured into my cloak, his noblemen were so bold as to put in their hands, so thick, that they had left me none, if I had not put a remainder up.

'At night he drinketh with all his nobility in rich plate. I was invited to that, but told I must not refuse to drink, and their waters are fire. I was sick and in a little flux of blood, and durst not stay to venture my health.
Letter from Sir Thomas Roe

The Theatres Closed

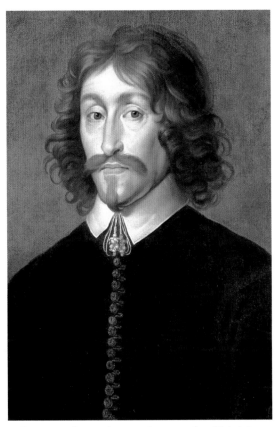

William Prynne by an unknown artist. Prynne kept his hair long to cover his mutilation

On this day in 1642, *An Ordinance Concerning Stage Plays* was published:

'And whereas public sports do not well agree with public calamities, nor public stage plays with the seasons of humiliation, this being an exercise of sad and pious solemnity, and the other being spectacles of pleasure, too commonly expressing lascivious mirth and levity; it is therefore thought fit and ordained by the Lords and Commons in this Parliament assembled, that while these sad causes and set-times of humiliation do continue, public stage plays shall cease and be forborne.'

Puritans had been railing against the theatre and actors for decades. Here, William Prynne fulminates against the stage in his huge tract, *Histrio-Mastix*, which ran to over a thousand pages:

'Stage plays are odious, unseemly, pernicious, and unlawful unto Christians. If we survey the style, or subject matter of all our popular interludes; we shall discover them to be either scurrilous, amorous and obscene; or barbarous, bloody and tyrannical; or heathenish and profane; or fabulous and fictitious, or impious and blasphemous; or satirical and invective; or at the best frothy, vain and frivolous: Our play haunters, adulterers, adulteresses, whoremasters, whores, bawds, panders, ruffians, roarers, drunkards, prodigals, cheaters, idle, infamous, base, profane, and godless persons.

'What wantonness, what effeminancy parallel to that which our men-women actors, in all their feminine, (yea sometimes in their masculine parts) express upon the theatre? And dare we men, we Christians, yet applaud it?'

Histrio-Mastix got Prynne into a lot of trouble. His denunciation of actresses was interpreted as an attack on Charles I's queen, Henrietta Maria, who had appeared in masques with her ladies. Prynne was sentenced to imprisonment, to pay a fine of several thousand pounds, to have his ears lopped, his nose slit, and to be branded 'S.L.', a Seditious Libeller. He was exiled to the Channel Islands.

The year before the *Ordinance* concerning stage plays was published, Prynne described his sufferings in a pamphlet. The officer executing his punishment had heated the iron so hot it had burnt his cheeks. He hacked the ears so close that a piece of Prynne's cheek was cut and his jugular vein nearly severed. But public opinion was to turn in Prynne's favour, and the theatres were closed.

'The Liquor of Life': Meads and Metheglins

He is given to fornications, and to taverns, and to sack and wine and metheglins, and to drinkings and swearings and starings, pribbles and prabbles.
The Merry Wives of Windsor (Act 5 Scene 5)

'On the first of September, Master Webb (who maketh the King's Mead) came to my house,' Sir Kenelm Digby boasts, in his recipe book *The Closet Opened*. Mead is made of honey and water boiled together. Strictly speaking, if herbs are added, it is called metheglin. Digby is a big fan of meads and metheglins, and includes 50 recipes in his book: some from his aristocratic friends, like Sir Baynam Throckmorton, or Lady Windebanke. There is even one from the Muscovian Ambassador's steward.

Here is his own:
Metheglin composed by myself out of sundry receipts:
'In sixty gallons of water, boil ten handfuls of sweet-
briar leaves; eyebright, liverwort, agrimony, scabious, balme, wood-betony, strawberry leaves, burnet, of each four handfuls; of rosemary, three handfuls; of mint, angelica, bays and wild-thyme, sweet marjoram, of each two handfuls: six eringo-roots. When the water hath taken out the virtue of the herbs and roots, let it settle, and the next day pour off the clear, and in every three gallons of it boil one of honey, scumming it well, and putting in a little cold water now and then to make the scum rise, as also some whites of eggs. When it is clear-scummed, take it off, and let it cool; then work it with ale-yeast; tun it up, and hang it in a bag, with ginger, cinnamon, cloves and cardamom. And as it worketh over, put in some strong honey-drink warmed. When it works no more, stop it up close.'
The Closet Opened, Sir Kenelm Digby

The Closet Opened also includes recipes for Humble Pie, Hotchpot, and Harts-Horn jelly. This last one begins; **'Take a small Cock-Chick, when it is scalded, slit it in two pieces, lay it to soak in warm water, until the blood be well out. Then take a calf's foot half boiled, slit it in the middle and pick out the fat and black of it.'** Cock-ale is exactly as it sounds: ale with a cock boiled in it. One recipe begins: 'Take a buttock of beef'.

There are recipes for good health, including one for plague-water, and another for a sucket of mallow stalks, of which he informs his readers, 'In Italy they eat much of them, for sharpness and heat of urine, and in gonorrhoeas to take away pain in urining.'

There are also a variety of desserts: possets and syllabubs, and others with delicious names like tansies, a flomery-caudle, quacking pudding, and a smoothening quiddany of quinces (made of mashed quince cores). But nearly half of *The Closet Opened* is made up of recipes for drinks: small ale, and ciders, and ones seldom heard of, like stepony and bragot.

Thomas Tusser
....

Thresh seed and to fanning September doth cry,
Get plough to the field, and be sowing of rye:
To harrow the ridges, ere ever ye strike,
Is one piece of husbandry Suffolk doth like.

September's Husbandry, Thomas Tusser

Thomas Tusser was born at Rivenhall in Essex and retired to Cattawade in Suffolk where he compiled his famous *100 Good points of Husbandry* in 1557. The cultural historian, Dorothy Hartley, gives perhaps the best account of Tusser's enduring appeal:

'You wrote that first small volume while you were farming down there [near Cattawade Bridges]; and every line of your rhyme grows from your land as if it grew from your own footprints. As of old was said, "The best dung for the land is its master's foot walking over it," so you walked your land, Tusser; studied your land; and wrote of your land. It has not changed

Bread making and pig killing by Simon Bening, 1530

beyond recall since you were down there; there is a factory on that sodden lower estuary now, but the slope up above the decoy pond is as fair and rich as you would wish, and they are keeping the mare's-tail under, though it will always be thick rooted where the stream banks up above the old sheep wash-pan. That sloe thicket has spread a bit, on that wild piece on top of the hill; they don't use the sloes for cow flux now as you suggested, though they still get them for gin.

'The old mill, down river, is still there, but the dyke waterway is silted up, and the wooden piles rotted under the marsh on either side. You'd have to use the upstream mill, that works on a sea dam, and will never "lack water". The old sea wall is pretty good on this side of the bridges, but lost lower down. There is a tablet to you in Manningtree Church, just across the river, where tradition says you worshipped because Brantham hill was too steep for your delicate wife.

'The swan still nests high and safely "for fear of a flood", the boats pass up and down the tide to London and Ipswich and Harwich and Dovercourt. All your land remembers you, Tusser, and we still read your book. Though seriously speaking, why we do is a puzzle. Why has this commonplace farmer's almanac survived year after year? It's the veriest doggerel, yet it sticks like burrs. It is coarse, crude and prosy. It deals with no romance, its flowers are cabbages, and it gloats on manure. The butcher, the baker, and the candlestick-maker are its heroes; the kitchen slut scouring the pans, and the farmer's boy whistling down the hedge, are its orchestra. The beauty of flowering orchards and the singing of wet earth are left to your contemporaries, but you, you write of dung, and of the carter "Hoying" out the hog from the cartwheel, and of purple faced turkeys, gobbling up the garden peas.

'Why then do we townsick ones read you, commonplace Tusser? Because... If there be magic through a quill, it is here; for between the uncouth lines we hear the year pass, as you heard it.'

Country Life edition 1931, Dorothy Hartley

First International Shakespeare Performance

'We gave the tragedy of *Hamlet*,' wrote Captain William Keeling in his diary on this day in 1607. Keeling was Captain of the East India ship, *Red Dragon* which was anchored off the coast of Sierra Leone, in the Bight of Benin. By the end of September, he was inviting his fellow East India Captain Hawkins from the *Hector*, on board for a production of *Richard II*, followed by a good fish supper. 'It keeps my people from idleness and unlawful games or sleep,' he explained.

British trading ships had been passing Sierra Leone for at least a quarter of a century by the time Captain Keeling introduced Africa to Shakespeare. Here is an account of a voyage made by Richard Madox in the autumn of 1582.

'I came from Blackwall in the *Edward Bonaventure* the 2nd April, and from Hampton in the galleon on Sunday the 29th April, and on Whitsunday the 3rd June we were out of sight of England and so came to the Canaries and after to Bonavista and lastly to Serra Liona where we now are [September 14th]. There are many lemons, red pepper that groweth on trees, grains growing in the ground, apples like great lily roots, many divers fine shellfish, many other fish, olyphants, monkeys, deer, buffs [wild oxen] and porcupines. 5 of our men, having leave to walk on Sunday, straggled so that they stayed out all night and were set in the bilboes for it when they came home and that worthily because they distressed the general and Captain Parker in thinking they had been lost.

'The Serra Liona standeth in 8 degrees and 2 terces. Here be many villainous vermin like wingless gnats which do much trouble us and make spoil of the bread. Here be arshires [perhaps a kind of newt] in the fresh water that eat the timber; almost no snails but those that are, very big. Here be great store of good sugar canes in the woods fast by where our ships road, for the master gunner got some. Here be also marlins and cranes.

'St Matthews Day: The Portingals having brought down their caravel with great store of negroes we went to see them where we found 50 of them trammeled like prisoners, all naked saving a rag like a dishclout to cover their members. There were women, one whose skin was finely pinked in this sort.

'There was taken in a cabin of the *Edward* a fine golden green snake of 2 foot long. Whether she came with wood or water or by herself is not known, for there was a great one taken a month past in the rudder of our ship and an other did bite the master of the *Elizabeth* aboard, but a Negro did suck it and it was quickly whole.'

The Diary of Richard Madox, Fellow of All Souls

Garrick's Shakespeare Jubilee

On this day in 1769, Garrick's Jubilee began in Stratford-upon-Avon.

It was to be a great event. Three days of celebrations to honour Stratford's greatest son. Stratford Council had managed to miss the bi-centenary of Shakespeare's actual birth by five years, but, needing to fill the empty niche in the front of their new Town Hall, they had invited leading actor-manager, and Shakespeare lover, David Garrick, to supply a statue of his beloved bard. In doing so, they bit off more than they could chew. The enthusiastic Garrick announced three days of events, surrounding the presentation of the new statue. These would include a procession of a hundred

characters from Shakespeare's plays through the town, fireworks across the Avon, an oratorio in Holy Trinity Church, a masked ball in an especially built rotunda, even a Shakespeare horse race. Garrick himself would be the master of ceremonies, special rainbow ribbons would be worn, and he would deliver an Ode to Shakespeare with music composed by Thomas Arne himself, the famous composer of *Rule Britannia*.

Unfortunately, being England, and September, it rained. The procession had to be called off, the fireworks got damp, and the Avon threatened to

burst its banks and sweep away the newly built rotunda. The entire event very nearly turned into the farce that many hoped and declared it would be, until Garrick rose to deliver his Ode: a man of the theatre speaking from his heart about another man of the theatre, to whom he had devoted much of his working life. The Ode was a triumph and turned around the fortunes and reputation of the whole Jubilee.

Back in London, there were special repeat performances of the great Shakespeare tribute, including the abandoned procession of Shakespeare's characters.

What no one seemed to mind was that not only were none of Shakespeare's plays performed during the Jubilee, but not one word of Shakespeare was spoken for the whole three days.

Also on this day in 1566, Suleiman the Magnificent died.

Suleiman was a great patron of culture. From his Imperial seat, the Topkapi Palace, he oversaw the golden age of the Ottoman Empire's artistic, literary and architectural development. He built his masterpiece the Süleymaniye, the Suleiman Mosque, in Istanbul, but also restored the Dome of the Rock in Jerusalem and renovated the Kaaba in Mecca.

In a break with Ottoman tradition, Suleiman married a Ruthenian harem girl, the infamous Roxelana. In a poem he wrote for her, under his pen name, Muhibbi, he called her, 'My wealth, my love, my moonlight, my most sincere friend, my confidante, my very existence, my Sultan, my one and only love,my springtime, my merry-faced love, my daytime, my sweetheart laughing leaf, my rose, the one only who does not distress me in this world. My Istanbul.'

The Birthday of Queen Elizabeth I

ELIZA TRIVMPHANS

Paul Hentzner saw the Queen at Greenwich on Sunday September 6th, the day before her sixty-fifth birthday, (she was born in 1533):

'Next came the Queen, in the 65th year of her age (as we were told), very majestic; her face oblong, fair but wrinkled; her eyes small, yet black and pleasant; her nose a little hooked, her lips narrow, and her teeth black (a defect the English seem subject to, from their too great use of sugar); she had in her ears two pearls with very rich drops; her hair was of an auburn colour, but false; upon her head she had a small crown, reported to be made of some of the gold from the celebrated Luneburg table; her bosom was uncovered, as all the English ladies have it till they marry; and she had on a necklace of exceeding fine jewels; her hands were slender, her fingers rather long, and her stature neither tall nor low; her air very stately; her manner of speaking very mild and obliging.

'That day she was dressed in white silk, bordered with pearls the size of beans, and over it a mantle of black silk shot with silver threads; her train very long,

the end of it borne by a marchioness; instead of a chain she had an oblong collar of gold and jewels. As she went along in all this state and magnificence, she spoke very graciously, first to one, then to another, in English, French, and Italian; for besides being well skilled in Greek, Latin and the languages I have mentioned, she is mistress of Spanish, Scotch, and Dutch. Whoever speaks to her, it is kneeling; now and then she raises some with her hand... Wherever she turns her face as she was going along, everybody fell down on their knees. The ladies of the court followed next to her, very handsome and well-shaped, and for the most part dressed in white. She was guarded on each side by the gentlemen pensioners, fifty in number, with gilt halberds.'
Travels in England, Paul Hentzner, 1598

Thomas Platter, seeing the Queen at Greenwich in 1599, warns of three questions not to ask her.

'For this is certain; the English esteem her, not only as their Queen, but as their God, for which reason three things are prohibited on pain of death. Firstly none may enquire whether she be still a virgin, for they hold her too holy to admit of doubt. Secondly no one may question her government or estates, so completely is she trusted. And lastly, it was forbidden, on pain of death, to make enquiries as to who is to succeed her on her decease, for fear that it were known, this person in his lust for government might plot against the Queen's life.'
Journal, Thomas Platter, 1599

And on a visit to Nonsuch Palace, Platter is surprised to be allowed into the Queen's private apartments:
'For since but a short time before, an attempt had been made to poison the Queen by smearing powder on the chair she was accustomed to sit and hold her hands on, she refused to allow anyone into her apartments without my lord Admiral's command.'

On the Death of Fathers
....

He was a man, take him for all in all,
I shall not look upon his like again.
Hamlet (Act 1 Scene 2)

On this day in 1601, Shakespeare's father was buried.
We don't know if William made it home for the
funeral. He was probably busy writing *Hamlet*, in
which a son converses with the ghost of his father
within two months of his sudden death.

   Here is perhaps the most famous bit of paternal
advice in all Shakespeare:

Polonius: Yet here, Laertes! aboard, aboard, for shame!
The wind sits in the shoulder of your sail,
And you are stay'd for. There; my blessing with thee!
And these few precepts in thy memory
See thou character. Give thy thoughts no tongue,
Nor any unproportioned thought his act.
Be thou familiar, but by no means vulgar.
Those friends thou hast, and their adoption tried,
Grapple them to thy soul with hoops of steel;
But do not dull thy palm with entertainment
Of each new-hatch'd, unfledged comrade. Beware
Of entrance to a quarrel, but being in,
Bear't that the opposed may beware of thee.
Give every man thy ear, but few thy voice;
Take each man's censure, but reserve thy judgment.
Costly thy habit as thy purse can buy,
But not express'd in fancy; rich, not gaudy;
For the apparel oft proclaims the man,
And they in France of the best rank and station
Are of a most select and generous chief in that.
Neither a borrower nor a lender be;
For loan oft loses both itself and friend,
And borrowing dulls the edge of husbandry.
This above all: to thine own self be true,
And it must follow, as the night the day,
Thou canst not then be false to any man.
Farewell: my blessing season this in thee!
Hamlet (Act 1 Scene 3)

On the Death of Mothers

O my mother! Mother! O!
Coriolanus (Act 5 Scene 3)

And seven years and one day later, in 1608, Shakespeare's mother was buried. Shakespeare probably wrote *Coriolanus* the following year. Volumnia is surely the most devastating portrait of a proud mother ever written.

In *All's Well That Ends Well*, the Countess of Rousillon advises her son Bertram, before he sets out from home:
Countess: Be thou blest, Bertram, and succeed thy father
In manners, as in shape! thy blood and virtue
Contend for empire in thee, and thy goodness
Share with thy birthright! Love all, trust a few,
Do wrong to none: be able for thine enemy
Rather in power than use, and keep thy friend
Under thy own life's key: be check'd for silence,
But never tax'd for speech. What heaven more will,
That thee may furnish and my prayers pluck down,
Fall on thy head! Farewell, my lord;
'Tis an unseason'd courtier; good my lord,

Advise him.
Lafeu: He cannot want the best
That shall attend his love.
Countess: Heaven bless him! Farewell, Bertram.
All's Well That Ends Well (Act 1 Scene 1)

On this day, a Tuesday, in 1746, the first Shakespeare play ever to be performed in Stratford was mounted in the Town Hall.
'For one night only *Othello* was played by a touring company run by Sarah Siddons' grandfather, John Ward. He had offered to donate the proceeds towards the restoration of Shakespeare's monument in Holy Trinity. "To begin punctually at 6 o'clock" the playbill announces, and that for extra measure there would be "several entertainments of singing" between the acts.

'The benefit raised £17, enough to pay John Hall, a Bristol limner, to revive the old colouring, renew the gilding and repair it "with ye original materials, sav'd for that purpose, whatsoever was by accident broken off".

'Having looked after his bust, Stratford again neglected Shakespeare's plays.'
Shakespeare's Country, J. C. Trewin

Harvest Home
....

...and his chin new reap'd
Showed like a stubble-land at Harvest-home.
Henry IV Part One (Act 1 Scene 3)

On this day the Brandenburg jurist Paul Hentzner
and his party, on their tour of England in 1598,
witnessed a harvest festival:
'As we were returning to our inn in Windsor, we
happened to meet some country people celebrating
their harvest-home; their last load of corn they
crowned with flowers, having besides an image richly
dressed, by which perhaps they would signify Ceres;
this they keep moving about while men
and women, men and maidservants,
riding through the streets in the cart,
shout as loud as they can till they arrive in
the barn. The farmers here do not bind up
their corn in sheaves as they do with us,
but directly they have reaped or mowed it,
put it into carts and convey it into their
barns.'

Come, sons of summer, by whose toil
We are the lords of wine and oil :
By whose tough labours, and rough hands,
We rip up first, then reap our lands.
Crowned with the ears of corn, now come,
And to the pipe sing harvest home.

Come forth, my lord, and see the cart
Dressed up with all the country art:
See here a maukin, there a sheet,
As spotless pure as it is sweet:
The horses, mares, and frisking fillies,
Clad all in linen white as lilies.

The harvest swains and wenches bound
For joy, to see the hock-cart crowned.
About the cart, hear how the rout

Of rural younglings raise the shout;
Pressing before, some coming after,
Those with a shout, and these with laughter.

Some bless the cart, some kiss the sheaves,
Some prank them up with oaken leaves:
Some cross the fill-horse, some with great
Devotion stroke the home-borne wheat:
While other rustics, less attent
To prayers than to merriment,
Run after with their breeches rent.
The Hock Cart, or Harvest Home, Robert Herrick

Forman 'Haleks' Avis Allen

On this day in 1611, Simon Forman died.

Forman, an astrologer, was the inspiration for *The Alchemist* by Ben Jonson. He left eye-witness accounts of at least three of Shakespeare's plays, (*Cymbeline*, *Macbeth* and *The Winter's Tale*) and a large number of Case Books, in which he details the people who came to consult him, from countesses to prostitutes. He also includes coded references to his sexual affairs, for example with a married woman called Avis Allen, with whom he was obsessed. 'She rose and came to me,' he wrote on December 15th, 1593, 'et halek Avis Allen.'

This extract from his autobiography rounds up one year, when he was beaten up by his maid, Bess, wrote a book on magic, but found it hard to make ends meet. It also bears witness to the way Elizabethans like Forman calculated the calendar:

'This year, 1590, from Christmas to our Lady day, the world went hard with me, and I wanted money and got little. Yet there was supplies and helps still at one time or other. But from our Lady day till fortnight after Midsummer, the world went very hard; I got little and spent much. I ran in debt much and, had not Mr Parkes been, I could not have told what to do. The 28th of May p.m. at 30 past 9, there rose a great brawl by Bess Vaughan against me: I was like to have come to much trouble by her, and to have been killed. I changed my lodging often. Between Easter and Whitsuntide I wrote a book of Necromancy. I lived hardly, yet found some small friends to help me sometimes. I was offered a wife many times this year between Easter and Whitsuntide, and had the sight and choice of four or five maids and widows. From Midsummer to Michaelmas the world went hard, and I sold many things to make money. After Michaelmas I removed to Sussex, where I went to dwell at Wickham, and was at another man's finding. At All Hallowtide I entered the circle for necromantical spells. And so lived hardly till our Lady day after, 1591. I spent much and got nothing; but found good friendship, and William lent me money.'

In January 1597, Forman records a steamy dream about Queen Elizabeth:

'... dreamt I was with the Queen, and that she was a little elderly woman in a coarse white petticoat all unready. She and I walked up and down through lanes and closes, talking and reasoning. At last we came over a great close where were many people,  and there were two men at hard words. One of them was a weaver, a tall man with a reddish beard, distract of his wits. She talked to him and he spoke very merrily unto her, and at last did take her and kiss her. So I took her by the arm and did put her away; and told her the fellow was frantic. So we went from him and I led her by the arm still, and then we went through a dirty lane. She had a long white smock very clean and fair, and it trailed in the dirt and her coat behind. I took her coat and did carry it up a good way, and then it hung too low before. I told her she should do me a favour to let me wait on her, and she said I should. Then I said, ' I mean to wait upon you and not under you, that I might make this belly a little bigger to carry up this coat and smock out of the dirt.' And so we talked merrily; then she began to lean upon me, when we were past the dirt and to be very familiar with me, and methought she began to love me. When we were alone, out of sight, methought she would have kissed me.'

Noisy London!
·················

Paul Hentzner came to England as companion to a young Silesian nobleman called Christoph Rehdiger in 1598. Here is his account of Londoners' addiction to noise:

'The English are vastly fond of great noises that fill the ear, such as the firing of cannon, drums, and the ringing of bells, so that in London it is common for a number of them that have got a glass in their heads to go up into the belfry for hours together, for the sake of exercise. If they see a foreigner well made, or particularly handsome, they will say, "It is a pity he is not an Englishman."'

And here is a vivid rendition of snatches of random conversation in the bustling shopping arcades of Thomas Gresham's Great Exchange.

What seek you, sir? Come here my friend: see here fine ruffs, falling bands, handkerchers, socks, coifs, and cuffs, wrought with gold and silver.

Have I nothing which likes you? I will use you well.

Would you have any fine Holland ? Any Cambric?
I have very fine, and of all prices.

Hark my love will you take a pint of wine ?
Thanks sir, not now.

Fine Venice glass, French garters, Spanish gloves, sweet, Flanders knives, fine silk stocks of Italy. What want you gentlemen? What lack ye?
Show me a peach-coloured nether stock.
There is a very fine hose, the price is an Angel, at word.

Will you take a noble?
I cannot truly.
There is a pair incarnate, take them for eight shillings.

Will you see a good hat, Sir? Lack you a good hat or a cap?
There is one which will fit you just, with a feather. It becometh you very well.
It is too large and too great for me.

It is after the Babylonian fashion, and the feather after the Polonian slant. It is all the fashion now-a-days.
Show me another after the French fashion, with a flat crown.

Will you see one in Spanish wool? with a Cyprus band, pinked with taffettas, and finely trimmed on the new cut?
Let me see it. Let us come to a price.

What lackest thou Welsh boy? What want ye sir? What would you buy mistress? What lackest thou fellow? What will it please you buy Gentleman ? What seekest thou honest man? Come hither: come to me, I will sell you a penny-worth.
The Chatter in the Pawn, John Eliot

Transvestite Boy Prostitutes in Jacobean London

Walking the city as my wonted use,
There was I troubled with this foul abuse;
Troubled with many thoughts pacing along,
It was my chance to shoulder in a throng,
Thrust to the channel I was, but crowding her,
I spied Pyander in a nymph's attire.

No nymph more fair than did Pyander seem,
Had not Pyander then Pyander been.
No lady with a fairer face more graced
But that Pyander's self himself defaced.
Never was boy so pleasing to the heart
As was Pyander for a woman's part.

Fool that I was in my affection,
More happy I, had it been a vision.
So far entangled was my soul by love
That force perforce I must Pyander prove.
The issue of which proof did testify
Ingling Pyander's damned villainy.

I loved indeed and to my mickle cost
I loved Pyander, so my labour lost.
Fair words I had, for store of coin I gave,
But not enjoined the fruit I thought to have.
O so I was besotted with her words,
His words, that no part of a she affords;

For had he been a she, injurious boy,
I had not been so subject to annoy.
A plague upon such filthy gullery!
Trust not a painted puppet as I have done
Who far more doted than Pygmalion.
The streets are full of juggling parasites
With the true shape of virgins' counterfeits,

But if of force you must a hackney hire,
Be curious in your choice, the best will tire.
The best is bad, therefore hire none at all
Better to go on foot than ride and fall.

Satire Five. Micro-cynicon (Six snarling satires), Thomas Middleton. (This is one of the satires burnt in the Bishops' bonfire of books in 1599)

As the sun entered the house of Libra on this day in Shakespeare's time, so September is seen next in Spenser's procession of the months in *The Faerie Queen*, carrying a pair of scales.

Next him, September marched eke on foot;
Yet was he heavy laden with the spoil
Of harvest's riches, which he made his boot,
And him enriched with bounty of the soil:
In his one hand, as fit for harvest's toil,
He held a knife-hook; and in th'other hand
A pair of weights, with which he did assoyle
Both more and less, where it in doubt did stand,
And equal gave to each as Justice duly scanned.

Mutabilitie Cantos, VII: XXXVIII

Holy Rood Day

A Fete at Bermondsey, c.1570 by Joris Hoefnagel, 1542-1600

No, by the Rood, not so.
Hamlet (Act 3 Scene 4)

Holy Rood Day was the Feast of the Exaltation of the Holy Cross (or Rood). The Empress Helena believed that she had discovered the very cross upon which Christ was crucified, and her son the Emperor Constantine built her a magnificent church in Jerusalem to house it. On this day in 335, the sacred relic was exalted in view of the people, an event commemorated throughout the Church ever since.

In Stratford-upon-Avon, a great fair was held on this day, as John Leland tells us, in this description of the town which he visited in his travels just before the birth of its most famous resident:
'The town of Stratford standeth upon a plain ground on the right hand of the ripe of Avon, as the water descendeth. It hath two or three very large streets beside back lanes. One of the principal streets leadeth east to west, another from north to south. The town is reasonably well built of timber. There is once a year a great fair at Holy Rood Day, which is a thing of a very great concourse of people for a two or three days.

'The parish church is a fair large piece of work and standeth at the south end of the town. There is a right goodly chapel in a fair street toward the south end of the town, dedicated to the Trinity, newly re-edified in mind of man by one Hugh Clopton, Mayor of London. This Clopton built also by the North side of this chapel a pretty house of brick and timber wherein he lay in his latter days, and died.

'There is a grammar school on the south side of this chapel, also an almshouse of ten poor folk. Clopton aforesaid made also the great and sumptuous bridge upon Avon, at the east end of town. This bridge hath fourteen great stone arches of stone, and a long causey made of stone. Afore the time of Hugh Clopton, there was but a bridge of timber.'
Itineraries, John Leland

Nut Time

I with my long nails will dig thee pignuts, show thee a jay's nest, and instruct thee how to snare the nimble marmoset; I'll bring thee to clustering filberts, and sometimes I'll get thee young scammels from the rocks.

The Tempest (Act 2 Scene 2)

An Old Irish Countess Goes Nutting

Why does the world report that Kate doth limp?
O sland'rous world! Kate like the hazel-twig
Is straight and slender, and as brown in hue
As hazel nuts, and sweeter than the kernels.

The Taming of The Shrew (Act 2 Scene 1)

In the early seventeenth century there lived an old lady who had been born when the Wars of the Roses were being waged.

Her name was Catherine, Countess of Desmond. Sir Walter Raleigh in his *History of the World* says he knew this old Countess when he was in Ireland in 1589. She had been 'married in Edward the Fourth's time', and according to the inscription on a portrait in Killarney 'and in y' course of her long Pilgrimage renewed her teeth twice'. She is reputed to have died 'above the age of one hundred and forty'.

There is another contemporary reference to the old Countess by the traveller Fynes Morrison. He was in Ireland from 1599 to 1603, and was shipwrecked on the very coast where the aged lady lived. He says in his *Itinerary*:

'In our time the Countess of Desmond lived to the age of about one hundred and forty years, being able to go on foot four or five miles to the market-town, and using weekly so to do in her last years; and not many years before she died, she had all her teeth renewed.'

The Earl of Leicester says that the old lady might have lived longer, but for an accident. 'She must needs climb a nut-tree to gather nuts; so, falling down, she hurt her thigh, which brought a fever, and that brought death.' Her ladyship died in 1604.

Tradition also has it that the Countess had danced at the English Court with the Duke of Gloucester (Richard III), of whom she had said that 'he was the handsomest man in the room, and was very well made'.

Old Thomas Parr was brought to London from his native Shrewsbury in 1635. He had been born in 1483, did not marry until he was 80 years old and had two children. He attributed his long life to his vegetarian diet and moral temperance. He became a national celebrity, painted by Rubens and Van Dyke, but died shortly after arriving in London. He was buried in Westminster Abbey. The inscription on his gravestone still reads: 'Thomas Parr of the county of Sallop. Born in AD 1483. He lived in the reign of ten princes, viz: King Edward IV, King Edward V, Richard III,King Henry VIII, King Henry VII, King Edward VI, Queen Mary, Queen Elizabeth, King James, and King Charles. Aged 152 years and was buried here November 15th 1635.'

Quaffing and Drinking

Olivia: *What is a drunken man like, Fool?*
Feste: *Like a drowned man, a fool and a madman: one draught above heat makes him a fool, the second mads him and the third drowns him.*
Twelfth Night (Act 1 Scene 5)

The Eight Kinds of Drunkenness by Thomas Nashe

'Nor have we one or two kinds of drunkards only, but eight kinds:

❋ The first is ape drunk, and he leaps, and sings, and holloes, and danceth for the heavens.

❋ The second is lion drunk, and he flings the pots about the house, calls his hostess whore, breaks the glass windows with his dagger, and is apt to quarrel with any man that speaks to him.

❋ The third is swine drunk, heavy, lumpish, sleepy,

and cries for a little more drink and a few more clothes.

❋ The fourth is sheep drunk, wise in his own conceit when he cannot bring forth a right word.

❋ The fifth is maudlin drunk when a fellow will weep for kindness in the midst of his ale, and kiss you saying 'By God, captain, I love thee; go thy ways, thou dost not think so often of me as I do of thee; I would (if it pleased God) I could not love thee as well as I do.' And then he puts his finger in his eye and cries.

❋ The sixth is martin drunk, when a man is drunk and drinks himself sober ere he can stir.

❋ The seventh is goat drunk, when, in his drunkenness, he hath no mind but on lechery.

❋ The eighth is fox drunk, when he is crafty drunk, as many of the Dutchmen be, that will never bargain but when they are drunk.'

By way of reply, a Dutchman, Levinus Lemnius, a physician from Zeeland, here describes the English temperament:
'Near approaching the Italians (but yet somewhat differing) are Englishmen: who being here more weak and less boiling, are of body lusty and well complexioned. And because they have somewhat thick spirits, they will stomach a matter vehemently, and a long time lodge and inward grudge in their hearts, whereby it happeneth that when their rage is up, they will not easily be pacified, neither can their high and haughty stomachs lightly be conquered, otherwise than by submission, and yielding to their mind and appetite.'
Notes on England, Levinus Lemnius

St Lambert's Day
• • • • • • • • • • • • • • • • • •

Be ready as your lives shall answer it
At Coventry upon St Lambert's day.
Richard II (Act 1 Scene 1)

This is the day that King Richard appointed for Bolingbroke to meet Mowbray in the lists at Coventry.

Jack-a-Lanterns

Hentzner witnessed Jack-a-lanterns, on a terrifying journey to Dover:

'On our way to it, which was rough and dangerous enough, the following accident happened to us. Our guide or postillion, a youth, was before with two of our company, about the distance of a musket shot, we (by not following quick enough) had lost sight of our friends; we came afterwards to where the road divided, on the right it was downhill and marshy, on the left was a small hill; whilst we stopped here in doubt, and consulted which of the roads we should take, we saw all on a sudden on the right hand some horsemen, their stature, dress and horses exactly resembling those of our friends; glad of having found them again, we determined to set on after them; but it happened through God's mercy that though we called to them, they did not answer us, but kept on down the marshy road at such a rate that their horses' feet struck fire at every stroke, which made us with reason begin to suspect that they were robbers, having had warning of such, or that they were nocturnal spectres, which as we were afterwards told are frequently seen in those places; there were likewise a great many jack-a-lanthorns (*ignes fatu*) so that we were quite seized with horror and amazement. But fortunately for us, our guide soon sounded his horn, and we following the noise, turned down the left-hand road, and arrived safe to our companions; who when we asked them if they had not seen the horsemen who had gone by us, answered not a soul. Our opinions, according to custom, were various upon this matter; but whatever the thing was, we were without doubt in imminent danger, from which that we escaped, the glory is to be ascribed to God alone.'
Travels in England, Paul Hentzner

In *Venus and Adonis* the young man abandons the Goddess of Love:
Whereat amazed as one that unaware
Hath dropped a precious jewel in the flood,
Or 'stonished as night wanderers often are,
Their light blown out in some mistrustful wood;
Even so confounded in the dark she lay
Having lost the fair discovery of her way.

In *A Midsummer Night's Dream*, one of Titania's fairies asks Puck if he is that 'shrewd and knavish sprite' that likes to 'mislead night wanderers, laughing at their harm'.

Bear and Bull Baiting

Rambures: *The Island of England breeds very valiant creatures. Their mastiffs are of unmatchable courage.*
Orleans: *Foolish curs: that run unwinking into the mouth of a Russian bear, and have their heads crushed like rotten apples.*
Henry V (Act 3 Scene 7)

Thomas Platter goes bear and bull baiting, and finds out how the English learn about the world: 'Every Sunday and Wednesday in London there are bear baitings on the other side of the water, and I ferried across on Sunday 18th September and saw the bear and bull baiting. The theatre is circular, with galleries round the top for spectators. In the middle of the place a large bear on a long rope was bound to a stake, then a great number of English mastiffs were brought in and shown first to the bear, which afterwards baited one after another: now the excellence and fine temper of such mastiffs was evinced, for although they were much struck and mauled by the bear, they did not give in, but had to be pulled off by sheer force, and their muzzles forced open with long sticks to which a broad ironpiece was attached at the top. The bears' teeth were not sharp so they could injure the dogs; they have them broken short. When the first mastiffs tired, fresh ones were brought in to bait the bear.

'When the first bear was weary another was supplied and fresh dogs to bait him, first one at a time, then more and more as it lasted, till they overpowered the bear, then only did they come to its aid. The second bear was very big and old, and kept the dogs at bay so artfully with his paws that they could not score a point off him until there were more of them. When this bear was tired, a large white powerful bull was brought in, and likewise bound in the centre of the theatre, and one dog only was set on him at a time, which he speared with his horns and tossed in such masterly fashion, that they could not get the better of him, and as the dogs fell on the floor again, several men held the sticks under them to break their fall, so that they would not be killed.

Afterwards more dogs were set on him, but could not down him. Then another powerful bear was fetched and baited by six or seven dogs at a time, which attacked him bravely on all sides, but could not get the better of him because of his thick pelt. 'Lastly they brought in an old blind bear which the boys hit with canes and sticks; but he knew how to untie his leash and he ran back to his stall.

'On leaving we descended the steps and went behind the theatre, saw the English mastiffs, of which there were one hundred and twenty together in one enclosure, each chained up to his own separate kennel however. And the place was evil-smelling because of the lights and meat on which the butchers feed the said dogs.

'In a stall adjoining were some twelve large bears, and several bulls in another, all of them kept there merely for the sport described above.

'With these, and many more amusements, the English pass their time, learning at the play what is happening abroad; indeed men and women visit such places without scruple, since the English for the most part do not travel much, but prefer to learn foreign matters and take their pleasures at home.'

The King's Cure
····················

This little scene in *Macbeth* is almost always cut in production:

Malcolm: *Comes the king forth, I pray you?*
Doctor: *Ay, sir; there are a crew of wretched souls*
That stay his cure; their malady convinces
The great assay of art; but, at his touch,
Such sanctity hath heaven given his hand
They presently amend.
Malcolm: *I thank you, Doctor.*
Macduff: *What's the disease he means?*
Malcolm: *'Tis called the evil:*
A most miraculous work in this good king,
Which often, since my here-remain in England,
I have seen him do. How he solicits heaven,
Himself best knows; but strangely-visited people,
All swoln and ulcerous, pitiful to the eye,
The mere despair of surgery, he cures;
Hanging a golden stamp about their necks,
Put on with holy prayers; and 'tis spoken
To the succeeding royalty he leaves
The healing benediction.

Macbeth (Act 4 Scene 3)

When the 19-year-old John Ernst, Duke of Saxe-Weimar visited James I at Theobalds in 1613, he witnessed the King's Cure:

'The service lasted about half an hour. When it was concluded, his majesty stood up, his chair was removed to the table, and he seated himself in it. Then immediately the Royal physician brought in a little girl, two boys and a tall strapping youth, who were afflicted with incurable diseases (the Evil), and bade them kneel down before his majesty; and as the Physician had already examined the disease (which he is always obliged to do, in order that no deception may be practised), he then pointed out the affected part in the neck of the first child to his majesty, who thereupon touched it, pronouncing these words: "Le Roi vous touche, Dieu vous guery" (The King touches, may God heal thee) and then hung a rose noble around the neck of the little girl with a white silk ribbon. He did likewise touch the other three. During the performance of this ceremony, the Bishop who stood close to the King, read from the gospel of St John, and lastly a prayer.

'This ceremony of healing is understood to be very distasteful to the King, and it is said he would willingly abolish it; but he cannot do so, because he assumes the title of King of 'France' as well; for he does not cure as King of England, by whom this power is said to have been never possessed, but as King of France, who ever had such a gift from God.'

An Account of the Visit to England by John Ernst, Duke of Saxe-Weimar, 1613

The First Shakespeare Film

F. R.Benson and his company in *Richard III*

On this day in 1899, audiences saw Shakespeare on film for the very first time. On the same day as Herbert Beerbohm Tree's production of *King John* opened at Her Majesty's Theatre in London, a short film of the play, starring Tree, was released in variety theatres, and as a peepshow Mutascope. One of the four scenes shot by the Biograph Company has survived. It lasts a mere four minutes and shows Tree as the tormented King John in the final moments of the play. John has been carried out into the air at Swinstead Abbey (*Ay marry, now my soul has elbow-room*). Death has laid siege to the feeble king's mind, and Tree raves extravagantly to express that, before expiring. It is possible that the short film served as an advert for the production.

In 1911, F.R. Benson's company made a half hour film of their production of *Richard III*, filmed on the stage of the Shakespeare Memorial Theatre in Stratford-upon-Avon. They also filmed short versions of *Julius Caesar*, *Macbeth*, and *The Taming of the Shrew*, but none of these have survived.

Actress Eleanor Elder records the filming in her diary. (Benson, the head of the company was known affectionately as 'Pa'):

'Pa was really comic in the rehearsal for the cinematograph today. Of course, everything has to be changed: business quickened, and a lot of talk left out altogether. Our instructions are to put plenty of movement into it – to keep within certain lines drawn on the stage; and to do as we are told, and to obey orders shouted at us without being disturbed, or letting it affect our acting. When they yell, "Stop!" we are to stop at once, to keep still, and not to move until we are told to look round at the camera. We shall be muddled when we go back to the play proper!'

Later, Eleanor describes the filming of *Julius Caesar*:
'We have done Caesar, a most trying performance, although the actual scenes run for about two-and-a-half-minutes each. We rehearse everything before we play it. Weird sights we are too – eyelashes and lips made up, and a little rouge. Awful blinding mauve light flickers at us all the time. The flying, hurried way we got through it was quite funny; and the language too ("Give your cue and get off"). Cassius exclaimed: "Good gracious, hullo!" when egged on to murder Caesar, Brutus made his exit saying: "I can't do it. You beasts!" Pa was yelling "Good!" or "Buck up! Do this!" etc. The funny little cine man with his vile cockney-American accent was most amusing: a clever keen-eyed little man who calls Pa "Old boy" and shuts him up every now and then. He said to Pa, "You may be alright on the stage, Mr Benson, but from our point of view, you're a bloody bad actor!" Pa took it all cheerfully.'

St Matthew's Day
····················

On this day in 1599, Thomas Platter mentions in his *Autobiography* that he saw *Julius Caesar*:

'On September 21st after lunch, about two o'clock, I and my party crossed the water, and there in the house with the thatched roof witnessed an excellent performance of the tragedy of the first Emperor Julius Caesar, with a cast of some fifteen people; when the play was over they danced very marvellously and gracefully together as is their wont, two dressed as men and two as women.

'On another occasion not far from our inn, in the suburb of Bishopsgate, if I remember, also after lunch, I beheld a play in which they presented diverse nations and an Englishman struggling together for a maiden; he overcame them all except the German who won the girl in a tussle, and then sat down by her side, when he and his servant drank themselves tipsy, so that they were both fuddled, and the servant proceeded to hurl his shoe at his master's head, whereupon they both fell asleep; meanwhile the Englishman stole into the tent and absconded with the German's prize, thus in turn outwitting the German; in conclusion they danced charmingly in the English and Irish fashion.

'Thus daily at two in the afternoon, London has sometimes three plays running in different places, competing with each other, and those which play best obtain most spectators.

'The playhouses are so constructed that they play on a raised platform, so that everyone has a good view. There are different galleries and places, however, where the seating is better and more comfortable and therefore more expensive. For whoever cares to stand below only pays one English penny, but if he wishes to sit he enters by another door, and pays another penny, while if he desires to sit in the most comfortable seats which are cushioned, where he not only sees everything well, but can also be seen, then he pays yet another English penny at another door. And during the performance food and drink are carried round the audience, so that for what one cares to pay one may also have refreshment.

'The actors are most expensively costumed for it is the English usage for eminent lords or Knights at their decease to bequeath and leave almost the best of their clothes to their serving men, which it is unseemly for the latter to wear, so that they offer them for sale for a small sum of money to the actors.'

Odd Frays
....

On this day in 1598, Ben Jonson killed the actor Gabriel Spencer in a duel near the Curtain Theatre.

A letter from Philip Henslowe to his son-in-law, Edward Alleyn:

To my well beloved son Mr Edward Alleyn at Mr Arthur Langworth's at the Brill in Sussex give this.

Now to let you understand the news, I will tell you some, but it is for me hard and heavy; since you were with me I have lost one of my company, which hurteth me greatly, that is Gabriel, for he is slain in Hoxton Fields by the hands of Benjamin Jonson bricklayer; therefore I would fain have a little of your counsel if I could. Thus with hearty commendations to you and my daughter, and likewise to all the rest of our friends, I end from London the 26th September 1598.

Your assured friend
to my power
Philip Henslowe

In October, Jonson was indicted for murder at the Old Bailey and imprisoned at Newgate. Within the month, he managed to escape the death sentence by claiming 'benefit of clergy', an old law which grants a reprieve on a first offence to anyone who can read their 'neck verse' in Latin. Jonson was released, though as a pardoned offender, he was branded on the thumb with a 'T' for Tyburn. Next time he would hang. Jonson converted to Catholicism, although he then renounced this faith twelve years later. Two years earlier, Spencer had himself killed a man called James Feake, who had attacked him with a candlestick. The following year, two playwrights fought in Southwark. John Day killed Henry Porter with his rapier. We don't know what either quarrel was about.

Here's an account of another particularly violent scrap:

'I know not whether I wrote you... of an odd fray that happened much about that time near the Temple twixt one Hutchinson of Gray's Inn and Sir Jermyn Poole, who assaulting the other upon advantage, and cutting off two of his fingers, besides a wound or two more before he could draw, the gentleman, finding himself disabled to revenge himself by the sword, flew in upon him and getting him down, tore away all his eyebrow with his teeth, and then seizing on his nose bit off a good part of it and carried it away in his pocket.'
John Chamberlain to Sir Ralph Winwood

For never-resting time leads summer on
To hideous winter and confounds him there;
Sap cheque'd with frost and lusty leaves quite gone,
Beauty o'er-snow'd and bareness everywhere:
Then were not summer's distillation left,
A liquid prisoner pent in walls of glass,
Beauty's effect with beauty were bereft,
Nor it nor no remembrance what it was:
But flowers distilled, though they with winter meet,
Lease but their show; their substance still lives sweet.
Sonnet V

Badgers and Foxes
· · · · · · · · · · · · · · · · · · · ·

Marry, hang thee, Brock.
Twelfth Night (Act 2 Scene 5)

Why Sir Toby Belch should call Malvolio a brock, (another name for the badger), is a bit of a mystery. It may refer to the fact that the steward is always soberly dressed in black and white, or perhaps because the badger has a reputation for solitariness, or latent aggression. Here is Edward Topsell on Badgers:

'They are in quantity as big as a Fox, but of a shorter and thicker body; their skin is hard, but rough and rugged, their hair harsh and stubborn of an intermingled grisard colour, sometime white, sometime black, his back covered with black and his belly with white, his head from the top thereof to the ridge of his shoulder, is adorned with streaks of white and black, being black in the middle and white at each side.

'These badgers are very sleepy, especially in the day time, and stir not abroad but in the night, for which cause they are called Luci-fugae; that is avoiders of the light. They eat honey, and worms, and hornets, and such things, because they are not very swift of foot to take other creatures. They love orchards, vines, and places of fruits also, and in the autumn they groweth very fat.

'In Italy and Germany they eat grays' flesh, and boil it with pears, which maketh the flesh taste like the flesh of a porcupine. The flesh is best in September if it be fat.'

Subtle as the fox for prey .
Cymbeline (Act 3 Scene3)

'His manner is when he perceiveth or seeth a flock of fowl to fly in the air, to roll himself in the red earth, making his skin to look bloody, and lie upon his back, winking with his eye, and holding in his breath as if he were dead, which thing the birds, namely crows, ravens, and such like observing, endureth for a good season, till opportunity serving his turn, and some of the fowl come near his snout, then suddenly he catcheth some of them in his mouth, feeding upon them like a living and not a dead fox, as the leopard doth devour and eat apes, and the sea frog other little fishes.

'In the like sort he deceiveth the hedgehog, for when the hedgehog perceiveth the Fox coming to him, he rolleth himself together like a foot-ball, and so nothing appeareth outward except his prickles, which the Fox cannot endure to take into his mouth, and then the cunning fox to encompass his desire, licketh gently the face and snout of the hedgehog, by that means bringing him to unfold himself again, and to stand upon his legs, which being done he instantly devoureth, or else poisons the beast with urine that he rendereth upon the hedgehog's face: at other times he goeth to the waters, and with his tail draweth fishes to the brim of the river, and when that he observeth a good booty, he casteth the fishes clean out of the water upon dry land, and then devoureth them.

'Avicen saw a fox and a crow fight together a long season, and the crow with his talons so be-gripling the fox's mouth that he could not bark, and in the meantime she beat and picked his head with her bill until he bled again.'
History of Four-Footed Beasts, Edward Topsell

Bright Soul of the Sad Year

Thomas Nashe's Pageant, *Summer's Last Will and Testament*, was written to entertain Archbishop Whitgift and his guests, sheltering from the plague which was ravaging London, at his house in Croydon. As Summer himself enters, 'leaning on Autumn and Winter's shoulders', this song of the dying season is sung:

Fair Summer droops, droop men and beasts therefore:
So fair a summer look for never more.
All good things vanish less than in a day,
Peace, plenty, pleasure, suddenly decay.
Go not yet away, bright soul of the sad year;
The earth is hell when thou leavest to appear.

What, shall those flowers that deck'd thy garland erst,
Upon thy grave be wastefully dispers'd?
O trees, consume your sap in sorrow's source;
Streams turn to tears your tributary course.
Go not yet hence, bright soul of the sad year;
The earth is hell, when thou leavest to appear.

Having introduced such characters as Spring, Sol (the Sun), Harvest, Vertumnus (the God of seasonal change) and a snudging Puritanical figure of Christmas, Nashe concludes with the dying Summer appointing Autumn as his heir, and this final song:

Autumn hath all the Summer's fruitful treasure:
Gone is our sport, fled is poor Croydon's pleasure.
Short days, sharp days, long night's come on apace;
Ah, but who shall hide us from the Winter's face?
Cold doth increase, the sickness will not cease,
And here we lie, God knows, with little ease:
From winter, plague and pestilence, good Lord, deliver us.

London doth mourn, Lambeth is quite forlorn,
Trades cry 'woe-worth' that ever they were born,
The want of term is town and city's harm,
Close chambers do we want to keep us warm;
Long banished must we live from our friends;
This low-built house will bring us to our ends.
From winter, plague and pestilence, good Lord, deliver us.

Tom Dallam and the Sultan's Wonderful Organ

On this day in 1599, Lancashire-born Thomas Dallam presented his marvellous mechanical organ, a present from Queen Elizabeth, to the Ottoman Sultan Mehmed III in his Seraglio in Constantinople. 'For a little space it should seem that at the Grand Sinyor's coming into the house the door (which I heard open) did set at liberty four hundred persons (which were locked up all the time of the Grand Sinyor's absence), and just at his coming in, they were set at liberty, and at the sight of the present, with great admiration did make a wondering noise.

'All being quiet, and no noise at all, the present began to salute the Grand Sinyor; for when I left it I did allow a quarter of an hour for his coming thither. First the clock struck 22; then the chime of 16 bells went off, and played a song of 4 parts. That being done, two personages which stood upon two corners of the second storey, holding two silver trumpets in their hands, did lift them to their heads and sounded a tantarra. Then the music went off, and the organ played a song of 5 parts twice over. In the top of the organ, being 16 foot high, did stand a holly bush full of blackbirds and thrushes, which at the end of the music did sing and shake their wings. Divers other motions there was which the Grand Sinyor wondered at.

Mehmed III, 1566 – 1603, by John Young

'When I came within the door, that which I did see was very wonderful unto me, I came directly upon the Grand Sinyor's right hand, some 16 of my paces from him, but he would not turn to look upon me. He sat in great state, yet the sight of him was nothing in comparison with the train that stood behind him, the sight whereof did make me almost to think I was in another world.

'Then the Coppagaw came unto me, and took my cloak from about me, and lay it down upon the carpets, and bid me go and play on the organ; but I refused to do so, because the Grand Sinyor sat so near the place whereat I should play, that I could not come at it, but I must needs turn my back towards him and touch his knee with my breeches, which no man on pain of death, might do, saving only the Coppagaw. So he smiled and let me stand a little. Then the Grand Sinyor spoke again, and the Coppagaw, with a merry countenance, bid me go with a good courage and thrust me on.

'He sat so right behind me that he could not see what I did; therefore he stood up, and his Coppagaw removed his chair to one side, where he might see my hands; but in his rising from his chair, he gave me a thrust forwards, which he could not otherwise do, he sat so near me, but I thought he had been drawing his sword to cut off my head.

'Then I saw the Grand Sinyor put his hand behind him full of gold, which the Coppagaw received and brought unto me forty and five pieces of gold called chickers, and then was I put out again where I came in, being not a little joyful of my good success.'

Diary, Thomas Dallam

St Cosmos and St Damian

The Queen takes Lunch

On this day in 1599, Thomas Platter saw Queen Elizabeth at Nonsuch Palace.

'On Sunday, September 26th, I and my party drove by coach through the borough of Tooting to see the royal palace of Nonsuch 12 English miles from London.

'We were led very soon into the presence chamber where we were placed well to the fore, so as better to behold the queen. This apartment like the others leading into this one was hung with fine tapestries, and the floor was strewn with straw or hay; only where the queen was to come out and up to her seat were carpets laid down in Turkish knot.

'After we had waited awhile there, somewhere between twelve and one, some men with white staffs entered from an inner chamber, and after them a number of lords of high standing followed by the queen, alone without escort, very straight and erect still, who sat down in the presence chamber upon a seat covered with red damask and cushions embroidered in gold thread, and so low was the chair that the cushions almost lay on the ground, and there

was a canopy above, fixed very ornately to the ceiling.

'She was most lavishly attired in a gown of pure white satin, gold embroidered, with a whole bird of paradise for panache, set forward on her head studded with costly jewels, wore a string of huge round pearls about her neck and elegant gloves over which were drawn costly rings. In short she was most gorgeously apparelled, and although she was already seventy four, was very youthful still in appearance, seeming no more than twenty years of age. She had a dignified and regal bearing, and rules her kingdom with great wisdom in peace and prosperity and the fear of God, has up till now successfully confronted her opponents with God's help and support, as can be testified by all the histories, and although her life has often been threatened by poison and many ill-designs, God has preserved her wonderfully at all times.

'As soon as the queen had seated herself, her lady-in-waiting, very splendidly arrayed, also entered the room, while her secretary stood on her right; those with the white staffs and several other knights stood on her left; and one of the knights handed her some books, kneeling when he approached her. (I am told that they even play cards with the queen in kneeling posture). When the prayer was ended, she withdrew. They bade us wait a little while in the audience chamber so as to see the queen's luncheon being served.'

The Journal of Thomas Platter

St Cosmos and St Damian are the twin patron saints of barbers, which is a slim excuse to include this quip by the Countess' clown, Lavache, in *All's Well That Ends Well*:

Like a barber's chair that fits all buttocks, the pin buttock, the quatch buttock, the brawn buttock, or any buttock.

All's Well that Ends Well (Act 2 Scene 2)

Paradise at Hampton Court

On this day in 1599, Thomas Platter visited Hampton Court and its gardens.

But first he had to get a passport:

'Having spoken to my lord Cobham about a passport he directed me to my lord Admiral. He straightway bade his secretary make a letter out for me to all those inhabiting royal residences, asking that I and my party should be shown not only the gardens, large apartments, chapels and chambers, but also the small royal cabinets and the treasures they contain, all of which we afterwards from time to time enjoyed.

'Hampton Court is the finest and most magnificent royal edifice to be found in England, or for that matter in other countries, and comprises without the park, ten different large courts, all adjoining one another. And the entire construction is built of brick.

'The first large forecourt is covered with lawn. In the second court is a beautiful clock, cleverly devised from which one can tell the time by the sun, and also observe the movements of the moon. The third court contains a fine large fountain of great height, artistically wrought of white marble, with an excellent water work with which one may easily spray any ladies or others standing around, and wet them well. And since the Queen recently progressed from Hampton Court to Nonsuch with some three hundred carts of bag and baggage as is her custom, the tapestries and other ornaments still hung in the apartments, for the latter, as will be noted shortly, contain such elegant tapestry of good gold, silver and pure silk that the like is nowhere to be found in such quantity in one place.

'And just as there is a park on the one hand so opposite this in the middle of the other side there is a maze, similarly decorated with plants and flowering trees, and two marble fountains so that time shall not drag in such a place; for should one miss one's way, not only are taste, vision and smell delighted, but the gladsome birdsongs and plashing fountains please the ear, indeed it is like an earthly paradise.

'After leaving this extensive and pleasant garden, and presenting our gratuity to the gardener, ... [they are given a guided tour of the royal apartments including] the paradise chamber, where the ceiling is adorned with very beautiful paintings and an extremely costly canopy or royal throne, from which amongst other precious stones, pearls, large diamonds, rubies, sapphires and the rest shine force, like the sun amongst the stars. Beneath this the Queen is accustomed to sit in her magnificence, upon a very stately chair covered with cushions.'

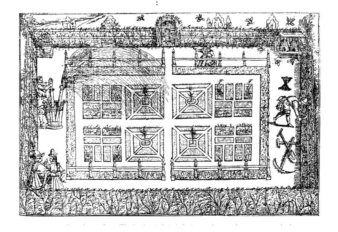

A New River for London

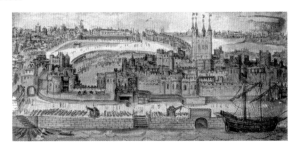

He'll turn your current in a ditch,
and make your channel his.
Coriolanus (Act 3 Scene 1)

On this day in 1610, London was about to gain a new water supply. It was all the work of a London goldsmith called Hugh Myddleton. Myddleton came from Wales originally. His house 'with Seven Eyes' stands in the town square in Ruthin till this day, and his statue stands at the corner of Islington Green.

'Warlike music of drums and trumpets liberally beat the air, and a troop of labourers, to the number of threescore or up-wards, all in green caps alike, bearing in their hands the symbols of their several employments in so great a business, marching twice or thrice about the cistern, orderly present themselves before the mount, and after their obeisance, the speech is pronounced:
Long have we labour'd, long desir'd, and pray'd
For this great work's perfection; and by the aid
Of heaven and good men's wishes, 'tis at length
Happily conquer'd, by cost, art, and strength:
After five years' dear expense in days,
Travail, and pains, beside the infinite ways
Of malice, envy, false suggestions,
Able to daunt the spirit of mighty ones
In wealth and courage, this, a work so rare,
Only by one man's industry, cost, and care,
Is brought to blest effect, so much withstood,
His only aim the city's general good.

'At which words, the flood-gate opens, the stream let into the cistern, drums and trumpets giving it triumphant welcomes, with a peal of small cannon concluding all.'
New River Speech, Thomas Middleton, 1613

The supply of pure spring water to the metropolis had often been canvassed but the expense and difficulty involved had prevented it. In May 1609, Myddleton, 'the dauntless Welshman', began his new river at Chadwell, near Ware. The engineering difficulties were huge, and the outcry from land-owners nearly stopped the project. They protested that the new river would cut up the country, flood arable land, and create quagmires. But the King came to Myddleton's aid, agreed to pay half of the expenses in consideration of a half-share in its ultimate profits, and silenced all opposition. In about fifteen months there was a grand opening at the New River Head, in the fields between Islington and London. Amwell Street, which runs down from Pentonville Road into Roseberry Avenue, marks the course of the new river today.

Also on this day in 1571, Anne Shakespeare was christened. She lived only seven short years and died in 1579, when William was 15. It was the first time he had to deal with the loss of an immediate member of his family.

Michaelmas and Goose Day

Today is the Feast of St Michael the Archangel, and the last day of the harvest season. It is also known as Goose Day because Queen Elizabeth is said to have heard of the defeat of the Armada when she was eating goose.

He who eats goose on Michaelmas Day
Shan't money lack or debts to pay.
Traditional Rhyme

Michaelmas was also one of the regular quarter-days for settling rents and accounts. It marked the end of the fishing season, and the beginning of the hunting season. It was also the traditional time to pick  apples and the time to make cider. But be warned, country lore has it that on this day, when the devil was hurled out of heaven by St Michael, he fell on some brambles. In his anger he pissed on the brambles, so don't pick blackberries after Michaelmas Day:

Saint Michael doth bid thee, amend the marsh wall,
The breck and the crab hole the foreland and all:
One noble, in season, bestowed thereon,
May save thee a hundred, ere winter be gone.

Now geld with the gelder, the ram and the bull,
Sew ponds, amend dams, and sell webster thy wool:
Out, fruit go and gather, but not in the dew,
With crab and the walnut, for fear of a shrew.

The moon in the wane, gather fruit for to last,
But winter fruit gather when Michael is past.
Fruit gathered too timely will taste of the wood,
Will shrink and be bitter,and seldom prove good:

So fruit that is shaken and beat off a tree,
With bruising in falling, soon faulty will be.

Now burn up the bees, that ye mind for to drive,
At Midsummer drive them, and save them alive;
Place hive in good air, set southly and warm,
And take in due season, wax, honey and swarm.
At Michaelmas, safely go sty up thy boar,
Lest straying abroad, ye do see him no more.
September's Husbandry, Thomas Tusser

'Here Cousin, Seize the Crown'

The Abdication of King Richard II, by M. Browne

On this day in 1399, Richard II abdicated.

Richard: *Give me the crown. Here, cousin, seize the crown;*
Here cousin:
On this side my hand, and on that side yours.
Now is this golden crown like a deep well
That owes two buckets, filling one another,
The emptier ever dancing in the air,
The other down, unseen and full of water:
That bucket down and full of tears am I,
Drinking my griefs, whilst you mount up on high.
Bolingbroke: *I thought you had been willing to resign.*
Richard: *My crown I am; but still my griefs are mine:*
You may my glories and my state depose,
But not my griefs; still am I king of those.
Bolingbroke: *Part of your cares you give me with*
    your crown.
Richard: *Your cares set up do not pluck my cares down.*
My care is loss of care, by old care done;
Your care is gain of care, by new care won:
The cares I give I have, though given away;

They tend the crown, yet still with me they stay.
Bolingbroke: *Are you contented to resign the crown?*
Richard: *Ay, no; no, ay; for I must nothing be;*
Therefore no no, for I resign to thee.
Now mark me, how I will undo myself;
I give this heavy weight from off my head
And this unwieldy sceptre from my hand,
The pride of kingly sway from out my heart;
With mine own tears I wash away my balm,
With mine own hands I give away my crown,
With mine own tongue deny my sacred state,
With mine own breath release all duty's rites:
All pomp and majesty I do forswear;
My manors, rents, revenues I forego;
My acts, decrees, and statutes I deny:
God pardon all oaths that are broke to me!
God keep all vows unbroke that swear to thee!
Make me, that nothing have, with nothing grieved,
And thou with all pleased, that hast all achieved!
Long mayst thou live in Richard's seat to sit,
And soon lie Richard in an earthly pit!
Richard II (Act 4 Scene 1)

Sir, the year growing ancient,
Not yet on summer's death, nor on the birth
Of trembling winter, the fairest flowers o' the season
Are our carnations and streak'd gillyvors,
Which some call nature's bastards: of that kind
Our rustic garden's barren; and I care not
To get slips of them.

The Winter's Tale (Act 4 Scene 4)

'It is now October, and the lofty winds make bare the
trees of their leaves, while the hogs in the woods
grow fat with the fallen acorns: the forward Deer
begin to go to rut, and the barren doe groweth good
meat : the Basket makers now gather their rods, and
the fishers lay their leaps in the deep: the load horses
go apace to the mill, and the meal market is seldom
without people: the hare on the hill makes the
greyhound a fair course, and the fox in the woods
calls the hounds to full cry: the multitude of people
raiseth the price of wares, and the smooth tongue
will sell much: the Sailor now bestirreth his stumps,
while the Merchant liveth in fear of the weather: the
great feasts are now at hand for the City, but the poor
man must not beg for fear of the stocks; a fire and a
pair of cards keep the guests in the ordinary, and
tobacco is held very precious for the Rheum: The
Coaches now begin to rattle in the street: but the cry
of the poor is unpleasing to the rich: Muffs and Cuffs
are now in request, and the shuttle cock and the
batteldore is a pretty house exercise: tennis and
Baloune are sports of some charge, and a quick
bandy is the court keeper's commodity: dancing and
fencing are now in some use, and kind hearts and
true lovers lie close to keep off cold: the Titmouse
now keeps in the hollow tree, and the blackbird sits
close in the bottom of the hedge: in brief, for little
pleasure I find in it, I thus conclude of it: I hold it a
messenger of ill news, and a second service to a cold
dinner. Farewell.'

Fantasticks, Nicholas Breton

**'In October and the beginning of November come
services, medlars, bullaces, roses cut or removed to
come late, hollyhocks, and such like. These
particulars are for the climate of London; but my
meaning is perceived, that you may have ver
perpetuum as the place affords.'**

Of Gardens, Francis Bacon

'October, in a garment of yellow and carnation
upon his hand with a garland of oak leaves and
acorns; in his right hand the sign of Scorpio, in his
left a basket of servises, medlars, and chestnuts and
other fruits that ripen late in the year; his robe the
colour of the leaves and flowers decaying.'

Emblems, Henry Peacham

Woodcock

Now is the woodcock near the gin.
Twelfth Night (Act 2 Scene 5)

Shooting season opens today on woodcock and pheasant.

The woodcock gained a reputation for being a stupid bird, because it was easily trapped in 'springes' or 'gins'. It was even thought by some to have no brain at all.

However, there is a rather magical tradition surrounding woodcocks, which for me reprieves the bird from this slow-witted reputation. Every autumn, on a change of wind to the easterly, woodcocks were thought to arrive all at once, from the moon.

Guided by moonbeams, it was said that they took two months to fly to the moon and two to fly back, spending three lunar months away.

As late as 1714, John Gay writes:
He sung where woodcocks in the summer feed,
And in what climes they renew their breed:
Some think to northern coasts their flight they tend
Or, to the moon in midnight hours ascend.
The Shepherd's Week

Jigs Banned

Also on this day in 1612, the Middlesex Court General session bans Jigs at the end of plays:

'An order for suppressing of Jigs at the end of plays. Whereas complaint hath been made at this last general sessions, that by reason of certain lewd jigs, songs, and dances used and accustomed at the playhouse called the Fortune in Golding Lane, divers cut-purses and other lewd and ill disposed persons in great multitudes do resort thither at the end of every play, many times causing tumults and outrages whereby His Majesty's peace is often broke and much mischief like to ensue thereby. It was hereupon expressly commanded and this city and liberties thereof and in the County of Middlesex that they and every of them utterly abolish all Jigs, Rhymes, and Dances after their plays.'

Fracischina.   Gian Farina.

Riciulina.   Metzetin

Vertumnus

Vertumnus by Giuseppe Arcimboldo, 1573

Grapes are hanging from my temples
Gently stroked by rays of sunshine.
Behold that summer fruit the melon,
Look how with its furrowed skin,
It produces wrinkles on my forehead.
Behold the apple and the peach
See how my two cheeks are formed
Round and full of life
Also have a look at my eyes,
Cherry-coloured one, and mulberry the other.

Look at those two hazelnuts:
With their green and empty skins
Side by side above my lip.
There's a chestnut's spiky case clinging to my chin.
Notice the fig which ripened
Then burst open and now dangles from my ear.

Though my aspect may be monstrous
I bear noble traits within
Hiding thus my kingly image.
Tell me now if you are willing
To discern what I conceal
Then my soul I will reveal.

Written by Don Gregorio Comanini (Archimboldo's friend
and contemporary)

⚙

How did Archimboldo paint me
The inventive genius ? Joyfully he set to work
Went through the fields and woods, and chose
A thousand flowers, thousand fruits,
Set to weave this cheerful mixture,
This great product of creation into an artistic garland.

Come behold my temples
Colourfully decked they are by so many ears of corn,

Rudolph II, King of Bohemia and Holy Roman Emperor (1576-1611), may have been an ineffectual ruler, but he was a great patron of the Arts, and a devotee of the occult, alchemy (he longed to discover the Philosopher's Stone), and astrology. He was a great patron of Tycho Brahe and Johannes Kepler. John Dee visited his court, and Nostradamus prepared his horoscope. He had a great Cabinet of Curiosities, which occupied three rooms of his palace in Prague.

Medlar Fruit

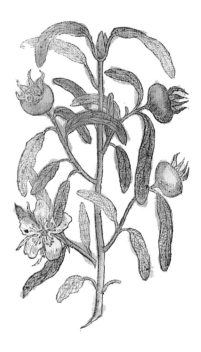

Mercutio: *Now will he sit under a medlar tree,*
And wish his mistress were that kind of fruit
As maids call medlars, when they laugh alone.
O Romeo, that she were, O that she were
An open-arse and thou a poperin pear!
Romeo and Juliet (Act 2 Scene 1)

Apemantus: *The middle of humanity thou never knewest,*
but the extremity of both ends: when thou wast in thy gilt
and thy perfume, they mocked thee for too much curiosity; in
thy rags thou knowest none, but art despised for the contrary.
There's a medlar for thee, eat it.
Timon: *On what I hate I feed not.*
Apemantus: *Dost hate a medlar?*
Timon: *Ay, though it look like thee.*
Apemantus: *An thou hadst hated meddlers sooner,*
thou shouldst have loved thyself better now.
Timon of Athens (Act 4 Scene3)

Medlar fruit are not seen very much these days. They are hard acidic and the bottom of the fruit has something of the appearance, as Mercutio rudely suggests, of an arsehole!

Medlars are ripe only when they are rotten, usually round about now, and once edible, after being 'bletted' or softened by frost, they have a distinctive taste, a bit like apple sauce.
   They can be eaten as a dessert, or with cheese. A nineteenth-century French food writer wrote of medlar preserve that it 'resembles a jam of dead leaves and evokes the loneliness of shepherds'.

Timon in his transformed state, as misanthropic hermit, expounds on the bounteous housewife nature, in an anthem for the natural food industry:
Why should you want? Behold, the earth hath roots;
Within this mile break forth a hundred springs;
The oaks bear mast, the briers scarlet hips;
The bounteous housewife, nature, on each bush
Lays her full mess before you. Want! why want?
Timon of Athens (Act 4 Scene 3)

Twelve Months of Fruits, by Robert Furber, c.1674-1756

Starlings Cause Air Crash!

On this day in 1960, a Lockheed Electra aeroplane setting off from Boston airport stirred up a flock of 10,000 starlings on the runway. It flew straight into the avian cloud which choked the engines and brought the aeroplane down: 62 people died in the crash.

And what has this tragedy to do with Shakespeare?

Starlings are not a species native to North America. They were introduced into the country at the end of the nineteenth century. In 1890 a drugs manufacturer called Eugene Schieffelin released 60 starlings into New York's Central Park, and another 40 the following year. Schieffelin was a Shakespeare fanatic. He decided that New York should be home to all the songbirds mentioned in Shakespeare. The thrushes and skylarks he released had no impact on the ecology of the continent, but the starlings did. They stayed on Manhattan for the first six years, even nesting in the eaves of the Natural History Museum, but then they headed west. By 1928 they had reached the Mississippi, and by 1942 they had arrived in California. Now they are found from Alaska to Florida, have ousted many native species, driving off bluebirds and woodpeckers, and form gigantic flocks of up to a million birds.

Eugene Schieffelin's romantic gesture brought about an ecological disaster. But where does Shakespeare even mention starlings, among the ousel cocks, cuckoos, and russet-pated choughs? In fact, there is just one reference. In *Henry IV Part One*, when, forbidden by the King to plead for the ransom of Mortimer, Hotspur rails:

He said he would not ransom Mortimer,
Forbade my tongue to speak of Mortimer;
But I will find him when he lies asleep
And in his ear I'll holla 'Mortimer !'
Nay,
I'll have a starling shall be taught to speak
Nothing but 'Mortimer' and give it him
To keep his anger still in motion.
Henry IV Part One (Act 1 Scene 3)

Also on this day in 1582, Pope Gregory's calendar jumps 11 days, so Oct 14th was followed by October 25th (see March 25th).

Ospreys

Ospreys have been making the headlines now on a regular basis for fifty years or so, since the early-1950s when a pair started to nest in the Scottish Highlands. They were thought to be extinct in the United Kingdom by the outbreak of World War II. They had been relentlessly persecuted on the pretext that they depleted stocks of salmon and trout in the lochs and rivers of Scotland. Then in 1954, a single pair returned to Speyside, and began to rear young in a nest high in a Caledonian pine in the Abernathy Forest at Loch Garten.

Was Shakespeare familiar with this magnificent raptor?

There is one single reference to the fish eagle in *Coriolanus*. Tullus Aufidius realizes he is being overshadowed by the brilliance of Coriolanus, who has sided with his Volscians to destroy Rome. He admires, yet detests Coriolanus' extraordinary genius as a soldier, and his popularity among his own men. When asked by his lieutenant if his rival will conquer his home city, Aufidius says:

... I think he'll be to Rome
As is the osprey to the fish, who takes it
By sovereignty of nature.
Coriolanus (Act 4 Scene 7)

Shakespeare's fellow poet and

Warwickshire lad, Michael Drayton (in his massive survey of his country, *Poly-Olbion*), describes the Fenlands of East Anglia, where the osprey then hunted for fish. Drayton uses the same image as Shakespeare:

The Osprey oft here seen, though seldom here it breeds,
Which over them the fish no sooner do espy,
But (betwixt him and them, by an antipathy)
Turning their bellies up, as though their death they saw,
They at his pleasure lie to stuff his glutt'nous maw.
Poly-Olbion, 25th Song, 1615

Shakespeare also refers to the Fens as the habitat of the lonely dragon that Coriolanus has become (see October 16th).

King James I experimented with trying to tame ospreys, in order to train them to fish. He had more luck with otters and cormorants. James even employed a Keeper of the Royal Cormorants on the Thames at Westminster to fish the river, a sight which today is more familiar on the rivers of rural China.

There are now, according to the Royal Society for the Protection of Birds, 148 breeding pairs of osprey the UK.

Tipping at the Tower

On this day in 1599, the Swiss physician Thomas Platter paid an expensive trip to the Tower of London, as recorded in his *Autobiography*:

'On the morning of October 6th, I and my party visited the castle, situated in London not far from the Thames and very magnificent and well fortified. In the entrance to the castle we were shown a large cannon on wheels which is said to have stood in like fashion in the court at Calais afterwards loaded with nails and chains, and when a monk tried to fire it, he was stabbed by an Englishman, or much harm would have been done. We were put in the charge of a guardsman, who was to act as a guide round the sights.

'We first of all entered an armoury where there were many shields, weapons and pikes. In this apartment we made the first gratuity to a keeper in attendance: 3 shillings. We were then led into another chamber in which were naught but squatting vaults, holster pistols and the like... here we made our second gratuity. Soon after we saw a suit of armour which had belonged to Henry VIII. From this room we went to another full of armour, a number of saddles girt with iron together with horse armour. There we gave largesse the third time.

'Having descended a little and entered another apartment, we saw a number of field pieces set on wheels, amongst them one with seven barrels which could be severally discharged. There was also a square one with three barrels, and here we made our fourth gratuity. Thence we came to the guard room, in the dungeon we saw ropes used to rack malefactors. Then we climbed up a wooden tower with a lead roofing. Afterwards in another room we were shown a very ancient tapestry which had been in this castle some five hundred years, this tapestry was very fine and large: here we gave our fifth gratuity.

'Then we climbed the tower erected by Julius Caesar, it was high and sixteen great pieces stood there which would fire a distance. Here we made the sixth gratuity. Descending again we entered the mint to watch all kinds of money being coined. We saw the gold minted and fanned with the bellows until the coals die out, a difficult and dangerous task. They informed me that some years ago 100,000 pounds sterling were minted monthly, while now they never exceed 30,000 pounds a month. There we made the seventh gratuity.

'We saw six lions and lionesses in this stronghold, in separate wooden cages, and two were over 100 years old. And if I remember one was named Edward, and one of the lionesses, Elizabeth. Not far from them was a lean ugly wolf, the only one in England, it is true, kept for this reason by the queen, as there is not another in the whole realm. Quite close to them were also a tiger and a porcupine. And but for a little a lion might have caught one of the party's servants, for it could get its claws through the bars of the cage in which they are fed. And having now for the eighth time also made a gratuity to the soldiers we returned to our hostel.'

The Pope's Premonition of Lepanto

On this day in 1572, just before five o'clock in the afternoon, Pope Pius V was busying himself with the affairs of the Vatican treasury when he suddenly hurried to an open window and stared out. After a few moments he turned back to face his staff and announced that a blessed victory had been granted to the Christian fleet at Lepanto.

His treasurer assiduously made a note of the time of this extraordinary announcement. Two weeks later, a messenger arrived in Rome having galloped all the way from Venice with the news of a decisive naval victory. Don John of Austria had smashed the Turkish fleet at Lepanto. The official report recorded the moment, just before 5 o'clock on October 7th.

Here is a contemporary account of the victory:
'Don John attired himself in a light suit of armour and boarded a small ship, called a frigate. Holding a crucifix in his hand, he visited one galley after the other, appointing to each its proper place in the battle and exhorting the crew to fight valiantly against the arch-enemy of the Christian faith. Not he, but Christ who had died for us upon the cross was the father of all, and the Patron of this Armada, and he hoped that they would find help and sustenance in His mercy. Thereupon the whole soldiery sent forth great shouts of jubilation and forthwith placed themselves in battle formation.

'Whereafter the above mentioned Don John of Austria again entered his galley and went to meet the Turkish Armada. Then the sea became quiet and still and the galleasses, which had sailed ahead, opened with heavy fire and brought great damage and terror to the Turks, causing them to cry, "Maom, Maom!" which in their language means, "Big ships, big ships with big cannon!" Thus the Turkish Armada which had been sailing ship to ship in half moon formation fell into disorder and split into three parts.

'The scales of Victory turned completely in our favour. There also sprang up a wind to our assistance. In the smoke of battle, Uluch Ali escaped. It is unknown whether he has fled to Africa or the Gulf of Lepanto.

'On several galleys there were also found a large number of Sultanas and Zechines and on Caragoggia's galley a beautiful young woman, a Christian. She was daintily and richly attired and her neck adorned with large pearls and other precious stones and jewels. She offered to buy her release with 60,000 ducats.

'Praise and glory be to God Almighty and His Blessed Mother in all eternity. Amen.'
Fugger Newsletter from the Christian Armada, sent October 8th, 1572

Rival Queens United in Death

The statue is but newly fix'd, the colour's not dry.

The Winter's Tale (Act 5 Scene 3)

On this day in 1612, the body of Mary, Queen of Scots, is finally laid to rest in Westminster Abbey, over a quarter of a century after her death.

When her son, King James I, came to the throne, after Elizabeth's death, he had a problem. The body of his mother lay in Peterborough Cathedral, where it had been taken after her execution at Fotheringay in 1587. He finally had the corpse disinterred and brought down to London and placed in the vault of Henry VII's Chapel on October 8th, 1612. He also had a monument constructed and placed in the South Aisle. There she lies, under an elaborate canopy, in her close-fitting coif and laced ruff and long mantle fastened by a brooch; the crowned Scottish Lion at her feet. The rival queens thus rest opposite one another in death.

The Medieval Theatre scholar, Professor Glynne Wickham, had a theory about this monument. The beautiful marble figure of Mary had been commissioned by King James from his Royal Master Mason, Cornelius Cure, sometime soon after his accession. Cure died in 1607 and the job passed to his son William, who continued to work on the statue at their workshop in Southwark, not far from the Globe. When the carving of the marble had been completed, William began on the painting. It seems odd to us now that sculptures should have been

painted, and in vivid life-like colours too.

The statue would have been moved to Westminster in plenty of time for the arrival of Mary's body in 1612. But it remained in Southwark until the paint was dry. So as Professor Wickham points out, when Simon Forman saw *The Winter's Tale* at the neighbouring Globe in 1611, and heard Paulina in the last Act reveal Hermione's statue and prevent Leontes from kissing it with the words:

Good my lord, forbear:
The ruddiness upon her lip is wet;
You'll mar it with much kissing; stain your own
With oily painting ...

then he and every member of the audience would be aware of the resonance. Professor Wickham's theory elaborates the significance of the two statues. King James' action in reinterring his mother was not just an act of filial piety, but of national reconciliation. He also points out that the time which had elapsed between the execution of the anointed queen and the ascent of her son to the throne was exactly sixteen years, the time period of Leontes' penance, until the restoration of his child, Perdita. That which was lost is found. Mary's monument would have been the very latest tourist attraction in Henry Peacham's poem (see June 8th).

For further monuments in Westminster Abbey see October 14th.

An Eskimo in London

Arnaq and Ntaaq, Inuit from Frobisher Bay, by John White, 1577

Were I in England now, as once I was, and had but this fish painted, not a holiday fool there but would give a piece of silver: there would this monster make a man; any strange beast there makes a man: when they will not give a doit to relieve a lame beggar, they will lazy out ten to see a dead Indian.

The Tempest (Act 2 Scene 2)

On this day in 1576, an Inuit man arrived in London.

The man had seen an English ship anchored in the Arctic Bay where his people, the Inuk, lived, and had rowed up in his kayak to see if he could trade with furs and red meat. He quickly found himself captured and brought on board with his kayak.

Unbeknownst to him, the ship, the *Gabriel*, captained by Martin Frobisher, had recently suffered heavy losses. For years Frobisher had been searching for a route to China, through the Arctic; a North-West Passage. The trip had started very well. The Queen herself had waved the little fleet off as they passed her palace at Greenwich. But after the Shetlands they had reached Greenland, where ice and fog prevented them landing.

Not only had they then been separated from their sister ship, the *Michael*, in a terrible storm, but five of their number had disappeared. They had left the ship in the company of another Inuit man who through sign language had promised to show them a passage through the ice. Not one of the five was ever seen again. Frobisher had waited for three days to see if they would reappear, and when the lone trader turned up, had decided to capture him in the hope of ransoming the missing crew.

In London, the man's somewhat Asiatic features persuaded the English that Frobisher was heading in the right direction in his mission to find a passage to China. Unfortunately the Inuit died of a cold. However, Frobisher set out again the following year, and this time returned with three more Inuit: a man called Calichoughe, and a woman with her infant child. Frobisher presumed they were a family unit, but in fact they were not.

Thomas Platter visiting Hampton Court in 1599 saw a portrait of these Inuit visitors, hanging in the Queen's Apartments. 'The man's face was much waled, and both looked like savages, wore skins and the woman carried a child in Indian dress in linen cloth upon her shoulder.' Platter also wrote down their names as they appeared on the picture. The mother was called Ginoct, and her daughter Nutioc.

All three of these Arctic people died very quickly in the alien climate of England.

The Gower Memorial Unveiled

On this day in 1888, the bronze statue of Shakespeare was unveiled in its original position behind the Theatre in Stratford looking towards the Church where he was baptized and is buried.

The statue was created by Lord Ronald Gower. In Millais' painting of Gower (which the RSC owns) you can see something of the aesthete and dilettante, who was accused by the Prince of Wales (later to be Edward VII) of being 'a member of an association for unnatural practices'. Oscar Wilde, who was present at the unveiling ceremony, had used Gower as the model for Sir Henry Wotton in *The Picture of Dorian Grey*.

Gower had been working on his statue for over a decade. He had struggled to get anyone to commission it. He had tried to persuade his friend John O'Connor, a leading theatre designer of his day, who had painted scenery for the Stratford Theatre since it opened in 1879, to influence the Flower family (largely responsible for financing the new building) to buy the statue for the Theatre. In the end he gave it to the town for nothing. It had cost him, at his own estimate, £500 annually. Gower himself wrote, **'A loud and approving cheer greeted the appearance of Shakespeare, which looked well in the soft sunshine which seemed to bathe it in a kindly benison of light and life. The volunteer band struck up "Warwickshire Lads and Lasses", and the bells pealed from Shakespeare's Church tower.'** The *Stratford Herald* described it as 'the most remarkable work executed by any British amateur sculptor'.

Gower had originally toyed ambitiously with the idea of surrounding the plinth on which Shakespeare sits with four couples: Antony and Cleopatra, Romeo and Juliet, Othello and Desdemona, and Lear and Cordelia. But he dropped that plan and when the plaster model was exhibited in Paris in 1881, and later at Crystal Palace, the bronze figures appeared as they do today. Falstaff represents Comedy, Lady Macbeth wrings her hands for Tragedy, a rather lithe Henry V holds the crown for History, and a moody Hamlet broods for Philosophy.

Gower was rather pleased with his figure of the Dane, writing:

'Hamlet is now on his pedestal; I think it successful, and has thought, melancholy, calm and character about it; not too mad, but the look of one half distraught by pity, sorrow, and the knowledge that a terrible destiny, that of the avenger, is his.'

Gower had a studio in the Boulevard Montparnasse, where one morning he entertained 'that wonder of the age', Sarah Bernhardt. She called him her '*cher confrère*' and advised him on the position of Lady Macbeth's hands.

The statue was moved after the Theatre fire in 1932 to its current position, at the edge of the canal basin, where it gazes out at the Moat House Hotel and the ring road bringing traffic in from Warwick and the M40.

Hamlet and the Pirates

On this day in 1924 there was a special morning performance of *Fratricide Punished* by William Poel in London at the New Oxford Theatre. *Fratricide Punished* is a translation of *Der bestrafte Brudermord*, a mangled version of *Hamlet* in German which was acted by 'English Comedians' in the seventeenth century. We know John Green's company performed *Hamlet* at Dresden in 1626, along with *Lear*, *Romeo and Juliet*, and *Julius Caesar*. This play may be a later burlesque version. At any rate, it clears up just exactly what happened when Hamlet was captured by those pirates!

The scene takes place on an island. The pirates are about to execute Hamlet:

Hamlet: *Hear me one word more. Since the very worst of malefactors is not denied a time of repentance, I, an innocent prince, beg you to let me raise to my Maker a fervent prayer; after that I am ready to die. But I will give you a signal, I will turn my hands towards heaven and the moment I stretch out my arms, fire !* (he puts the banditti in position) *Aim both pistols at my sides, and when I say 'shoot' give me as much lead as I need and be sure to hit me, so that I shall not be long in torture.*

2nd Pirate: *Well, we'll easily grant him this favour.*

1st Pirate: *Go ahead.*

Hamlet: (kneels between these two men praying then spreading out his hands) **Shoot!** (Throwing himself forward on his face between the two, who shoot each other. The two banditti fall to the ground) *Oh, just heaven! Thanks be to thee for this angelic idea. I will praise forever the guardian angel who through my*

own idea has saved my life. But these villains - as was their work so is their pay. The dogs are still stirring - out of revenge I'll give them their death-blows to make surer, or else one of the rogues might escape. (Stabs them with their own swords) *I'll search them out to see whether, by chance they have any warrant of arrest about them. This one has nothing. Here on this murderer I find a letter. I will read it. This letter is written to an arch-murderer in England. Should this attempt fail, they had only to hand me over to him and he would soon enough blow out the light of my life. But the Gods stand by the righteous. Now I will return to my father, to his horror. But I will not trust any longer to water, who knows, but what the captain of the ship is a villain too? I will go back to the first town and take the post. The sailors I will order back to Denmark. These rascals I will throw into the water.* (Exit)

Stratford Mop

He is wit's pedlar, and retails his wares
At wakes and wassails, meetings, markets, fairs.
Love's Labour's Lost (Act 5 Scene 1)

Stratford-upon-Avon Mop Fair has its origins some time during the reign of Edward III. Farmers and householders gathered to employ their servants for the coming year. It was the custom for workers to display an item which showed their trade. A groom might wear a knot of horse hair, or a waggoner some whipcord in his hat, while a servant with no particular skill would carry a mophead – hence the phrase, Mop Fair.

Autolycus Displays His Wares, by Charles Robert Leslie (1836)

As a pleasure fair the Stratford Mop remains a key date in the Warwickshire calendar. Nowadays, the streets are closed off for the dodgem cars, the ghost train, the coconut shies and the candy-floss stalls. In Shakespeare's day, gingerbread was as popular at fairs as candy floss is today.

To make Coarse Ginger Bread
Take a quart of Honey clarified, and seethe it till it be brown, and if it be thick, put to it a dash of water: then take fine crumbs of white bread grated, and put to it, and stir it well, and when it is almost cold, put to it the powder of Ginger, Cloves, Cinnamon, and a little Licorice and Anise seeds: then knead it, and put it into

a mould and print it. Some use to put to it also a little Pepper, but that is according unto taste and pleasure.
The English Housewife, Gervase Markham

Queen Elizabeth I is credited with the invention of the gingerbread man, which became a popular Christmas treat. Loaves of gingerbread, like squares of quince and other fruit pastes, were often stamped with decorative designs.

Ginger was one of the most commonly traded spices during the thirteenth and fourteenth centuries. Arabs carried bulbs of ginger on their voyages to East Africa to plant on the island of Zanzibar. When ginger arrived in England at this period, it was much sought after: one pound of ginger was equivalent to the cost of a sheep. By Shakespeare's day it wasn't quite so expensive; as the clown Costard attests:
An' I had but one penny in the world, thou shouldst have it to buy gingerbread.
Love's Labour's Lost (Act 5 Scene 1)

Almanacs usually included an annual calendar listing the 'principal fairs kept in England', beginning with the Salisbury Fair on January 12th and ending with a fair on December 29th at Canterbury. Shakespeare mentions two fairs in *Henry IV Part Two*, at Hinckley and Stamford.

Furry Jellies

Robert Carr, Earl of Somerset, and Frances, Countess of Somerset, attributed to Reginold Elstrack, 1615

On this day in 1615, the great Jacobean beauty Frances Carr and her husband were detained on suspicion of the murder of Sir Thomas Overbury. Frances with her accomplice Mrs Turner, attempted to poison Overbury while he was imprisoned in the Tower of London. She smuggled in poisoned jellies.

At the age of 13, Frances had married the 14-year-old Earl of Essex. Essex went abroad and Frances began an affair with the King's favourite, Robert Carr, Earl of Somerset. In 1610, Essex returned and tried to remove his wife to the country, but she brought an action of annulment against him.

However, Robert Carr's secretary, Sir Thomas Overbury, tried to dissuade Carr from marrying Frances. Carr and Frances' powerful family contrived to have Overbury sent to the Tower, where he died of poisoning on the September 14th. Frances married Carr that December.

But in 1615 an enquiry began into Overbury's death and the Earl and Countess were both arrested.

This is Frances' letter to the Lieutenant of the Tower, presented with the jellies. It was a crucial piece of evidence against her:

'Sir, I pray deliver not these things till supper. I would have you change the tarts in place of these now come, and at four of the clock I will send a jelly to him as it was sent to me; the tarts and jellies taste you not of, but the wine you may drink, for in it is no letters, I know. Do this at night I pray you.'

And in her trial she was charged thus:
'These tarts were taken from you by Mr Lieutenant and the same being kept but a while were strangely furred and appeared to be corrupted with poison. Then came the glister which gave him sixty stools, thereof he died.'

At her trial in 1616, the Countess confessed to Overbury's murder and was condemned to death with her husband. In fact, both escaped the sentence.

Also on this day in 1566, Gilbert, Will's next brother, was christened.

The Death of Kings
·······················

Henry V is buried in Westminster Abbey.

'Here lieth... Henry V, with a royal image of silver and gilt, which Katherine his wife caused to be laid upon him, but the head of this image, being of massy silver, is broken off, and conveyed away with the plates of silver and gilt that covered his body; Katherine was buried in the old Lady Chapel in 1438, but her corpse being taken up in the reign of Henry VII, when a new foundation was to be laid, she was never since buried, but remaineth above ground in a coffin of boards, behind the east end of the presbytery.'

Survey of London, John Stow

Neither the saintly Henry VI, nor his murderer (according to Shakespeare at any rate) the Duke of Gloucester, the future Richard III, is buried in Westminster Abbey. Henry VI was eventually laid to rest in St George's Chapel at Windsor. But in *Richard III*, Lady Anne is accompanying the corpse of her father-in-law, the 'poor key-cold figure of a holy king', on its journey towards Chertsey Abbey, when the funeral cortège is intercepted by Crookback Richard. Having wooed Lady Anne with astonishing speed, Richard sends the corpse of Henry VI to Whitefriars. But he was finally interred in St George's Chapel in 1484, the year after Edward IV (the man who probably actually did order Henry's death) was buried there too.

After the Battle of Bosworth Field, when Richmond defeated Crookback, the last of the Plantagenet kings was succeeded by the first of the Tudors, Henry VII. Richard's naked body was bundled onto a pack horse and transported to the Greyfriars' church in Leicester, where he was finally interred in the Cathedral. His body is now lost. Some say his corpse was exhumed under orders from Henry VII and cast into the River Soar.

The new Tudor king began to consider where he himself wanted to be buried, and determined on Windsor, partly as a result of a cult that had arisen around the body of Henry VI, which was said to have inspired a number of miracles. So he started building himself a new Chapel, pulling down most of the old St George's. But it was determined in a law case that Henry VI had actually wanted to be buried at Westminster, and that the body should be exhumed and moved. Having been shoved about throughout his life, Henry VI was shoved around in death too. In fact his body was never actually taken to Westminster, but Henry Tudor did start building him a new chapel there, in expectation of the move. This is now known as the Henry VII Chapel.

Henry's son, Henry VIII, the subject of Shakespeare and Fletcher's *All is True*, was also buried at Windsor in St George's Chapel. Bloody Mary's heart and bowels were buried in the Chapel Royal in St James's but her corpse, without a monument, was buried in the Abbey. Her half-sister, Elizabeth I, lies nearby in a glorious monument in the North Aisle.

On the Tombs in Westminster Abbey
Mortality, behold and fear!
What a change of flesh is here!
Think how many royal bones
Sleep within this heap of stones!
Here they lie had realms and lands;
Who now want strength to stir their hands:
Where from their pulpits, sealed with dust,
They preach 'In greatness is no trust!'
Here's an acre sown indeed
With the richest royall'st seed,
That the earth did e'er suck in;
Since the First Man died for sin.
Here the bones of birth have cried,
'Though Gods they were; as Men they died!'
Francis Beaumont

Beaumont was buried in the Abbey in 1616.

Priest Holes

· · · · · · · · · · · · · ·

Early one mid-October morning in 1591, priest hunters arrived at Baddesley Clinton, a Jesuit safe house, a few miles from Stratford-upon-Avon. Father John Gerard describes in his autobiography how he and seven other priests, concealed in a hiding hole in a medieval sewer beneath the house, narrowly avoided capture:

'On one occasion we were all at the house where Father Garnet was living – it was the time he was still in the country.

'It was about five o'clock the following morning. I was making my meditation, Father Southwell was beginning Mass and the rest were at prayer, when suddenly we heard a great uproar outside the main door. Then I heard a voice shouting and swearing at a servant who was refusing them entrance. It was the priest hunters, or pursuivants, as they were called. There were four of them altogether, with swords drawn, and they were battering at the door to force an entrance. But a faithful servant held them back, otherwise we should all have been caught.

'Father Southwell heard the din. He guessed what it was all about, and he slipped off his vestments and stripped the altar bare. While he was doing this, we laid hold of all our personal belongings: nothing was left to betray the presence of a priest. Even our boots and swords were hidden away – they would have aroused suspicions if none of the people they belonged to were to be found. Our beds presented a problem; as they were still warm and merely covered in the usual way preparatory to being made, some of us went off and turned the beds and put the cold side up to delude anyone who put his hand in to feel them.

'Outside the ruffians were bawling and yelling, but servants held fast the door. They said the mistress of the house, a widow, was not yet up, but was coming down at once to answer them. This gave us enough time to stow ourselves and all our belongings into a very cleverly built sort of cave.

View of Baddesley Clinton in 1898 by Rebecca Dulcibella Orpen

'At last these leopards were let in. They tore madly through the whole house, searched everywhere, pried with candles into the darkest corners. They took four hours over the work but fortunately they chanced on nothing. All they did was to show how dogged and spiteful they could be, and how forbearing Catholics were. In the end they made off, but only once they had got paid for their trouble. As if it is not enough to suffer, Catholics are charged for their suffering.

'When they had gone, and gone a good way, so there was no danger of their turning back suddenly, as they sometimes do, a lady came and called us from our den, not one but several Daniels. The hiding place was well below ground level; the floor was covered with water and I was standing with my feet in it all the time. Father Garnet was there; also Father Southwell and Father Oldcorne (three future martyrs), Father Stanney and myself, two secular priests and two or three laymen.

'So we were all saved that day.'

Baddesley Clinton is now a National Trust property, and the priest hole (one of three in the house) can still be seen to this day.

An Italian Tragedy
····················

Murder's as near to lust as flame to smoke.
Pericles (Act 2 Scene 4)

On this night in 1590 in the Italian city of Naples, Carlo Gesualdo, the composer of sublime sacred music and exquisite madrigals, murdered his wife and her lover. The following account of the discovery of the scene of the brutal crime is taken from the court records:

'On entering the upper apartments of the said house of the aforesaid Don Carlo Gesualdo, in the furthermost room thereof was found dead, stretched out upon the ground, the most illustrious Don Fabrizio Carafa, Duke of Andria. The only clothing upon the body was a woman's night-dress, worked with lace, with a collar of black silk and with one sleeve red with blood. He was wounded in many places, as follows: an arquebus wound in the left arm passing from one side of the elbow to the other and also through the breast, (the sleeve of the said night-dress being scorched); many and diverse wounds in the chest made by sharp steel weapons; also in the arms, in the head, and in the face; and another arquebus wound in the temple above the left eye whence there was an abundant flow of blood.

'And in the selfsame room was found a gilt couch with curtains of green cloth and within the same bed was found the aforementioned Donna Maria d'Avalos clothed in the night-dress, and the bed was filled with blood. She was lying dead with her throat cut; and also with a wound in the head, in the right temple, a dagger thrust in the face, more dagger wounds in the right hand and arm; and in the breast and flank, two sword thrusts. And on the said bed was found a man's shirt with frilled starched cuffs, and on the chair covered in crimson velvet, near the said bed, was discovered a pair of breeches of green cloth, a doublet of yellow cloth, a pair of green silk hose, and a pair of cloth shoes, all of which vestments were without

injury, whether sword thrusts or blood stains.'

On hearing of his wife's affair with the Duke of Andria, Gesualdo had devised a plot. In order to give the lovers the opportunity to meet, he had announced he was going on a hunting trip. Before leaving he ensured that all the locks in his house were broken. On his return, Gesualdo summoned three servants. Carrying flaming torches, and bristling with weaponry, they marched into Donna Maria's apartments. A manservant heard shots, and later observed men leave the room. His testimony continues:

'Then Don Carlo himself came out, his hands covered in blood but he turned back and re-entered the chamber of Donna Maria saying, "I do not believe they are dead." The said Don Carlo went up to the bed of Donna Maria and dealt her still more wounds saying, "I do not believe she is dead." He then commanded the witness not to let the women scream and the said Don Carlo Gesualdo descended the staircase: and the witness heard a great noise of horses below and in the morning saw neither the Lord Don Carlo nor any members of his court or household.'

Midnight Mushrumps

As October can be a great time to forage for mushrooms and fungi in the woodlands, here is Shakespeare on their inextricable association with the fairy world:

... you demi-puppets that
By moonshine do the green sour ringlets make,
Whereof the ewe not bites, and you whose pastime
Is to make midnight mushrooms, that rejoice
To hear the solemn curfew.

The Tempest, (Act 5 Scene 1)

A fairy ring appears from time to time on the lawn of the Avonbank gardens in Stratford, between the Theatre and Holy Trinity Church, under a large holm oak tree. Its dark inkstain outline recalls Prospero's green sour ringlets, or Titania and her fairies dancing with their ringlets ruffled by the whistling wind.

Folklore suggests that fairy rings can be dangerous, and that the unwary can be lured inside and never seen again, but another superstition says that wearing a hat backwards can confuse the fairies and prevent them from pulling you into their ring.

In reality, of course, fairy or elf rings are a naturally occurring arc of mushrooms, detectable either by the fungi themselves, or (as in Avonbank gardens) by the necrotic zone of dark green grass. Shakespeare calls mushrooms by the much more descriptive name of mushrumps, and would have known toadstools also as puddockstools. As fairy rings can last for hundreds of years, perhaps Shakespeare knew this particular one.

And the phenomenon does not only occur in England. Travelling in Namibia a few years ago, I came across a sort of African fairy ring. In the middle of the desert there was a strange circular barren patch of earth. My guide told me mushrooms were common around there, but no one knew what caused them. Scientists suspect they might be caused by termite activity or radioactive soil but have no real explanation. The local Himba people, however, say they are made by spirits.

Elinor Fettiplace includes this delicious mushroom pickle in her Elizabethan recipe book:
'To pickle mushrooms: Take your buttons, clean them with a sponge and put them in cold water as you clean them, then put them dry in a stew pan, and shake a handful of salt over them, then stew them in their own liquor till they are a little tender; then strain them from the liquor and put them upon a cloth to dry till they are quite cold. Make your pickle before you do your mushrooms, that it may be quite cold before you put them in. The pickle must be made with white wine, white pepper, quartered nutmeg, a blade of mace, and a race of ginger.'

St Luke (Patron Saint of Doctors)
••••••••••••••••••••••••••••••••••••••

Throw Physic to the dogs, I'll none of it.
Macbeth (Act 5 Scene 3)

Dr John Hall, Shakespeare's son-in-law, kept a series of medical case notes about the patients he treated around Stratford, all 'cruelly tormented' with this affliction, and 'miserably vexed' with that. The case notes provide a rare picture of provincial medical practice at the time.

Among the salves and unguents made of maiden-hair, and hyssop, the capillaries of herbs, snails and shavings of ivory, and the gold-covered pills, Hall records some of the extraordinary ingredients he used. Fifteen-year-old John Emes of Alcester is 'cured of pissing in bed thus: the windpipe of a cock, dried, and made into a powder and with Crocus Martis [iron oxide] given in a rear egg every morning'. A 'rear egg' is partially cooked. Mrs Fiennes was diagnosed with a scorbutic dropsy. Among several preparations, she was given a clyster (an enema) containing a child's urine. A young woman called Mary Wilson 'afflicted with a Hectic Fever', drank off a number of caudles and cordials and 'sucked woman's milk', which continued to be recommended by doctors long after Hall's time.

Lady Rouse, 'being with child, was miserably troubled with the mother', or hysteria. Hall has 'a fume of Horse hoofs burnt, which restored her as soon as it was drawn into her nostrils'. And a Stratford widow with an 'immoderate cough' is given a pipe to smoke, filled with tobacco, coltsfoot, aniseed and orpiment, or yellow arsenic sulphide, 'and so was cured'.

John Smith of Aston Cantlow was in 'hazard of his life' when Dr Hall was sent for. He was suffering from the stone. Hall administered a delicious-sounding posset made of bruised winter cherries and syrup of marshmallows, and then he took a 'good big onion and head of garlic', fried them with butter and vinegar, and applied them hot to John Smith's backside 'between the yard (genitalia) and the anus'. Hall concludes his observation: 'and so he was delivered from that long pernicious and eminent danger for which God be praised'.

A Stratford barber, suffering from bad stomach pains, is given a medicinal wine made of bugloss, rhubarb, hops and horehound, mixed with 'the juice of goose-dung half a pint'. A local pauper, 'labouring of a swimming in the head', is purged and given a dram of peacock dung dried and infused in white wine: 'And this he continued from New Moon to Full Moon and was cured'. But the Lord of Northampton 'vexed with a desperate squinsy', is treated with perhaps the most unusual concoction, which includes, among other things, a cataplasm of 'swallows' nests, straw, dirt and all, to which was added white dog's turd'.

In later life, Hall himself contracted a 'deadly burning fever'. He became 'not only much maciated, but also weakened so that I could not move myself in my bed without help. Then was a pigeon cut open alive; and applied to my feet, to draw down the vapours; for I was often afflicted with a light delirium. Then my wife [Susanna] sent for two physicians'.

Autumn Spiders

'Avonside:
This morning, in the early light, a dense grey mist, rising off the weir has revealed a silken treasury all along the bank outside my window. The reeds are hung with webs which seem to be strung with dew pearls. The labouring spiders are weaving tedious snares to trap their enemies, to quote that

famous bottled spider, the Duke of Gloucester, soon to be Richard III. A large female has constructed her fantastic net right outside my window, and safe inside, I can examine her at leisure. She is the colours of autumn itself, dappled orange and brown, and she has a cross of white dots on her back. In September and October in particular, the female garden orb spiders (for such these are) build their gossamer traps, and then sit upside down in the middle, awaiting their prey. I'm not a great spider fan, I have to admit. But I suspect that is largely because I don't like being surprised by their sudden appearance.'

Diary, Greg Doran

Shakespeare most horrifyingly creates such an entrance in the diseased jealous mind of Leontes in *The Winter's Tale*:

There may be in the cup
A spider steep'd, and one may drink, depart,
And yet partake no venom, for his knowledge
Is not infected: but if one present
The abhorr'd ingredient to his eye, make known
How he hath drunk, he cracks his gorge, his sides,
With violent hefts. I have drunk, and seen the spider.
The Winter's Tale (Act 2 Scene 1)

The Bastard, Falconbridge, when he considers King John's involvement in the death of young Prince Arthur, draws on a gentler image of the spider's silken threads:

... If thou didst but consent
To this most cruel act, do but despair;
And if thou want'st a cord, the smallest thread
That ever spider twisted from her womb
Will serve to strangle thee, a rush will be a beam
To hang thee on; or wouldst thou drown thyself,
Put but a little water in a spoon,
And it shall be as all the ocean,
Enough to stifle such a villain up.
I do suspect thee very grievously.
King John (Act 4 Scene 3)

Falcons

But what a point my Lord, your falcon made
And what a pitch she flew above the rest !
To see how God in all his creatures works
Yea, man and birds are fain of climbing high.
Henry VI Part Two (Act 2 Scene 1)

Give me the lie, do, and try whether I am not now a
gentleman born.
The Winter's Tale (Act 5 Scene 2)

On this day in 1596, Shakespeare applied to the
Garter King of Arms for permission for his father,
John, to bear a coat of arms. It was approved on the
basis that John's great-grandfather had performed
'faithful and approved service to Henry VII', and
because he had married Mary, 'the daughter and one
of the heirs of Robert Arden of Wellincote'. It cost 30
guineas, and allowed John and 'his issue and
prosperity' to sign themselves 'gentlemen'. A sad
irony then that Shakespeare's own male line, his son
Hamnet, had died two months before.

The hand-written application is still kept in the
College of Arms. It shows a sketch of the design. The
description is as follows: 'Gold, on a bend sable, a
spear of the first, steeled argent [a gold spear with a
silver tip on a black diagonal bar]; and for his crest,
or cognizaunce a falcon his wings displayed argent,
standing on a wreath of his colours, supporting a
spear gold, steeled as aforesaid, set upon a helmet of
mantles and tassels.' The motto would read 'Non
Sans Droit': 'Not Without Right'. The applicant
would choose their design which would then be
ratified and approved by the College. If this was so in
this case, it shows a degree of heraldic wit to render
the family name as a spear being shaken. But why did
Shakespeare choose that particular bird as his
cognizaunce, and which falcon had he in mind?

Falcons were widely used in hunting at the time.
The hobby was the poor man's hunting bird. It

wasn't useful for much more than catching songbirds like larks; while the merlin was the choice of the ladies. Mary, Queen of Scots, went hunting with a merlin on her arm. The ubiquitous kestrel is
the famous windhover of Gerard Manley Hopkins'
poem; the 'dapple-dawn-drawn falcon in his riding',
hovering almost motionless over the verge of the
road 'upon the rein of a wimpling wind'. The largest
of our native falcons is the beautiful blue peregrine,
the fastest living creature on earth. It can achieve
phenomenal speeds in its swooping plunges,
perhaps up to 240 miles per hour. Surely, if
Shakespeare was choosing a falcon to surmount
his crest and shake his spear, this would be the bird
to select.

Shakespeare shows his understanding of falconry in
this speech of Petruchio's:
My falcon now is sharp and passing empty
And till she stoop, she must not be full gorg'd
For then she never looks upon her lure.
Another way I have to man my haggard,
To make her come, and know her keeper's call,
That's to watch her, as we watch these kites,
That bate and beat and will not be obedient.
The Taming of the Shrew (Act 4 Scene 1)

Hyssop Ale and 'Huff-Cap'

There shall be no more cakes and ale.

Twelfth Night (Act 2 Scene 3)

John Taylor describes a series of different 'real' ales he tasted in Manchester on his journey North:

... And there eight several sorts of ale we had.
All able to make one stark drunk or raving mad.
We had at one time set up in the table,
Good ale of hyssop, 'twas no Aesop fable:
Then we had ale of sage, and ale of malt,
And ale of wormwood, that can make one halt,
With ale of rosemary, and bettony,
And two ales more, or else I needs must lie,
But to conclude this drinking ale tale
We had a sort of ale called 'scurvy ale'.

The Pennyless Pilgrimage – London to Edinburgh, John Taylor

In William Harrison's *Description of England*, 1577, he writes of the appetite for strong ales and beers, and of one particularly lethal brand called 'Huff-cap':

'There is such heady ale and beer... commonly called "Huff-cap", "the mad dog", "Father Whoreson", "angels' food", "dragon's milk", "go-by-the-wall", "stride wide", and "lift leg" etc.

'It is incredible to say how our "maltbugs" lug at this liquor, even as pigs should lie in a row lugging at their dame's teats, till they lie still again and be not able to wag. Neither did Romulus and Remus suck their she-wolf with such eager and sharp devotion as these men hale at their "huff-cap", till they be red as cocks and as little wiser than their combs.'

In Edmund Spenser's parade of the months in The *Faerie Queen*, October staggers in with his head 'totty of the must' or reeling with the new wine produced at this season. He rides a dreadful scorpion, the very one sent to kill Orion when he bragged to Diana that he could hunt and kill any animal on earth:

Then came October full of merry glee:
For, yet his noll was totty of the must,
Which he was treading in the wine-vats see,
And of the joyous oil, whose gentle gust
Made him so frolic and so full of lust:
Upon a dreadful Scorpion he did ride,
The same which by Diana's doom unjust
Slew great Orion: and eke by his side
He had his ploughing share, and coulter ready tide.

Mutabilitie Cantos, VII: XXXIX

Theatre is Banned

Bare ruin'd choirs, where late the sweet birds sang.
Sonnet LXXIII

An ordinance 'for the suppression of stage plays, interludes and common players is this day ordered'. On this day in 1647, the theatres were finally shut down for the next thirteen years.

There is surely nothing so forlorn as a theatre which has been closed down. The King's Men had survived the catastrophe of the Globe Theatre fire in 1613 and had been moved into their new premises within a year. Now its doors were shut by law, and the place fell silent. Within two years the developers had moved in and the place was turned into tenements. The Fortune Theatre in Golden Lane (just behind today's Barbican), once regarded as 'the fairest playhouse in London', had burned down, within the space of two hours, in 1618. Although the company had lost 'all their apparel and play books', the Fortune was rebuilt. By 1649, however, 'it was very ruinous, decayed and fallen down', and was also redeveloped, into '20 tenements, with backsides, gardens, and other conveniences'.

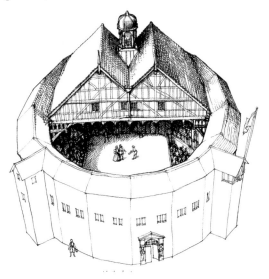

The Swan, 'in times past as famous as any other theatre', had not even made it to the official termination of playing, but had fallen into decay 'and like a dying Swan, hanging down her head, seemed to sing her own dirge'; while the Blackfriars Theatre, the King's Men's second indoor home, was to be gutted in 1655 and again turned into a housing project. Davenant wrote sadly of its broken shell:

Poor house, that in days of our grandsires
Belongst unto the mendicant friars,
And where so often in our fathers' days
We have seen so many of Shakespeare's plays,
So many of Jonson's, Beaumont's or Fletcher's,
Until I know not what puritan teachers
Have made with their rantings the players as poor
As were the friars and poets before.

But perhaps the saddest story of the theatre closures came from the Hope Theatre, just across the road from the Globe. It baited bears on Tuesdays and Thursdays, and staged plays for the rest of the week. However, by 1656, it too was scheduled for demolition. One bleak Saturday morning in the February of that year, Thomas Godfrey, who had been Keeper of the King's Game, on the command of Thomas Pride, the High Sheriff of Surrey, gave his seven bears over to a company of soldiers, who shot them all dead.

Only the Red Bull in Clerkenwell carried on, sometimes staging shows illegally and enduring raids by the militia. After the Restoration, in 1662, Pepys saw *Dr Faustus* performed at the Red Bull, 'but so wretchedly and poorly done, that we were sick of it'. And by the following year, the theatre finally closed, even to prize fights, and Davenant wrote:

Tell 'em the Red Bull stands empty of fencers,
There are no tenants in it but old spiders.

Will Adams and the Shogun

William Adams, from Gillingham in Kent, was the pilot of a Dutch merchant ship wrecked off Japan in 1600. The first Englishman in Japan, he became a close adviser to the Shogun, Tokugawa Ieyasu. On this day, after eleven years, hearing that an English ship had arrived in Java, he wrote to his countrymen: 'So we in safety let our anchor fall about a league from a place called Bongo, at which time came to us many boats, and we suffered them to come aboard us, being not able to resist them; which people did us no harm, neither of us both understanding the other one. Within two or three days after our arrival came a Jesuit from a place called Langasack, which was not to our good.

'We had sick and whole 24 men, of which the next day three died. In which time of our being here the Emperor hearing of us, sent presently five galleys to us to bring me to the court where his Highness was, which was distant about eighty English leagues. So that as soon as I came before him he demanded of me what country we were. So that in all points I answered him, so that there was nothing that was not demanded of concerning wars and peace between country and country, so that the particulars here to write would be too tedious. And for that time I was commanded to prison.

'So that a two days

Shogun Tokugawa Ieyasu, from a painted scroll

after, th'Emperor called me again, demanding the reason for our coming so far. I answered we were a people that sought friendship with all nations, and to have trade with all countries, bringing such merchandise as our country did afford into strange lands in the way of traffic. So in the end I was commanded into prison, hearing no more news either of our ship nor captain. In which time of imprisonment the Jesuit and the Portingales gave many evidences against us and the rest, that we were all thieves and robbers of all nations.

'But God that is always merciful at need showed mercy unto us and would not suffer them to have their wills of us. In the end the Emperor gave them an answer that we as yet had done to him nor to none of his land any harm or damage, therefore against reason and justice to put us to death, with which they were out of heart that their cruel pretence failed them, for which God be for ever more praised.

'So in the process of time, th'Emperor called me, as divers times he had formerly done, so one time above the rest he would have me make him a small ship. I answered him that I was no carpenter and had no knowledge thereof. "Well, do you endeavour," sayeth he. I built him a ship, about the burthen of eighty tons. The which ship being made in all respects as our manner is, he came aboard to see it, the sight whereof gave him great content, and by which I came in favour, that always I must be in his presence.

'In the end of five years I made supplication to the King to depart his land, desiring to see my poor wife and children according to conscience and nature: the which request th'Emperor was not well pleased withal and would not let me go any more for my country, but to bide in his land.'

William Adams, writing 'to his unknown friends and countrymen, at Bantam' October 23rd, 1611

Adams never returned to England, and died in Japan.

The Pilgrimage to Mecca

On this day in 1599, Richard Hakluyt wrote the dedication to his second edition of his great life's work, *Voyages*. The full title describes exactly what they contain: 'The Principal Navigations, Voyages, Traffiques and Discoveries of the English Nation made by sea or overland to the remote and farthest distant quarters of the earth at any time within the compass of these 1600 years.'

The following is taken from that edition:

THE YEARLY VOYAGE OR PILGRIMAGE OF THE MAHUMETANS, TURKS AND MOORS TO MECCA IN ARABIA.

'In the midst of the city is the great Mosquita, with the house of Abraham standing in the very midst thereof, which Mosquita was built in the time the prophet lived. This famous and sumptuous Mosquita hath 99 gates and 5 steeples, from whence the Talismani call the people to the Mosquita. And the pilgrims which are not provided of tents, resort hither...

'The house of Abraham is four square, and made of speckled stone, 20 paces high and 40 in circuit. And upon one side of this house within the wall, there is a stone of a span long and half a span broad, which stone (as they say) before the house was builded fell down from heaven, at the fall whereof was heard a voice, that wheresoever this stone fell, there should be built the house of God, wherein God will hear sinners. Moreover, they say that when this stone fell from heaven it was white as the whitest snow, and by reason it hath been so oft kissed by sinners it is therewith become black: for all the pilgrims are bound to kiss this stone, otherwise they carry their sins home with them again. The house hath without 31 pillars of brass, set upon cubic or square stones being red and green, which pillars sustain nought else save a thread of copper, which reacheth from one to another, whereunto are fastened many burning lamps. These pillars of brass were caused to be made by the Sultan Soliman, grandfather to Sultan Amurath now Emperor. In the midst there are three pillars of aloes-wood not very thick, and covered with tiles of India of 1000 colours, which serve to underprop the Terrartza. It is so dark that they can hardly see within for want of light, not without an evil smell. Without the gate five paces is the pond Zun Zun, which is that blessed pond that the angel of the Lord showed unto Hagar whiles she went seeking water for her son Ishmael to drink.

Mecca depicted in a tile of the period

'Departing from the Caravan, and being guided by such as are experienced in the way, the pilgrims go unto the city twenty or thirty in a company as they think good, walking unto a certain gate, the gate of health. And from this place is descried the great Mosquita, which environeth the house of Abraham, which being descried they reverently salute twice saying, "Salem Alech Jara sul Alla," that is to say, "Peace be to thee Ambassador of God." This salutation being ended they ascend five steps, upon which is a great void place made of stone.

'The pilgrims enter the Mosquita and drawing near unto the house of Abraham, they go round about it seven times always saying "This is the house of God, and of his servant Abraham"; this done they go to kiss the black stone abovesaid. After they go unto the pond Zun Zun, and in their apparel as they be, they wash themselves from head to foot saying "Tobah Allah, Tobah Allah," that is to say, "Pardon Lord, Pardon Lord," drinking also of that water, which is muddy and filthy and of an ill savour, and in this wise, washed and watered, everyone returneth to his place of abode. And these ceremonies everyone is bound to do once at least.'

St Crispin's and St Crispian's Day

The Martyrdom of Saints Crispin and Crispinian, by Aert van den Bossche, 1494

The Battle of Agincourt took place on this day in 1415.

This day is called the Feast of Crispian:
He that outlives this day, and comes safe home,
Will stand a-tiptoe when the day is named,
And rouse him at the name of Crispian.
He that shall see this day and live t'old age,
Will yearly on the vigil feast his neighbours,
And say 'To-morrow is Saint Crispian':
Then will he strip his sleeve and show his scars
And say 'These wounds I had on Crispin's day.'
Old men forget: yet all shall be forgot,
But he'll remember with advantages
What feats he did that day. Then shall our names,
Familiar in his mouth as household words
Harry the King, Bedford and Exeter,
Warwick and Talbot, Salisbury and Gloucester,
Be in their flowing cups freshly remembered.
This story shall the good man teach his son;
And Crispin Crispian shall ne'er go by,
From this day to the ending of the world,
But we in it shall be remember'd;

We few, we happy few, we band of brothers;
For he today that sheds his blood with me
Shall be my brother; be he ne'er so vile,
This day shall gentle his condition:
And gentlemen in England now abed
Shall think themselves accursed they were not here,
And hold their manhoods cheap whiles any speaks
That fought with us upon Saint Crispin's day.
Henry V (Act 4 Scene 3)

Today is traditionally the feast day of Saint Crispin and St Crispinian – the patron saints of shoemakers, cobblers, tanners and leather workers. Like St George, they were decanonized during the Vatican II reforms because there was not enough evidence that they actually existed.

Also on this day, Richard Quinney, a neighbour, wrote to Shakespeare asking for a £30 loan.

A Counterfeit Crank

To speak puling like a beggar at Hallowmas.
The Two Gentlemen of Verona (Act 2 Scene 1)

As Hallontide approaches, here is an account of a beggar who turned up at Thomas Harman's door one Hallowmas, while he was writing his book about tricksters and con-men, *A Caveat for Common Cursitors*.

'Upon Allhallow Day in the morning last, Anno Domini 1566, ere my book was half printed, there came early in the morning a counterfeit crank under my lodging at the Whitefriars. This crank there lamentably lamenting and pitifully crying to be relieved, declared his painful and miserable disease. I being risen, and not half ready, heard his doleful words and rueful moanings; hearing him name the falling sickness, thought assuredly to myself, he was a deep dissembler. So coming out at a sudden, and beholding his ugly irksome attire, his loathsome and horrible countenance, it made me in a marvellous perplexity what to think of him, whether it were feigned or truth.

'For after this manner he went: he was naked from the waist upward saving he had on an old jerkin of leather patched, and that was loose about him that all his body lay bare. A filthy cloth about his head, having a narrow place to put out his face with a beaver made to truss up his beard and a string that tied the same about his neck; with an old felt hat which he still carried to receive the charity and devotion of the people, that would he hold out from him; having his face from his eyes downward all smeared with fresh blood, as though he had new fallen, and been tormented with his painful pangs.'
A Caveat for Common Cursitors, Thomas Harman

🕮

Harman's suspicions are aroused when a woman offers this 'crank' a cloth to wipe his face of the blood, and he refuses it. On being questioned, the beggar tells Harman that his name is Nicholas Jennings, he is from Leicestershire, has had the falling sickness for eight years, and has spent eighteen months in 'Bethlem'. Harman sends secretly to Bethlehem Hospital to verify the crank's story, and, when he discovers he has been conned, gets his printer to send two of his boys to spy on the crank. They find him begging at the backside of Clement's Inn without Temple:
'There is a lane that goeth into the fields. There he renewed his face again with fresh blood which he carried about him in a bladder, and daubed on fresh dirt upon his jerkin, hat and hosen, and so back again to the Temple, and sometime to the waterside, and begged of all that passed by. And when it began to be somewhat dark, he took a sculler and was set over the water at St George's Fields. But these boys with Argus' and lynxes' eyes set sure watch upon him, and the one took a boat and followed him and the other went back to tell his master.'

The Counterfeit Crank Pursued
....

'The boy that followed him by water, had no money to pay for his boat hire, but laid his penner and his inkhorn to gage for a penny.' The printer joins him, and they dog the crank through the fields into Newington, where the printer gets a constable to arrest him. They take Jennings to the constable's house, interrogate him and discover he has begged thirteen shillings and threepence halfpenny.

'Then they stripped him stark naked; and as many as saw him said they never saw a handsomer man, with a yellow flaxen beard, and fair skinned, without any spot or grief.'

The printer and the constable, now in a particularly zealous mood, decide to go and apprehend some more rogues and leave the crank in the custody of the housekeeper:
'This crafty crank espying all gone, requested the goodwife that he might go out on the backside and make water, and to exonerate his paunch. She bade

him draw the latch of the door and go out, neither thinking or mistrusting that he would have gone away naked. But to conclude, when he was out, he cast away the cloak, and as naked as ever he was born, he ran away over the fields.'

Two months later, the printer runs into the same man, this time decently dressed and professing to be a hatter, who has come from Leicester to find work but who has run out of money. The printer finds the constable and has Jennings arrested again:
'And as they were going under Ludgate, this crafty crank took to his heels and ran down the hill as fast as he could drive, the constable and the printer after him as fast as they could. But the printer of the twain being lighter of foot, overtook him at Fleet Bridge and with a strong hand carried him to the Counter and safely delivered him.'

They discover that Jennings has:
'a pretty house, well stuffed, with a fair joint table and a fair cupboard garnished with pewter.

'And so remaining in the Counter three days he was removed to the Bridewell, where he was stripped stark naked. For which offence he stood upon the pillory in Cheapside, both in his ugly and handsome attire; and after that went in the mill while his ugly picture was a-drawing; and then was whipped at a cart's tail through London, and his displayed banner carried before him unto his own door, and so back to Bridewell again, and there remained for a time and at length, let at liberty, on that condition he would prove an honest man, and labour truly to get his living. And his picture remaineth in Bridewell for a monument.'

Also on this day in 1607, Halley's comet passed.

St Simon and St Jude
....

St Jude is the patron saint of lost causes. This is thought to be because his name was dangerously close to that of Judas the betrayer so no one dare invoke him except in the most hopeless of circumstances! Western tradition says that he joined his fellow Apostle, Simon, in Persia where they were both martyred.

Today the Lord Mayor of London's Procession traditionally takes place.

   William Smith, a haberdasher, has left us a description of the Lord Mayor's Procession in his *Brief Description of the Royal City of London*, 1575:
'**The day of St Simon and St Jude the Mayor enters into his state and office. The next day he goes by water to Westminster in most triumphant-like manner. Next before him goeth the barge of the livery of his own company, decked with their proper arms; and then the Bachelors' barge and so all the companies in order every one having their own proper barge with the** arms of their company. And so passing along the Thames he landeth at Westminster, where he taketh his oath in the Exchequer before the judge there: which done he returneth by water as aforesaid and landeth at St Paul's Wharf where he and the rest of the Aldermen take their horses and in great pomp pass through Cheapside.'

Autumn Vegetables
I'd rather be set quick in the earth
And bowled to death with turnips.
The Merry Wives of Windsor (Act 3 Scene 4)

The Colewort, Cauliflower, and Cabbage, in their season,
The Rouncefall, great beans, and early ripening peason:
The Onion, Scallion, Leek, which housewives highly rate;
Their kinsman Garlic then, the poor man's Mithridate;
The savoury Parsnip next, and Carrot pleasing food;
The Skirret (which some way) in sallats stirs the blood;
The Turnip, tasting well to clowns in winter weather.
Thus in our verse we put, roots, herbs, and fruits together.
The great moist Pumpkin (pumpion) then that on the ground
     doth lie,
A purer of his kind, the sweet Muskmullion by;
Which dainty palates now, because they would not want,
Have kindly learned to set, as yearly to transplant.
The Radish somewhat hot, yet urine doth provoke;
The Cucumber as cold, the heating Artichoke;
The Citrons, which our soil not easily doth afford.
Poly-Olbion, Michael Drayton

Also: remember – clocks tend to go back around this date.

Light thickens
And the crow makes wing to the rooky wood
Macbeth (Act 3 Scene 2)

The Death of Raleigh
· ·

What is our life? A Play of Passion!
Our mirth? The Music of Division!
Our mothers' wombs, the Tiring Houses be;
Where we are dressed for this short Comedy!
Heaven, the judicious sharp Spectator is,
That sits and marks still, Who do act amiss?
Our graves, that hide us from the searching sun,
Are like Drawn Curtains, when the play is done.
Thus march we, Playing, to our latest rest;
Only we die in earnest! That's no jest!
On the Life of Man, Sir Walter Raleigh, 1612

Sir Walter Raleigh had been released from the Tower after 13 years of imprisonment in order to prove his contention that the fabled gold mines of El Dorado actually existed. He failed to find them and was executed on this day in 1618, after his final return from Guiana empty-handed.

'He took a pipe of tobacco a little before he went to the scaffold, which some formal persons were scandalized at, but I think it was well and properly done, to settle his spirits.

'The time of his execution was contrived to be on my Lord Mayor's day (viz the day after St Simon and St Jude) 1618 that the Pageants and fine shows might draw away the people from beholding the Tragedy of one of the gallantest worthies that ever England bred.

'Mr Elias Ashmole told me that his son Carew Raleigh told him that he had his father's skull; that some years since, upon digging up the grave, his skull and neck bone being viewed, they found the bone of his neck lapped over, so that he could not have been hanged.

'A scaffold was erected in the old Palace yard, upon which after 14 years repreivement, his head was cut off: at which time, such abundance of blood issued from his veins, that showed he had stock of nature enough left to have continued many years in life,

Sir Walter Raleigh by William Segar, 1598

though now above three score old, if it had not been taken away by the hand of violence.'
Execution of Sir Walter Raleigh, John Aubrey

The seasons change their manners, as the year
Had found some months asleep, and leapt them over.
Henry IV Part Two (Act 4 Scene 4)

Walter Raleigh on El Dorado
••••••••••••••••••••••••••••••

She is a region in Guiana, all gold and bounty.
The Merry Wives of Windsor (Act 1 Scene 3)

'The Empire of Guiana is directly east from Peru towards the sea, and lieth under the equinoctial line, and it hath more abundance of Gold than any part of Peru, as I have been assured by such of the Spaniards as have seen Manoa, the imperial city, which the Spaniards call El Dorado, that for the greatness, for the riches, and for the excellent seat, it far exceedeth any city in the world, at least of so much of the world as is known to the Spanish Nation.'
The Discovery of Guiana, Sir Walter Raleigh, 1595

Here Raleigh quotes a chapter of Lopez's *History of the Indies* 'wherein he describeth the court and magnificence of Huaynacapa, ancestor to the Emperor of Guiana':
'All the vessels of his home, table, kitchen were of Gold and Silver, and the meanest of silver and copper for strength and hardness of metal. He had in his wardrobe hollow statues of gold which seemed giants, and the figures in proportion and bigness of all the beasts and birds, trees and herbs that the earth bringeth forth: and of all the fishes that the sea or waters of his kingdom breedeth. Finally there was

nothing in his country, whereof he had not the counterfeit in gold: Yea and they say, the Incas had a garden of pleasure in an island near Puna where they went to recreate themselves, which had all kind of garden herbs, flowers and trees of Gold and Silver, an invention, and magnificence till then never seen. Besides all this, he had an infinite quantity of silver and gold unwrought in Cuzco which was lost, for the Indians hid it, seeing that the Spaniards took it, and sent it to Spain.

'Now although these reports may seem strange, yet if we consider the many millions which are daily brought out of Peru into Spain, we may easily believe the same. If other princes foreslow the good occasions offered, and suffer him to add this empire to the rest, which by far exceedeth all the rest: if his gold now endanger us, he will then be unresistible.'

He goes on to describe the man who first saw El Dorado:
'This Martinez was he that first christened the city of Manoa by the name of El Dorado. Those Guianians are marvellous great drunkards, in which vice I think no nation can compare with them: and at times of their great solemn feasts when the emperor carouseth with his captains, the manner is thus: All those that pledge him are first stripped naked, and their bodies anointed all over with a kind of white balsamum of which there is great plenty and yet very dear amongst them, whereof we have had good experience: when they are anointed all over, certain servants of the Emperor having prepared gold made into fine powder blow it through hollow canes upon their naked bodies, until they be all shining from the foot to the head, and in this sort they sit drinking by twenties and hundreds and continue in drunkenness sometime six or seven days together. Upon this sight, the images of gold in their temples, the plate armours and shields of gold which they use in their wars, he called it El Dorado.'

Hallowe'en

The Lancashire Witch Trials

The witches of Pendle Hill in Lancashire have always held a strange fascination. At the time, their sensational story inspired the playwrights down in London at the Globe to cash in on the breaking news. They didn't even wait for the outcome of the trial to dramatize the events which had taken place in far-away Lancashire. Nor does the plot of one of the plays even faintly resemble the detail of what had unfolded in the frightened community in the Forest of Pendle. The accused women were still in prison awaiting their death sentences as the comedy, with its entirely fabricated narrative, packed them in for three days on Bankside.

'Here hath been lately a new comedy at the Globe called "The Witches of Lancashire", acted (by reason of the great concourse of people) 3 days together; the 3rd day I went with a friend to see it, and found a greater appearance of fine folk (gentlemen and gentlewomen) than I thought had been in town in the vacation: the subject was of the slights and passages done or supposed to be done, by these witches sent from thence hither and other witches and the familiars; Of their nightly meetings in several places: their banqueting with all sorts of meat and drink conveyed unto them by their familiars upon the pulling of a chord: the walking of pails of milk by themselves and (as they say of children) a highlone: the transforming of men and women into the shapes of several creatures and especially of horses by putting an enchanted bridle in their mouths; their posting to and from places far distant in an incredible short time: the cutting off a witch-gent woman's hand in the form of a cat, by a soldier turned miller, known to her husband by a ring thereon [the only tragical part of the story] ... And though there be not in it any poetical genius, or art, or language, or judgement to state or tenet of witches, or application to virtue but full of ribaldry and of things improbable and impossible; yet in respect of the newness of the subject [the witches being still visible and in prison here] and it consisteth from the beginning to the end of odd passages and fopperies to provoke laughter, and is mixed with divers songs and dances, it passeth for a merry and excellent new play.'

Letter from Nathaniel Tomkyns to Sir Robert Phelps (August 1634)

The play Tomkyns describes is Heywood and Brome's *The Late Lancashire Witches*, which was written in the summer of 1634 to capitalize on the trial of the Pendle 'witches', four women – Alice Nutter, Alizon Device, her 80-year-old mother, Old Demdyke, and Chattox, who had been accused of witchcraft. The play was, as Andrew Gurr describes it, 'a rabble-rousing case for the prosecution... It was mere clowning about a topical piece of news.'

At Hallon-tide, slaughter-time entereth in,
And then doth the husbandman's feasting begin:
From thence unto Shrovetide, kill now and then some,
Their offal for household the better will come.

Five Hundred Good Points of Husbandry, Thomas Tusser

It is now November, and according to the old proverb:
Let the Thresher take his flail
And the Ship no more sail.

'For the high winds and the rough seas will try the ribs of the ships, and the hearts of the sailors: Now come the country people all wet to the market, and the toiling carriers are pitifully moiled: The young Heron and the Shoulerd are now fat for the great Feast, and the woodcock begins to make toward the cockshoot; the Warreners now begin to ply their harvest, and the Butcher after a good bargain drinks a health to the grazier: the Cook and the Comfit maker make ready for Christmas, and the Minstrel in the Country, beat the boys for false fingering: Scholars before breakfast have a cold stomach to their books, and a master without Art is fit for an A.B.C. A red herring and a cup of sack, make war in a weak stomach, and the poor man's fast, is better than the glutton's surfeit: trenchers and dishes are now necessary servants, and a lock to a Cupboard keeps a bit for a need: Now begins the Goshawk to weed the wood of the Pheasant, and the Mallard loves not to hear the bells of the falcon: the winds now are cold, and the Air chill, and the poor die through want of Charity: Butter and Cheese begin to raise their prices, and kitchen stuff is a commodity that every man is not acquainted with. In sum, with a conceit of the chilling cold of it, I thus conclude in it: I hold it the discomfort of Nature, and Reason's patience. Farewell.'

Fantasticks, Nicholas Breton

'November in a garment of changeable green and black with a garland of olives on his head, a bunch of parsnips and turnips in his left hand and the sign of Sagittarius in his right.'

Emblems, Henry Peacham

Hallowmas

Hallowmas or All Hallows is the feast day honouring all the saints.

Yes, by St Anne, and ginger shall be hot i' the mouth too.
Twelfth Night (Act 2 Scene 3)

Feste deliberately provokes the resolutely Puritan Malvolio by invoking the cult of saints, in the person of the mother of the Virgin Mary, St Anne.

Many saints were invoked against particular diseases: St Agatha for sore breasts, St Antony against inflammations, St Apollonia against the toothache, St Benedict against poison, St Blaise against bones sticking in your throat, St Mark against sudden death, St Job against venereal disease, St John against epilepsy, St Margaret against danger in child bearing, St Quintain against coughs, St Roch against the plague.

'If we were sick of the pestilence we ran to Saint Roch, if of the ague to St Pernel; if men were in prison they prayed to St Leonard, if a wife were weary of her husband she offered otes at Paul's at London to St Uncumber. Thus we have been deluded with these images.'
Dialogue (Palm Sunday), Michael Woode, 1554

Other saints provided protection for different trades. St Sebastian presided over archers and pin makers, St Valentine, not surprisingly, over lovers, St Gregory over literati, St Andrew and St Joseph over carpenters. St Antony was patron saint of swineherds and grocers, St Arnold of millers, St Catherine of spinners, St Clement of tanners, St Cloud of nailsmiths, St Urban of ploughmen, St Martin of master shoemakers, and St Crispin of cobblers, St Nicholas of butchers, and St Peter of fishmongers. St Hubert protected dogs and was invoked against the bite of mad ones, St Loy for horses, St Magnus against locusts and caterpillars.

The abolition of the cult of saints was part of Henry VIII's reform of the church, and although the cult had been briefly revived under her sister Mary, when Elizabeth came to the throne in 1558, she pressed on with the same policy. The Golden Legend of Saints was replaced with Foxe's Book of Martyrs.

Shakespeare's parents saw three major religious transformations in England in a dozen years. It is possible that folk like them retained a fondness for the old faith, that they were papist at heart, and hankered after the familiar old ways. But Shakespeare was of a generation that knew little of that. Perhaps he was unaffected by any nostalgia for a Catholic past, but he would certainly have been aware of the devotion to the saints that flourished in pre-Reformation England. And on one occasion he seems to satirize the exploitation of the cult.

In an odd little scene in Act 2 of Henry VI Part Two, a cripple called Saunder Simpcox is brought before King Henry, claiming that St Alban appeared to him in a dream and bade him make his way from Berwick in the North to the saint's shrine, where he was cured of the blindness that had plagued him since birth. When the Duke of Gloucester exposes this fraud, by asking him to tell him the colour of various garments, he is whipped and sent away. Simpcox's wife pleads, 'Alas, sir, we did it for pure need.'

Also on this day in 1604, Othello was performed at Whitehall; in 1611 The Tempest was performed, and on this day in 1610, Jonson's The Alchemist received its first performance.

All Souls Day

All Souls Day commemorates the faithfully departed souls. It is sometimes referred to as the Day of the Dead. At the Reformation it was fused with All Saints' Day.

'Our holy and festival days are very well reduced unto a less number; for whereas (not long since) we had under the pope four score and fifteen, called festival, and thirty profesti, beside the Sundays, they are all brought unto seven and twenty, and, with them, the superfluous numbers of idle wakes, guilds, fraternities, church-ales, help-ales, and soul-ales called also dirge-ales, with the heathenish rioting at bride-ales, are well diminished and laid aside. And no great matter were it if the feasts of the Virgin Mary, with the rest, were utterly removed from the calendars, as neither necessary nor commendable in a reformed church.'

Description of England, William Harrison, 1577

Before Henry VIII's reforms, over ninety days in the year were Holy Days dedicated to the saints on which work was forbidden. Folk were expected to fast on the night before and to attend mass, matins and evensong on the day.

Cromwell had personally supervised an Act 'for the abrogation of certain holydays' on the grounds that they caused the decay of industry, and encouraged sloth, and all sorts of other sins 'being enticed by the licentious vacation and liberty of those holydays'. The Act was the first overt attack on the traditional pattern of religious observance. The ritual year was decimated, wiping out many local festivals.

The patronal festival or 'Church Holiday' was no longer to be kept as a feast day at all, and all feasts (with very few exceptions) which occurred during harvest were abolished. In July, St Martin, St Swithin, and Becket's main feast were all abrogated, and in August, St Laurence and St Augustine, and from September were swept away St Giles, Cuthbert and Holy Cross Day. Some were restored, but the boy bishop and misrule ceremonies traditionally kept on the feasts of St Nicholas and St Catherine, St Clement and Holy Innocents were all abolished. It would be true to say that the Reformation eliminated familiar beloved observances, and a vast and resonant world of symbols was destroyed.

For example, it used to be traditional for bells to be rung at midnight on All Souls to comfort the souls in purgatory. Of all Henry VIII's reforms, the abolition of this custom was perhaps the most unpopular. If the whole concept of purgatory was to be denied, then bells, or indeed prayers for the dead, were redundant. But the population, anxious for the welfare of their dearly departed, were reluctant to suppress these rituals. However, after the Gunpowder Plot, in order to commemorate the King's deliverance, bells were to be rung as part of the annual celebration. As this occurred only three days after All Souls, perhaps it helped to mitigate the people's distress. Bells were rung again a fortnight or so later for Queen Elizabeth's Accession Day on the 17th.

The tradition of making a kind of oat cake called soul cakes on All Souls, however, seemed to survive well into the next centuries, and according to John Aubrey a high heap of soul cakes would be placed on the table for visitors to take, with the rhyme: 'A soul cake, a soul cake. Have mercy on all Christian souls, for a soul cake.'

The Hundred Merry Tales

Benedick in *Much Ado About Nothing* is furious with Beatrice's suggestion that he got his wit out of *The Hundred Merry Tales*. To see why he was so offended, here is one of those merry tales, published this month in 1526:

'In Essex, there dwelled a merry gentleman which had a cook called Thomas that was greatly diseased with a toothache and complained to his master thereof. Which said he had a book of medicines and said he would look up his book to see if he could find any medicine there for it. And so he sent one of his daughters to his study for his book, and incontinent looked upon it a long season and then said thus to his cook: "Thomas (quod he), here is a medicine for thy toothache and it is a charm. But it will do you no good except ye kneel on your knees and ask for Saint Charity."

'This man, glad to be released of his pain, kneeled and said "Master, for Saint Charity, let me have that medicine." Then quod this gentleman: "Kneel on your knees and say after me..." – which kneeled down and said after him as he had bid him.

'This gentleman began and said thus: "The sun on the Sunday."
"The sun on the Sunday," quod Thomas.
"The moon on the Monday."
"The moon on the Monday."
"The Trinity on the Tuesday."
"The Trinity on the Tuesday."
"The wit on the Wednesday."
"The wit on the Wednesday."
"The holy, holy Thursday."
"The holy, holy Thursday."
"And all that fast on Friday."
"And all that fast on Friday."
"Shite in thy mouth on Saturday."
'This Thomas cook, hearing his master thus mocking him, in an anger started up and said: "By God's body, mocking Churl, I will never do thee service more" – and went forth to his chamber to get his gear together to th'intent to go thence by-and-by.

'But, what for the anger that he took with his master for the mock he gave him, and what for the labour that he took to gather his gear – so shortly together the pain of the toothache went from him incontinent, that his master came to him and made him tarry still, and told him that his charm was the cause of the ease of the pain of his toothache.

'By this tale ye may see that anger oftimes putteth away bodily pain.'

Actors Behaving Badly

In early-November 1602, an actor called Christopher Beeston was accused of fornication at the Bridewell Court.

'Margery White, sent to Bridewell prison for having a child in whoredom by one Henry Noone of the Star and Cock in Fenchurch Street, deposes as follows: '… And further she saith that one Christopher Beeston, a player, at one Winter's house in Star Alley without Bishopsgate had the use of her body, but as she saith he did it forcibly, for, he said, "I have lain with a hundred wenches in my time."'

Then:

'Christopher Beeston, a player, accused by Margaret White, a prisoner of this house, to have had the use of her body at one Goodwife Winter's house without Bishopsgate on Midsummer Even last, being himself examined as touching the premises, utterly denieth it and saith it is done of malice.'

Then:

'Mr Knevett utterly denieth that ever he used any such speeches as concerning one Beeston, a player, which was to this effect, that Beeston himself said that he had lain with a hundred women in his time.'

And then:

'And forasmuch as the said Christopher Beeston is by one Margaret White, a prisoner of this house, accused to have committed with her the abominable sin of adultery in most filthy and brutish manner in one Winter's house in an alley without Bishopsgate on Midsummer Eve last, and he being examined utterly denieth the fact, notwithstanding she justifieth it to his face. At which time also the said Beeston and others his confederate players did very unreverently demean themselves to certain governors and much abused the place. It is ordered by a general consent that such a course shall be in law proceeded against him as is and shall be thought fit for so great a crime.'
Bridewell Court Minute Books

Also on this day in 1604, *The Merry Wives of Windsor* was acted for King James.

Gunpowder Plot, 1605

'It is said of the gunpowder plot that it seemed a piece rather hammered in hell by a conventricle of cacodemons, than traced by human invention.'

Rev. John Ward, Vicar of Stratford

'This day was meant to be the day of all our deaths; and many were appointed as sheep to the slaughter, nay worse than so. There was a thing doing on it, if it had been done, we all had been undone. And the very same day wherein that appointment was disappointed by God, and we all saved, that we might not die but live, and declare the prise of the Lord: the lord of whose doing, that marvellous deed was, of whose making, this joyful day is that we celebrate.

'Of keeping remembrance, many ways there be: Among the rest, this is one, of making days; set solemn days to preserve memorable acts, that they be not eaten out, by them, but ever revived, with the return of the year, and still kept fresh in continual memory. God himself taught us this way. In remembrance of the great delivery from the destroying angel, He himself ordained the day of the Pass-over be yearly kept. The destroyer passed over our dwellings, this day: It is our Passover. We have therefore well done and upon good warrant, to tread in the same steps, and by law to provide, that this day should not die, nor the memorial thereof perish, from our selves or from our seed, but be consecrated to perpetual memory, by a yearly acknowledgment to be made of it through all generations.'

Lancelot Andrewes' Sermon, November 5th, 1606

'I cannot but remember what you have at diverse times told me touching Thomas Percy, that you suspected him to be a subtle, flattering, dangerous knave. He hath not only verified your judgement but exceeded all degrees of comparison and gone beyond Nero and Caligula, that wished all Rome but one head that they might cut it off at a stroke ...

'He had hired the house or lodging next to the Parliament, together with the cellar or vault under the upper house, into which by the means of one Johnson [Guy Fawkes' pseudonym] his man – a superstitious papist, or rather a priest as is thought – he hath conveyed any time this twelve month as much powder in satchels as four or five and thirty barrels, hogsheads and firkins could contain, with intent the first day of the parliament, when the King should be in his speech, to blow them all up; and had so cunningly covered them with billets, faggots, and such trash, that without long search they could not be discovered. And but that God blinded him to send this enclosed, without name or date, to the Lord Mounteagle, it was very like to take effect.

'But carrying it to the Lord of Salisbury, it gave such light, that watch being set, the fellow was taken making his trains at midnight with a blind lantern and presently confessed the plot, yet with such show of resolution that he seemed to be chiefly grieved that it had wanted success. The next day he was carried to the tower, but what Sir William Waud and other examiners have wrang out of him I cannot learn. On Tuesday at night we had great ringing and as great store of bonfires as ever was seen.'

Letter to Dudley Carlton, John Chamberlain

England Mourns the Future King Henry IX

On this day in 1612, Henry, Prince of Wales died of typhoid, aged 18.

The sudden death of the heir apparent was regarded as a national tragedy. Henry had shown great promise and leadership. He was an excellent swordsman, and an avid patron of the arts. He had revived the codes of chivalry, which had been encouraged by Queen Elizabeth but which were of little apparent interest to his father James.

The timing of his death was particularly sad, as his younger sister, Elizabeth, was about to be married to Frederick Elector Palatine, and the country was preparing for great celebrations.

It is hard to imagine how the history of England might have been changed had the stoutly Protestant prince become King Henry IX, instead of his younger brother being crowned Charles I.

Bacon wrote with elegant diplomacy of the prince that:

'His person was strong and erect; his stature of a middle size; his limbs well made; his gait and deportment majestic; his face long and inclining to leanness; his habit of body full; his look grave, and the motion of his eyes rather composed than spirited. In his countenance were some marks of severity, and in his air some appearance of haughtiness. But whoever looked beyond these outward circumstances, and addressed and softened him with a due respect and seasonable discourse, found the prince to be gracious and easy, so that he seemed wholly different in conversation from what he was in appearance.

'He was devoted to the magnificence of buildings and works of all kinds, though in other respects rather frugal, and was a lover of both antiquity and arts. His affections and passions were not strong, but rather equal than warm. With regard to that of love, there was a wonderful silence, so that he passed that dangerous time of his youth in the highest fortune, and in a vigorous state of health. He had certainly strong parts, and was endowed both with curiosity and capacity, but in speech he was slow, and in some measure hesitating. But whoever diligently observed what fell from him, either by way of question or remark, saw it to be full to the purpose, and expressive of no common genius.

'He died in the nineteenth year of his age, of an obstinate fever, which during the summer, through the excessive heat and dryness of the season, unusual to the islands, had been epidemical, though not fatal, but in autumn became more mortal. Fame which, as Tacitus says, is more tragical with respect to the deaths of princes, added a suspicion of poison: but as no signs of this appeared, especially in his stomach, which uses to be chiefly affected by poison, this report soon vanished.

'The same day sevennight he died, there fell out a very ridiculous accident. A very handsome young fellow, much about his age and not unlike him, came stark naked to St James's whiles they were at supper, saying he was the Prince's ghost come from heaven with a message to the King. But by no manner of examination or threatening could they get anymore out of him, or who set him awork. Some say he is simple, others mad. All the penance they gave him was two or three lashes, which he endured as it seemed without sense, and keeping him naked as he was all night and the next day in the Porter's lodge, where thousands came to see him. The King sent to have him dismissed without more ado or enquiry.'

John Chamberlain, letter of November 19th, 1612

Miraculous Face on a Blade of Straw

Knock, knock, knock! Who's there i' the other devil's name!
Faith, here's an equivocator, that could swear in both the
scales against either scale; who committed treason enough for
God's sake, yet could not equivocate to heaven : O! Come in,
equivocator.

Macbeth (Act 2 Scene 3)

Henry Garnet and the Famous Straw

The audience at *Macbeth* would have been perfectly well aware to whom the Porter was referring as the 'equivocator'. In the aftermath of the Gunpowder Plot, the Jesuit priest Henry Garnet was arrested, tortured and finally executed. At his trial, he had equivocated when asked whether his actions were treasonable or not and was found guilty in fifteen minutes. Jesuits developed the practice of equivocation in order to facilitate giving untruthful responses while under interrogation. They would speak words with equivocal or unclear meanings so as to avoid self-incrimination.

At the site of his execution a devout Catholic collected a piece of straw, spattered with the Jesuit father's blood. Some time later, he realized a miracle had occurred. Father John Gerard spread the story further:

'Here I will add something about the way we obtained the straw on which the miraculous likeness of Father Garnet appeared, for I attended the death bed of the man who found the straw, or rather the man to whom God gave it.

'A short time before he died, this man told me that he had felt an unusual fervour of soul on the morning of the holy priest's death. He wanted to attend the execution in order perhaps to secure some small relic. So he pushed his way close to the place where the executioner was hacking up the martyr's body, but he was afraid to touch anything as there were officers surrounding it. Just at that moment the butcher cut the venerable head from the body and threw it into a basket full of straw. As he did this an ear of straw came up into his hand, or at least so near his hand, that he was able to pick it up without drawing notice on himself. This ear was stained with blood, and he kept it with great reverence.'

Autobiography, John Gerard

Apparently some months later, the man showed it to a fellow Catholic. He noticed that the blood had congealed upon one of the husks in the form of a minute face, resembling Garnet's own portrait.

The straw, though carefully preserved by the English Jesuits at Liège, was lost during the upheavals of the French Revolution.

The First Folio: In Praise of Hemmings and Condell

On this day in 1623, the First Folio was entered in the Stationers' Register. The two men who collected all Shakespeare's plays together were his friends, Hemmings and Condell.

A couple of years younger than Shakespeare, John Hemmings was originally from the West Midlands too. His father was a Droitwich man. Hemmings acted as the company business manager; he is listed as the man who received the cash for the company's performances at court. One of the 'house-keepers' of the Globe and the Blackfriars, having a one-sixth sharehold in the company, he was the tapster at the Globe Tavern too and lived in St Mary's Aldermanbury near his friend Henry Condell. Hemmings and his wife Rebecca had a huge family, at least a dozen children. We know he played Corbaccio in Volpone, and might have been the original Falstaff too. There's a later reference to him (in the ballad about the Globe fire (see June 30th) as 'Stuttering Hemmings', but I can't believe that.

Harry Condell (also a sharer and housekeeper) actually appeared on stage as himself in the Induction to The Malcontent, alongside Dick Burbage, to shoo away a pair of rowdy toffs before the play could start. He was clearly a good actor, playing opposite Burbage as Mosca in Volpone, Surly in The Alchemist and the Cardinal in The Duchess of Malfi. Like his friend and neighbour Hemmings, Condell and his wife Elizabeth had a large family – nine children in their case. Thank God this philoprogenitive pair decided to collect Shakespeare's works into this edition. Had they not done so, the only plays of Shakespeare's we might now have are those which had already been published in the Single Quarto editions (19 of them), and the 18 or so remaining, plays like Antony and Cleopatra, The Winter's Tale and Macbeth, might have been lost for ever.

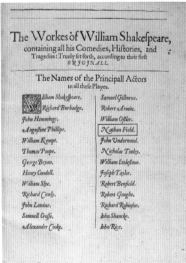

They dedicated the book to the Herbert brothers, William and Philip, the Earls of Pembroke, proffering 'these remains of your servant', saying 'the Volume asked to be yours'. They protested that they had published it 'only to keep the memory of so worthy a friend and fellow alive... without ambition, either of self profit or fame'.

The address to the general public ('From the most able, to him that can but spell') is more chatty, and much less formal, and from it we learn something more about their motivation for collecting the plays together. There had evidently been many pirated editions already: 'diverse stolen, and surreptitious copies, maimed and deformed by the frauds of stealth of injurious imposters'. We can also derive a picture of their great friend in his lifetime, delivering to them the 'foul papers' or first drafts of his plays to be copied out: 'as he was a happy imitator of Nature, he was a most gentle expresser of it. His hand and thought went together: And what he thought he uttered with that easiness, that we have scarce received from him a blot in his papers'.

Having begged the reader to dig into his purse and fork out a shilling (bound) or five shillings (bound in calf skin), Hemmings and Condell make an appeal to the reader as valid today as then:

'Read him, therefore, again and again.'

'The Names of the Principall Actors in all these Playes'

At the front of the *First Folio* of Shakespeare's *Complete Works*, a page lists the names of his principal actors. Without these actors Shakespeare wouldn't have written as he did. They all acted, and some ran the company as well.

Tom Pope and **George Bryan** were also original sharers, and Pope was housekeeper of the Globe from the start. He lived nearby in Southwark, but had died before the company received their Royal patronage in 1603. Bryan, who lived in the parish of St Andrew in the Wardrobe, with his wife and son, is recorded as a groom of the chamber in 1603, so may have left the company for a position at court.

William Sly is the last in the list of the original six sharers in the company. He was housekeeper of the Globe by 1605, and of Blackfriars in 1608. He was clearly a good comic actor, to pull off the role of a noisy gallant in the *Induction* to *The Malcontent* who clambers on stage and demands to see himself: 'Where's Harry Condell, Dick Burbage and Will Sly?' The gallant pretends he's seen the play before and has copied down all the jokes in his table-book.

When Burbage asks him why he takes off the ridiculous feather in his hat, he says, 'Why? Do you think I'll have jest broken upon me in the play to be laughed at?' He may have been the original Osric in *Hamlet*. He lived in Southwark with his bastard son.

Richard Cowley (probably pronounced 'Cooley') is the first 'hired man' in the list. He was with the company right through, though never a sharer (probably didn't have the money), and he played Verges in *Much Ado*, alongside Will Kemp's Dogberry.

Perhaps Cowley was not a very good actor, but reliable and worth having around the company all the same. Just as well, as he had four children to support. He lived up in Shoreditch in the parish of St Leonards, so he had quite a long walk in to work.

John Lowin is the first of the next generation of actors. He started as a hired man and became a sharer (he might have bought Phillips' share when he died in 1605). He seems to have taken over the running of the company eventually with Joseph Taylor. His portrait hangs in the Ashmolean. We have a better idea of the kind of parts he played: Bosola in Webster's *The Duchess of Malfi*, Domitian in *The Roman Actor*, and Flaminius in *Believe as You List*, both by Philip Massinger. He may also have originated the part of Henry VIII,

and took over the roles of Falstaff and Volpone. You can see from his portrait he's a man of 'great beard and bulk'. When the theatres closed in 1647 he ran the Three Pigeons Tavern in Brentford.

Samuel Cross we know very little about, but next in the list is **Alexander Cook** and it is clear that Sander was a boy player to start with, and ended up a sharer in the company. If Sam and Sander were boy players together, I wonder if one of them was short and dark, and the other tall and fair. Were they the original Silvia and Julia, Hermia and Helena, Beatrice and Hero, Rosalind and Celia, Viola and Maria ? Which of them was the original Juliet, and which of them graduated to play Lady Macbeth and Cleopatra?

Samuel Gilbourne was Austin Phillips' apprentice and inherited his bass viol.

'Here Come the Players'

Little Robert Armin came from King's Lynn and was apprenticed to a goldsmith in Lombard Street. But Richard Tarleton saw him busking in a pub in Gracechurch Street and took him on. He did a ventriloquist's act with his 'bauble' and seems to have joined Shakespeare's company when Kemp left. He took over as Dogberry. Armin introduced a new kind of fool; more of a court jester than a clown. He was the first Touchstone, Feste and Lear's Fool. He lived in St Botolph's with four kids and had his own coat of arms.

William Ostler married the boss's daughter, Thomasine Hemmings. He'd been a boy player in Blackfriars and was with the King's Men by 1609. By 1611, he was having poems written about him. John Davies of Hereford wrote an epigram to Ostler ending:
But if thou playest thy dying part as well
As thy stage parts thou hast no part in hell.

Nathan Field (Nid) had been a 'little eyass' in the Blackfriars boys' company as well. In fact his father was a preacher in Blackfriars who attacked playgoing. No wonder his son wrote a defence of the stage. In fact, Field was something of an activist on behalf of his profession, as he wrote a letter of protest to a preacher at St Mary Overie in Southwark, objecting to his use  of the pulpit to attack the theatre. 'It is not condemned in scripture, and being patronized by the King, it is disloyal to preach against it.' Nid was Ben Jonson's favourite actor and his portrait hangs in Dulwich Picture Gallery. He is a good-looking man, in his beautiful embroidered shirt, and rakish earring. He holds his hand over his heart, perhaps in

a gesture of sincerity or fidelity. He had to leave the King's Men when a scandal erupted over him getting the Countess of Argyll pregnant.

John Underwood was another 'little eyass' who graduated into the King's Men. Nicholas Tooley was Burbage's apprentice, and witnessed his Will in 1619.

William Ecclestone joined the company aged 19 and played parts like Kastril in *The Alchemist*.

Joseph Taylor is a big name on the list. He took over from Burbage when he died. So Taylor was the second Hamlet in a very long and unbroken line; unbroken because it seems that Davenant saw Taylor play it and passed on the role to Betterton, thus bridging the hiatus of the closure of the theatres during the Civil War and the interregnum. From Betterton to Garrick, and so on through Kean, Irving, Gielgud, Olivier, right up to David Tennant, preparing to go into rehearsal with me as I write this. Taylor also inherited Iago, Mosca, Face (*The Alchemist*) and created the role of Paris, *The Roman Actor*, and Antiochus in *Believe as You List*, becoming the new double act with John Lowin. In 1648, he and Lowin were playing together in an illegal production of Rollo at the Cockpit when it was raided by soldiers who dragged the company off in their costumes to prison. He died four years later, in 1652.

Robert Benfield became a sharer in the company but Robert Gough never did.

Richard Robinson was a boy player, who later witnessed Burbage's Will. John Shanks, composer, comedian and weaver, played clowns. He was famous for his jigs, but gave them up in order to join the King's Men. John Rice might have been the first Desdemona.

Martinmas
··············

(For Easter) at Matrilmas, hang up thy beef,
For stall-fed and pease-fed, play pickpurse and thief:
With that and the like, ere a grass beef comes in,
Thy folk shall look cheerly, when others look thin.
November's Husbandry, Thomas Tusser

The feast of St Martin of Tours, the Roman soldier saint, who divided his cloak with a beggar at the gates of Amiens. In Scotland an ox used to be called a 'mart' because Martinmas was traditionally the time for slaughtering beef ready for winter use.

As November 11th is now a day marked for remembrance, here are two of Shakespeare's thoughts on the subject from *All's Well That Ends Well*:
His good remembrance, sir,
Lies richer in your thoughts than on his tomb;
So in approof lives not his epitaph
As in your royal speech.
(Act I Scene 2)

Praising what is lost
Makes the remembrance dear.
(Act 5 Scene 3)

As Ophelia reminds us, rosemary is for remembrance. 'There's rosemary, that's for remembrance, pray you, loves remember.' But she also proffers another herb whose very name suggests regret: rue: 'There's rue for you, and here's some for me; we may call it herb-of-grace o' Sundays.' Here, in *Richard II*, the gardener is moved by the plight of the queen and promises to plant a bank of rue for her.
Poor queen! so that thy state might be no worse,
I would my skill were subject to thy curse.
Here did she fall a tear; here in this place
I'll set a bank of rue, sour herb of grace:
Rue, even for ruth, here shortly shall be seen,
In the remembrance of a weeping queen.
Richard II (Act 3 Scene 4)

The Pope's Present

Dorothy Tutin kneels in rehearsal

In 1964, during Pope John XXIII's Second Vatican Council, a party of RSC actors travelled to Rome to present a short entertainment, a selection of pieces from Shakespeare's plays, for the pontiff in the Vatican itself. The company included Dorothy Tutin, Tony Church and Timothy West. It was apparently the first time His Holiness had ever been entertained to a theatrical performance.

All went well until the end of the proceedings when the company advanced to the papal chair, holding the precious edition of the First Folio of Shakespeare's plays, which was the pride of the Theatre's Collection. It had been donated to the Shakespeare Memorial Theatre at its inception by Sir Archibald Flower.

The idea was (perhaps with regard to Shakespeare's own suspected secret observation of the Catholic Faith) that the Folio should be blessed by the present occupant of St Peter's holy office.

However, as the 1623 edition, in its beautiful Victorian binding of Morocco leather and gilt embossing, was proffered up for his special benediction, the Pope, misunderstanding the gesture, and thinking it was a gift, handed it to one of his cardinals. A swift and urgent act of diplomacy was required to prevent the treasured book from disappearing for ever into the papal libraries.

As the sun prepares to move into the house of Sagittarius (in Shakespeare's day), here is the entrance of November in Edmund Spenser's *The Faerie Queen*. He is all sweaty from the hog slaughter that traditionally happens this month. And he rides upon Chiron, the superlative and sober centaur, last of his kind, who taught Achilles to shoot with the bow and arrow, and became the constellation of the archer Sagittarius:

Next was November, he full gross and fat,
As fed with lard, and that right well might seem;
For, he had been a-fatting hogs of late,
That yet his brows with sweat, did reek and steam,
*And yet the season was full sharp and breem; ***
In planting eke he took no small delight:
Whereon he rode, not easy was to deem;
For it a dreadful Centaur was in sight,
The seed of Saturn, and fair Nais, Chiron hight.
Mutabilities Cantos VII: XL

* boisterous

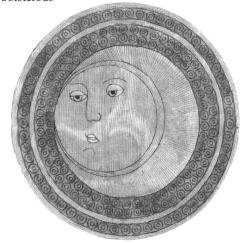

Comets and Fiery Trigons

Comets importing change of times and states
Brandish your crystal tresses in the sky.
   Henry VI Part One (Act 1 Scene 1)

A fiery comet was seen all over Europe in the middle of November 1577, when Shakespeare was thirteen. It was seen by Tycho Brahe around this date. He made a drawing of it, noting that it was seven to eight arc minutes in diameter and bluish white, the colour of Saturn. Its tail was reddish, like a flame seen through smoke, and it moved at about three degrees of arc per 24 hours.

But more significant still was the timing of its appearance. Within the next decade, a Fiery Trigon was about to occur.

Falstaff: Kiss me, Doll.
Prince: Saturn and Venus this year in conjunction?
What says the almanac to that?
Poins: And look whether the Fiery Trigon, his man, be not lisping to his master's old tables, his notebook, his counsel-keeper!
Falstaff: Thou dost give me flattering busses.
   Henry IV Part Two (Act 2 Scene 4)

A Fiery Trigon is a term used in astrology to denote the upper planets, closest to God (Jupiter and Saturn), meeting in a fiery sign. The twelve signs of the zodiac are divided into four trigons, each dominated by its own element, either fire, air, earth or water. The fiery signs are Aries, Leo and Sagittarius. This greatest of all conjunctions happens perhaps once in a thousand years. Elizabethan astrologers believed that it had happened at Noah's Flood, when Moses received the Ten Commandments, at the birth of Christ, and was due to occur in 1583. Brahe conjectured that as Jupiter and Saturn entered this Fiery Trigon, the effect would in fact be magnified by the arrival of the brand new super nova. The almanacs buzzed with possible predictions. Some thought the end of the world was nigh (see January 4th); some that it heralded the second coming of Christ.

❖

Also on this day in 1986, Her Majesty Queen Elizabeth II opened the Swan Theatre. Shakespeare and Fletcher's *The Two Noble Kinsmen* was the opening production.

Yellow Ruffs!

On this day in 1615 one Mrs Turner was executed for her part in the murder of Sir Thomas Overbury. According to a contemporary account, Mrs Turner was the inventor of yellow starch and she 'was hanged in a cobweb lawn ruff of that colour at Tyburn and with her I believe that yellow starch that disfigured our nation and rendered them so ridiculous and fantastic will receive its funeral. The executioners also wore ruffs of yellow paper'.

'They have great and monstrous ruffs, made either of Cambric, Holland, Lawn, or else of some other the finest cloth that can be got for money, whereof some be a quarter of a yard deep, yea, some more, very few less; so that they stand a full quarter of a yard (and more) from their necks, hanging over their shoulder points, instead of a veil. But if Aeolus with his blasts, or Neptune with his storms chance to hit upon the crafty bark of their bruised ruffs, then they go flip flap in the wind, like rags flying abroad, and lie upon their shoulders like the dishclout of a slut.

Elegant couple courting by Willem Buytewech, 1618

'But wot you what? The devil, as he in the fullness of his malice first invented these great ruffs, so hath he now found out also two great stars to bear up and maintain his kingdom of great ruffs: the one arch or pillar whereby his kingdom of great ruffs is under-propped, is a certain kind of liquid matter which they call Starch, wherein the devil hath willed them to wash and dive his ruffs well, which when they be dry, will then stand stiff and inflexible about their necks.

The other pillar is a certain device made of wires, crested for the purpose, whipped over either with gold, thread, silver or silk, and this he calleth a supportasse, or under-propper. This is to be applied round about their necks under the ruff, upon the outside of the band, to bear up the whole frame and body of the ruff from falling and hanging down.

'So few have them, as almost none is without them; for every one, how mean or simple soever they be otherwise, will have of them three or four apiece forsayling. And as though the finest cloth that may be got any where for money, were not good enough, they have them wrought all over with silk work, and peradventure laced with gold and silver, or other costly lace of no small price. And whether they have Argent to maintain this gear withal, or not, it forceth not much, for they will have it by one mean or another, or else they will either sell or mortgage their Lands (as they have good store) on Suters hill & Stangate hole, with loss of their lives at Tyburn in a rope, & in sure token thereof, they have now newly found out a more monstrous kind of ruff of 12, yea, 16 lengths apiece, set 3 or 4 times double, & is oftsome, fitly called: 'Three steps and a half to the Gallows.'

Anatomy of Abuses, Phillip Stubbes

A statute of 1580 forbade neckwear beyond a certain size. Members of the Ironmongers' and Grocers' companies were stationed at Bishopsgate to stop people with monstrous ruffs from entering the city.

How a Gallant Should Behave Himself at a Playhouse

Thomas Dekker has advice for the young gallant at the theatre:

'Present yourself not on the stage, especially at a new play, until the quaking Prologue hath by rubbing got colour into his cheeks, and is ready to give the trumpets their cue that he's upon point to enter: for then it is time, as though you were one of the properties, or that you had dropped out of the hangings, to creep from behind the arras, with your tripos or three-footed stool in one hand and a teston [sixpence] mounted between a forefinger and a thumb in the other; for if you should bestow your person upon the vulgar, when the belly of the house is but half full, your apparel is quite eaten up, the fashion lost, and the proportion of your body in more danger to be devoured than if it were served up in the Counter amongst the poultry. Avoid that as you would the bastone [bastinado or beating with a stick].

'It shall crown you with rich commendation, to laugh aloud in the midst of the most serious and saddest scenes of the terriblest tragedy, and there to let the clapper, your tongue, be tossed so high that all the house may ring of it. All the eyes in the galleries will leave walking after the players, and only follow you.

'Now, sir; if the writer be a fellow that hath either epigrammed you, or hath had a flirt with your mistress, or hath brought either your feather, or your red beard, or your little legs, etc. on the stage; you shall disgrace him worse than tossing him in a blanket, or giving him the bastinado in a tavern, if, in the middle of his play, you rise with a screwed and discontented face from your stool to be gone; no matter whether the scenes be good, or no; the better they are the worse do you distaste them; and being on your feet, sneak not away like a coward, but salute all your gentle acquaintance, that are spread either on the rushes, or on the stools about you; and draw what troop you can from the stage after you; the mimics are beholden to you for allowing them elbow-room; their poet cries, perhaps "a pox go with you"; but care not you for that; there's no music without frets.'

The Gull's Hornbook, Thomas Dekker, 1609

Dangerous Theatre
....

Here are two letters which attest to just how dangerous theatre could be in Shakespeare's day.

The first is a letter from one Philip Gawdy to his father dated this day, 1587:

'You shall understand of some accidental news here in this town, though myself no witness thereof, yet I may be bold to verify it for an assured truth. My Lord Admiral's men and players, having a device in their play to tie one of their fellows to a post and so shoot him to death, having borrowed their cavaliers [pistols], one of the player's hands swerved: his piece, being charged with bullet, missed the fellow he aimed at and killed a child, and a woman great with child forthwith, and hurt another man in the head very sore. How they will answer it I do not study unless their profession were better, but in Christianity I am very sorry for the chance; And yet I find by this an old proverb verified, that never comes more hurt than comes of fooling.'

In the following 'turbulent and rebellious' letter, John Gill, a felt maker's apprentice, sends a challenge to an actor called Richard Baxter, for a wound he received sitting on the stage of the Red Bull theatre. 'Mr Baxter, So it is that upon Monday last... I happened to be upon your stage intending not hurt to anyone, where I was grievously wounded in the head as may appear, and in the surgeon's hands, who is to have 10s for the cure, and in the meantime my master refuses to give me maintenance. I suffered great loss and hindrance, and, therefore, in kindness I desire you to give me satisfaction, seeing I was wounded by your own hand and weapon. If you refuse, then look to yourself and avoid danger which shall this day ensue upon your company and playhouse, as you can, for I am a felt maker's apprentice, and have made it known to at least one hundred and forty of our fellow apprentices, who are all here present, ready to take revenge upon you, unless willingly you will give present satisfaction. And as you have a care of your own safeties, so let me have answer forthwith.'

Baxter gave this letter to the authorities, who arrested Gill at the Red Bull, where he was accompanied by a hundred of his mates, 'assembled riotously' to the terror of the neighbourhood.

St Hugh and Accession Day Tilts

Every year on this day, to celebrate Queen Elizabeth's accession to the throne in 1558, a great joust was held at Whitehall. The queen's champion fought against all comers in the palace tilt yard. The tradition was begun by Sir Henry Lee who continued the custom until he resigned and recommended that office unto the right noble George, Earl of Cumberland

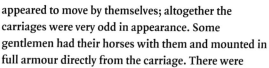

'Now approached the day, when on November 17 the tournament was to be held. About twelve o'clock the queen and her ladies placed themselves at the windows in a long room at Whitehall palace, near Westminster, opposite the barrier where the tournament was to be held. From this room a broad staircase led downwards, and round the barrier stands were arranged by boards above the ground, so that everybody by paying 12d. would get a stand and see the play. Many thousand spectators, men, women, and girls, got places, not to speak of those who were within the barrier and paid nothing.

'During the whole time of the tournament all those who wished to fight entered the list by pairs, the trumpets being blown at the time and other musical instruments. The combatants had their servants clad in different colours, they, however, did not enter the barrier, but arranged themselves on both sides. Some of the servants were disguised like savages, or like Irishmen, with the hair hanging down to the girdle like women, others had horses equipped like elephants, some carriages were drawn by men, others appeared to move by themselves; altogether the carriages were very odd in appearance. Some gentlemen had their horses with them and mounted in full armour directly from the carriage. There were some who showed very good horsemanship and were also in fine attire. The manner of the combat each had settled before entering the lists. The costs amounted to several thousand pounds each.

'When a gentleman with his servants approached the barrier, on horseback or in a carriage, he stopped at the foot of the staircase leading to the queen's room, while one of his servants in pompous attire of a special pattern mounted the steps and addressed the queen in well-composed verses or with a ludicrous speech, making her and her ladies laugh. When the speech was ended he in the name of his lord offered to the queen a costly present. Now always two by two rode against each other, breaking lances across the beam. The fete lasted until five o'clock in the afternoon.'

Description by Lupold von Wedel of the Accession Day Tilt in 1584

Cold's the wind, and wet's the rain;
Saint Hugh be our good speed !
Ill is the weather that bringeth no gain;
Nor helps good hearts in need !
The Shoemaker's Holiday, Thomas Dekker

Accession Day was the first public holiday not to be associated with a religious feast day.

England Joins the Slave Trade

In 1562, John Hawkins set out on a voyage that would mark the beginning of the English slave trade. He left England with the purpose of capturing Africans along the Guinea Coast. In this extract from his third voyage (recorded in Richard Hakluyt's *Voyages*), he describes one such raid:

'Arrived eighteenth November, where we landed 150 men, hoping to obtain some negroes, where we got but few, and those with great hurt and damage to our men, which chiefly proceed of their envenomed arrows; and though in the beginning they seemed to be but small hurts, yet there hardly escaped any that had blood drawn out of them, but died in strange sort, with their mouths shut some ten days, before they died, and after their wounds were whole, where I myself had one of the greatest wounds, yet thanks be to God escaped. From thence we past the time upon the coast of Guinea, searching with all diligence the rivers from Rio Grande, unto Siera Leona, till the twelfth of January, in which time we had not gotten together a hundred and fifty negroes; yet notwithstanding, the sickness of our men, and the late time of the year commanded us away.

'But even in that present instant, there came to us a Negro, sent from a king, oppressed by other kings his neighbours, desiring our aid, with promise that as many negroes by these wars might be obtained, as well of his part as

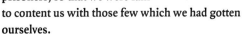

of ours, should be at our pleasure whereupon we concluded to give aid.

'Considering that the good success of this enterprise might highly further the commodity of our voyage, I went myself, and with the help of the king of our side, assaulted the town, both by land and sea, and very hardly with fire (their houses being covered with dry palm leaves) obtained the town, put the inhabitants to flight, where we took 250 persons, men, women and children; and by the king of our side, there were taken 600 prisoners whereof we hoped to have our choice: but the Negro (in which nation is seldom or never found truth) meant nothing less; for that night he removed his camp and prisoners, so that we were fain to content us with those few which we had gotten ourselves.

'Now we had obtained between four and five hundred negroes, wherewith we thought it somewhat reasonable to seek the coast of the West Indies, and there for our negroes we hoped to obtain whereof to countervail our charges with some gains.'

In *The Tempest*, Ariel compares the old Counsellor Gonzalo's grief to rain falling off a thatched roof, a melancholy image which must have been only too familiar to Shakespeare's audience:

His tears run down his beard, like winter's drops
From eaves of reeds.

The Tempest (Act 5 Scene 1)

Hoax at the Swan

A spectacular play was advertised to be performed at the Swan Theatre on Bankside. Called *England's Joy* and said to stage famous events from the reigns of Edward III to Elizabeth, a broadside produced by its creator, Edward Vennar, promised:

'A great triumph... with fighting of twelve gentlemen at barriers'... The queen ' taken up to heaven, when presently a throne of blessed souls and beneath under the stage, set forth with strange fireworks, divers black and damned souls wonderfully described in their several torments.'

In a letter written this day in 1602, John Chamberlain described what happened next:

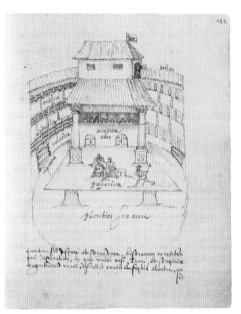

'I must tell you of a cozening prank of one Vennar, of Lincoln's Inn, that gave out bills of a famous play on Saturday was seven-night on the Bankside to be acted only by certain gentlemen and women of account. The price at coming in was 2s or 18d at least. And when he had gotten most part of the money into his hands, he would have showed them a fair pair of heels, but he was not so nimble to get up onto horseback, but he was fain to foresake that course and betake himself to the water, where he was pursued and taken and brought before the Lord Chief Justice, who would make nothing of it but a jest and merriment and bound him over in £5 to appear at the sessions. In the meantime, the common people, when they saw themselves deluded, revenged themselves upon the hangings, curtains, chairs, stools, walls, and whatsoever came in their way, very outrageously, and made great spoil. There was a great store of good company, and many noblemen.'

John Chamberlain to Dudley Carleton

A Beargarden Banquet of Dainty Conceits

Another theatrical debacle took place in October 1614. John Taylor, the Water Poet and self-publicist, challenged a rival poet to a public trial of wit on stage at the Hope Theatre on Bankside. But his rival, William Fennor, didn't turn up.

'Be it therefore known unto all men that I, John Taylor, waterman, did agree with William Fennor (who arrogantly and falsely entitles himself the king's majesty's rhyming poet) to answer me at a trial of wit on the seventh of October last, 1614, on the Hope stage; and the said Fennor received of me 10s in earnest of his coming to meet me. Whereupon I caused 1,000 bills to be printed and divulged my name 1,000 ways and more, giving my friends and divers of my acquaintance notice of this Beargarden banquet of dainty conceits. And when the day came that the play should have been performed, the house being filled with a great audience who had all spent their moneys extraordinarily, then this companion for an ass ran away and left me for a fool amongst thousands of critical censurers, where I was ill thought of by my friends, scorned by my foes, and, in conclusion, in a greater puzzle than the blind bear in the midst of all her whip-broth.'

Works II, John Taylor

St Edmund the King
·······················

An Anatomy of Wit

On this day in 1606, the writer John Lyly was buried at St Bartholomew-the-Less.

Lyly had written one of the literary sensations of the age of Queen Elizabeth, but his reputation declined and he died in poverty. *Euphues: The Anatomy of Wit*, published in 1578, when Lyly was a struggling Oxford graduate, had given its name to a whole style of English prose, and influenced a generation of young writers like William Shakespeare. The euphuistic style was highly mannered and artificial, employing balanced phrases, patterns of sounds and syllables, and elaborate comparisons derived from classical mythology and the natural world.

Winter by Arcimboldo, c. 1571

The story of *Euphues: The Anatomy of Wit* is mirrored by Shakespeare's *The Two Gentlemen of Verona*. Two young men, Euphues and Philautus, have their friendship tested when Euphues falls in love with Philautus' intended, Lucilla. Here Philautus writes to his false friend:

'Although heretofore, Euphues, I have enshrined thee in my heart, for a trusty friend, I will shun thee hereafter as a trothless foe; and although I cannot see in thee less wit than I was wont, yet do I find less honesty. I perceive at the last [although, being deceived, it may be too late] that musk, though it be sweet in the smell, is sour in the smack; that the leaf of the cedar tree, though it be fair to be seen yet the syrup depriveth sight; that friendship, though it be plighted by shaking the hand, yet it is shaken off by fraud of the heart.

'Dost though not know that a perfect friend should be like the glaze-worm which shineth most bright in the dark; or like the pure frankincense which smelleth most sweet when it is in the fire; or, at least, not unlike to the damask rose which is sweeter in the still than on the stalk ? But thou Euphues, dost rather resemble the swallow which in the summer creepeth under the eaves of every house and in the winter leaveth nothing but dirt behind her; or the humble bee which having sucked honey out of the fair flower doth leave it and loathe it; or the spider which in the finest web doth hang the fairest fly.'

Today is the feast of St Edmund, King of East Anglia. In 869, when the Danes made one of their periodic raids on the country, King Edmund was captured by the enemy forces and decapitated. When his men returned to the scene and found his headless corpse, they discovered the saintly king's head between the paws of a white wolf, who had protected it. The saint gives his name to Bury St Edmunds, and is seen in the Wilton Diptych, behind King Richard II, who bore a special devotion to the saint. Edmund's banner was carried into battle by the troops of Henry V at Agincourt.

Set garlic and beans at St Edmund the king.
The moon in the wane, thereon hangeth a thing:
Th'increase of a pottle (well proved off some),
Shall pleasure thy household, ere peascod time come.
100 Good Points of Husbandry, Thomas Tusser

Thomas Tusser's reminder to set garlic bulbs at this time of year recalls Thomas Nashe's description of garlic in *The Unfortunate Traveller*:
Garlic hath three properties – to make a man wink, drink and stink.

The Persian Sophy

They say he has been fencer to the Sophy.
Twelfth Night (Act 3 Scene 4)

Shah Abbas and a pageboy, Muhammed Qasim, 1627

The Sherley brothers witnessed the Persian 'Sophy' make a triumphal Entry:

'When the Shah Abbas returned to Qazvin he camped some distance from the city to prepare a triumphal entry. He sent word that the English were to ride out to meet him in Persian costume, which they did. Sir Anthony for the occasion wore a turban worth a thousand pounds, and a jewelled scimitar swung at his side. Robert Sherley was attired in cloth of Gold, and all others wore silk and velvet. As the two parties approached each other, the Shah was accompanied by a band of courtesans, "riding astride in disorder and shouting and crying in every direction as if they had lost their senses, making such cries as the Wild Irish make".

'Persian troops also accompanied the Shah, carrying the heads of slain Uzbegs on their lances. Some said there were twenty thousand heads on the lance tips, but others counted only twelve hundred. Sherley dismounted and kissed the Shah's foot. "My speech was short unto him, the time being fit for no other." He tells the Shah, "the fame of his royal virtues had brought me from a far country". He begged Abbas to consider "the danger and expense of my voyage, only to see him, of whom I had received such magnificent and glorious relations".

'The Shah kissed Sir Anthony three or four times and swore a great oath that Sir Anthony would be henceforth as his brother. A magnificent banquet was held in the Sherleys' honour at which were served pears, melons, quinces, pomegranates, oranges, lemons, pistachios, almonds, grapes, sweets and wine.'
Sir Anthony Sherley, His Relation of his Travels into Persia, 1613

The scene is enacted in *The Travels of the Three English Brothers* (1607).
A battle presented. Excursion; the one half drive out the other, then enter with heads on their swords.
Sophy: *These are our victories, to see those tongues*
That lately threw defiance in our teeth
Quite put to silence in the caves of the earth.
Then are we sure our enemy is dead
When from the body we divide the head.
How likes the Christian our Persian wars?
Sir Anthony: *As themselves deserve, renowned Sophy.*

St Cecilia

••••••••••

The Concert by Hendrick ter Brugghen

St Cecilia was the patron saint of music. Perhaps Shakespeare's most haunting and eloquent description of it comes in the last act of *The Merchant of Venice* and helps to calm the violence of the play:

Lorenzo: *How sweet the moonlight sleeps upon this bank!*
Here will we sit and let the sounds of music
Creep in our ears: soft stillness and the night
Become the touches of sweet harmony.
Sit, Jessica. Look how the floor of heaven
Is thick inlaid with patines of bright gold:
There's not the smallest orb which thou behold'st
But in his motion like an angel sings,
Still quiring to the young-eyed cherubins;
Such harmony is in immortal souls;
But whilst this muddy vesture of decay
Doth grossly close it in, we cannot hear it. (Enter Musicians)
Come, ho! and wake Diana with a hymn!
With sweetest touches pierce your mistress' ear,
And draw her home with music. (Music)

Jessica: *I am never merry when I hear sweet music.*
Lorenzo: *The reason is, your spirits are attentive:*
For do but note a wild and wanton herd,
Or race of youthful and unhandled colts,
Fetching mad bounds, bellowing and neighing loud,
Which is the hot condition of their blood;
If they but hear perchance a trumpet sound,
Or any air of music touch their ears,
You shall perceive them make a mutual stand,
Their savage eyes turn'd to a modest gaze
By the sweet power of music: therefore the poet
Did feign that Orpheus drew trees, stones and floods;
Since nought so stockish, hard and full of rage,
But music for the time doth change his nature.
The man that hath no music in himself,
Nor is not moved with concord of sweet sounds,
Is fit for treasons, stratagems and spoils;
The motions of his spirit are dull as night
And his affections dark as Erebus:
Let no such man be trusted. Mark the music.
The Merchant of Venice (Act 5 Scene 1)

Francis Fry's 'Aerial Journey'

'About November last, in the Parish of Spreyton, in the County of Devon...'

So begins a sensational letter. It gives an account of what happened to a 21-year-old serving man called Francis Fry, when he became haunted by a terrifying spirit.

'Fry's head was thrust into a narrow space, where a man's fist could not enter, between a bed and a wall; and forced to be taken thence by the strength of Men, all bruised and bloody; upon this it was thought fit to bleed him, and after that was done, the binder was removed from his arm, and conveyed about his middle and presently was drawn so very straight, it had almost killed him, and was cut asunder, making an ugly uncouth noise. Several other times, with handkerchiefs, cravats, and other things he was near strangled, they were drawn so close upon his throat.

'He lay one night in his periwig which was all torn to pieces. His best periwig he enclosed in a little box (with a joint-stool and other weight upon it); the box was snapped asunder, and the wig torn all to flitters. His master saw his buckles fall all to pieces on his feet: But first I should have told you the fate of the shoestrings, a gentlewoman assured me that she saw it come out of his shoe, without any visible hand, and fling itself to the far end of the room; the other was coming out too, but a maid prevented and helped it out, which crisp'd and curl'd about her hand like a living eel.

'But the most remarkable of all happened in that day that I passed by the door, on my return hither (which was Easter Eve), when Fry, returning from work (that he can little do) he was caught by the woman spectre by the skirts of his doublet and carried into the air. He was quickly missed by his master and the workmen, and great enquiry was made for Fran. Fry; but half an hour after Fry was heard whistling and singing in a kind of quagmire, but coming to himself an hour after, he solemnly protested, that the daemon carried him so high that he saw his master's house underneath him, no bigger than a haycock, that he was in perfect sense and prayed God not to suffer the devil to destroy him. The workmen found one shoe on one side of the house, and the other shoe on the other side; his periwig was espied next morning hanging on top of a tall tree.'

A letter to John Aubrey from the Rev. Mr Andrew Paschal, Rector of Chedzoy in Somerset

Also on this day in 1616, Shakespeare Quinney was christened. His grandfather died in April.

It is My Birthday

Both Cleopatra (in *Antony and Cleopatra*) and Cassius (in *Julius Caesar*) suddenly announce their birthdays at unexpected moments in the course of the action. After the devastating defeat at Actium, when Cleopatra has fled the sea battle, Antony

collapses in despair. But he rallies, whips Octavius' messenger out of his presence, and dares his master to single combat. Inflated once more with self-confidence, he proposes 'one other gaudy night', to which Cleopatra replies:

It is my birthday;
I had thought to've held it poor; but since my lord
Is Antony again, I will be Cleopatra.
Anthony and Cleopatra (Act 3 Scene 9)

In *Julius Caesar* on the plains of Philippi, as the two sides square up for the decisive battle, Cassius draws his colleague Messala apart:
Messala: What says my general ?
Cassius: Messala,
This is my birthday; as this very day was Cassius born.
(Act 5 Scene 1)
Rather than being a joyful occasion, Cassius perceives terrible omens which predict defeat. His birthday will also be his last on earth. He kills himself with the very sword he used to help assassinate Julius Caesar.

On the subject of growing older, Shakespeare's Sonnet XII reminds everyone of the inevitable process of ageing, and, as he proposes to the young Earl of Southampton, the only way of countering its effects:
When I do count the clock that tells the time,
And see the brave day sunk in hideous night;
When I behold the violet past prime,
And sable curls, all silvered o'er with white;
When lofty trees I see barren of leaves,
Which erst from heat did canopy the herd,
And summer's green all girded up with sheaves,
Borne on the bier with white and bristly beard,
Then of thy beauty do I question make,
That thou amongst the wastes of time must go,
Since sweets and beauties do themselves forsake
And die as fast as they see others grow;
And nothing gainst Time's scythe can make defence
Save breed, to brave him when he takes thee hence.

Feast of St Katherine

The *Golden Legend* is a collection of stories about saints. It was assembled by Jacobus de Voragine, the Bishop of Genoa, in 1275, and 'englished' by William Caxton, England's first printer. According to a colophon at the end of his book, Caxton finished it in the first year of the reign of King Richard III, on November 20th, 1483. For sixty years it was the most often printed book in Europe.

Here is part of the story of St Katherine, whose feast day is celebrated today. The Emperor Maxentius fell in love with Katherine, but she rejected him and was tortured by him as a result. Rather surprisingly the instrument of her prospective martyrdom, the famous Katherine Wheel, was the lurid invention of one of the Emperor's sadistic captains, but it didn't work. So she was beheaded. Milk flowed from her body instead of blood, and the angels buried her on Mount Sinai.

Detail from St Katherine Altarpiece by Lucas Cranach, 1506

'And when the emperor was returned, he commanded Katherine to be brought before him, and when he saw her so shining, whom he supposed to have been tormented by great famine and fasting, and supposed that some had fed her in prison, he was filled with fury and commanded to torment the keepers of the prison, and she said to him: Verily, I took never sith meat of man, but Jesu Christ hath fed me by his angel. I pray thee, said the emperor, set at thine heart this that I admonish thee, and answer not by doubtable words. We will not hold thee as a chamberer, but thou shalt triumph as a queen in my realm, in beauty enhanced. To whom the blessed virgin Katherine said: Understand, I pray thee, and judge truly, whom ought I better to choose of these two, or the king puissant, perdurable, glorious and fair, or one sick, unsteadfast, not noble, and foul? And then the emperor having disdain, and angry by felony, spake: Of these two choose thee one, or do sacrifice and live, or suffer divers torments and perish. And she said: Tarry not to do what torments thou wilt, for I desire to offer to God my blood and my flesh like as he offered for me; he is my God, my father, my friend and mine only spouse.

'And then a captain warned and advised the king, being wood for anger, that he should make four wheels of iron, environed with sharp razors, cutting so that she might be horribly all detrenched and cut in that torment, so that he might fear the other Christian people by ensample of that cruel torment. And then was ordained that two wheels should turn against the other two by great force, so that they should break all that should be between the wheels, and then the blessed virgin prayed our Lord that he would break these engines to the praising of his name, and for to convert the people that were there. And anon as this blessed virgin was set in this torment, the angel of our Lord brake the wheels by so great force that it slew four thousand paynims.'

The Golden Legend

The Discovery of Witchcraft

'Aroint thee witch!' the rump-fed ronyon cries!
Macbeth (Act 1 Scene 3)

Reginald Scot published his *Discovery of Witchcraft* in 1584. It is a damning account of the superstitious nonsense he found all around him. Here Scot describes how elderly women are accused of being witches:

'One sort of such as are said to be witches, are women which be commonly old, lame, blear-eyed, pale, foul, and full of wrinkles; poor, and sullen, superstitious: in whose drowsy minds the devil hath gotten a fine seat; so as, what mischief, mischance, calamity, or slaughter is brought to pass, they are easily persuaded the same is done by themselves; imprinting in their minds an earnest and constant imagination hereof.

'These miserable wretches are so odious unto all their neighbours, and so feared, as few dare offend them, or deny them any thing they ask: whereby they take upon them; yea, and sometimes think, that they can do such things as are beyond the ability of human nature. These go from door to door for a pot full of milk, yeast, drink, pottage, or some such relief; (without the which they could hardly live). It falleth out many times, that their expectation is [not] answered or served, in those places where they beg or borrow; but rather their lewdness is by their neighbours reproved. And further, in tract of time the witch waxeth odious and tedious to her neighbours; and they again are despised and despited of her: so as sometimes she curseth one, and sometimes another; and that from the master of the house, his wife, children, cattle, &c. to the little pig that lieth in the sty. Thus in process of time they have all displeased her, and she hath wished evil luck unto them all. Doubtless (at length) some of her neighbours die, or fall sick; or some of their children are visited with diseases that vex them strangely: as apoplexies, epilepsies, convulsions, hot fevers, worms, &c., which by ignorant parents are supposed to be the vengeance of witches.

'The witch on the other side expecting her neighbours' mischances, and seeing things sometimes come to pass according to her curses, being called before a justice, is driven to see her imprecations and desires, and her neighbours' harms and losses to concur, and as it were to take effect: and so confesseth that she hath brought such things to pass. Wherein, not only she, but the accuser, and also the justice are foully deceived and abused.

'And because it may appear unto the world what treacherous and faithless dealing, gross and fond absurdities, what cankered and spiteful malice, what lewd and false packing, what cunning and crafty intercepting, what bald and peevish interpretations, what abominable and devilish inventions, and what flat and plain knavery is practised against these old women; I will set down the whole order of the inquisition, to the everlasting shame of all witchmongers. He that can be persuaded that these things are true, may soon be brought to believe that the moon is made of green cheese.'

The King's Demons
....

The prince of darkness is a gentleman;
Modo he's called, and Mahu.
King Lear (Act 3 Scene 4)

King James I wrote his own treatise about Witchcraft, *The Demonology*, specifically to discredit Reginald Scot, as he states in his preface:
'The fearful abounding at this time in this country, of these detestable slaves of the Devil, the Witches or enchanters, hath moved me (beloved reader) to dispatch in post, this following treatise of mine, not in any way (as I protest) to serve for a show of my learning, but only (moved of conscience) to press thereby, so far as I can, to resolve the doubting hearts of many; both that such assaults of Satan are most certainly practised, and that the instruments thereof, merits most severely to be punished: against the damnable opinions of two principally in our age, whereof the one called Scot an Englishman, is not ashamed in public print to deny, that there can be such a thing as Witch-craft: and so maintains the old error of the Sadducees, in denying of spirits.
The Demonology

When he came to the throne of England in 1603, James had Scot's book destroyed.

He also attacked a German doctor called Johann Weyer. His *Praestigiis Daemonum* (1563) was a point-by-point rebuttal of the witch-hunter's handbook, *Malleus Maleficarum*. Sigmund Freud called it one of the ten most significant books of all time. Weyer was a pioneer in the field of psychiatry, and was said to have been the first person to use the term 'mentally ill' to designate those women accused of practising witchcraft. However, unlike Scot, Weyer was also a firm believer in magic.

The *Pseudo-monarchia daemonum*, an appendix to his book, is a catalogue of demons.

ANDRAS is seen in an angel's shape with a head like a black night raven, riding upon a black wolf, with a sharp sword in his hand.

ANDREALPHUS is a great marquis, appearing as a peacock, he raiseth great noises, and perfectly teacheth geometry, he maketh a man cunning in astronomy.

SITRI appears with the face of a leopard, and wings as a griffin: when he taketh human shape, he is very beautiful, he inflameth a man with a woman's love.

VUALL is seen as a great and terrible dromedary, but in human form. He soundeth out in a bass voice the Ægyptian tongue. This man above all other procureth the especial love of women.

Also on this day in 1582, a Bishop's Licence was granted for the marriage of Will Shakespeare and Anne Hathaway.

The North Berwick Witch Trials

The witch in Smithfield shall be burned to ashes,
And you three shall be strangled on the gallows.

Henry VI Part Two (Act 2 Scene 3)

'The King and Council is occupied with the examinations of sundry witches taken in this country, and confessing both great numbers and the names of their fellows; and also strange and odious facts done by them; which upon the full trials of their causes are intended to be hereafter published. And some of good qualities are like to be blotted by the dealings of the wicked sort.

'The King by his own especial travail has drawn Sampson, the great witch, to confess her wicked doings, and to discover sundry things touching his own life, and how the witches sought to have his shirt or other linen for the execution of their charms. In this Lord Claud and other noblemen are evil spoken of. The witches known number is over thirty, and many others accused. Their acts are filthy, lewd, and phantastical.'

News from Scotland

The trials ran for two years and implicated some seventy people. The witches, who held their coven at St Andrew's auld kirk overlooking the harbour, were

convicted of having used witchcraft to conjure a storm to sink the King's ship as he brought his bride Anne from Denmark to Scotland.

On this day in 1590, Agnes Sampson was examined by James himself at Holyrood House. Agnes had been kept in a cell, not allowed to sleep and made to wear a witch's bridle chained to the wall. The bridle had iron prongs which pressed into her cheeks and tongue. She finally confessed to the fifty-three indictments against her, and was strangled and burned as a witch.

'Agnes Sampson, questioned on "sundry articles laid to her charge" admitted healing the sick by natural remedies and prayer, helping people who had been bewitched, having dealings with the devil in the form of a dog; that she had been moved to serve the devil by poverty after the death of her husband and received the devil's mark; the devil sometimes took the form of a foal or stag, or a truss of hay; confessed to taking part in assemblies, and the baptism of cat to raise storms.

'Sundry of the witches confessed they had sundry times company with the devil at the kirk of North Berwick, where he appeared to them in the likeness of a man with a red cap, and a rump at his tail, and made a harangue in manner of a sermon to them; his text, "Many go to the market, but all buy not." Playing to them upon a trump, he said, "Cummer, go ye before; cummer go ye!" and so they danced. When they had done, he caused every one, to the number of threescore, kiss his buttocks. John Gordon, alias called Greymeal, stood behind the door, to eschew, yet it behoved him also to kiss at last. John Feane, schoolmaster of Saltpreston, confessed he was clerk to their assemblies; yet at his execution he confessed only he had committed adultery with two and thirty women, but denied witchcraft.'

News from Scotland

Shakespeare Arrested

On this day in 1596, Shakespeare was arrested.

'England. Be it known that William Shakespeare, Francis Langley, Dorothy Soer, wife of John Soer, and Anne Lee, for fear of death and so forth. Writ of Attachment issued and directed to the Sheriff of Surrey, returnable the eighteenth of St Martin.'
The Rolls of the Court of the Queen's Bench

The Justice of the Peace in Southwark tried to stop the Lord Hunsdon's Men from performing at the Swan. He sent his stepson, William Wayte, to evict the players. There was an altercation outside the playhouse between Wayte, his companions and several players, including Shakespeare. The Sheriff of Surrey issued an arrest warrant on this day, November 29th, which named Francis Langley and Shakespeare among others, charging them with threatening Wayte's life. According to the Court record, William Wayte 'swore before the Judge of Queen's Bench that he stood in danger of death, or bodily hurt' from 'William Shakespere' and three others. The matter was settled out of court – and in Shakespeare's favour apparently. He and his company performed at Whitehall for the Queen a month later. The fact that Shakespeare had recently acquired that coat-of-arms, and therefore the social standing of a gentleman, might have helped.

The Trial of Queen Katherine by George Henry Harlow, 1817

Cardinal Wolsey

Also on this day in 1530, Cardinal Wolsey died. Shakespeare and Fletcher's play *All is True* is not as highly regarded these days as it used to be. But it has at its centre an extraordinarily well-drawn character: Wolsey, the Ipswich butcher's son. Here he is at his great fall from grace:

Wolsey: *... I have ventured*
Like little wanton boys that swim on bladders
This many summers, in a sea of glory,
But far beyond my depth: my high blown pride
At length broke under me, and now has left me
Weary and old with service, to the mercy
Of a rude stream, that must forever hide me.
All is True (Act 3 Scene 2)

When Katherine of Aragon, in sick retirement at Kimbolton, hears of the Cardinal's death, she cannot find a generous word to say about her old adversary. Her man Griffith gently upbraids her:
Noble Madam,
Men's evil manners live in brass; their virtues
We write in water.
All is True (Act 4 Scene 2)

St Andrew's Day
....

O, Scotland, Scotland.
Macbeth (Act 4 Scene 3)

On the feast day of St Andrew, patron Saint of Scotland, here is Fynes Moryson on the Scots: 'Touching their diet, they eat much red colewort and cabbage, but little fresh meat, using to salt their mutton and geese, which made me the more wonder that they used to eat their beef without salting.

'Myself was at a Knight's house, who had many servants to attend him, that brought in his meat with their heads covered with blue caps, the table being more than half furnished with great platters of porridge, each having a little piece of sodden meat; and when the table was served, the servants did sit down with us, but the upper mess instead of porridge, had a pullet with some prunes in the broth. And I observed no Art of cookery, or furniture of Household stuff, but rather rude neglect of both, though myself and my companion were entertained after the best manner.

'They vulgarly eat hearth cakes of oats, but in the cities have also wheaten bread, which for the most part was bought by Courtiers, Gentlemen, and the best sort of citizens. When I lived at Barwick, the Scots weekly upon market day, obtained leave of the governor, to buy peas and beans, whereof as also of wheat, their merchants at this day send great quantities from London into Scotland.

'They drink pure wines, not with sugar as the English, yet at feasts they put comfits in the wine, after the French manner. I did never see nor hear that they have any public inns with signs hanging out, but the better sort of citizens brew ale, their usual drink (which will distemper a stranger's body).

'The country people and merchants used to drink largely, the gentlemen some-what more sparingly, yet the very courtiers, at Feasts, by night meetings, and entertaining any stranger, used to drink healths not without excess and (to speak the truth without offence), the excess of drinking was then far greater in general among the Scots than the English. Myself being at court invited by some gentlemen to supper, and being forewarned to fear this excess, would not promise to sup with them but upon condition that my inviter would be my protection from large drinking, which I was many times forced to invoke, being courteously entertained and much provoked to garaussing, and so for that time avoided any great intemperance. As myself will not accuse them of great intemperance, so I cannot altogether free them from the imputation of excess, wherewith the popular voice chargeth them.

'The inferior sort of Citizens' wives and the women of the country, did wear cloaks made with coarse stuff, of two or three colours in checker work, vulgarly called Plodan.'
Itinerary, Fynes Moryson

Charles Kean as Macbeth, 1838

At Christmas I no more desire a rose
Than wish a snow in May's new-fangled mirth;
But like of each thing that in season grows.
Love's Labours Lost (Act 1 Scene 1)

When we shall hear the wind and rain beat dark December.
Cymbeline (Act 3 Scene 3)

'It is now December, and he that walks the streets shall find dirt on his shoes, except he go all in boots: Now doth the lawyer make an end of his harvest, and the client of his purse: Now Capons and Hens, besides Turkeys, Geese and Ducks, beside beef and Mutton, must all die for the great feast, for in twelve days a multitude of people will not be fed with a little; Now plums and spice, Sugar and Honey, square it among pies and broth, and Gossip I drink to you, and you are welcome, and I thank you, and how do you do, and I pray you be merry: Now are the tailors and the Tire makers full of work against the Holidays, and Music now must be in tune, or else never: the youth must dance and sing and the aged sit by the fire. It is the Law of Nature and no contradiction in reason: the Ass that hath borne all the year now must take a little rest, and the lean ox must feed till he be fat: the Footman now shall have many a foul step, and the Ostler will have work enough about the heels of the Horses, while the

Tapster, if he take not heed, will lie drunk in the cellar: the prices of meat will rise apace and the apparel of the proud will make the tailor rich; Dice and cards will benefit the Butler: And if the Cook do not lack wit, he will sweetly lick his fingers: Starchers and launderers will have their hands
full of work, and periwigs and painting will not be a little set by.'
Strange stuffs will be well sold,
Strange tales well told,
Strange sights much sought,
Strange things much bought.
And what else falls out thus.
To conclude, I hold it the costly Purveyor of Excess, and after breeder of necessity, the practice of Folly, and the Purgatory of Reason. Farewell.'
Fantasticks, Nicholas Breton

'**December must be expressed with a horrid and fearful aspect, clad in Irish rugge or a coarse freeze girt upon him, instead of a garland upon his hand, three or four night caps with a Turkish Turban over them. His nose red, his mouth and beard clogged with icicles, at his back a bundle of holly and ivy, mistletoe, holding a furred mitten in the sign of Capricornus.**'
Emblems, Henry Peacham

Advent

. . . .

Within the infant rind of this small flower
Poisoin hath residence, and medicine power.
Romeo and Juliet (Act 2 Scene 3)

Gerard's Herbal

On this day in 1597, a History of Plants called *Gerard's Herbal* was published. And with the start of Advent, it's a good time to read about flowers. Here is the original gardening book for Christmas.

John Gerard's *Herbal* is a delight. It combines so many fascinating details with personal anecdotes of Gerard's own field research. Here he runs for his life when he tastes the poisonous Sea Spurge by mistake: 'Some write by report of others, that it enflameth exceedingly, but myself speak by experience; for walking along the sea coast at Lee in Essex (with a gentleman called Mr Rich, dwelling in the same town), I took but one drop of it into my mouth; which nevertheless did so inflame and swell in my throat that I hardly escaped with my life. And in the like case was the gentleman, which caused us to take to our horses, and post for our lives unto the next farm house to drink some milk to quench the extremity of our heat, which then ceased.'

And there's lots of practical advice too. For example, he recommends neesewort, which not surprisingly, when ground to a powder and drawn up the nose 'causeth sneezing', but he warns, 'it kills rats'. Cowslips on the other hand, when 'snuffed through a quill', will cure migraine.

Devilsbit 'cleanseth slimy phlegm'. Rue is good for earache. Wearing a garland of penny-royal is useful in preventing giddiness. Use hellebore for melancholy and madness. Syrup of borage also purges melancholy. French women put wild bugloss on their faces. Rosemary is a great breath freshener. Vervain is very potent, but (he cautions) 'keep to Mother Bombie's rules'.

Occasionally, Gerard does a little advertising of his own products, declaring his own balm, an oil made of St John's Wort, to be excellent for deep wounds.

And there are shopping tips. Golden rod is sold by the apothecaries in Bucklersbury for half a crown an ounce, but it is found locally in good old Hampstead Wood, proving the old saw 'far fetched and dear bought is best for ladies'

Gerard's Herbal Continued

In his *Herbal*, John Gerard creates a picture of London bursting with wild flowers and herbs, and details with great precision where they can be found. Bitter-sweet (a kind of Nightshade) he says: **'I found in a ditch side, against the right honourable the Earl of Sussex his garden wall, at his house in Bermondsey...** Betony, continues Gerard, **'loves shadowy woods... and is seldom seen. I found it in a wood by a village called Hampstead, near unto a Worshipful Gentleman's house, one of the clerks of the Queen's council called Mr Wade, from whence I brought plants for my garden.'** Dead Nettle or Yellow Archangel, is not common either, but again he finds it in Hampstead, **'under the hedge on the left hand as you go ...to the church.'** Kippernut covers a field next to **'the conduit heads by Maribone, near the way that leads to Paddington by London'.** And Clown's Wound-wort turns up **'in the moist meadows by Lambeth near London',** just as Frogs-bit flourishes **'in all the ditches about St George his fields, where any that is disposed may see it'.**

Of nature's rich abundance of foods, Gerard recommends pickling the leaves of Dover samphire; informs us that in Cheshire people eat worts and wortleberries like strawberries, and the Dutch eat kipper nuts like carrots; but Jerusalem artichokes are only fit for swine.

Gerard's descriptions of the plants he has collected for his own garden convey the depth of his passion. He has the crown imperial, **'lilies of all kinds, the flower de luce being one',** as well as lily of the valley (**'the red type'**), and a special Persian lily, thanks to his friend, Mr Garret. And there are thorn apples from Constantinople, and Golden Apples of Love from Spain. In his herb garden, there is hyssop, and borage, and wild marjoram (which lasts all winter); and there was some sammonie (or bindweed) but his gardener threw it away.

But there are some flowers that Gerard simply appreciates for their beauty.

Of Sweet Williams, he says:

'We have in our London gardens a kind here of bearing most fine and pleasant white flowers, spotted very confusedly with reddish spots, which setteth forth the beauty thereof. It is commonly in most places called London Pride... These plants are not used either in meat or medicine, but esteemed for their beauty to deck up our gardens, the bosoms of the beautiful, garlands and crowns for pleasure.'

John Gerard is buried in St Andrew's Church, Holborn.

Also on this day in 1603, *As You Like It* was performed before King James I.

'We Have the Man Shakespeare With Us'

In early-December 1603, the King's Men performed at the Earl of Pembroke's home at Wilton, near Salisbury, before their new monarch.

There is no record of the original performance of *All's Well That Ends Well*, Shakespeare's most

Mary Sidney, Countess of Pembroke, and Portrait of an Unknown Man Clasping a Hand, both by Nicholas Hilliard

vassalage', whom he addressed intensely private sonnets, and also perhaps the person on whom he based the character of Bertram in *All's Well*.

Mary Pembroke was a great patroness of the Arts and Sciences, and Wilton at that time was described as both an arcadia and an academy. It has been

melancholy and in some ways problematic comedy, but scholars usually place it as having been written in 1604. If this is true then Shakespeare may have used his experiences of visiting Wilton House, the home of the Pembroke family, a few months earlier in December 1603. The new King, James I, had fled the plague that was ravaging London, and arrived for an extended stay at Wilton. His host, the recently widowed Countess, Mary, invited Shakespeare's company to perform for the royal party. The King's Men had only just been granted the patronage of James, and they were sitting out the pestilence at Mortlake while all the city theatres had been closed for the entire year.

There was apparently a letter in the library at Wilton (now lost) from Mary to her son, William Herbert, begging him to join them. It read, 'We have the man Shakespeare with us.'

The Double Cube Room at Wilton is one of the most beautiful grand rooms in England. On one side of the fireplace hangs a Van Dyck painting of William Herbert, 3rd Earl of Pembroke. It is interesting to ponder if the subject of this rather gloomy, scowling portrait was once the beautiful young man Shakespeare adored, Mr W.H., the 'Lord of my

suggested that this was not Shakespeare's first visit to Wiltshire, and that the Countess had invited him before to sort out her troublesome son.

When he was seventeen, a marriage had been arranged for the young man by his parents with Bridget Vere, the granddaughter of Lord Burleigh, Queen Elizabeth's greatest minister, but William Herbert had refused to obey. Two years earlier, a marriage had been negotiated with Elizabeth Carey, the granddaughter of the Lord Chamberlain, the patron of Shakespeare's company, but William had declared it 'not to his liking'. So the Countess is supposed to have commissioned Shakespeare to write seventeen sonnets to celebrate his seventeenth birthday, urging the headstrong William to marry.

Perhaps Shakespeare himself fell in love with the young earl...

William Herbert did eventually get a wife, in the year after Shakespeare's visit with the King's Men. It is perhaps the reason he's scowling in his portrait. He married a wealthy heiress, Lady Mary Talbot, who (it was reported) was 'dwarfish and unattractive'. Clarendon said 'he paid much too dear for his wife's fortune, by taking her into the bargain'.

All's Well That Ends Well?

St Clement's Day
....

Until the seventeenth century, St Clement's feast was celebrated on this day. He was patron saint of ironworkers, including blacksmiths and anchor-makers. Shakespeare has this memorable picture of a smith in *King John*.

Old men and beldams in the streets
Do prophesy upon it dangerously:
Young Arthur's death is common in their mouths:
And when they talk of him, they shake their heads
And whisper one another in the ear;
And he that speaks doth gripe the hearer's wrist,
Whilst he that hears makes fearful action,
With wrinkled brows, with nods, with rolling eyes.

I saw a smith stand with his hammer, thus,
The whilst his iron did on the anvil cool,
With open mouth swallowing a tailor's news;
Who, with his shears and measure in his hand,
Standing on slippers, which his nimble haste
Had falsely thrust upon contrary feet,
Told of a many thousand warlike French
That were embattailed and rank'd in Kent:
Another lean unwash'd artificer
Cuts off his tale and talks of Arthur's death.
King John (Act 4 Scene 2)

St Clement is not the only patron saint of smiths. St Dunstan is another contender for the honour. The story goes that St Dunstan:
Once pull'd the devil by the nose
With red-hot tongs, which made him roar,
That he was heard three miles or more.

Until St Thomas à Becket's fame overshadowed his, St Dunstan was the favorite saint of the English people.

It was the custom on St Clem's Night to 'go about to beg drink to make merry with', sometimes with an effigy of Old Clem himself, in wig, beard and pipe.

Cock a doodle doo, Peggy has lost her shoe.
This nursery rhyme dates back to Shakespeare's time and is associated with a gruesome murder. Thieves broke into the house of a rich yeoman called Anthony James, while his servants were out at the fair. James and his pregnant wife were brutally murdered in front of their two children, who were carried away by the thieves along with the loot.

They were taken to Bishop's Hatfield in Hertfordshire, to an inn kept by one Annis Dell and her son George. The boy was drowned in Bottomless Pond just outside the town. His little sister, Elizabeth, witnessed her brother's murder, but then, like Lavinia in *Titus Andronicus*, her tongue was cut out so she could not reveal the identity of the culprits. Then Elizabeth was given to a beggar who took her away with him but she managed to make her escape.

On the morning of St Peter's Day, hunters beating the reeds around Bottomless Pond to flush out wild fowl, discovered the body of a red-headed-boy in a green jacket, tied to a stake with a hair rope, but no one could identify the corpse.

Some years later, having wandered from town to town begging for food, Elizabeth found herself back in Bishop's Hatfield. She recognized the inn, but was unable to tell anyone what she knew. But one day, a month before Christmas, while she was playing in the King's Park with a friend, a cock began to crow. Her friend 'mocked the cock', a familiar children's game, to add words to the cockerel's call, crying out 'Cock a doodle doo, Peggy has lost her shoe'. The girl invited her dumb friend to join in. Whereby young Bess suddenly repeated the cry. Miraculously, the child had recovered the power of speech.

Annis Dell and her son were finally arrested for the murder of Bess's little brother, and hanged on August 4th, 1606 in Hatfield.

Apocalyptic Stratford

'For three hundred years, while its fame spread across the world, the little town had stood here at the river's bend. Time and change had touched it lightly: it had heard from afar both the coming of the Armada and the fall of the Third Reich, and all Man's wars had passed
it by.

'Now it was gone, as though it had never been...'

A stray nuclear rocket has landed on Stratford-upon-Avon. In the apocalypse that follows, the river bursts its banks and reaches the church:

'Timidly the waters touched the worn gravestone that for more than three hundred years had lain before the vanished altar. The church that had sheltered it so long had given it some protection at the last, and only a slight discolouration of the rock told of the fires that had passed this way. In the corpse-light of the dying land, the archaic words could still be traced as the waters rose around them, breaking at last in tiny ripples across the stone. Line by line the epitaph upon which so many millions had gazed slipped beneath the conquering waters. For a little while the letters could still be faintly seen; then they were gone forever.

Good friend for Jesus sake forbeare,
To digg the dust enclosed heare
Blest be ye man yt spares these stones,
And curst be he yt moves my bones.

'Undisturbed through all eternity the poet could sleep in safety now; in the silence and darkness above his head, the Avon was seeking its new outlet to the sea.'

In December 1595, a pamphlet entitled *A Most Strange and Wonderful Prophesy upon this Troublesome World* was published in London. Allegedly written by two German astrologers, it forecast the end of the world in the following year. Happily, the Company of Stationers confiscated all copies immediately.

The end of the world as we know it is the subject of a short story by Arthur C. Clarke.

'The Curse' was written in 1953, and was published in Cosmos. Clarke had spent his war years in Stratford-upon-Avon in the RAF, as a specialist involved in the early warning radar defence system. The story, he later admitted, 'now appears perhaps somewhat less imaginative than when it was first published in the distant dawn of the Atomic Age'. It begins thus:

'It was written,' Clarke said, 'within a few miles of the small and famous slab of stone whose ultimate fate it describes.'

St Nicholas' Night

Gadshill: *Sirrah, if they meet not with St Nicholas' Clerks, I'll give thee this neck.*
Chamberlain: *No, I'll none of it: I prithee keep that for the hangman, for I know thou worship'st St Nicholas as truly as a man of falsehood may.*
Henry IV Part One (Act 2 Scene 2)

St Nicholas, more usually associated with the gift-bearing Santa Claus nowadays, was regarded as the patron saint of thieves in Shakespeare's day.

Saint Nicholas by Jacob de Punder, 1563

'In the late days of Queen Mary, a godly matron named Gertrude Crokehay, the wife of master Robert Crokehay dwelling then at Saint Katherine's by the Tower of London, abstained herself from the popish church. And she being in her husband's house it happened in 1556, that the Pope's childish Saint Nicholas went about the parish, which she understanding shut her doors against him, and would not suffer him to come within her house.

'Then Doctor Mallet hearing thereof (and being then master of the said Saint Katherine's) the next day came to her with 20 at his tail, thinking belike to fray her, and asked why she would not the night before let in Saint Nicholas and receive his blessing. To whom she answered thus. "Sir, I know no Saint Nicholas that came hither." 'Yes," quod Mallet, "here was one that represented St. Nicholas."

"Indeed sir," said she, "he was one that is my neighbour's child, but not St Nicholas. For St Nicholas is in heaven. I was afraid of them that came with him to have had my purse cut by them. For I have heard of men robbed by St Nicholas' clerks."

'So Mallet, perceiving nothing to be gotten at her hands, went his way as he came, and she for that time so escaped.'
Foxe's Book of Martyrs

The custom of electing a boy bishop, dressing him in episcopal vestments and parading him around town from house to house as St Nicholas, goes back to medieval times. Edward I allowed such a boy to sing the Vespers before him at Heaton near Newark in 1299. Sometimes a mock mass would be celebrated. Henry VIII suppressed the custom, but it was revived by Mary and finally abolished by Elizabeth, though it lingered on in some rural areas.

Song for Winter

Thus sometimes hath the brightest day a cloud;
And after summer evermore succeeds
Barren winter, with his wrathful nipping cold:
So cares and joys abound, as seasons fleet.

Henry VI Part Two (Act 2 Scene 4)

How like a winter hath my absence been
From thee, the pleasure of the fleeting year!
What freezings have I felt, what dark days seen!
What old December's bareness everywhere!
And yet this time remov'd was summer's time;
The teeming autumn, big with rich increase,
Bearing the wanton burden of their prime,
Like widow'd wombs after their lord's decease:
Yet this abundant issue seemed to me
But hope of orphans and unfather'd fruit;
For summer and his pleasures wait on thee,
And, thou away, the very birds are mute:
Or, if they sing, 'tis with so dull a cheer,
That leaves look pale, dreading the winter's near.

Sonnet XCVII

Blow, blow, thou winter wind,
Thou art not so unkind
As man's ingratitude;
Thy tooth is not so keen,
Because thou art not seen,
Although thy breath be rude.
Heigh-ho! sing heigh-ho! unto the green holly.
Most friendship is feigning, most loving mere folly.
Then, heigh-ho, the holly!
This life is most jolly.

Freeze, freeze, thou bitter sky,
That dost not bite so nigh
As benefits forgot;
Though thou the waters warp,
Thy sting is not so sharp
As friend rememb'red not.
Most friendship is feigning, most loving mere folly.
Then, heigh-ho, the holly!
This life is most jolly.

As You Like It (Act 2 Scene 7)

Under the greenwood tree
Who loves to lie with me,
And turn his merry note
Unto the sweet bird's throat,
Come hither, come hither, come hither.
Here shall he see
No enemy
But winter and rough weather.

As You Like It (Act 2 Scene 5)

The First Shakespeare Actress

On this day in 1660, a woman appeared on the stage in a Shakespeare play for the first time, in the role of Desdemona in *Othello*.

Here is an account by another actress, Fanny Kemble, of playing the same part, opposite Macready in 1848. In letters to her devoted friend, Harriet St Leger, Fanny describes the problems of working with an actor who is out of control on stage:

MISS FANNY KEMBLE AS PORTIA.

'Macready is not pleasant to act with, as he keeps no specific time for his exits or entrances, comes on while one is in the middle of a soliloquy, and goes off while one is in the middle of a speech to him. He growls and prowls, and roams and foams, about the stage in every direction, like a tiger in a cage, so that I never know on what side of me he means to be; and keeps up a perpetual snarling and grumbling, like the aforesaid tiger, so that I never feel quite sure when he has done, and that it is my turn to speak...

'I do not know how Desdemona might have affected me in other circumstances, but my only feeling about acting it with Mr Macready is dread of his personal violence. I quail at the idea of his laying hold of me in those terrible passionate scenes; for in *Macbeth* he pinched me black and blue, and almost tore the point lace from my head. I am sure my little finger will be re-broken, and as for that smothering in bed, "Heaven have mercy upon me!" as poor Desdemona says. If that foolish creature wouldn't persist in talking long after she has been smothered and stabbed to death, one might escape by the off side of the bed and leave the bolster to be questioned by Emilia, and apostrophized by Othello; but she will uplift her testimony after death to her husband's amiable treatment of her, and even the bolster wouldn't be stupid enough for that.'

And in a later letter to Harriet, she continues:
'My rehearsal of Desdemona tried me severely, for I was frightened to death of Macready, and the horror of the play itself took such hold of me that at the end I could hardly stand for shaking, or speak for crying; and Macready seemed quite mollified by my condition, and promised not to re-break my little finger, if he could remember it. He lets down the bed-curtain before he smothers me and as the drapery conceals the murderous struggle, and therefore he need not cover my head at all, I hope I shall escape alive.

'I was told by a friend of mine who was at *Hamlet* the other evening, that in the closet scene with his mother, he had literally knocked the poor woman down who was playing the Queen. I thought this an incredible exaggeration, and asked her afterwards if it was true, and she said so true that she was bruised all across her breast with the blow he had given her; that, happening to take his hand at a moment when he did not wish her to do so, he struck her so violently, and knocked her literally down; so I suppose I may consider it "relenting" that he never knocked me down.'

Records of Later Life, Fanny Kemble, 1882

Angels in Stratford
····················

In the bar of the White Swan Hotel in Stratford are a series of Elizabethan wall paintings, which were discovered in 1927 when the hotel was being renovated. They are from the apocryphal *Book of Tobit*, and though the story is set in Nineveh, under the rule of King Sennacherib, here the ancient Assyrian city looks pretty much like Rother Market, just outside the hotel.

The first painting shows Tobit, and his wife Anna, in the dress of ordinary Elizabethan yeomanry, handing a letter to their son Tobias. Tobit has apparently been blinded by birds dropping lime into his eyes. The Angel Raphael hides behind a drape. He has been sent by God to accompany Tobias to Media.

Next we see the angel with Tobias and his dog, on their journey; while the third scene depicts the most famous event in the story. A giant fish jumped out of the River Tigris and tried to swallow Tobias, but Raphael protected him, and here they are seen removing the giant fish's heart, liver and gall bladder.

Alas, that is as far as the existing paintings go. What a shame they do not show us the story of Tobias' bride to be, Sarah, who is doomed to lose her husband on her wedding night to the Demon Asmodeus. She has already lost seven husbands in this way when Tobias turns up. Luckily with the help of that giant fish bladder, Tobias and Raphael smoke the demon out, and send him packing to Upper Egypt. The happy couple return to Nineveh, and even manage to cure Tobit's blindness with the rest of the fish paste.

How they would have depicted that persistent bride frustrator, Asmodeus, would have been interesting to see. Asmodeus is interpreted by some scholars as the sin of homosexuality, because of his penchant for ruining all those prospective bridegrooms.

But no one seems to have any explanation as to why, of all biblical tales, the story of Tobias and the Angel should be illustrated here. Shakespeare must have known the paintings, and the story. Polonius' advice to Laertes in *Hamlet* echoes old Tobit's instructions to his departing son:

For if thou deal truly, thy doings shall prosperously succeed to thee, and to all them that live justly.

In Shakespeare's day the White Swan was called the King's House.

Wittenberg Student in Duel: Tycho Brahe's Gold Nose

Tycho Brahe takes measurements of the stars with a giant mural quadrant, 1598

On this day in 1566 the Danish Astronomer Tycho Brahe attended a betrothal ceremony in Rostock. He was at the time a student, like Hamlet, at the University of Wittenberg, but had had to flee to Rostock because of an outbreak of plague. During the dancing a quarrel broke out with a fellow student called Parsberg. But the dispute was not settled and a couple of weeks later, at another party, it broke out again.

Tycho's own consultation of the stars warned him that there were serious omens to be heeded, and he decided to stay indoors. But that night at supper he and Parsberg started to row all over again. Parsberg told him to draw his sword, and they went out into the churchyard. The party that followed them found a bloody scene. Parsberg's broadsword had cut off most of Tycho's nose. It was just two weeks after his twentieth birthday.

Doctors could do nothing for his disfigurement. But eventually Tycho came up with his own solution. He made himself a false nose out of gold and silver blended to a flesh colour. And he had a copper nose for everyday wear. He held the nose in place with an adhesive salve, which he kept in his pocket in a little box.

In later life Tycho was to become one of the most revered astronomers in the world. At the age of thirty he was given the island of Hveen, in the Sound, by the King of Denmark, where he built his Uraniborg or 'Castle of the Heavens', a great observatory. From here he logged a total of 777 stars.

O who can hold a fire in his hand
By thinking on the frosty Caucasus?
Or cloy the hungry edge of appetite
By bare imagination of a feast?
Or wallow naked in December snow
By thinking on fantastic summer's heat?
O, no! the apprehension of the good
Gives but the greater feeling to the worse:
Fell sorrow's tooth doth never rankle more
Than when he bites, but lanceth not the sore.

Richard II (Act I Scene 3)

An Amateur Macbeth
·······················

... what the dickens.
The Merry Wives of Windsor (Act 3 Scene 2)

Charles Dickens was an avid amateur actor. He organized a benefit performance of *The Merry Wives of Windsor* for the instalment of his friend Sheridan Knowles as curator of the newly purchased Shakespeare's birthplace in 1848. He played Justice Shallow himself. In *Sketches by Boz*, he describes the scene backstage before an amateur performance of *Macbeth*:

'The little narrow passages beneath the stage are neither especially clean nor too brilliantly lighted; and the absence of any flooring together with the damp mildewy smell which pervades the place, does not conduce in any great measure to their comfortable appearance. Don't fall over the plate-basket – it's one of the "properties" – the cauldron for the witches' cave; and the three uncouth-looking figures, with broken clothes pegs in their hands, who are drinking gin and water out of a pint pot, are the weird sisters. This miserable room, lighted by candles in sconces placed at lengthened intervals round the wall, is the dressing room, common to the gentleman performers, and the square hole in the ceiling is the trap door of the stage above. You will observe that the ceiling is ornamented with beams that support the boards and tastefully hung with cobwebs.

'The characters in the tragedy are all dressed, and their own clothes are scattered in hurried confusion over the wooden dresser which surrounds the room. The snuff-shop-looking figure, in front of the glass, is Banquo, and the young lady with the liberal display of legs, who is kindly painting his face with a hare's foot, is dressed for Fleance. The large woman who is consulting the stage directions in Cumberland's edition of *Macbeth*, is the Lady Macbeth of the night; she is always selected to play the part, because she is tall and stout, and looks a little like Mrs Siddons – at a considerable distance. That stupid looking milksop, with light hair and bow legs – a kind of man whom you can warrant town-made – is fresh caught; he plays Malcolm tonight, just to accustom himself to the audience. He will get on better by degrees; he will play Othello in a month, and in a month more will very probably be apprehended on a charge of embezzlement. The black-eyed female with whom he is talking so earnestly, is dressed for the gentlewoman. It is her first appearance, too – in that character. The boy of fourteen, who is having his eyebrows smeared with soap and whitening, is Duncan, King of Scotland; and the two dirty men with the corked countenances, in very old green tunics, and dirty drab boots, are "the army".

"Look sharp below there, gents," exclaims the dresser, a red-headed and red-whiskered Jew, calling through the trap, "they're a going to ring up. The flute says he be blowed if he plays any more, and they're getting precious noisy in front."

'A general rush immediately takes place to the half-dozen little steps leading to the stage, and the heterogeneous group are soon assembled at the side scenes, in breathless anxiety and motley confusion.'

Boy Kidnapped to be a Stage Player

Nay, their endeavour keeps in the wonted pace; but there is,
sir, an eyrie of children, little eyases, that cry out on the top of
question and are most tyrannically clapp'd for't. These are
now the fashion, and so berattle the common stages (so they
call them) that many wearing rapiers are afraid of
goosequills and dare scarce come thither.
Hamlet (Act 2 Scene 2)

In an extraordinary bill of complaint, Henry Clifton
informed the Queen that his young son, Thomas,
aged about thirteen, had been abducted in the street.
Apparently, while walking from school in mid-
December, he was attacked, and taken to the
Blackfriars Playhouse, where he had been forced to
act in plays. The bill seethes with Clifton's fierce
indignation, and almost drowns in his strict
adherence to the legal terminology of the day.

'Mr Clifton, a Norfolk gentleman living in London,
accuses Nathaniel Giles, Master of the Children of the
Queen's Chapel, with certain confederates (among
them one James Robinson) of arranging to surprise
the said Thomas Clifton as he should pass between
your said subject's house and the said grammar
school and him (with like violence and force) to carry
unto the said playhouse in the Blackfriars aforesaid
and there to sort him with mercenary players and
such other children as they had there placed, and by
the like force and violence him there to detain and
compel to exercise the base trade of mercenary
interlude player to his utter loss of time, ruin and
disparagement.

'About the thirteenth day of December (1600), the
said confederates did waylay the said Thomas Clifton
as he should pass from your said subject's house to
the said school, and as he was walking quietly from
your subject's house to the said school, (and with
great force and violence) did seize and surprise him
and, with like force and violence, did (to the terror
and hurt of him, the said Thomas Clifton), haul, pull,
drag, and carry away to the said playhouse in
Blackfriars aforesaid, threatening him that if the said
Thomas would not obey him (the said Robinson), that
he (the said Robinson) would charge the constable
with him (the said Thomas Clifton). By which
violence, threats and terror the said James
Robinson then brought the said Thomas
Clifton into the said playhouse in Blackfriars
aforesaid where the other confederates
committed him to the said playhouse
amongst a company of lewd and dissolute
mercenary players, purposing in that place
(and for no service of your majesty) to use
and exercise him, (the said Thomas Clifton),
in acting of parts in base plays and
interludes, to the mercenary gain and private
commodity of them (the said confederates).'

O, the twelfth day of December.
Twelfth Night (Act 2 Scene 3)

St Lucy's Day: **The Shortest Day**

She came adorned hither like Sweet May
Sent back like Hallowmas or short'st of day.
Richard II (Act 5 Scene 1)

St Lucy's Day used to be the shortest day in the year, by the old reckoning, the Julian calendar (now December 21st). Lucy means 'light', and in medieval accounts of her martyrdom, St Lucy's eyes were gouged out before her execution. In art, she is often depicted holding a plate on which lie her eyes. Lucy is the patron saint of the blind.

As her brief day brings the longest night of the year, John Donne's poem, *A Nocturnal upon St Lucie's Day*, expresses, in a mourning piece, the withdrawal of the world-spirit into sterility and darkness. It begins thus:

'Tis the year's midnight, and it is the day's,
Lucy's, who scarce seven hours herself unmasks;
The sun is spent, and now his flasks
Send forth light squibs, no constant rays;
The world's whole sap is sunk...

In Trevelyon's *Miscellany* (1608), a precise account is given of exactly how long the days and nights are throughout the year. In a time when the most would be made of the daylight hours this was an important factor. In the darkest days of deep December daylight dwindled down to a mere seven hours and thirty-six minutes, while the night stretched out to a lengthy sixteen hours and twenty-four minutes.

Also on this day in 1784, Dr Johnson died.

Dr Johnson caught Shakespeare's genius in the following couplet from a prologue he wrote for his friend David Garrick to speak at the opening of the Theatre Royal, Drury Lane, in 1747:
Each change of many-coloured life he drew,
Exhausted worlds, and then imagined new.

Elsewhere, in the Preface to his edition of *Shakespeare* (published in October 1765), Dr Johnson defines the difficulty of persuading others of that genius:
'Yet his real power is not shown in the splendour of particular passages, but by the progress of his fable, and the tenor of his dialogue: and he that tries to recommend him by select quotations, will succeed like the pedant in Hierocles, who, when he offered his house for sale, carried a brick in his pocket as a specimen.'

Herne's Oak
. . . .

There is an old tale goes that Herne the hunter,
Sometime a keeper here in Windsor Forest,
Doth all the winter-time, at still midnight,
Walk round about an oak, with great ragg'd horns;
And there he blasts the tree, and takes the cattle,
And makes milch-kine yield blood, and shakes a chain
In a most hideous and dreadful manner.
You have heard of such a spirit, and well you know
The superstitious idle-headed eld
Receiv'd, and did deliver to our age,
This tale of Herne the hunter for a truth.
The Merry Wives of Windsor (Act 4 Scene 4)

Herne is said to have been a favourite huntsman of King Richard II in Windsor Great Forest. One day while out hunting, King Richard was cornered and attacked by a white hart, ironically his own emblem. Herne saved the King's life but was mortally wounded himself. A dark stranger from Bagshot Heath brought Herne back to health by tying the dead animal's antlers on Herne's brow. But in return, Herne had to sacrifice his hunting skills. The other king's huntsmen framed him as a thief. As a result he lost the favour of the king. He was found the next day, by a pedlar, hanging dead from a lone oak tree. That same oak tree became known as Herne's Oak. His ghost appears with a phosphorescent glow, accompanied by demon hounds and a horned owl in a terrifying spectral hunt.

There is some speculation as to the exact whereabouts of the Herne's Oak that Shakespeare described. According to the Ordnance Survey map, Herne's Oak was situated in the Home Park, a little to the north of Frogmore House. This tree was felled in 1796.

Queen Victoria had Herne's Oak replanted, but put it in a different place. However, it was blown down in a gale in 1863. Perhaps the spirit of Herne was angry at the repositioning. Victoria had a new cabinet made from the old trunk.

Edward VII replanted the current Herne's Oak in 1906. It survived the great gales of 1987, but is nevertheless in a sorry state today.

In 1976, a young guardsman posted to the East Terrace at Windsor Castle was found unconscious. When he came to, he swore that he had seen a statue grow horns and come to life.

The Merry Wives of East Kent

· ·

When researching his book *A Caveat for Common Cursitors*, (see October 26th), Thomas Harman met another colourful vagrant who came to his gate. She was a 'Mort', a wandering beggar.

"'Last summer," quoth she, "I was great with child, and I travelled into East Kent by the sea coast, for I lusted marvellously after oysters and mussels, and gathered many, and in the place where I found them, I opened them and ate them still. At last, in seeking more, I reached after one, and stepped into a hole and fell in, into the waist, and there did stick, and I had been drowned if the tide had come in, and espying a man a good way off, I cried as much as I could for help. I was alone. And

whether it was with striving and forcing myself out, or for joy of his coming to me, I had a great colour in my face, and looked well coloured. And to be plain with you, he liked me so well as he said that I should there lie still, and I would not grant him that he might lie with me. And by my troth I wist not what to answer, I was in such a perplexity. For I knew the man well. He had a very honest woman to his wife, and was of some wealth; and on the other side, if I were not holp out, I should have perished, and I granted

him that I would obey to his will. Then he plucked me out."'

The mort manages to persuade the husband to take her home to his house and let her sleep in his barn, where he can come to her that night and have his way. But the mort goes straight to the man's wife and tells her everything, and (together with five of the goodwife's friends) they hatch a plot to humiliate him. That night, when her husband gets home, the goodwife sends the mort out to her lodgings in the barn to sleep.

"'Away," saith this goodwife "to your lodging!" "Yes, good dame," saith she, "as fast as I can." Thus by looking one on the other each knew the other's mind, and so departed to her homely couch.

'The goodman of the house shrugged him for joy, thinking to himself, "I will make some pastime with you anon," and, calling to his wife for his supper, set him down, and was very pleasant, and drank to his wife, and fell to his mammerings and munched apace, nothing understanding of the banquet that was a-preparing for him after supper, and according to the proverb, that sweet meat will have sour sauce.

'Thus feeding her with friendly fantasies, consumed two hours and more...

[The story continues on the following page.]

The Merry Wives of East Kent (continued)

'Then feigning how he would see in what case his horse were in, repaired covertly to the barn, where his friendly foes lurked privily. "What, are you come?" quoth she, "By the mass, I would not for a hundred pound that my dame should know that you were here, either any else of the house." "No, I warrant thee," saith this Goodman, "they will all be safe and fast enough at their work, and I will be here at mine anon"; and lay down by her and straight would have had to do with her. "Nay, fie," saith she, "I like not this order. If ye lie with me, you must surely untruss you and put down your hosen, for that way is the easiest and best." "Sayest thou so?" quoth he. "Now, by my troth, agreed." And when he had untrussed himself and put down, he began to assail the insatiable fort.

'"Why," quoth she that was without shame saving her promise, "and are you not ashamed?." "Never a whit," saith he, "Lie down quickly."

'"Now, fie for shame, fie," saith she aloud, which was the watchword. At which word, these five furious, sturdy, muffled gossips flings out, and takes sure hold of this betrayed person, some plucking his hosen down lower, and binding the same fast about his feet, then binding his hands, and knitting a handkercher about his eyes, that he should not see. And when they had made him sure and fast, then they laid him on until they were windless.

'"Be good," saith this mort, "unto my master, for the passion of God !" and laid on as fast as the rest and still ceased not to cry upon them to be merciful unto him, and yet laid on apace. And when they had well beaten him, that blood brast plentifully out of most places, they let him lie still bound - with this exhortation, that he should from that time forth know his wife from other men's, and that this punishment was but a flea-biting in respect of that which should follow if he amended not his manners.

'Thus leaving him blustering, blowing, and foaming for pain and melancholy that he might nor could be revenged on them, they vanished away, and had this mort with them and safely conveyed her out of town.'

The Robben Island Shakespeare

On this day in 1977 Nelson Mandela, while in prison on Robben Island, read a copy of Shakespeare's plays and autographed the following lines from *Julius Caesar*:

Cowards die many times before their deaths
The valiant only taste of death but once.
Of all the wonders that I yet have heard,
It seems to me most strange that men should fear;
Seeing that death a necessary end,
Will come when it will come.

(Act 2 Scene 2)

The copy of Shakespeare was the property of Indian ANC inmate, Sony Venkatrathnam. He had disguised his Collins schoolboy edition behind pictures of Rama and Sita, taken from a Hindu calendar. The guards thought it was a prayer book and allowed Sony to keep it. No other books were allowed in the prison. Sony lent the book to his colleagues, who read the plays at night. Many autographed their favourite passages.

Walter Sisulu underlined Shylock's lines from *The Merchant of Venice*: 'For sufferance is the badge of all our tribe', while someone else highlighted Caliban's lines from *The Tempest*: 'This Island's mine, by Sycorax my mother'. Between those two lines lay the whole apartheid struggle.

South African actor John Kani, who played Caliban in the 2009 RSC Baxter Theatre co-production of *The Tempest*, describes his introduction to Shakespeare, through the Xhosa translation of *Julius Caesar* by B.B. Mdledle, which they performed at high school. He didn't realize it was by Shakespeare. When he read Shakespeare's original play many years later, he couldn't help feeling it had failed to capture the beauty of Mdledle's writing.

Girl Drowns in River

A sad tale's best for winter.
The Winter's Tale (Act 2 Scene 1)

The poor soul sat sighing by a
  sycamore tree,
Sing all a green willow,
Her hand on her bosom, her head on
  her knee,
Sing willow, willow, willow,
The fresh stream ran by her and
  murmur'd her moans,
Sing willow, willow, willow,
Her salt tears fell from her and
  soften'd the stones
Sing willow, willow, willow,
Sing all a green willow must be my
  garland.
Othello (Act 4 Scene 3)

The Death of Ophelia by Eugène Delacroix, 1853

When Shakespeare was only a boy of 15, a local girl, called, incredibly, Katherine Hamlet, drowned in the River Avon at Tiddington. He must have recalled her tragic death when he came to write *Hamlet* many years later:

There is a willow grows aslant a brook,
That shows his hoar leaves in the glassy stream;
There with fantastic garlands did she come
Of crow-flowers, nettles, daisies, and long purples
That liberal shepherds give a grosser name,
But our cold maids do dead men's fingers call them:
There, on the pendent boughs her coronet weeds
Clambering to hang, an envious sliver broke;
When down her weedy trophies and herself
Fell in the weeping brook.
Hamlet (Act 4 Scene 7)

According to John Gerard, 'long purples', or purple loosestrife (wild willow herb), are very goodly to behold for the decking of houses and gardens:

'It groweth hard by the Thames, as you go from a place called the Devil's Handkerchief to Redreffe, near unto a stile that standeth in your way upon the Thames bank, among the planks that do hold up the same bank. It groweth also in a ditch side not far from the place of execution, called Saint Thomas Waterings.'

These plants also grow in abundance in July, along the Avon, towards the weir and lock in Stratford. Richard Mabey suggests however that long purples may actually be early purple orchids and that the 'grosser name' was 'dogstones', meaning dog's testicles, referring to the pair of testicle-like root tubers. Orchis apparently means testicle, which shocked John Ruskin.

Christmas Fare

Good Husband and Huswife, now chiefly be glad,
Things handsome to have, as they ought to be had.
They both do provide, against Christmas to come,
To welcome their neighbours, good cheer to have some.

Good bread and good drink, a fire in the hall,
Brawn, pudding, and souse, and good mustard withal.
Beef, mutton and pork, and good pies of the best,
Pig, veal, goose, and capon, and turkey well dressed,
Cheese, apples and nuts and good carols to hear,
As then, in the country is counted good cheer.

What cost to the husband, is any of this?
Good household provision only it is:
Of the other the like, I do leave out a many,
That costeth the husband never a penny.

Christmas Husbandly Fare, Thomas Tusser, 1571

Also on this day in 1604, *The Tragedy of Gowrie* (a play about the attempt to assassinate James I four years earlier, in 1600) was performed by the King's Men. '**The Tragedy of Gowrie with all the action and actors hath been twice represented by the King's Players, with exceeding concourse of all sorts of people. But whether the matter or manner be not well handled, or that it be thought unfit that princes should be played on the stage in their lifetime, I hear that some great Councillors are much displeased with it, and so is thought shall be forbidden.**'
Letter from John Chamberlain

On August 5th, 1600 at Gowrie House in Perth, King James had escaped assassination by the Master of Ruthven and his brother the Earl of Gowrie. August 5th was made a day of national thanksgiving.

A romanticized engraving of the incident at Gowrie House

A Young Nip at the Bull
••••••••••••••••••••••••

'Of a Young Nip that cunningly beguiled an ancient Professor of that trade, and his quean with him at a play in the Christmas Holidays (*A nip is a young thief. A quean is a prostitute. The Bull is an inn-yard theatre*):

'A good fellow that was newly entered into the nipping craft, and had not yet attained to any acquaintance with the chief and cunning masters of that trade, in the Christmas holidays last came to see a play at the Bull within Bishopsgate, there to take his benefit as time and place would permit him. Not long had he stayed in the press, but he had gotten a young man's purse out of his pocket, which, when he had, he stepped into the stable to take out the money, and to convey away the purse. But looking on his commodity he found nothing therein but white counters, a thimble and a broken threepence, which belike the person that ought [owned] it, had done of purpose to deceive the cutpurse withal, or else had played at the cards for counters, and so carried his winnings about him till his next sitting to play.

'Somewhat displeased to be so overtaken he looked aside and espied a lusty youth entering at the door, and his drab with him. This fellow he heard to be one of the finest nippers about town, and ever carried his quean with him for conveyance when the stratagem was performed. He puts up the counters into the purse again and follows close to see some piece of their service. Among a company of seemly men was this lusty companion and his minion gotten where best they might behold the play, and work for

advantage, and ever this young nip was next to him, to mark when he should attempt any exploit, standing as it were more than half between the cunning nip and his drab, only to learn some part of his skill.

'In short time the deed was performed, but how, the young nip could not easily discern, only he felt him shift his hand toward his trug, to convey the purse to her, but she, being somewhat mindful of the play, because a merriment was then on stage, gave no regard, whereby, thinking he had pulled her by the coat, he twitched the young nip by the cloak, who taking advantage of this offer, put down his hand and received the purse of him.

'Then, counting it discourtesy to let him lose all his labour, he softly plucked the quean by the coat, which she feeling, and imagining it had been her companion's hand, received of him the first purse with the white counters in it. Then, fearing lest his stay should hinder him, and seeing the other intended to have more purses ere he departed, away goes the young nip with the purse he got so easily, wherein, as I have heard, was thirty-seven shillings in gold and odd money, which did so much content him, as that he had beguiled so ancient a stander in that profession. What the other thought when he found the purse, and could not guess how he was cozened, I leave to your censures. Only this make me smile, that one false knave beguile another, which bids honest men look the better to their purses.'

The Third and Last Part of Coney-Catching, Robert Greene (1592)

Hamlet as Toilet Paper

Thou whoreson zed! thou unnecessary letter! My lord, if you'll give me leave, I will tread this unbolted villain into mortar and daub the walls of a jakes with him.

King Lear (Act 2 Scene 2)

In a Hogarth engraving of 1724, sheets of *Hamlet* are being used as toilet paper. What is happening? The management of Drury Lane Theatre are being criticized for presenting a dreadful crowd-pleaser to rival the popular pantomimes produced at Lincoln's Inn Fields. *Harlequin Shepherd* was based on the real-life exploits of a criminal called Jack Shepherd, who made his escape from Newgate Prison by squeezing down a privy.

In Hogarth's engraving, the Drury Lane impresarios are shown manipulating puppets of the characters, one of which is disappearing down the close-stool. The sheets of toilet paper, hanging on a nail on the wall, are pages from the scripts of *Hamlet*, *Macbeth* and *Julius Caesar*. On the other side of the stage, Ben Jonson's ghost howls in outrage, and a note at the bottom informs us that the excrement used on the

hero is chewed gingerbread 'to prevent offence'.

In Shakespeare's day, the first flushing toilet was invented by Elizabethan 'bad boy', Sir John Harrington. He had offended his godmother, the Queen, by translating one of the naughty books of Ariosto's *Orlando Furioso* (in which a queen is spied playing sex games with her dwarf); and he followed it up with a cloacan satire, *The Metamorphosis of Ajax*. This 'discourse upon a stale subject' described his new invention and puns on the current word for a lavatory – a jakes (Shakespeare has several such puns). Harrington's Christian name, John, became a euphemism for a toilet, just as in the nineteenth century his fellow lavatorial pioneer, Thomas Crapper, was to lend his name to a related bodily function.

The term 'loo' came from the cry 'gardez-l'eau', used to warn passers-by below, when emptying chamber pots (or jordans) into the street from above.

And what, as every schoolboy needs to know, did Elizabethans use as toilet paper? In fact all sorts of things were used: from moss and rags, to wood shavings and corn husks. But the sixteenth-century French satirist, François Rabelais, has his giant, Gargantua, delight in his discovery of the perfect bum-wiper:

'But, to conclude, I maintain, that of all arsewisps, bumfodders, tail-napkins, bunghole cleansers, and wipe-breeches, there is none in the world comparable to the neck of a goose, that is well downed, if you hold her head betwixt your legs. And believe me, you will thereby feel in your nockhole a most wonderful pleasure, both in regard of the softness of the said down and of the temperate heat of the goose, which is easily communicated to the bum-gut.'

Gargantua and Pantagruel, Book 14

St Thomas' Day Christmas Pudding

Queen Elizabeth and the Middle Temple Christmas Pudding

Queen Elizabeth was a great patron of the Middle Temple. The Bench Table which still stands at the head of the hall was a gift from the Queen. It is a staggering twenty-nine feet long and is made of continuous planks taken from a single oak. The wood for the table came from a tree felled in Windsor Great Park which was then sailed down the river to Middle Temple Hall.

Upon this table, the lawyers of Middle Temple enjoyed a Christmas pudding made by the fair hands of the Queen herself, so pleased was she by the way she had been received by the benchers. A little of the recipe was saved to mix into the following year's recipe and the tradition continued until 1966, when it died out. It was then revived by the Queen Mother, who stirred a new pud for the benchers in 1971.

For a Christmas pudding:
Take twelve eggs and break them, then take crumbs of bread, and mace, and currants, and dates cut small, and some ox suet small minced and some saffron, put all these in a sheep's maw [stomach bag or paunch] and so boil it.
Lady Elinor Fettiplace's Receipt Book

Come guard this night the Christmas-Pie,
That the thief, though ne'er so sly,
With his flesh-hooks, don't come nigh
To catch it.

From him, who all alone sits there,
Having his eyes still in his ear,
And a deal of nightly fear
To watch it.
Christmas Eve, Robert Herrick

Come, bring with a noise,
My merry, merry boys,
The Christmas Log to the firing;
While my good Dame, she
Bids ye all be free;
And drink to your heart's desiring.

With the last year's brand
Light the new block, and
For good success in his spending,
On your Psaltries play,
That sweet luck may
Come while the log is a-tending.

Drink now the strong beer,
Cut the white loaf here,
The while the meat is a-shredding;
For the rare mince-pie
And the plums stand by
To fill the paste that's a-kneading.
Ceremonies for Christmas, Robert Herrick

The Ruddock and the Wren

Shakespeare calls that most Christmassy of birds, the robin redbreast, the ruddock.

In *Cymbeline*, as Arviragus and Guiderius cover the supposedly dead body of their 'brother', Fidele, we hear:

... the ruddock would
with charitable bill – O bill sore shaming
Those rich-left heirs, that let their fathers lie
Without a monument – bring thee all this;
Yea, and furred moss besides, when flowers are none
To winter ground thy corse.

Cymbeline (Act 4 Scene 2)

In an odd (and often cut) parenthesis, Shakespeare recalls the robin's reputation for charity, in covering with leaves those who have been lost in snowy woods.

Covering with moss the dead's unclosed eye
The little redbreast teacheth charity.

And, in his poem *To the Nightingale and the Robin Redbreast*, Robert Herrick wrote:

When I departed am, ring thou my knell,
Thou pitiful and pretty Philomel :
And when I'm laid out for a corse, then be
Thou sexton, redbreast, for to cover me.

Robins were captured not so much for food but as songbirds, to be kept in a cage, a practice still followed in the nineteenth century when William Blake famously denounced it:

A robin redbreast in a cage,
Puts all heaven in a rage.

Auguries of Innocence, William Blake

The robin is often linked in popularity with the wren:

Kill a robin or a wren
Never prosper, boy or man

Traditional Rhyme

For centuries, according to folklore, the wren was hunted around Christmas, particularly on St Stephen's Day, perhaps because it was thought to have betrayed St Stephen's hiding place, or more likely as a midwinter sacrifice to ensure the spring's return to the earth. Little boys would try to catch a wren on Boxing Day and parade it in a cage, or its dead body nailed to a pole, around local hostelries, singing:

The wren, the wren, the king of all birds,
St Stephen's Day was caught in the furze,
Although he is little, his family's great
I pray you, good landlady, give us a treat.

Traditional Rhyme

Burning Babe

. . . .

As I in hoary winter's night stood shivering in the snow,
Surprised I was with sudden heat which made my heart
    to glow;
And lifting up a fearful eye to view what fire was near,
A pretty babe all burning bright did in the air appear;
Who, though scorched with excessive heat, such floods of
    tears did shed,
As though his floods should quench his flames, which with
his tears were fed.
'Alas,' quoth he, 'but newly born, in fiery heats I fry,
Yet none approach to warm their hearts, or feel my
    fire but I!
My faultless breast the furnace is, the fuel wounding
thorns,
Love is the fire, and sighs the smoke, the ashes shame
    and scorns;
The fuel justice layeth on, and mercy blows the coals,
The metal in this furnace wrought are men's defiled souls,
For which, as now on fire I am to work them to their good,
So will I melt into a bath to wash them in my blood.'
With this he vanished out of sight and swiftly
    shrunk away,
And straight I called unto mind that it was
    Christmas Day.

The Burning Babe, Robert Southwell

On this day in 1595, Robert Southwell, a Jesuit priest,
was executed. Ben Jonson reported to his friend
Drummond of Hawthornden:
'that Southwell was hanged yet, so he had written that
piece of his, ye burning babe , he would have been
content to destroy many of his'.

In the parade of the months in The Faerie Queen by
Edmund Spenser, chill December rides upon a
shaggy-bearded goat. Spenser identifies the goat as
Amalthea, who fed the infant Jove with goat's milk
and honey on Mount Ida, on the island of Crete. The
goat represents Capricorn.

And after him, came next the chill December.
Yet he through merry feasting which he made,
And great bonfires, did not the cold remember;
His Saviour's birth his mind so much did glad:
Upon a shaggy-bearded Goat he rode,
The same wherewith Dan Jove in tender years,
They say, was nourished by th'Idaean maid;
And in his hand a broad deep bowl he bears;
Of which, he freely drinks an health to all his peers.

Mutabilitie Cantos, VII: XLI

Christmas Eve

Some say that ever 'gainst that season comes
Wherein our Saviour's birth is celebrated,
The bird of dawning singeth all night long;
And then, they say, no spirit can walk abroad,
The nights are wholesome, then no planets strike,
No fairy takes, nor witch hath power to charm,
So hallowed and so gracious is the time.

Hamlet (Act 1 Scene 1)

'It is now Christmas, and not a Cup of drink must pass without a carol: the beasts, fowl and fish come to a general execution, and the corn is ground to dust for the bakehouse, and pastry: Cards and Dice purge many a purse, and the Youth show their agility in shoeing of the wild Mare: now good cheer and welcome, and God be with you, and I thank you: and against the new year, provide for the presents: the Lord of Misrule is no mean man for his time, and the guests of the high table must lack no wine: the lusty bloods must look about them like men, and piping and dancing puts away much melancholy: stolen Venison is sweet, and a fat Coney is worth money: Pit-falls are now set for small birds, and a woodcock hangs himself in the gin: a good fire heats all the house, and a full Alms-basket makes the Beggar's Prayers: the Maskers and Mummers make their merry sport: but if they lose their money, their Drum goes dead: Swearers and Swaggerers are sent away to the Ale-house, and unruly Wenches go in danger of Judgement: Musicians now make their Instruments speak out and a good song is worth the hearing. In sum, it is a holy time, a duty of Christians, for the remembrance of Christ, and a custom among friends, for the maintenance of good fellowship: In brief, I thus conclude of it: I hold it a memory of the Heaven's Love, and the world's peace, the mirth of the honest, and the meeting of the friendly. Farewell.'

The Kalendar of the Months, Nicholas Breton

Mistletoe and Oak Trees

'There was one Oak in the great wood called Norwood, that had mistletoe, a Timber tree, which was felled about 1657. Some persons cut this mistletoe, for some apothecaries in London, and sold them a quantity for ten shillings, each time, and left only one branch remaining for more to sprout. One fell lame shortly after: Soon after, each of the others lost an eye, and he that felled the tree, about 1678 (tho' warned of these misfortunes of the other men) would not withstanding adventure to do it, and shortly after broke his leg; as if the Hamadryades had resolved to take an ample revenge for the injury done to that sacred and venerable oak.'

Miscellanies, John Aubrey

John Stow reports that every man's house was decked with holly and ivy at this season. Queen Elizabeth herself paid for holly and ivy to decorate the parish churches which flanked the royal winter palace of Whitehall at Christmas.

Christmas Day

On Christmas Day, 1605, the month after the Gunpowder Plot, Bishop Lancelot Andrewes delivered his first Christmas sermon to the King, after which he became the most popular preacher at the Court of King James, and preached at nearly every major Christian festival until his death.

As Dean of Westminster Abbey, Andrewes had participated at the funeral of Elizabeth and the coronation of James. He was so learned it was said he could have been an interpreter in the Tower of Babel. He attended the Hampton Court Conference and was appointed chairman of the translation of the first twelve books of the Bible, from *Genesis* to *Kings*.

He delivered this Christmas sermon, about the coming of the three kings, at Christmas 1622. This extract might seem familiar:

'**We consider the way that they came, if it be pleasant, or plain and easy; for if it be, it is so much the better. This was nothing pleasant, for through deserts, all the way waste and desolate. Nor secondly, easy neither; for over the rocks and crags of both Arabias, specially Petra, their journey lay. Yet if safe, but it was not, but exceeding dangerous, as lying through the midst of the black tents of Kedar, a nation of thieves and cutthroats; to pass over the hills of robbers, infamous then, and infamous to this day. No passing without great troop or convoy.**

'**Last we consider the time of their coming, the season of the year.**

'**It was no summer progress. A cold coming they**

had of it at this time of the year, just the worst time of the year to take a journey, and specially a long journey. The ways deep, the weather sharp, the days short, the sun farthest off, in solsitio brumali, the very dead of winter. Venimus, we are come, if that be one, venimus, we are now come, come at this time, that sure is another.

'**And these difficulties they overcame, of a wearisome, irksome, troublesome, dangerous, unseasonable journey; and for all this they came.**'

Sermon of the Nativity, Lancelot Andrewes before King James, at Whitehall

In the opening five lines of T.S. Eliot's *Journey of the Magi*, Eliot directly quotes from Bishop Andrewes, whose sermons had a profound influence on his conversion to Catholicism:

A cold coming we had of it,
Just the worst time of the year
For a journey, and such a journey;
The ways deep and the weather sharp,
The very dead of winter.

'This great light was extinguished' in 1626. Andrewes was buried in St Mary Overie in Southwark, his effigy carved by the sculptor who made William Shakespeare's effigy in Holy Trinity Church in Stratford, Gerard Jansen. Andrewes is shown in ruff and rochet with his mantle, as prelate of the Most Noble Order of the Garter.

St Stephen's Day: **Boxing Day**

The King's Men played *Measure for Measure* at court:

Accounts exist for payments made to the King's Men for their performances at Court before King James. *Measure for Measure* by Shaxberd was performed on the evening of this very day, St Stephen's Night, 1605, and in 1606, *King Lear*. Here are the records for the performances at Hallowmas and over the Christmas holidays of 1604-5 (for which John Hemmings records a payment of £60), as well as the Shrovetide performances.

Edmund Tilney was the Master of the Revels responsible for the arrangements.

1604 & 1605 Edd. Tylney
Sunday after Hallowmas - *Merry Wives*
perfd. by the K's players.
Hallamas - in the Banqueting hos. at Whitehall the
   ***Moor of Venis* – perfd. by the K's players**
On St Stephens Night – *Mesure for Mesur* **by Shaxberd**
   – perfd. by the K's players
On Innocent's Night *Errors* **by Shaxberd - perfd. by**
   the K's players.
On Sunday following *How to learn of a woman to wooe*
   by Heywood, perfd. by the Q's players.
On New Year's Night – *All fools* **by G. Chapman perfd.**
   by the Boyes of the Chapel.
bet New yrs day & twelfth day – *Loves Labour lost*
   perfd. by the K's prs.
On 7th Jan *K.Hen. the fifth* **perfd. by the K prs.**
On 8th Jan – *Everyone out of his humour*
On Candlemas night – *Everyone out of his humour*
On Shrove Sunday – *the Marchant of Venis* **by**
   Shaxberd - perfd. by the K's Prs -

George Arbuthnot, Vicar of
Holy Trinity

The same repeated on Shrove tuesd. by the K's command.

Measure for Measure may have been played before the King and his court on this day in 1605, but, three centuries later, when the Stratford Memorial Theatre wanted to stage a production of the play, it received some stiff opposition.

George Arbuthnot was Vicar of Holy Trinity from the very opening of the Shakespeare Theatre in Stratford in 1879. He was not generally against the works of Shakespeare; in fact, he had given a talk at the opening of the Parish Parlour built for Queen Victoria's Diamond Jubilee, on the Life of the Immortal Bard, illustrated 'with Limelight Views'. However, he wrote to the *Herald* in the last year of his incumbency to rail against the inclusion of *Measure for Measure* in the Festival Season in 1908, a play he considered thoroughly unsuitable:

'I have challenged them to say that any of them will take a young lady to see it, and all I can do now is to state my opinion that no respectable and modest woman ought to go to it. I am sorry if this statement advertises it, but as Vicar of this parish I feel obliged to make it.'

❁

Also on St Stephen's Night, at the Inner Temple one year, when Robert Dudley had been invited to be the Lord of Misrule called Prince Palaphiles, a fox and a cat were let loose in the hall, hunted down by a score of hounds, and ripped apart in front of the fire. After which there was a banquet.

St John the Evangelist's Day

The Yuletide Season at the Rose

Ten years before the court performances described above, Philip Henslowe recorded what repertoire was playing over Christmas at the Rose Theatre. On this day in 1594, Marlowe's *Dr Faustus* was playing, and had also played just before Christmas, on the 20th.

Henslowe had three other Marlowe plays in the repertoire (the playwright himself had been murdered eighteen months before): *The Jew of Malta* (December 9th) and *Tamburlaine the Great*, which had earned him £1 11 shillings on the 17th (*Part One*) and £2 6s (*Part Two*) on the 19th. Both parts were repeated over New Year, with *Part One* pulling in £2 2s on December 30th, while *Part Two* on January 1st attracted another great house, making Henslowe £3 2s 0d.

And the hard-working company also performed on Christmas Day itself. They played in a now long-lost and long-forgotten play called *The Grecian Comedy*. It made a healthy profit of £2 6s.

Edward Alleyn as Tamburlaine the Great

St Stephen's Day (Boxing Day) featured what was possibly also a new play called *The Siege of London*.

One of the pleasures of reading Henslowe's diaries is to ponder the titles of many long-forgotten plays. *Crack Me This Nut* sounds like good seasonal fare. But *The Tanner of Denmark* didn't pass muster, for some reason, and only had one recorded performance. And what might *Clorys and Orgasto* or *Bendo and Richardo* have been like, or, come to that, a play called simply *Mahomet*?

There were plays about the Roman emperors Constantine and Diocletian; Sir John Mandeville, the great traveller and tall-story teller; the Italian poet Torquato Tasso; and King Lud. Titles recorded by Henslowe like *Zenobia*, *Long Meg* and *Pope Joan* suggest that there were some good parts written about women too.

During Yuletide, 1595, *The Jew of Malta* was still in the repertoire, but the Christmas play that year was *The Wonder of a Woman*, reaping Henslowe £3 2s 0d.

But a favourite Christmas entry is for the following year, 1596, when the company played a third performance of their new 'get-penny' or hit play *Nabucadonizer* on Christmas Day. Presumably it was a play about Nebuchadnezzar, the greatest King of Babylon. A nice big ancient epic for the holidays, then. Nothing changes. Perhaps it starred that snappy biblical trio Shadrach, Meshach, and Abednego.

Childermas

Herod the king
In his raging,
Charged he hath this day
His men of might
In his own sight
All young children to slay.

The Coventry Carol

Holy Innocents' Day, or Childermas, was observed as a commemoration of the massacre of the innocents by Herod. It was considered to be a very unlucky day. To marry on Childermas was especially inauspicious, and Edward IV postponed his coronation to avoid this feast day.

Did Shakespeare ever see the slaughter of the innocents enacted? As it happens, one of only two play texts remaining from Coventry's mystery cycle, the *Shearmen and Tailors' Play*, contains this episode. It also has a particularly splendid Herod. Here he is at full throttle (and this is just his opening speech); the original spellings are retained, as they seem to add an extra earthy shudder to it:

The myghttyst conquerowre that eyver walkid on grownd;
For I am evyn he thatt made bothe hevin and hell,

And of my myghte powar holdith up this world rownd.
Magaog and Modroke, both them did I confownde,
And with this bryght bronde there bonis I brak onsunder,
Thatt all the wyde worlde on those rappis did wonder.
I am cawse of this grett lyght and thunder;
Ytt ys throgh my fure that they soche noyse dothe make.
My feyrefull contenance the clowdis so doth incumbur
That oftymis for drede ther-of the verre yerth doth quake.
Loke when I with males this bright brond doth schake,
All the whole world from the north to the sowthe
I ma them dystroie with won worde of my mowthe.

In his advice to the Players, Hamlet forbids any over-acting from his company. It would be difficult not to over-act the speech above.

O it offends me to the very soul to hear a robustious, periwig-pated fellow tear a passion to tatters, to very rags, to split the ears of the groundlings, who for the most part are capable of nothing but inexplicable dumb-shows and noise; I would have such a fellow whipped for o'er-doing Termagant; it out-herods Herod;
I pray you, avoid it.

Hamlet (Act 3 Scene 2)

Pocahontas
. . . .

On this day in 1607 Captain John Smith was 'rescued' by Pocahontas.

'Not long after, early in the morning a great fire was made in a long house, and a mat spread on the one side, as on the other. On the one they caused him to sit, and all the guard went out of the house, and presently came skipping in a great grim fellow, all painted over with coal, mingled with oil; and many snakes and weasels skins stuffed with moss, and all their tails tied together, so they met on the crown of his head in a tassle; and around about the tassle was as a coronet of feathers, the skins hanging about his neck, back and shoulders, and in a manner covered his face; with a hellish voice and a rattle in his hand. With most strange gestures and passions he began his invocation, and environed the fire with a circle of meal, which done, three more such like devils came rushing in with the like antique tricks, painted half black, half red: but all their eyes were painted white, and some red strokes like moustachoes, along their cheeks: around about him those fiends dance a pretty while, and then came in three more as ugly as the rest; with red eyes and white strokes over the black faces, at last they all sat down right against him; three of

them on the one hand of the chief priest and three on the other.

'At last they brought him to Meronocomoco, where was Powhatan, their Emperor. Here more than two hundred of those grim courtiers stood wondering at him, as he had been a monster; till Powhatan and his train had put themselves in their greatest braveries. Before a fire upon a seat like a bedstead, he sat covered with a great robe, made of racoon skins, and all the tails hanging by. On either side did sit a young wench of 16 or 18 years, and along on each side of the house, two rows of men, and behind them as many women, with all their heads and shoulders painted red; many of their heads bedecked with the white down of birds; but everyone with something; and a great chain of white beads about their necks. At his entrance before the King, all the people gave a great shout. The Queen of Appamatuck was appointed to bring him water to wash his hands, and another brought him a bunch of feathers instead of a towel to dry them: having feasted after their best barbarous manner they could, a long consultation was held, but the conclusion was, two great stones were brought before Powhatan: then as many as could laid hands on him, dragged him to them, and thereon laid his head, and being ready with their clubs, to beat out his brains, Pocahontas the king's dearest daughter, when no entreaty could prevail, got his head in her arms, and laid her own upon his to save him from death.'

A True Relation, Captain John Smith, 1608

Captain Smith was a great self-publicist. Read his autobiography (perhaps the first of its kind) and you discover that Pocahontas was not the first lady to rescue him from certain death. When he was fighting as a mercenary in Transylvania, and was captured and taken into slavery, he was rescued by the love of the lady Charatza Tragabizanda; and, a little later in Crym's Country, by the Lady Callamata.

Weaving Rainbows

On this day in 1460, during the Wars of the Roses, Richard of York (Richard III's father) and his forces were intercepted near Wakefield by a larger Lancastrian force. York's son, the Duke of Rutland, was killed, and then York himself. The scene where Queen Margaret taunts York with a handkerchief dipped in his son's blood, and then places a paper crown on his head, is one of the most memorable from Shakespeare's early *Henry VI* trilogy:

Queen Margaret: *A crown for York! and, lords,
    bow low to him:*

Hold you his hands, whilst I do set it on.

(Putting a paper crown on his head)

Ay, marry, sir, now looks he like a king!

Ay, this is he that took King Henry's chair.

Henry VI Part Three, Act 1 Scene 4

The events of this day are oddly commemorated in the well-known mnemonic, designed to allow you to remember the order of the colours of the rainbow: **'Richard Of York Gave Battle In Vain.'**

Shakespeare admires the perfection of the rainbow, and describes the impossibility of improving it, in a list of impossibilities cited by the Earl of Salisbury to prove to King John the needless waste of having a second coronation:

To gild refined gold, to paint the lily,

To throw a perfume on the violet,

To smooth the ice, or add another hue

Unto the rainbow, or with taper-light

To seek the beauteous eye of heaven to garnish,

Is wasteful and ridiculous excess.

King John (Act 4 Scene 2)

John Keats' poem *Lamia* is about tampering with the perfection of the rainbow, by scientific analysis:

Do not all charms fly

At the mere touch of cold philosophy?

There was an awful rainbow once in heaven:

We know her woof, her texture; she is given

In the dull catalogue of common things.

Philosophy will clip an Angel's wings,

Conquer all mysteries by rule and line,

Empty the haunted air, and gnomed mine –

Unweave a rainbow…

Lamia, John Keats

'The Ever Running Year'

Henry V (Act 4 Scene 1)

On this day in 1607, Edmund Shakespeare, 'player', Will's brother, was buried.

Shakespeare's youngest brother and fellow actor, Edmund, died on December 29th at the age of 27, four months after the death of his illegitimate son. The cause and circumstances of Edmund's death remain a mystery. His funeral took place in the morning. It was more expensive to be buried before noon. The tolling of the forenoon bell cost twenty shillings, and was probably ordered and paid for by Shakespeare himself, perhaps so that the actors could attend the service before the matinee at the Globe.

Edmund was laid to rest at St Saviour's Church in Southwark.

'We have had here a very merry Christmas and nothing to disquiet us save brabbles amongst our ambassadors, and one or two poor companions that died of the plague. The first holy days we had every night a public play in the great hall, at which the king was ever present and liked or disliked as he saw cause, but it seems he takes an extraordinary pleasure in them. The queen and the prince were more the players' friends, for on other nights they had them privately and have since taken them to their protection.

'On New Year's night we had a play of Robin Goodfellow and a mask brought in by a magician of China. There was a heaven built at the lower end of the hall out of which our magician came down, and after he made a long sleepy speech to the King of the nature of the country whence he came, comparing it with ours for strength and plenty, he said he had brought in clouds, certain Indian and China knights to see the magnificency of this court; and thereupon a traverse was drawn and maskers sitting in a vaulty place with their torchbearers and other lights, which was no unpleasing spectacle.

'The first gave the king an impresa in a shield with a sonnet in a paper to express his device and presented a jewel of £40,000 value which the king is to buy from Peter van Lore. It made a fair show to the French ambassador's eye, whose master would have been very well pleased with such a masker's present, but not at that price.

'The Sunday following was the great day of the Queen's mask. The hall was much lessened by the works that were in it, so as none could be admitted but men of appearance; the one end was made into a rock and, in several places, the waits placed, in attire like savages, loose mantles and petticoats, but of different colours, the stuffs embroidered satins and cloth of gold and silver, for the which they were beholden to Queen Elizabeth's wardrobe... So ended that night's sport with the end of our Christmas gambols.'

Letter from Sir Dudley Carleton to his friend, John Chamberlain

Do nothing but eat, and make good cheer
And praise God for the Merry Year.

Justice Silence's song, Henry IV Part Two (Act 5 Scene 3)

The Shakespeare Centre Library and Archive, Stratford-upon-Avon

The most important Shakespeare Library in Europe, covering Shakespeare's works, life and times, and the performance of his plays. The Shakespeare Collections received Designated Status in 2005, acknowledging their national and international importance.

Maintained by the Shakespeare Birthplace Trust, the Library and Archive contains:

The combined printed book collections of the Shakespeare Birthplace Trust and the Royal Shakespeare Company, including almost every significant edition of Shakespeare's works from the 1623 First Folio onwards, over 600 early printed books, and a major collection of modern Shakespearean criticism.

The archive of the Royal Shakespeare Company.

Shakespeare-related ephemera from all periods such as playbills and programmes, newspaper articles, manuscripts, original artwork, engravings, photographs and videos.

Approximately half the existing contemporary documents connected with Shakespeare, other original material relating to his life, and official records of the town of Stratford-upon-Avon.

The Library and Archive is freely available to anyone wishing to use it.
Appointments are not necessary except for video viewing but it is helpful to know your requirements in advance. Identification must be provided.

email: library@shakespeare.org.uk
Telephone: 01789 201816
Opening hours are 10-5, Tuesday to Friday, 9.30-12.30 Saturday
Website, including catalogues and RSC Performance Database:
www.shakespeare.org.uk/content/view/19/19

Prelims: *A description of pride; Ecclesiasticus 10th Chapter*, from Trevelyon's Miscellany. By Permission of the Folger Shakespeare Library; *Shakespeare and his Friends*, Faed, John (1820-1902) / Private Collection / The Bridgeman Art Library.

January: *Portrait of Johanna Le Maire* by Nicolaes Eliasz Pickenoy, 1622 © Rijksmuseum, Amsterdam; *Embroidered wedding glove* by Unknown, 1622 © Rijksmuseum, Amsterdam; *January hath 31 days*, from Trevelyon's Miscellany. By Permission of the Folger Shakespeare Library; *Masquer: A Daughter of the Niger*, Inigo Jones, 1573-1652 © Devonshire Collection, Chatsworth. Reproduced by permission of Chatsworth Settlement Trustees; *A Torchbearer: An Oceania*, Inigo Jones, 1573-1652 © Devonshire Collection, Chatsworth. Reproduced by permission of Chatsworth Settlement Trustees; *Frozen River* from *Collection of Emblems: Ancient and Modern* by George Wither, 1635. By permission of the Shakespeare Birthplace Trust; *Icon bearing the portrait of Ivan IV Vasilievich, called "Ivan the Terrible"* (1530-84) / Nationalmuseet, Copenhagen, Denmark / The Bridgeman Art Library; *Ganymede* from *Collection of Emblems: Ancient and Modern* by George Wither, 1635. By permission of the Shakespeare Birthplace Trust; *Portrait of a gentleman, said to be Edmund Spenser* (c.1552-99), the Kinnoull Portrait (panel), English School, (16th century) / Private Collection / © Philip Mould Ltd, London / The Bridgeman Art Library; *Pattern: borage; roses; honeysuckle*, from Trevelyon's Miscellany. By Permission of the Folger Shakespeare Library; *Detail from Motifs: rose and buds/ two abstract flowers/ two abstract lilies*, from Trevelyon's Miscellany. By Permission of the Folger Shakespeare Library; *Hunters in the Snow - January*, 1565, Bruegel, Pieter the Elder (c.1525-69) / Kunsthistorisches Museum, Vienna, Austria / The Bridgeman Art Library; *Illustration from Titus Andronicus*, by William Shakespeare (ink on paper) (b/w photo), Peacham, Henry (c.1576-1643) / Bibliotheque Nationale, Paris, France / Lauros / Giraudon / The Bridgeman Art Library; *Benjamin Jonson*, by Abraham van Blyenberch, 1618 © National Portrait Gallery; *Covered Jar with Carp Design*, 1522-66 (porcelain), Chinese School, Ming Dynasty (1368-1644) / Indianapolis Museum of Art, USA / Gift of Mr and Mrs Eli Lilly / The Bridgeman Art Library; *Sir Walter Raleigh* by Nicholas Hilliard © National Portrait Gallery; *Panorama of London and the Thames, part three showing Southwark, London Bridge and the churches in the City*, c.1600 (engraving) (see also 7214, 64730 & 64732), Visscher, Nicolaes (Claes) Jansz (1586-1652) / Guildhall Library, City of London / The Bridgeman Art Library.

February: *The Flute Player or Knave Playing a Fife* (oil on canvas), Brugghen, Hendrick Ter (1588-1629) / Gemaeldegalerie Alte Meister, Kassel, Germany / © Museumslandschaft Hessen Kassel / The Bridgeman Art Library; *February hath 28 days*, from Trevelyon's Miscellany. By Permission of the Folger Shakespeare Library; *Portrait of Robert Devereux* (1566-1601) c.1596 (oil on canvas), Gheeraerts, Marcus, the Younger (c.1561-1635.) (after) / National Portrait Gallery, London, UK / The Bridgeman Art Library; *Henry Wriothesley, 3rd Earl of Southampton* (1573-1624), 1603 (oil on canvas), Critz, John de, the Elder (c.1552-1642)(attr. to) / Boughton House, Northamptonshire, UK / The Bridgeman Art Library; *Mary Queen of Scots*, from Trevelyon's Miscellany. By Permission of the Folger Shakespeare Library; *Caprimulgus* from Francis Willughby's

Ornithology, 1676. By permission of the Shakespeare Birthplace Trust; *Seeming Lover* from *Collection of Emblems: Ancient and Modern* by George Wither, 1635. By permission of the Shakespeare Birthplace Trust; *Detail from Motifs: vase with carnations/ abstract borage; abstract flower*, from Trevelyon's Miscellany. By Permission of the Folger Shakespeare Library; *Sir Philip Sidney*, (1554-86), 1577 (panel), English School, (16th century) / Longleat House, Wiltshire, UK / The Bridgeman Art Library; *Ivan and Boris*, Doughty, C.L. (1913-85) / Private Collection / © Look and Learn / The Bridgeman Art Library; *Shrovetide Revellers (The Merry Company)* c.1615 (oil on canvas), Hals, Frans (1582/3-1666) / Metropolitan Museum of Art, New York, USA / The Bridgeman Art Library; *Winter Landscape*, 1623 (oil on panel), Velde, Esaias I van de (1587-1630) / National Gallery, London, UK / The Bridgeman Art Library; *Portrait thought to be Michel Eyquem de Montaigne* (1533-92) (oil on panel), French School, (16th century) / Musee Conde, Chantilly, France / Lauros / Giraudon / The Bridgeman Art Library; *Job*, from the *Tres Riches Heures du Duc de Berry*, early 15th century (vellum), Colombe, Jean (c.1430-c.93) / Musee Conde, Chantilly, France / The Bridgeman Art Library.

March: *Saint Peter*, from Trevelyon's Miscellany. By Permission of the Folger Shakespeare Library; *March hath 31 days*, from Trevelyon's Miscellany. By Permission of the Folger Shakespeare Library; *Violets* from *Gerard's Herbal*. By permission of the Shakespeare Birthplace Trust; *Primroses* from *Gerard's Herbal*. By permission of the Shakespeare Birthplace Trust; *The Shakespeare Memorial Theatre goes up in flames*, 1926, RSC Archive. By permission of the Shakespeare Birthplace Trust; *Theatre producer, William Bridges Adams, and others stare down into the burnt out shell of The Shakespeare Memorial Theatre*, RSC Archive. By permission of the Shakespeare Birthplace Trust; *Daffodils* from *Gerard's Herbal*. By permission of the Shakespeare Birthplace Trust; *Sowing seed* from *Collection of Emblems: Ancient and Modern* by George Wither, 1635. By permission of the Shakespeare Birthplace Trust; *John Fletcher* by Unknown Artist © National Portrait Gallery; *Portrait of Richard Burbage* (1573-1619) (oil on canvas), English School, (17th century) / © Dulwich Picture Gallery, London, UK / The Bridgeman Art Library; *Illustration from The Compleat Horseman* by Gervase Markham and illustrated by Pauline Baynes, published by Robson (1976); *The New World Arch in Fleet Street*. This can be found in the Warder Collection; *Knight*, Trinity College Library, Dublin, MS 1440 fol 19r. By permission of Trinity College Library, Dublin; *Hoary Plantain* from *Gerard's Herbal*. By permission of the Shakespeare Birthplace Trust; *The Ermine portrait of Elizabeth I*, attributed to William Segar © The Marquess of Salisbury; *The entry of Richard II and Bolingbroke into London*, Northcote, James (1746-1831) / Royal Albert Memorial Museum, Exeter, Devon, UK / The Bridgeman Art Library; *St. George and the Dragon, after an original painting in the Chapel of the Trinity at Stratford Upon Avon, Warwickshire*, 1804 (colour litho), Hoxton, Thomas Fisher (fl.19th century) / Private Collection / The Bridgeman Art Library; *Man with a ring* by Werner van den Valckert, 1617 © Rijksmuseum, Amsterdam; *Sir Henry Wotton* by Unknown Artist © National Portrait Gallery; *Portrait of John Donne*, c.1595 (oil on canvas), English School, (16th century) / National Portrait Gallery, London, UK / The Bridgeman Art Library.

April: Richard Tarleton (litho) (b/w photo), English School, (17th century) / Private Collection / The Bridgeman Art Library; *April hath 30 days*, from Trevelyon's Miscellany. By Permission of the Folger Shakespeare Library; Sir Francis Drake, 1581, Hilliard, Nicholas (1547-1619) / Kunsthistorisches Museum, Vienna, Austria / The Bridgeman Art Library; Ostrich from Francis Willughby's *Ornithology*, 1676. By permission of the Shakespeare Birthplace Trust; Royal, military and court costumes of the time of James I [graphic], Folger Library, ART Vol. c91 no.8c. By Permission of the Folger Shakespeare Library; Walter Scott at Shakespeare's Tomb, attributed to David Roberts. By permission of the Shakespeare Birthplace Trust; Portrait of Francis Bacon (1561-1626) Viscount of St. Albans Writing at his Desk, 1640 (engraving), Marshall, William (fl.1617-49) / Private Collection / The Stapleton Collection / The Bridgeman Art Library; Francis Bacon by Nicholas Hilliard © National Portrait Gallery; Ox from *Collection of Emblems: Ancient and Modern* by George Wither, 1635. By permission of the Shakespeare Birthplace Trust; Early designs for the Flag of the Union, 1604, by the Earl of Nottingham. National Library of Scotland MS. 2517, f. 67v. Reproduced by permission of the National Library of Scotland; Elizabethan Football (woodcut print) (b/w photo), English School, (16th century) / Private Collection / The Bridgeman Art Library; Illustration from *The Compleat Horseman* by Gervase Markham and illustrated by Pauline Baynes, published by Robson (1976); *The Misery of man's life: Live to die* [in verse], from Trevelyon's Miscellany. By Permission of the Folger Shakespeare Library; Cuckoo from Francis Willughby's *Ornithology*, 1676. By permission of the Shakespeare Birthplace Trust; Parrot from Francis Willughby's *Ornithology*, 1676. By permission of the Shakespeare Birthplace Trust; Macbeth, the Three Witches and Hecate in Act IV, Scene I of 'Macbeth' by William Shakespeare (1564-1616) published 1805 (engraving), Boydell, John (1719-1804) & Josiah (1760-1817) / Private Collection / The Stapleton Collection / The Bridgeman Art Library; Hanging bird from Francis Willughby's *Ornithology*, 1676. By permission of the Shakespeare Birthplace Trust; Akbar Tames the Savage Elephant, Hawa'i, Outside the Red Fort at Agra, miniature from the Akbarnama of Abul Fazl, c.1590 (left hand side of double page miniature, see 4042) (gouache on paper), Basawan and Chatai (fl.1590) / British Museum, London, UK / The Bridgeman Art Library; Oxslips from *Gerard's Herbal*. By permission of the Shakespeare Birthplace Trust.

May: Illustration for *As You Like It* from *Shakespeare: The Animated Tales*. Illustration by Valentin Olschwang; Joan Alleyn, 1596 (oil on panel), English School, (16th century) / © Dulwich Picture Gallery, London, UK / The Bridgeman Art Library; Nightingale from Francis Willughby's *Ornithology*, 1676. By permission of the Shakespeare Birthplace Trust; *Mr Garrick as Steward of the Stratford Jubilee, September 1769* by Benjamin Van der Gucht (1769), Folger Library, Shelfmark ART 242301. By Permission of the Folger Shakespeare Library; Mulberries from *Gerard's Herbal*. By permission of the Shakespeare Birthplace Trust; Pyramus and Thisbe from *Collection of Emblems: Ancient and Modern* by George Wither, 1635. By permission of the Shakespeare Birthplace Trust; Gospel sermon from *Collection of Emblems: Ancient and Modern* by George Wither, 1635. By permission of the Shakespeare Birthplace Trust; Homo Bulla: A Boy Blowing Bubbles, c.1665 (oil on canvas), Helst, Bartolomeus van der (1613-70) / Private Collection / © Lawrence Steigrad Fine Arts, New York /

The Bridgeman Art Library; Illustration for *The Winter's Tale* from *Shakespeare: The Animated Tales* illustrated by Elena Livanova and Stanilav Sokolov; Eternity/Time from *Collection of Emblems: Ancient and Modern* by George Wither, 1635. By permission of the Shakespeare Birthplace Trust; Bluebells from *Gerard's Herbal*. By permission of the Shakespeare Birthplace Trust; Dandelions from *Gerard's Herbal*. By permission of the Shakespeare Birthplace Trust; The Thames at Richmond, with the Old Royal Palace, c.1620 (oil on canvas) (detail) (see also 65997), Flemish School, (17th century) / Fitzwilliam Museum, University of Cambridge, UK / The Bridgeman Art Library; *The Yellow Dress* by Dame Laura Knight, Collection of Worcester City Museums © Reproduced with permission of The Estate of Dame Laura Knight DBE RA 2009. All rights reserved; Chequered Daffodil (Snakeshead Fritallaria) from *Gerard's Herbal*. By permission of the Shakespeare Birthplace Trust; Daisies from *Gerard's Herbal*. By permission of the Shakespeare Birthplace Trust; *A description of pride; Ecclesiasticus 10th Chapter*, from Trevelyon's Miscellany. By Permission of the Folger Shakespeare Library; Detail from *May hath 31 days*, from Trevelyon's Miscellany. By Permission of the Folger Shakespeare Library; Lark from Francis Willughby's *Ornithology*, 1676. By permission of the Shakespeare Birthplace Trust; *Richard III*, from Trevelyon's Miscellany. By Permission of the Folger Shakespeare Library; Rose from *Gerard's Herbal*. By permission of the Shakespeare Birthplace Trust; King Henry VI of England at Towton, 1860 (oil on board), Dyce, William (1806-64) / © Guildhall Art Gallery, City of London / The Bridgeman Art Library; Lavender from *Gerard's Herbal*. By permission of the Shakespeare Birthplace Trust; Book and Picture Shop by Saloman de Bray, 1628 © Rijksmuseum, Amsterdam; Stratford's New Shakespeare Memorial Theatre in 1923, RSC Archive. By permission of the Shakespeare Birthplace Trust; Portrait believed to be of Christopher Marlowe (artist unknown), 1585. Reproduced by permission of Corpus Christi College, Cambridge.

June: *June hath 30 days*, from Trevelyon's Miscellany. By Permission of the Folger Shakespeare Library; Drawing of Table Bay by Wouter Schouten, 1658, from the William Fehr Collection © Iziko Museums of Cape Town; Herdsmen bartering sheep for copper in Table Bay by Thomas Herbert, 1627, reproduced by permission of the National Library of South Africa (Shelfmark PHA: Koisan); Double Eglantine from *Gerard's Herbal*. By permission of the Shakespeare Birthplace Trust; Icon depicting the Assassination of Dmitri Ivanovich (1583-91) in Ouglicht, 16th-17th century (oil on panel), Russian School / Private Collection / Giraudon / The Bridgeman Art Library; Saskia as Flora, 1634 (oil on canvas), Rembrandt Harmensz. van Rijn (1606-69) / Hermitage, St. Petersburg, Russia / The Bridgeman Art Library; Lady-smock from *Gerard's Herbal*. By permission of the Shakespeare Birthplace Trust; Blackbird from Francis Willughby's *Ornithology*, 1676. By permission of the Shakespeare Birthplace Trust; Land Crab (w/c on paper), White, John (fl.1570-93) (after) / British Museum, London, UK / The Bridgeman Art Library; Tree planter from *Collection of Emblems: Ancient and Modern* by George Wither, 1635. By permission of the Shakespeare Birthplace Trust; *Ecclesiasticus the 25th Chapter*, from Trevelyon's Miscellany. By Permission of the Folger Shakespeare Library; Honeysuckle (or woodbine) from *Gerard's Herbal*. By permission of the Shakespeare Birthplace Trust; *July hath*

31 days, from Trevelyon's Miscellany. By Permission of the Folger Shakespeare Library; St.John's Wort from *Gerard's Herbal*. By permission of the Shakespeare Birthplace Trust.

July: Elisabeth Scott is congratulated by HRH The Prince of Wales at the opening of the New Shakespeare Memorial Theatre, 1932, RSC Archive. By permission of the Shakespeare Birthplace Trust; Detail from Boy Playing the Flute (oil on canvas), Leyster, Judith (1600-60) / © Nationalmuseum, Stockholm, Sweden / The Bridgeman Art Library; Floure-de-luce from *Gerard's Herbal*. By permission of the Shakespeare Birthplace Trust; The Arrest and Supplication of Sir Thomas More (1478-1535) (oil on panel), Caron, Antoine (1520-99) / Musee de Blois, Blois, France / Lauros / Giraudon / The Bridgeman Art Library; Illustration by William Heath Robinson from Random House Children's Books by kind permission of Random House Group Ltd.; Final Design for Oberon's Dress, Inigo Jones (1573-1652) © Devonshire Collection, Chatsworth. Reproduced by permission of Chatsworth Settlement Trustees; Indian ritual dance from the village of Secoton, book illustration, c.1570-80 (w/c on paper) (see 87469), White, John (fl.1570-93) / British Museum, London, UK / The Bridgeman Art Library; Christian IV, King of Denmark and Norway and Sweden, etc. © Bettmann/Corbis; A Presumptuous Woman, from Trevelyon's Miscellany. By Permission of the Folger Shakespeare Library; Holland Rose from *Gerard's Herbal*. By permission of the Shakespeare Birthplace Trust; Swan from Francis Willughby's *Ornithology*, 1676. By permission of the Shakespeare Birthplace Trust; Indian in Body Paint (litho), White, John (fl.1570-93) (after) / Private Collection / The Bridgeman Art Library; Daphne and Apollo, c.1470-80 (oil on panel), Pollaiolo, Antonio (1432/3-98) / National Gallery, London, UK / The Bridgeman Art Library; Illustration by Peter Jackson from *London is Stranger than Fiction*. Reproduced by permission of Associated Newspapers Ltd; Skull from *Gerard's Herbal*. By permission of the Shakespeare Birthplace Trust.

August: *August hath 31 days*, from Trevelyon's Miscellany. By Permission of the Folger Shakespeare Library; Table laid with cheese and fruit by Floris Van Dijck, 1615 © Rijksmuseum, Amsterdam; Pomewater (apple) from *Gerard's Herbal*. By permission of the Shakespeare Birthplace Trust; The Standard of the Earl of Shrewsbury, College of Arms MS. I.2, p.19. Reproduced by permission of the College of Arms; Child and Ram from *Collection of Emblems: Ancient and Modern* by George Wither, 1635. By permission of the Shakespeare Birthplace Trust; Poppy from *Gerard's Herbal*. By permission of the Shakespeare Birthplace Trust; A Sculptor's Workshop, Stratford-Upon-Avon by Henry Wallis, 1617, RSC Archive. By permission of the Shakespeare Birthplace Trust; Apricocks from *Gerard's Herbal*. By permission of the Shakespeare Birthplace Trust; Large double white daisy from *Gerard's Herbal*. By permission of the Shakespeare Birthplace Trust; Diana and Actaeon from *Collection of Emblems: Ancient and Modern* by George Wither, 1635. By permission of the Shakespeare Birthplace Trust; Illustration for *King Richard III* from *Shakespeare: The Animated Tales*. Illustration by Peter Kotov; Massacre de la Saint Barthelemy le 24, 1572, by François Dubois / Musee d'Art et d'Histoire Lausanne / © Photo Scala, Florence; Portrait of Galileo Galilei (1564-1642) Astronomer and Physicist (Drawing), Leoni, Ottavio Mario (c.1578-1630) / Biblioteca Marucelliana, Florence, Italy / The Bridgeman Art Library; Swallow from Francis Willughby's *Ornithology*, 1676. By

permission of the Shakespeare Birthplace Trust; *James the first*, from Trevelyon's Miscellany. By Permission of the Folger Shakespeare Library.

September: *William Prynne* by Hanneman or Jonson, at Lincoln's Inn. By kind permission of the Honourable Society of Lincoln's Inn. Photograph: Photographic Survey, The Courtauld Institute of Art; *September hath 30 days*, from Trevelyon's Miscellany. By Permission of the Folger Shakespeare Library; Bread-making and Pig-Killing by Simon Bening, 1530 (Image ref. 064757). By permission of the British Library; Illustration by William Heath Robinson from Random House Children's Books by kind permission of Random House Group Ltd.; A Fete at Bermondsey, c.1570, Hoefnagel, Joris (1542-1600) / Hatfield House, Hertfordshire, UK / The Bridgeman Art Library; Thomas Parr illustration by Peter Jackson from *London is Stranger than Fiction*. Reproduced by permission of Associated Newspapers Ltd; James I of England (1566-1625) at Court (engraving) (b/w photo), English School, (17th century) / Private Collection / The Bridgeman Art Library; F.R. Benson & co. in *Richard III*, RSC Archive. By permission of the Shakespeare Birthplace Trust; Illustration for *Julius Caesar* from *Shakespeare: The Animated Tales*. Illustration by Vicotr Chuguyevski, Yuri kulakov and Galina Melko; Duel from *Collection of Emblems: Ancient and Modern* by George Wither, 1635. By permission of the Shakespeare Birthplace Trust; Mahomet (Mehmed) III (1566-1603) Sultan 1595-1603, from 'A Series of Portraits of the Emperors of Turkey', 1808 (w/c), Young, John (1755-1825) / Private Collection / The Stapleton Collection / The Bridgeman Art Library; Adaption of The Tower of London and the River Thames, 1615 (pen and ink on paper), Dutch School, (17th century) / British Museum, London, UK / The Bridgeman Art Library; Brambles from *Gerard's Herbal*. By permission of the Shakespeare Birthplace Trust; *The Abdication of King Richard II* by M. Browne (Photo by Archive Photos/Getty Images).

October: Woodcock from Francis Willughby's *Ornithology*, 1676. By permission of the Shakespeare Birthplace Trust; Vertumnus, Giuseppe Arcimboldo, 1573 (Photo by Imagno/Getty Images); October, from 'Twelve Months of Fruits', by Robert Furber (c.1674-1756) engraved by Henry Fletcher, 1732 (colour engraving), Casteels, Pieter (1684-1749) (after) / Victoria & Albert Museum, London, UK / The Bridgeman Art Library; Medlar from *Gerard's Herbal*. By permission of the Shakespeare Birthplace Trust; Detail of crows from *October hath 31 days*, from Trevelyon's Miscellany. By Permission of the Folger Shakespeare Library; Starling from Francis Willughby's *Ornithology*, 1676. By permission of the Shakespeare Birthplace Trust; Osprey from Francis Willughby's *Ornithology*, 1676. By permission of the Shakespeare Birthplace Trust; Cormorant from from Francis Willughby's *Ornithology*, 1676. By permission of the Shakespeare Birthplace Trust; *Queen Elizabeth*, from Trevelyon's Miscellany. By Permission of the Folger Shakespeare Library; *Queen Mary*, from Trevelyon's Miscellany. By Permission of the Folger Shakespeare Library; Eskimo (Inuit) Woman and Baby (colour litho), White, John (fl.1570-93) (after) / Private Collection / The Bridgeman Art Library; Autolycus, scene from 'A Winter's Tale', 1836 (oil), Leslie, Charles Robert (1794-1859) / Victoria & Albert Museum, London, UK / The Bridgeman Art Library; View of Baddesley Clinton in 1898 (oil on canvas), Orpen, Rebecca Dulcibella (19th century) / Baddesley Clinton,

Warwickshire, UK / National Trust Photographic Library/John Hammond / The Bridgeman Art Library; Fickle woman from *Collection of Emblems: Ancient and Modern* by George Wither, 1635. By permission of the Shakespeare Birthplace Trust; Mushroom from *Gerard's Herbal*. By permission of the Shakespeare Birthplace Trust; Drawing for Shakespeare's Coat of Arms, College of Arms MS Shakespeare Grants 1, reproduced by permission of the College of Arms; Portrait of Tokugawa Ieyasu (1543-1616), Japanese, 17th century, Japanese School, (17th century) / Private Collection / The Bridgeman Art Library; Tile with the Great Mosque of Mecca (underglazed fritware), Turkish School, (17th century) / © Walters Art Museum, Baltimore, USA / The Bridgeman Art Library; Torture of Crispin and Crispianian, 1500 (tempera on board), Bossche, Aert van den (fl.1490-94) / Wilanow Palace, Warsaw, Poland / The Bridgeman Art Library; St. Simon, from Trevelyon's Miscellany. By Permission of the Folger Shakespeare Library; Portrait of Sir Walter Raleigh, 1598 (oil on panel), Segar, William (fl.1585-d.1633) (attr. to) / National Gallery of Ireland, Dublin, Ireland / The Bridgeman Art Library.

November: *The Proverbs of Salomon the 7th Chapter*, from Trevelyon's Miscellany. By Permission of the Folger Shakespeare Library; *Robert Keyes gentleman/Guydo Faux gentleman* [Guy Fawkes], from Trevelyon's Miscellany. By Permission of the Folger Shakespeare Library; Henry Garnett (1555—1606), circa 1600, by an unknown artist (Photo by Hulton Archive/Getty Images); Head of a Man, traditionally called William Sly, Elizabethan actor, English School, (17th century) / © Dulwich Picture Gallery, London, UK / The Bridgeman Art Library; Portrait of John Lowin by Anonymous British Artist, Ashmolean Museum, University of Oxford (WA1898.22 (F741)); Portrait of Nathan Field (1587-c.1634), Elizabethan actor (panel), English School, (17th century) / © Dulwich Picture Gallery, London, UK / The Bridgeman Art Library; *November hath 30 days*, from Trevelyon's Miscellany. By Permission of the Folger Shakespeare Library; Rue from *Gerard's Herbal*. By permission of the Shakespeare Birthplace Trust; Dorothy Tutin kneels in rehearsal (photograph), RSC Archive. By permission of the Shakespeare Birthplace Trust; Detail from Motifs: sun in roundel/moon with face in roundel, from Trevelyon's Miscellany. By Permission of the Folger Shakespeare Library; Astronomer and stars from *Collection of Emblems: Ancient and Modern* by George Wither, 1635. By permission of the Shakespeare Birthplace Trust; *Elegant couple courting*, Willem Buytewech, 1618 © Rijksmuseum, Amsterdam; Ape-man from *Collection of Emblems: Ancient and Modern* by George Wither, 1635. By permission of the Shakespeare Birthplace Trust; Drawing of a Shakespeare performance at the Swan Theatre, London, England, late 1590s. Probably drawn (or copied) by Arendt van Buchell and based on an original by Jan de Witt, there is some debate over which play is shown being produced. (Photo by Mansell/Time & Life Pictures/Getty Images); Portrait of Shah Abbas I with one of his pages, signed Muhammad Qasim, 10th February 1627, Persian, from Isfahan, Iran, (drawing enhanced with colours, gold and silver on paper), / Louvre, Paris, France / The Bridgeman Art Library; Concert, c.1626 (oil on canvas), Brugghen, Hendrick Ter (1588-1629) / National Gallery, London, UK / The Bridgeman Art Library; Illustrations by William Heath Robinson from Random House Children's Books by kind permission of Random House Group Ltd; Death and True Love

from *Collection of Emblems: Ancient and Modern* by George Wither, 1635. By permission of the Shakespeare Birthplace Trust; St. Catherine Altarpiece, 1506 (oil on panel), Cranach, Lucas, the Elder (1472-1553) / Gemaeldegalerie Alte Meister, Dresden, Germany / © Staatliche Kunstsammlungen Dresden / The Bridgeman Art Library.

December: Frontispiece from *Gerard's Herbal*. By permission of the Shakespeare Birthplace Trust; Giant double carnation from *Gerard's Herbal*. By permission of the Shakespeare Birthplace Trust; Flour-de-luce from *Gerard's Herbal*. By permission of the Shakespeare Birthplace Trust; Mary Sidney, Countess of Pembroke by Nicholas Hilliard © National Portrait Gallery; Man clasping hand from a cloud, possibly William Shakespeare, 1588, Hilliard, Nicholas (1547-1619) / Victoria & Albert Museum, London, UK / The Bridgeman Art Library; St. Nicholas, 1563 (oil on panel), Poindre, Jacques de (c.1527-post 1572) / © Walters Art Museum, Baltimore, USA / The Bridgeman Art Library; Miss Fanny Kemble as Portia in 'The Merchant of Venice', pub. by M & M Skelt (coloured engraving), English School, (19th century) / Smallhythe Place, Kent, UK / National Trust Photographic Library/Derrick E. Witty / The Bridgeman Art Library; Circa 1587, Tycho Brahe (1546—1601) in his observatory at Uraniborg, the 'Castle of the Heavens' on the island of Hven (Ven) with a young assistant and a clerk. (Photo by Hulton Archive/Getty Images); *December hath 31 days*, from Trevelyon's Miscellany. By Permission of the Folger Shakespeare Library; Detail from Pattern: oak leaves and acorns, from Trevelyon's Miscellany. By Permission of the Folger Shakespeare Library; The Death of Ophelia, 1844 (oil on canvas), Delacroix, Ferdinand Victor Eugene (1798-1863) / Louvre, Paris, France / Lauros / Giraudon / The Bridgeman Art Library; Dogstones from *Gerard's Herbal*. By permission of the Shakespeare Birthplace Trust; Detail from Pattern: holly leaves, holly berries, from Trevelyon's Miscellany. By Permission of the Folger Shakespeare Library; Illustration of Queen Elizabeth making Christmas Pudding by Peter Jackson from *London is Stranger than Fiction*. Reproduced by permission of Associated Newspapers Ltd; Ruddock/ Robin Redbreast from Francis Willughby's *Ornithology*, 1676. By permission of the Shakespeare Birthplace Trust; Mistletoe from *Gerard's Herbal*. By permission of the Shakespeare Birthplace Trust; Bishop Circa 1620, Anglican clergyman and scholar Lancelot Andrewes (1555—1626), consecrated Bishop of Winchester in 1618. (Photo by Hulton Archive/Getty Images); George Arbuthnot, Photograph: Felicity Howlett, from a pamphlet from the Holy Trinity Church, Stratford; *Henry the sixth*, from Trevelyon's Miscellany. By Permission of the Folger Shakespeare Library; Detail from Motifs: carnation, strawberries, leaves / acorns, strawberries, leaves, from Trevelyon's Miscellany. By Permission of the Folger Shakespeare Library.

Every effort has been made to contact all copyright holders. If notified, the publisher will be pleased to rectify any errors or omissions at the earliest opportunity.